Feminist Interventions
in International Communication

Critical Media Studies
INSTITUTIONS, POLITICS, AND CULTURE

Series Editor
Andrew Calabrese, University of Colorado

For a complete listing of series titles, visit www.rowmanlittlefield.com.

Feminist Interventions in International Communication

Minding the Gap

Edited by Katharine Sarikakis and Leslie Regan Shade

ROWMAN & LITTLEFIELD PUBLISHERS, INC.
Lanham • Boulder • New York • Toronto • Plymouth, UK

ROWMAN & LITTLEFIELD PUBLISHERS, INC.

Published in the United States of America
by Rowman & Littlefield Publishers, Inc.
A wholly owned subsidiary of The Rowman & Littlefield Publishing Group, Inc.
4501 Forbes Boulevard, Suite 200, Lanham, Maryland 20706
www.rowmanlittlefield.com

Estover Road, Plymouth PL6 7PY, United Kingdom

British Library Cataloguing in Publication Information Available

Library of Congress Cataloging-in-Publication Data
Feminist interventions in international communication : minding the gap / edited by Katharine Sarikakis and Leslie Regan Shade.
    p. cm. — (Critical media studies)
  Includes bibliographical references and index.
  ISBN-13: 978-0-7425-5304-0 (cloth : alk. paper)
  ISBN-10: 0-7425-5304-3 (cloth : alk. paper)
  ISBN-13: 978-0-7425-5305-7 (pbk. : alk. paper)
  ISBN-10: 0-7425-5305-1 (pbk. : alk. paper)
  1. Communication, International. 2. Mass media and women. 3. Feminism. I. Sarikakis, Katharine, 1970– II. Shade, Leslie Regan, 1957–
  P96.I5F46 2008
  302.2082—dc22
                                                                    2007021579

Printed in the United States of America

♾ ™ The paper used in this publication meets the minimum requirements of American National Standard for Information Sciences—Permanence of Paper for Printed Library Materials, ANSI/NISO Z39.48-1992.

Contents

PART ONE

REVISITING INTERNATIONAL COMMUNICATION STUDIES

CHAPTER ONE

Revisiting International Communication: Approach of the Curious Feminist

Katharine Sarikakis and Leslie Regan Shade

International relations scholar Cynthia Enloe (2004) admonishes feminists to be curious about the world around them and to ask questions about their everyday political and social life that not only warrant consideration but that are also often dismissed or ignored by the mainstream media—and often by feminists themselves. Taking the stance of the Curious Feminist(s), this anthology asks why an accounting of feminist activities and theorizations has been typically neglected in standard texts on and about international communication (IC). It undertakes a theoretical accounting of feminist IC, provides a feminist political-economic critique of the current global mediascape, and sheds light into the neglected areas of IC.

Women's use of communication techniques and technologies for development and grassroots initiatives around the world has been flourishing, with concomitant attention paid to policy and programming initiatives that include "gender mainstreaming" by governments and nongovernmental organizations (NGO). At the same time, global media structures and flows have had an enormous impact upon women's lives, through not only their representations of women but also their utilization of women in production and consumption. This runs the gamut from community-based telecenters that encourage Internet use for women's craft entrepreneurialism, to the manufacturing of news reports that perpetuate women as victims of violence or as vacuous celebrities. Media continue to advertise consumer goods through depictions of women's sexualization, while pressuring them to consume objects and celebrate lifestyles not necessarily in their best interests.

Despite nearly forty years of systematic feminist scholarship and intervention, it is sadly the case that basic political claims about the representation of women or their equal and dignified treatment at work have neither been met by the global media industries nor have they been sufficiently prioritized by national governments or intergovernmental organizations. Mirroringly or unreflexively, scholarly attention to these issues within the context of international communication has not been given its due in the mainstream publications in the field. We, like many feminists before us, ask where are the women and where are women's theorizations and perspectives in our field? Rakow and Wackwitz (2004), referring to the broader field of communication studies, write

> That an area of scholarly work is identified by a term such as feminist communication theory reveals as much about nonfeminist communication theory as it does about itself. The field of communication, existing as disciplinary departments in universities and scholarly divisions in professional associations, has largely developed out of the Western worldview, which expresses the thinking of white men and falsely universalizes their particular experiences. Thus despite the potential for communication scholarship to recognize, support, and give voice to the great diversity of human experience, the field, in this regard, is largely marked by failure. (2)

We argue here that the study of *international* communication echoes the same failure. *Feminist Interventions in International Communication* applies feminist political-economic and policy analysis, combined with postcolonial and cultural studies, to explore the dynamics of the globalization of the media industries in selected geopolitical areas in the world, issues of transnational and international policy, questions of women's employment in transnational media industries, and matters of content consumed and produced at a global level. It seeks to make visible the intersections between human experience and global structures by shedding light into the ways in which women's experience through production, consumption, representation, and agency are influenced by and shape international communication processes and cultures. Moreover, the book makes an argument for the revisiting of IC as a field of study by expanding the scope of research into areas such as cultural representation and mediation, pornography, and the construction of girlhood, among others, and by investigating the complex links between the operation of international and global forms of media—and mediated cultures—and the locality (but also transcendent nature) of women's material and immaterial experience. It seeks to move beyond the dualistic thinking of "hard" IC themes such as propaganda, global media ownership, and so on, and "soft" IC foci such as cultural imperialism or flow of meanings. This book's central axis—the recognition of the processual character of IC transformation and phenomena, the role of power, and the inadequacy of rigid scholarship—points to the need for a more comprehensive understanding of the workings of IC.

It is not the intention of this chapter to exhaustively map the territory and development of the field of IC but rather to discuss several major themes in the field as represented through some of the most utilized readings taken up by scholars and adopted in IC curricula. The chapter also highlights feminist contributions to IC, outlines the themes explored in this book, and points to necessary further research in feminism and IC.

International Communication, Globalization, and Transnationalism

The study of international communication has rarely been straightforward (Mowlana 1997). Its development has reflected social, political, and economic issues in world society at large, affecting mass communication and cultures. At an epistemological level, IC is considered to have derived from international relations, itself a once turbulent and "illegitimate" field of study. As such, IC scholarship has concentrated on the ways in which communication among nations has been conditioned and has affected regions of the world, as well as the ways in which communication has been used as a tool of international diplomacy or foreign policy (Taylor 1997).

The field of IC is not uncontested; indeed, Semati (2004) argues that there is probably no such thing as a discipline of international communication, because IC issues have been explored and studied by many disciplines. Semati argues that as a field of inquiry IC is interdisciplinary by nature and that the best strategy for probing and furthering the boundaries of this field is most probably through a new organization of inquiry. Semati thus follows an issues-oriented approach to the study of IC, illustrating how the field is shaped by the concerns and political dispositions of scholars, journalists, and activists, as much as it has been influenced by the role of government or state-driven and -funded research, by the intellectual power of concepts, and by world processes such as modernization and development.

Thussu (2006) is concerned with the economic and political dimensions of IC, identifying a recurrent theme of dependency intertwined with economic and political supremacy of the global North and its effects on the global South. Hamelink (1996) argues that the "international" is better expressed as "world," whereby world communication is entangled to world politics, and in particular with regulation that affects the everyday lives of billions of people. As he notes, "The politics of world communication determines the variety of contents in the media, the representation of diverse social interests, the charges for use of telephone and postal services, and the quality of information networks" (2). Downing's (2000) and Rodriguez's (2001) work on alternative media and attention paid to "dewesternizing" media theory (Curran and Park 1999) point to the ways in which epistemological questions in IC are intertwined with the quality of our understanding of nondominant media and communication systems and with the ability of researchers and activists to "imagine" and conceptualize communication cultures.

From the "international," scholarship and activism have moved to address the "global" in communication and politics; this (for some, paradigmatic) shift took place with the influence of various disciplines such as politics, economics, and sociology, through their attention to processes that have been taking place at a global scale. Globalization literature has equally affected our ways of understanding communication processes and structures, as parts of "global" or "world" or "universal" processes, similarly so experienced as well. Rantanen's (2005) *Media and Globalization* attempts to bring together the study of such experiences by four generations of culturally and nationally distinct families through a century of "globalization" and the study of their use of media and their development during this period.

The study of globalization has led to that of transnational networks, such as diasporic communities and their uses of communication technologies to connect, maintain, and develop cultural affiliations with the lacing of origins and their current locations. Transnationalism, diaspora, and media studies (Karim 2003) explore emerging and understudied conditions in IC, such as patterns of transnational media production and consumption that are attached to growing human mobility; the political and cultural challenges attached to the expansion of diasporic communications for the nation-state and the media industry; and the growing role of the city for mediated communications and political and cultural representation (Georgiou 2006). Transnational communication consists of the interaction among not institutions and systems but rather citizens, social groups, and organizations of a civil society character.

In 1989 a unique anthology on women and international communication, *Communication at the Crossroads: The Gender Gap Connection*, edited by Donna Allen and Ramona Rush, challenged dominant views by arguing that communications globally were at a crossroads due to both women's difference from men's realities and experiences and their work and analysis based on that difference. In their book *Women Transforming Communications: Global Intersections*, Allen, Rush, and Kaufman (1996) addressed IC as a question of networking, and in particular women's international networking and its impact upon systems and ideas of communication. The shift of emphasis to transnational networks, citizens, connectivity, and social movements, coupled with the strategies employed by media companies around the world to appear to their "local" audiences, have led scholars to argue that we are witnessing a paradigmatic shift in scholarship that corresponds to contemporary sociopolitical changes.

Many argue that we are moving into a third-level paradigm in IC studies: that of transnationalization, which emerges after internationalization and globalization (Chalaby 2005). This neat separation is largely based on the impact of communication technologies on the operational strategies of media industries around the world. A particular emphasis is given to the ways in which local—or national—contexts are considered in their own cultural terms for the promotion of media products, through the use of local media workers and nationally focused strategies which, however, utilize central audiovisual and archive libraries and promote the same brand. Without ignoring their differences, but rather concentrating on possible common concerns of distinct intellectual traditions, such as the North American emphasis on international and the European focus on the cultural and global dimensions of communication, it is possible to identify a more complex trend in the study of IC, as this derives from the many writings of feminist media and cultural scholarship across the world. Shome (2006) illustrates this intellectual liveliness by arguing that transnational feminist perspectives recognize that gender *is* global, and that "gender troubles always manifest global troubles" (255). Space and place, their interconnections and asymmetries, are at the vanguard of transnational feminist frameworks.

Feminist Perspectives in International Communication

Major feminist writers in the field of international communication, such as Gertrude Robinson (1998, 2005), Annabelle Sreberny-Mohammadi (1996), Donna Allen and Ramona Rush (1989), Donna Allen, Ramona R. Rush, and Susan Kaufman (1996), Margaret Gallagher (1979, 2001), and third-world feminist theorists such as Pilar Riaño (1994) and Kiran Prasad (2005) have explored the international dimensions of communication in national and local contexts, while theorizing their connections to international affairs, systems of governance, and domination. A rich multiperspectival body of literature, which remains largely either unacknowledged or ignored by the vast majority of considered key texts in the IC field, has been systematically addressing IC questions almost as if in a parallel universe. This literature, however, finds better reception among certain international organizations and disciplines and has influenced international policy and programs on the information society, abundantly evident with the World Summits on the Information Society (WSIS) in Geneva (2003) and Tunis (2005) and its Gender Caucus (Gurumurthy et al. 2006; Jensen 2005; Sreberny 2005).

Interdisciplinary attempts to explore the complex issues in the field come from authors in varied fields, including international relations (Gillian Youngs's work on gender, technology, and IR); political science (Saskia Sassen's work on digital cities and global assemblages); women's studies and communication (Lisa McLaughlin's work on the global public sphere and feminism and Carolyn Byerly's work on international news and women); law (Catherine McKinnon's work on pornography and civil rights, and the legal recognition of rape as a weapon of war); social policy (Catherine Itzin's work on pornography and civil liberties); and science and technology studies (Donna Haraway's pioneering manifesto on the emancipatory potential for communication technologies).[1]

Minding the Gap

In all these accounts and others, which space prohibits a definitive exploration thereof, the levels of "international," "global," and "transnational" are addressed through the lenses of sensitivity to and awareness of the female human condition. Feminist accounts therefore bring together in an unconventional manner the study of the inter-, trans-, and supra-national with the global, shedding light on and challenging the perceived dichotomies of local and global, difference and universality, public and private, national and international. In this vein, this book approaches international communication with "feminist curiosity" and through an organization of inquiry that is both conventional to the field's major conceptual themes, such as international flows of information, international communication technologies, and the question of hegemony and inequity. At the same time, its approach makes visible the gaps in IC scholarship through an attention not only to representation but to the possibilities of new technologies, the realities of labor conditions, the sway of consumption cultures, and local, national, and international policy.

Feminist political economy is at the fore of these chapters. An increasingly dynamic and critical scholarship points to the resiliency and pertinence of applying a feminist lens to crucial issues surrounding media institutions and policies. In their lively and ground-breaking book *Sex & Money*, Riordan and Meehan (2002) argue that "all media structures, agents, processes, and expressions find their raison d'être in relationships shaped by sex and money" (x). They therefore encourage communication scholars to rethink ontological and epistemological assumptions to further understand communication processes at various levels—personal, structural, and institutional; to further interrogate the blurring boundaries of the private and the public; and to stress how "vested economic interests shape one's leisure and personal identity" (x).

In its orientation toward feminist political economy, this book examines several themes: how women are targeted as consumers within various media enterprises; women's access to and participation in diverse communication technologies, from the Internet to book publishing; the relationship between gender and the ownership of media and cultural industries; the impact of gender on global information flows; media structuring and organization of social relations; the impact of information and communication technologies (ICTs) on women's work and working conditions; international divisions of labor; media and ICT policy at local, national, and international levels; and feminist activism and praxis.

Part I, Revisiting International Communication Studies, takes a fresh look at origins, themes, and tensions in feminist IC. Margaret Gallagher, whose pioneering work on gendered media representation and policies has bridged the gap between academia and nongovernmental policy forums, presents a synopsis of the structures and processes of the contemporary global media system in terms of content, representation, and policies. She reminds us that many of the issues we face today—related to power, hegemony, access, autonomy, and equitable working conditions—are the same issues we faced three decades ago, albeit wrapped in a new technological and political guise. Reviewing a decade of work on the Global Media Monitoring Project, she reports the continued dismal coverage—or absence—of women in news reporting and news production. While internationally women's groups have demanded accountability from media organizations, global trends toward conglomeration and hypercommercialization often render these efforts futile, and it is debatable whether the Internet presents more opportunities for women. Inflecting gender issues into media policy interventions, while increasing, has often muddied the public's perception toward "women's issues" as being against freedom of expression. Recent mainstream media spins on "women's oppression" in Afghanistan and Iraq, coupled with activist reactions against the Bush administration, highlight the possibilities of a transnational "politics of solidarity."

Gillian Youngs considers the epistemological relation between IC and international relations (IR) and how an application of the "private/public" is essential to feminist theorizing of IC. Masculinist conceptions of the state, politics, and markets dominate IC and IR scholarship and discourse; this public paradigm lords over the private paradigm that is relegated to women. Feminists rightly protest, she argues, about the continuing dominance of masculine worldviews in IC and IR and are correct in their contention that this partial perspective produces a skewed view of the world. Feminist IR has made notable gains in that field related to gender and spatial politics which can benefit feminist IC. Mobile communications create fresh opportunities for feminist IC scholars to reconsider the tangled notions of the public and private, a theme that is further explored in Crow and Sawchuk's chapter on spectrum policy.

Debunking discourses that posit the "information society" as a democratic and gender-free space is the focus of Ursula Huw's chapter. Historically access to communication technologies has been a key requisite for women's participation, but contradictions abound. As with Youngs, Huw points out how shifts in the public and private have both inhibited women and have created new opportunities. Increases in global inequities in technologies; the blurring of the citizen and the consumer; the domestication, delocalization, and outsourcing of work; erratic or unreliable labor legislation or collective agreements for workers; and the spontaneous emergence of new forms of collectivities constitute the often disembodied parameters of the information society.

The gendering of media and cultural policy is the focus of part II. Alison Beale considers how international cultural policy and governance deploys the ideal of women to formulate international treaties and conventions, but she argues that these policies do not benefit women. As a burgeoning area of concern for national and international governments and with its reconceptualization of citizenship and cultural security, feminists, Beale argues, need to be active in these debates. Kiran Prasad's panoramic accounting of development communication and policy with a focus on India details the challenges faced by the dominance of Western norms in efforts to create and enforce policy on women's fair representation. She also describes international and local forums to promote women's media participation and empowerment and the use of appropriate technology, such as radio, to meet community needs. Women-led NGO energy has been crucial in partnering with government to create innovative and effective development programs. Barbara Crow and Kim Sawchuk look at the communications spectrum from the purview of international communication policy, and international communication policy from the purview of feminism, with particular attention to the technical, political, and economic conditions that support everyday media consumption. They advocate that feminists become cognizant of gender infrastructure development and ownership to ensure that spectrum remains a public good and that it be a crucial element of feminist media democracy platforms.

Making visible the invisible mobile communication devices and using them for social justice is a key challenge for feminists. Sarikakis and Shaukat sketch the enormous contours of the global pornography industry, with its staggering revenues and complicity with major media conglomerates and governments. International policy has grappled with how to regulate porn; differing cultural norms and national conceptions of speech rights make this an enormous challenge. Moreover, there seems to be a more subtle, untold understanding that porn is largely based on "choice," the basis of individualistic neoliberalism, but also that its laborers are not "worthy" of protection. Implicated are querulous labor rights issues of women in the industry, the "pornofication" of culture, and its impact on gender equity and human rights—issues that IC has to date not sufficiently addressed.

Part III considers the mediation of meanings within regimes of power in various media—print, music videos, and the Internet—in Canada, the Arab countries, Africa, and Western countries. Yasmin Jiwani reflects on international mediations of violence within Canada and specifically the effect of race and gender for indigenous and racialized minority women, arguing that transnational imagery is central to the complicity of mainstream media in framing gender and racializing women of color and indigenous women unless they acquiesce and assimilate. Her case studies of news coverage of Muslim women post–September 11 and missing and murdered Aboriginal women in Canada reveal how the news media construct notions of "legitimate" victimhood versus invisibility.

Salam Al-Mahadin's political economy of the female body in Arab media examines the nexus between "media subjectivity" and the political, social, religious, and economic realities of Arab societies through the inscription of the "female body politic" in music videos. In their analysis of news agency coverage of the United Nations' Millennium Development Goals (MDGs), Nancy Van Leuven, C. Anthony Giffard, Sheryl Cunningham, and Danielle Newton argue that media often ignore issues related to women's human rights, empowerment, and equality, especially crucial development issues of reproductive and sexual rights. Rather than repeatedly utilize the frames of poverty and maternity, media should create new framings that value women's human rights and autonomy. While the global HIV/AIDS pandemic continues to devastate Africa, women and children are the real victims here, yet media coverage rarely focuses on how gender discrimination and human rights violations perpetrate this disaster. Patricia Made challenges South African media to cease its gender-blind coverage of HIV/AIDS, a symbolic annihilation whose invisibility is devastating. Journalists, she contends, must mainstream gender in their media coverage as a matter of basic human rights and dignity. The gendering of news is also explored by Jayne Rodgers in her chapter, where she looks both at news as a gendered product and at the creation of independent online media. Do online media replicate, or deviate from, gendered patterns of employment and coverage? Surveying the independent landscape, she advocates for more inclusion of feminist voices and news within existing forums, as well as the creation of new, exciting venues.

The authors in part IV recognize that, in both IC and feminist communication studies, labor has been a conspicuously absent yet vital element. Vincent Mosco, Catherine McKercher, and Andrew Stevens reflect on the interrelationship among feminist political economy studies of labor and communication and the increasingly blurring boundaries between home and work, thanks to technological convergence and neoliberal trade agendas. In order to understand the relationship of gender to the workplace, they argue, it is imperative to understand the relationship of the workplace to the home. ICTs that enable home-based work, immigrant women's labor that is cheap and "flexible," women's immaterial labor, transnational outsourcing, and how trade unions are address-ing this contingent workforce of permatemps all point to the necessity of femi-nist political-economic analyses. Lisa McLaughlin argues that policies and proj-ects in ICT for development are not gender-blind, as claimed by many gender and development advocates. Rather they often are gender-biased in a way that defines and targets women specifically as information workers. She analyzes the "corporatization of development" at WSIS—propelled through multistake-holder processes defined as democratic and cooperative efforts, but which ulti-mately privileged the private sector and neoliberal supporters of market-based development—through a focus on United Nations agency gender initiatives and the major router manufacturer Cisco Systems, which promised to empower women by training them in the manufacture and repair of their routing hard-ware. The fantastic revenues of the young twins Mary-Kate and Ashley Olsen, American entertainment-lifestyle moguls, whose billion-dollar empire is lauded in celebrity and business magazines, are contrasted to the lives and livelihoods of the exploited Bangladeshi women who sew their branded line of clothing, re-tailed by megagiant Wal-Mart. Leslie Shade and Nikki Porter consider the ab-sence of "girls studies" in IC, and the disjointed global labor conditions that em-power some but disempower many others.

The negotiation of glocal media and technology cultures is addressed in the last part of this anthology. Simone Murray outlines the trajectory of the femi-nist book industry, a neglected area of study in communication and women's studies, and shows how trends in the political economy of the global publishing industry have curtailed independent and innovative publishing initiatives. While mainstream publishers are loathe to solicit and market feminist content, the Internet offers some possibilities for feminist publishers, but much work needs to be done to achieve wider success, such as in feminist book distribution. The relationship of gender/women to communication in Eastern European countries is explored by Valentina Marinescu; in particular she examines the impact of women's communicative actions in shaping the "democratic sphere" in the EE. She finds that in order to gain public and political visibility and so-cioeconomic empowerment, women's rights within and through the media must be advanced. Innovative use and adoption of ICTs is also a requisite, as well as gender mainstreaming within media organizations. Mary Griffiths examines de-bates in New Zealand around media classification and censorship conducted by the Office of Film and Literature Classification (OCFL) and how a new politi-cal regime that is avowedly conservative has swayed consensus on what are con-sidered to be traditional family values and gender roles. Adopting the Associa-tion for Progressive Communication's Gender Evaluation Methodology (GEM), Claire Buré's case studies focus on how communities in the Philippines and Ecuador negotiated this evaluative tool. She recommends that GEM be locally grounded and oriented to the needs of the telecentre and community and that there be a sensitivity toward communities where gender issues and gender equality are not routinely considered.

Interrelated themes explored in this anthology include that of the public-private dichotomy and its blurring in everyday social, economic, and cultural life (Youngs; Huws; Beale; Al-Mahani; Crow and Sawchuk; Mosco et al.; Marinescu); violence, as a matter of inequality, symbolic and material discrimination, and abuse (Sarikakis and Shaukat; Jiwani; Al-Mahadin; Made); and the impact of ICTs on women's lives and gender relations (Youngs; Huws; Prasad; Crow and Sawchuk; Rodgers; Mosco et al.; McLaughlin; Murray; Buré). Throughout the chapters, the impact of patriarchal cultures in the structures and functions of media and the culture industry is a common thread, as an underlying, nearly universal "language" in IC, which, despite its various expressions, itself constitutes a field of inquiry.

The anthology also extends its analysis to identify the rationale and need for the integration of "mainstream" international studies with the analysis of gender as a factor inherent in both the micropolitics of everyday life and therefore the materialization of citizenship and the macropolitics of elite and long-term decision-making processes and settings which affect the human condition across cultures and nations. It therefore critically examines policy regimes in the cultural as well as more conventionally understood front of media structures, raising questions of development, emancipation, and human dignity, while critically analyzing "cultures" of discrimination that endanger women's lives, use women (but not to their benefit), and exclude women from communicative processes and resources (Beale; Prasad; Sarikakis and Shaukat; Crow and Sawchuk; Made; McLaughlin; Shade and Porter).

Future Research for the Curious Feminist

Enloe's Curious Feminist listens carefully, digs deep, challenges assumptions, and welcomes surprises. As we end the first decade of the millennium, the Curious Feminist can find many research gaps to fill within academia, policy, and activism. Byerly and Ross's Model of Women's Media Action (2006) is useful, as are considerations of various "right to communicate" platforms and entreaties toward preservation of the global commons. We highlight four interconnected spheres:

1. *Critique and accountability of local, national, and international media regimes.* As with the pioneering work from the Global Media Monitoring Project (1995, 2000, 2005), considered effort and coordination needs to be exercised in analysis of media institutions and content at multiple sites. Methodologically these analyses can take the form of mixed quantitative

and qualitative exercises; as Fonow and Cook (2005) outline, feminist methodologies for the social sciences include a rich array of resources to produce and distribute feminist knowledge.

2. *Education and awareness, advocacy, and activism around intersections of local, national, and international media and cultural policy.* Media and cultural policy issues do not take place in a vacuum; the transnationalization of media industries is impacted by international policy regimes and governance structures constructed by the interests of international trade agendas, the private sector, and to a certain extent civil society. Knowledge of and participation in media policy forums is central; dissecting the policy language and distilling it for communities is crucial.

3. *Support of independent women's and community media.* As a counter to the prevalence and power of mainstream corporate-controlled media, innovative forms of independent media—print, digital, or radio, created with open access principles—need to be nurtured and supported. Some of the more exciting initiatives have been created with the sheer stamina and pluckiness of community-based groups. Involving youth is crucial.

4. *Detailed, large-scale international, comparative, ethnographic research in coordinated themes, such as those studied in this book, is urgently needed in order to produce a cartography of the female human condition, as this is affected by the processes, cultures, and structures of international communication.* Not only research on those with access to ICTs and media, but also those without access must be undertaken, as their lives too are vividly impacted.

It is our hope that this anthology will excite more scholarship in IC with avowedly feminist orientations. We are hoping that our invocation of the Curious Feminist as evidenced by the stimulating work of our creative contributors will serve to edify, enrich, and instigate a veritable flurry of scholarship that adds immensely to feminist interventions in international communication. Finally we hope that our effort to provide visibility and a common platform for neglected or obscured questions such as those explored in this book will enrich IC mainstream scholarship and will contribute to a more synergetic and collaborative approach to the study of IC among scholars from different traditions and backgrounds.

Note

1. A few representative references to this work include Gillian Youngs, "Virtual Voices, Real Lives," in *Women@Internet*, edited by Wendy Harcourt, 55–68 (London: Zed, 1999) and "Ethics of Access: Globalization, Feminism and Information Society," *Global Ethics* 1, no. 1 (2005): 69–84; Saskia Sassen, "Women's Burden: Countergeographies of Globalization and the Feminization of Survival," *Journal of International Affairs* 53, no. 2 (2000): 503–24 and *Territory, Authority, Rights:*

From Medieval to Global Assemblages (Princeton, NJ: Princeton University Press, 2006); Lisa McLaughlin, "Feminism and the Political Economy of Transnational Space," *The Sociological Review* 52, no. 1 (2004): 156–75; Carolyn Byerly, "Feminist Interventions in Newsrooms," in *Women and Media: International Perspectives*, edited by Karen Ross and Carolyn M. Byerly, 109–31 (Oxford: Blackwell Publishing, 2004); Catharine A. McKinnon, *Feminism Unmodified* (Cambridge, MA: Harvard University Press, 1987) and *Are Women Human? And Other International Dialogues* (Belknap Press, 2006); Catherine Itzin, *Pornography: Women, Violence and Civil Liberties* (Oxford: Oxford University Press, 1993); Donna Haraway, "A Cyborg Manifesto: Science, Technology, and Socialist-Feminism in the Late Twentieth Century," in *Simians, Cyborgs and Women: The Reinvention of Nature*, 149–81 (New York: Routledge, 1991).

References

Allen, Donna, and Ramona R. Rush, eds. 1989. *Communication at the Crossroads: The Gender Gap Connection.* Norwood, NJ: Ablex.

Allen, Donna, Ramona R. Rush, and Susan J. Kaufman, eds. 1996. *Women Transforming Communications: Global Intersections.* New York: Sage.

Alleyne, Mark. 1995. *International Power and International Communication.* New York: St. Martin's Press.

Byerly, Carolyn M., and Karen Ross. 2006. *Women and Media: A Critical Introduction.* Oxford: Blackwell.

Chalaby, Jean L. 2005. "From Internationalization to Transnationalism." *Global Media and Communication* 1 (1): 28–33.

Curran, James, and Myung-Jin Park. 1999. *De-Westernizing Media Studies.* London: Routledge.

DeVereaux, Constance, and Martin Griffin. 2006. "International, Global, Transnational: Just a Matter of Words?" *Eurozine.* http://eurozine.com/pdf/2006-10-11-devereauxgriffin-en.pdf (accessed 22 February 2007).

Downing, John D. H. 2000. *Radical Media: Rebellious Communication and Social Movements.* Thousand Oaks, CA: Sage.

Enloe, Cynthia. 2004. *The Curious Feminist: Searching for Women in a New Age of Empire.* Berkeley: University of California Press.

Fonow, Mary Margaret, and Judith A. Cook. 2005. "Feminist Methodologies: New Applications in the Academy and Public Policy." *Signs* 30 (4): 2221–36.

Fortner, Robert S. 1992. *International Communication: History, Conflict and Control of the Global Metropolis.* Belmont, CA: Wadsworth Publishing.

Gallagher, Margaret. 1979. *The Portrayal and Participation of Women in the Media.* Paris: UNESCO.

———. 2001. *Gender Setting: New Agendas for Media Monitoring and Advocacy.* London: Zed Books.

Georgiou, Myria. 2006. *Diaspora, Identity and the Media: Diasporic Transnationalism and Mediated Spatialities.* Cresskill, NJ: Hampton Press.

Gurumurthy, Anita, Parminder Jeet Singh, Anu Mundkur, and Mridula Swamy, eds. 2006. *Gender in the Information Society: Emerging Issues.* Bangkok: Asian-Pacific Development Information Programme, United Nations Development Program and Elsevier. www.apdip.net/publications/ict4d/GenderIS.pdf (accessed 1 March 2007).

Hamelink, Cees. 1996. *World Communication: Disempowerment and Self-Empowerment.* London: Zed Books.

Jensen, Heike. 2005. "Gender and the WSIS Process: War of the Words." In *Vision in Process.* Berlin: Heinrich Böll Foundation. www.boell.de/de/04_thema/2271.html (accessed 1 March 2007)

Karim, Karim H., ed. 2003. *The Media of Diaspora: Mapping the Globe.* London: Routledge.

Meehan, Eileen R., and Ellen Riordan. 2001. *Sex & Money: Feminism and Political Economy in the Media*. Minneapolis: University of Minnesota Press.

Mowlana, Hamid. 1997. *Global Information and World Communication: New Frontiers in International Relations*. London: Sage.

Prasad, Kiran, ed. 2005. *Women and Media: Challenging Feminist Discourse*. Delhi: The Woman Press.

Rakow, Lana F., and Laura A. Wackwitz. 2004. *Feminist Communication Theory: Selections in Context*. Thousand Oaks, CA: Sage.

Rantanen, Tehri. 2005. *The Media and Globalization*. London: Sage.

Riaño, Pilar, ed. 1994. *Women in Grassroots Communication: Furthering Social Change*. Thousand Oaks, CA: Sage.

Riordan, Ellen, and Eileen R. Meehan. 2002. Introd. to *Sex & Money: Feminism and Political Economy in the Media*. Minneapolis: University of Minnesota Press.

Robinson, Gertrude J. 1998. "Monopolies of Knowledge in Canadian Communication Studies: The Case of Feminist Approaches." *Canadian Journal of Communication* 23 (1). www.cjc-online.ca/viewarticle.php?id=446 (accessed 28 February 2007).

———. 2005. *Gender, Journalism, and Equity: Canadian, US, and European Perspectives*. Cresskill, NJ: Hampton Press.

Rodriguez, Clemencia. 2001. *Fissures in the Mediascape: An International Study of Citizen's Media*. Creskill, NJ: Hampton Press.

Ross, Karen, and Carolyn M. Byerly, eds. 2004. *Women and Media: International Perspectives*. Oxford: Blackwell Publishing.

Semati, Mehdi, ed. 2004. *New Frontiers in International Communication Theory*. Lanham, MD: Rowman and Littlefield.

Shome, Raka. 2006. "Transnational Feminism and Communication Studies." *The Communication Review* 9: 255–67.

Sreberny, Annabelle. 2005. "Why Sis! Gender, WSIS and Tunis." *Media Development* 3. www.wacc.org.uk/wacc/publications/media_development/2005_3/why_sis_gender_wsis_and_tunis (accessed 1 March 2007).

Sreberny-Mohammadi, Annabelle. 1996. "International Feminism(s): Engendering Debate in International Communications." *Journal of International Communication* 3 (1): 1–3.

Taylor, Philip. 1997. *Global Communications, International Affairs and the Media since 1945*. New York: Routledge.

Thussu, Daya Kishan. 2006. *International Communication: Continuity and Change*, 2d ed. London: Hodder Arnold.

CHAPTER TWO

Feminist Issues
and the Global Media System
Margaret Gallagher

When the Taliban successfully captured Kabul in September 1996, they
immediately did two things: they barred women from . . . any participation
in the public sphere, and they banned television. Control over these two
elements—women and the media—lay at the heart of the Taliban regime. It
is interesting to note that the state of each is increasingly taken as a key index of the democratization and development of a society.

— Annabelle Sreberny, "Seeing Through the Veil"[1]

Over the past twenty-five years, analytical critique of the interconnections between women, media, and sociopolitical processes has occupied an ever more
central place on the international agenda. This has occurred against a background of dramatic transformations brought about by changes in the global media system. Well-documented trends include the emergence of a small number
of global conglomerates that dominate transnational media production and
flows; the spread of commercialized, consumer-oriented media; the diffusion of
Western-inspired program genres and formats; and the spread of promarket media regulatory frameworks (Zhao and Hackett 2005).

From a feminist perspective, the general thrust of the emerging global media
system is challenging at various levels. The trends are not conducive to pluralism, to diversity, or to public interest values—which many feminists have argued are among the foundations on which greater equality of representation in

17

media structures and content depend. Moreover, the convergence of media technology and services—a gradual merging of television, radio, print, computers, and the Internet—has blurred the boundaries between definitions of "old" and "new" media, as well as of "mainstream" and "alternative" media. At the same time, the globalization of media distribution systems, formats, and applications calls into question what have traditionally been considered national media and local identities.

These convergences and shifting boundaries make it increasingly problematic to maintain distinctions that have traditionally characterized the study of women and communications internationally—production, content, users, and policies. Having said that, the remainder of this chapter will explore global patterns within some of these broad categories, which continue to be helpful in shedding light on empirical trends and emerging issues around the world. Nevertheless, these separate issues should be understood as belonging to a multilayered conceptualization of the structure and process of gender representation in the media; the political, cultural, and economic formations that support this structure and process; the social relations that produce gendered subjects; and the nature of gendered identity.

Powerful Issues: Media Employment and Decision Making

It is salutary to be reminded that—despite today's theoretical sophistication, and even though the global political and communication environment has changed dramatically—feminist communication analysis still wrestles with issues that are fundamentally similar to those it faced thirty years ago. They revolve around the most basic questions of power, values, access, and exclusion. Indeed, one of the key contributions of feminist scholarship has been to uncover the embedded nature of gender-based judgements and assumptions—assumptions that permeate not just the media but all social, economic, and political institutions. Thus although early diagnoses called for a "critical mass" of women in the media as part of the solution to the problem, it is now clear that "the problem" is both more deeply rooted and more overarching than can be solved by a numerical redistribution.

Women are now an important middle-level cohort of producers, directors, journalists, and reporters in the media of many countries round the world. The only available international comparative study (Gallagher 1995) found that approximately a third of radio and television producers in Southern Africa and in Latin America were women; in Europe the equivalent figure was 37 percent. Of particular significance is the increasing presence of women as newscasters and program presenters in television. The phenomenon is widespread. For example, the 2005 Global Media Monitoring Project (GMMP), which monitored the news in seventy-six countries, found that 57 percent of television news items were presented by women on the monitoring day. Yet only 29 percent of newspaper stories were reported by women (Gallagher 2006).

The disproportion is intriguing—and not necessarily reassuring. In their study of women in journalism in the U.S. and the UK, Chambers et al. (2004) speak of "women journalists as spectacle," claiming that "in television where spectacle counts—emphasis on the decorative value and even sexualization of women journalists is overt" (1). And indeed global data show that female television reporters and presenters disappear from the screen once they reach age fifty, though up to their midthirties women are in the majority in both of these roles (Gallagher 2006).

This increased presence of women on the screen and in a few other high-profile positions almost certainly contributes to a gulf between perceptions and reality. Women still have very little real decision making power within the media. In 2000 the International Federation of Journalists (IFJ) conducted a survey covering 70 percent of its membership in thirty-nine countries. It found that although more than a third of journalists are women, less than 3 percent of senior media executives and decision makers are female (Peters 2001). In the newly emerging media industries, the picture does not look much better. A study of the major telecommunications and e-companies in the U.S. established that only 13 percent of top executives are women (Jamieson 2001).

Why do so few women break through the glass ceiling? The 2000 IFJ survey compared results with those from a similar survey conducted a decade earlier. Ten years after that first study, many issues remain unresolved. Women still lose out in appointments to the top jobs; have less access to training; earn less than their male coworkers; are confronted with job segregation, limited promotion perspectives, and sexual harassment; and continue to face impossible choices between career and family life. But by far the most common obstacle to advancement that women media professionals report is the problem of male attitudes (de Bruin and Ross 2004). In certain countries, the overwhelmingly male media culture makes it almost impossible for women to feel comfortable and thus to thrive professionally. For instance in Korea, according to Kim (2006), authoritative news-gathering methods, informal communication between (male) journalists, and traditional perceptions of women all come together as exclusion mechanisms that result in the alienation of female journalists.

The implicit "rules of the game" that permeate media organizations are most starkly apparent when it comes to the reporting of war. When British journalist Yvette Ridley was arrested by the Taliban in Afghanistan in 2001, she was vilified in the press for having risked "making her daughter an orphan" (quoted in Magor 2002, 143). As Magor points out, the parallel case of French journalist Michel Peyrard, also a parent, provoked no accusations of irresponsibility toward his family. Men's professional role is accepted as paramount. Women's professional role is conditional and secondary. In the context of war and conflict, deeply inscribed gender distinctions come to the fore in relation to whose voices prevail. Feminist analyses of twenty-first-century wars—particularly in Afghanistan and Iraq—have focused on the manipulation, ridiculing, or exclusion of women's voices in news coverage of these conflicts (for instance, *Feminist Media Studies* 2002 ; *Feminist Media Studies* 2005; Lemish 2005).

The experience of "otherness" expressed by many female media professionals is widespread. Interviews with journalists in Mumbai, Toronto, Sydney, and Melbourne reveal that in all these cities women encounter discrimination in newsrooms—experiences that "represent a global scenario . . . in regards to gendered professional practices" (Mahtani 2005, 309). Not surprisingly, these gendered experiences and practices are rarely recognized as such by men. In her study of British journalists, Margareta Melin-Higgins (2004) found that though most of her male interviewees did not believe that female journalists today face gender-based obstacles, all of the women she interviewed did report such problems. This experience of gender-based discrimination is one of the main reasons why women decide to leave the industry (American Press Institute/Pew 2002, Mahtani 2005, Opoku-Mensah 2004).

There is no easy way of dismantling the obstacles faced by women media professionals. For example, Goga (2001) found that affirmative action policies in the South African media have increased the number of women and people of color, even in higher grades. But because white males continue to be concentrated in top management, inequality persists in the "power relations" at work within media organizations. These are rooted in much deeper structures of privilege and are infinitely more difficult to breach. Moreover, as studies in Canada (Aldridge 2001) and the UK (Antcliff 2005) have shown, changes in the commercial ethos of the media can lead to the reversal of gains. Apparent progress in women's employment in the media is thus contingent and fragile in the context of today's increasingly market-driven media system.

Critical Issues: Content and Portrayal

If women's lack of power within the media industries is an international phenomenon, gender portrayal in the media seems to conform to an equally universal pattern. Wherever one looks, media content reflects a masculine vision of the world and of what is important.

Every five years since 1995, the Global Media Monitoring Project (GMMP) has provided a one-day snapshot of "who makes the news" in the newspapers, radio, and television of more than seventy countries. The 1995 study found that women were only 17 percent of the world's news subjects—the people who are interviewed or whom the news is about (MediaWatch 1995). Five years later, the figure was 18 percent (Spears and Seydegart 2000). By 2005 the number had risen to 21 percent (Gallagher 2006). Regional differences are slight, ranging from a high of 26 percent in North America to a low of 15 percent in the Middle East. Everywhere, expert opinion is overwhelmingly male; men are 83 percent of experts and 86 percent of spokespersons. When popular opinion is solicited in news stories, the views of women—52 percent of the world's population—account for only 34 percent of those interviewed. There is not a single major news topic in which women outnumber men as newsmakers. In stories on politics and government, only 14 percent of news subjects are women. Even in stories that affect women profoundly, such as gender-based violence, it is the male voice (64 percent of news subjects) that prevails.

The results across the three studies (1995–2005) are strikingly consistent, and they have been replicated in research carried out over a longer time frame. For instance, a one-month study in twelve Southern African countries in 2002 found that 17 percent of news subjects were women (Gender and Media Baseline Study 2003). The numbers tell only a tiny part of the story. Behind them lies a power structure—social, political, and economic—in which men are predominant. News values intertwine with political priorities to portray a particular view of what is important. Issues that are central in women's lives come low down in the scale of what is regarded as newsworthy, and specific categories of women are practically invisible. The 2005 GMMP found that only 4 percent of news stories deal in any way with issues of gender equality or inequality (Gallagher 2006; Byerly 2002). Older women are virtually absent from media content (Tielen and Groombridge 2000). And if women are underrepresented or misrepresented in media content, this is doubly so for those women who are not members of the dominant national culture (Valdivia 2000; Shields 2003; Media Monitoring Project 1999).

As state-run media cede control to commercial interests, the struggle for change has become more complicated. Contradictions abound. In her study of women in the Indian press, Ammu Joseph concludes that with the trend towards market-driven, consumer-oriented media, "journalists who take strong positions on issues of justice risk derision, if not marginalisation. They are often referred to as crusading, campaigning or 'committed journalists' or even 'Mother Teresa's of the press'" (2000, 285). In the U.S. and the UK, say Chambers, Steiner, Fleming (2004), news organizations' search for increased market share has led to the exploitation of women journalists with a brief to produce materialist and consumerist stories that are devoid of political content. This is the paradox: as more women enter the media profession, proprietors and managements with profit-oriented agendas are exercising greater control on editorial matters, making it difficult for journalists of either sex to swim against the tide.

These contradictions attain heightened political resonance at a time when "corporate globalization is eager to capture new territories *and* religious fundamentalism endeavours to capture the imagination of local and transnational diasporic communities" (Parameswaran 2003, 311, emphasis in original). Nowhere are these political and ideological tensions more clear than in contemporary representations of veiled Muslim women (Macdonald 2006; Jiwani 2005). In the wake of 9/11, images of women in chadors, burqas, and hijabs have provided the Western media—and Western politicians—with a visual spectacle that is apparently both threatening and incomprehensible. The crude political manipulation of these images—to justify wars of "liberation" in both Afghanistan and Iraq—is clear (Stabile and Kumar 2005; Winegar 2005). Equally clear is the lack of analysis of—or indeed interest in—the nature of women's oppression. That countless Afghan women chose to retain the burqa after the overthrow of the Taliban was thus deemed inexplicable by many Western media commentators. One of the most extraordinary reasons advanced—in a widely reported news story about plans to establish a beauty school in Kabul, with help from U.S. cosmetic giant Revlon—was that the burqa helped women to "hide their unfashionable clothing" (BBC News 2002).

The deep-seated sexism evident in contemporary media content, despite the measurable presence of more women working in media organizations, has increasingly preoccupied feminist activists and researchers internationally. In an important 1994 essay, the late Donna Allen, founder of the Women's Institute for Freedom of the Press, emphasized the need to bridge the gap between women's groups and associations outside and inside the media, if women's experiences and viewpoints were to get a better hearing (Allen 1994). At more or less the same time, groups such as Cotidiano Mujer in Uruguay, the Media Advocacy Group in India (now known as the Centre for Advocacy and Research), Women's Media Watch in Jamaica, and later Gender Links in South Africa, were thinking along the same lines (Gallagher 2001; Byerly and Ross 2006). Such groups believe that without interaction and professional dialogue—between researchers, activists, audiences, advertisers, journalists, radio and television producers—there can be no progress. Inevitably initiatives of this sort are most likely to succeed in a media environment of public responsibility. But the global trend toward rabidly commercial, market-driven media must place a question mark over the future viability of these strategies.

Frontier Issues: The Internet Era

In her essay "Cyberspace: The New Feminist Frontier?" Gillian Youngs argues that the Internet is "actually and potentially revolutionary for women and feminist activism" (2004, 190) because it disrupts both patriarchal as well as national and international boundaries. It is in this sphere above all others that the notion of "globalization from below"—using communication networks to challenge dominant transnational media—seems potentially attainable. However, as Youngs points out, the historically embedded nature of gender inequality—and the specific history of male domination in science and technology—means that the radical potential of new communication technologies is far from guaranteed.

A determining issue is accessibility. Women represent a growing proportion of Internet users in many parts of the world. But truly significant numbers of women are currently online in only a small number of countries beyond the OECD (Organisation for Economic Co-operation and Development) group. In most regions, home access to a computer and to the Internet are rare outside the upper income strata. For many women, the Internet is frustrating and inaccessible—often because of technical problems and costs of access, but also due to lack of training and knowledge (AWORC 2001; Morna and Khan 2000). But for those who do have access, the Internet can indeed be a force for change. Examples range from broad-based initiatives to share concerns about women's roles and give "voice to the voiceless" in South Asia (Mitra 2004) to specific, issue-based applications, such as a campaign for women's suffrage in Kuwait (Wheeler 2004).

However, despite the hyperbole that often surrounds them, the new communication technologies are inherently no better than the old ones—print, radio, television, and so on. Just as we have had to deconstruct traditional media beliefs, such as "news is news," so we now have to challenge the idea that "technology is technology"—that it is gender-neutral. In fact, patterns of gender segregation, which are well known in the established media industries, are already being reproduced in the new information and technology sector worldwide. Men are more likely to be found in the high-paying, creative work of software development or Internet start-ups, whereas employees in single-tasked ICT work, such as cashiers or data-entry workers, are predominantly female and low-paid (ILO 2001). Women are virtually absent from senior decision making and politically influential positions in the sector.

The almost complete absence of women from the production of new media software (and hardware) raises the question of how women's viewpoints, knowledge, and interests can be adequately represented in the new media. One of the reasons given by women to explain their low attendance at telecenters in Africa is language and content that does not "speak to them" (Morna and Khan 2000). Language in this sense means mode of address rather than proficiency in a foreign language—though the latter is also a major problem. The relative presence of English on the Internet is declining (an estimated decrease from 75 percent of Web pages in 1998 to 45 percent in 2005), but English remains by far the dominant language of Internet content (Funredes 2006). The fundamental issue, however, is lack of relevance. Despite the vast amount of content available on the Web, little can be of use to most women in most parts of the world. A Web search in early 2000 found some 200,000 websites related to women and gender, but only a fraction of these originated in developing countries (Fontaine 2002).

The picture that emerges from many analyses of Internet content is of a masculinist rhetoric and a set of representations that are frequently sexualized and often sexist. Pornography, e-mail harassment, "flaming" (abusive or obscene language), and cyber-stalking are well documented (van Zoonen 2002). Revenue from sex sites is said to be between several hundred million dollars and over two billion dollars annually (Hamelink 2000, 32; see also Sarikakis and Shaukut in this volume). The Internet is heavily implicated in the growth of the global sex industry, including sex tourism and trafficking in women (Hughes 2000). While women and nongovernmental organizations have used the Internet extensively to campaign against all forms of violence against women, the battle is daunting. Illustrative of this is a study of how women in Thailand tried to use a Thai-managed, English-language website to refute widespread Internet stereotypes of "the Thai woman" as either a potential prostitute or a mail-order bride. For the small group of educated, English-speaking women involved, the experience seemed affirming. But their postings were largely ignored by the (Western) male contributors, who continued to "talk directly to other men" in postings that fetishized Thai women as better wives or sexy companions (Enteen 2005, 475).

The Internet era promises even greater corporate concentration in the global distribution of news and information, with the intermingling of digital news networks, converging newsrooms, and advertisers. Given the monolithic nature of these institutions, and the lack of gender sensitivity within them, the struggle to have women's voices heard in the international news agenda is set to move into even more difficult terrain. But the emergence of another tier of information providers—from citizen journalists to Web logs to online communities—presents an independent, if fragile, alternative. Enterprises such as Women's eNews, Women's Feature Service, WINGS, and others (Byerly and Ross 2006) allow women's voices to be heard across national boundaries. The combination of Internet and radio can be especially powerful. For instance, FIRE (Feminist International Radio Endeavour) uses audio, print, and pictures to broadcast women's perspectives on issues and events around the world (Thompson, Gómez, and Todo 2005). These new linkages and new approaches to information provision hold great promise in terms of bringing women in from the margins of media and communication developments.

Foundational Issues: Policies and Their Implementation

The increasingly globalized nature of communication media, and the emergence of a market logic in the international policy arena (Ó Siochrú 2005) introduce new complexity into an already problematic, and potentially divisive, area for media reform activists. Feminists striving for genuine diversity in the media face enormous difficulties in convincing media industry bodies, practitioners, and policy makers that the search for a policy framework within which rights and freedoms can be fairly evaluated has nothing to do with censorship, but everything to do with openness and inclusiveness.

While many media organizations have policies and guidelines to prevent discrimination in employment, most are wary of equivalent provisions for media content. Where they exist, self-regulatory measures are frequently entrusted to compliance/complaints bodies that lack monitoring capacity. Action is often left to private citizens, who must watch, challenge, and litigate. However, a 2000 survey of Canadian women and men found that only 6 percent had tried to complain when they were offended by something they saw or heard in the media. This suggests that a complaints-based system of regulation will catch only a very small proportion of those who encounter offensive content, and that other channels of public criticism are needed (MediaWatch 2000).

One of the difficulties in mounting successful challenges is that media codes tend to be too general to allow unambiguous interpretation. Another problem is that when codes are specific vis à vis the portrayal of women, this tends to be expressed in moralistic terms that proscribe provocative or obscene imagery. Often these exhortations reflect obsolete interpretations of public taste. Even newly developed codes do not necessarily take account of gender. For instance, although women are frequently portrayed as sex objects in the Thai press, this was ignored in the initial draft of the Thai Press Council's 1998 Code of Ethics. Intense pressure from activists did result in the addition of a new clause stating that news reports must not victimize women or violate their dignity (Siriyusavak 1999). The example illustrates the need for gender specialists to be consulted when policies, codes, and guidelines are discussed and developed. Useful approaches to policy development based on broad consultation and dialogue have been initiated in countries such as Jamaica, Japan, South Korea, and Sri Lanka (Gallagher 2001, 39–42).

In this undeniably contentious area, the temptation to cede to a laissez-faire position is compelling. But it is certainly possible to develop frameworks that encourage reflection on the potential conflicts between human rights, freedoms, and responsibilities. Two examples—from Canada and South Africa— illustrate different approaches to the dilemma. Canada has long been acknowledged as having the most detailed codes of conduct on gender portrayal. But intense commercial pressures in Canada's media marketplace have weakened existing implementation mechanisms. An analysis commissioned by Media-Watch (Coulter and Murray 2001) concluded that in this new media environment it is important to address issues of gender equality in the context of human rights. Media regulation, says the report, is essentially a matter of balancing "collective human rights" and "individual freedom of speech"—a balance that could best be achieved in a "co-regulatory model" that would include tripartite coordination of government, industry, and civil society. South Africa's 2003 Code of Conduct for Broadcasters deals explicitly with the tension between "rights" and "freedoms," stating that in disputes

> rights of free expression will have to be weighed up against many other rights, including the right to equality, dignity, privacy, political campaigning, fair trial, economic activity, workplace democracy, property and *most significantly the rights of children and women*. (ICASA 2003, para. 7, emphasis added)

These developments offer some ways of conceptualizing the pursuit of rights and freedoms and some possible routes toward their reconciliation. But the contradictions remain profound. In Indonesia in early 2006, two almost diametrically opposed matters of public concern provoked widespread protest. One was a proposed law against pornography currently before the Parliament, against which almost all women's rights organizations, together with other civil society groups, campaigned. They were fearful that the passing of the bill—which included measures to regulate women's dress and public behavior—would open the way for greater oppression of women (Mardzoeki and Lane 2006). The second was the launch of the Indonesian edition of *Playboy* (which quickly sold out). Alongside its pictures of partly dressed women, the magazine carried an interview with Pramoedya Ananta Toer, Indonesia's most famous writer and dissident[2]—thus situating itself in a discourse of freedom of expression (IFEX 2006). These struggles around "freedom of speech" are indicative of the ways in which women's rights are threatened as politicians and media moguls pursue their disparate goals—goals over which women themselves have relatively little control.

Enduring Issues: New Spin, New Politics

> Because of our recent military gains in much of Afghanistan, women are no longer imprisoned in their homes . . . Yet the terrorists who helped rule that country now plot and plan in many countries. And they must be stopped. The fight against terrorism is also a fight for the rights and dignity of women. (Laura Bush, radio broadcast, 18 November 2001; quoted in Stabile and Kumar 2005, 765).

In a specific and disturbing way, women have come to occupy a central position in international discourses of geopolitics, media, and society. The appropriation of feminist language to sell products is nothing new (Shields 2003). But use of the rhetoric of women's rights to peddle colonial expansion, while certainly not born in the twenty-first century (Ahmed 1992), has assumed an almost emblematic position in the post-9/11 era. The invocations of women's liberation used by the Bush administration to rationalize its wars in Afghanistan and Iraq ring hollow in the aftermath of the two invasions. Each has left the women of those countries in a parlous situation (Human Rights Watch 2002; Stork and Abrahams 2004).

Large sections of the media were complicit in spinning the discourse of women's oppression that preceded those wars. Yet while the news media subsequently focused much attention on the nondiscovery of weapons of mass destruction—another chimera used to justify the bombing of Iraq—the "monumental lie" of women's liberation has gone unchallenged (Stabile and Kumar 2005, 779). In some respects, this is part of the wider issue of what Chris Paterson calls the systematic "new spin," in which politicians in both the U.S. and the UK now exercise "unprecedented control over international representations of their policies" in the media (2005, 53).

But there is an additional phenomenon at work, in terms of the priority given to particular issues. This is as true of academic analysis as it is of news coverage. Notwithstanding the plethora of scholarly articles and books on the role of the media in reporting on Iraq (e.g., Miller 2003; Tumber and Palmer 2004; Calabrese 2005), it has been left to feminist researchers to highlight the specific symbolic uses and abuses of women as vehicles in the representation of these colonialist policies. Despite the wealth of feminist scholarship in all areas of media and communication studies, these insights are rarely assimilated into "mainstream" theories and analyses (Gallagher 2003). In the field of international communication studies—to which analysis of the social impact of globalization, geopolitical propagandizing, and corporate media expansion is germane—it is especially poignant that feminist work continues to be regarded as parallel, rather than integral, to the canon.

Armand Mattelart (2003) has reminded us that it was a feminist— Flora Tristán—who coined the term "democratic cosmopolitanism" in her 1843 L'Union ouvrière, considered a forerunner of Marx and Engels' Communist Manifesto (1848). Tristán was the first to propose a Socialist International, and she devoted her short life to the promotion of women's and workers' rights and to the doctrine of international solidarity. Notions such as solidarity and internationalism came to seem outdated or utopian in the individualistic climate produced by corporate control of global communications in the late twentieth century. But recent attempts by civil society activists and academics to (re)frame the World Summit on the Information Society (WSIS) debate in terms of communication rights—though largely a failure, and a spectacular one in relation to women's communication rights—have helped to revitalize these concepts and to mobilize reflection and action around common goals.

Among the many voices today calling for interconnections between media reform movements and social networks, both local and global, feminist voices are again raised. For instance, Chandra Mohanty (2003) calls for a "politics of solidarity" and for "feminism without borders" to address the injustices of global capitalism. Ellen Riordan (2004) pleads for feminist theory to be allowed to inform political-economic analysis, so as to bring new perspectives to the study of media and communication internationally. Carolyn Byerly and Karen Ross (2006) propose a model of women's media action to explore the role of women's media activism both in women's liberation and in social transformation, within and across nations. These and other contemporary voices situate feminist scholarship within a global political economy framework, whose agenda is social change.

It has been a central argument of this chapter that the tendency to ignore women's voices is universally embedded in normative cultural and social practices. The result is an impoverishment of analysis and a weakening of the transformational potential of civil society action. In a world where the forces of globalization have simultaneously repositioned women in new systems of inequality and destabilized geopolitical boundaries, a transnational "politics of solidarity" as proposed by Mohanty is imperative. This, she argues, must be built on "mutuality, accountability, and the recognition of common interests as the basis for relationships between diverse communities" (2003, 7). This is a feminist politics—one that embraces difference while seeking inclusivity, and one that can strengthen theory and praxis in international communication studies.

Notes

This is an updated and abridged version of a paper entitled "Women, Media and Democratic Society: In Pursuit of Rights and Freedoms," written for the United Nations Expert Group Meeting on the Participation and Access of Women to the Media, organized by the UN Division for the Advancement of Women and held in Beirut, Lebanon, in November 2002. See www.un.org/womenwatch/daw/egm/media2002/reports/BP1Gallagher.PDF.

1. Annabelle Sreberny, "Seeing Through the Veil: Regimes of Representation," *Feminist Media Studies* 2, no. 2 (2002): 270–72.
2. Pramoedya Ananta Toer died on 30 April 2006.

References

Ahmed, Leila. 1992. *Women and Gender in Islam: Historical Roots of a Modern Debate.* New Haven: Yale University Press.

Aldridge, Meryl. 2001. "Lost Expectations? Women Journalists and the Fall-Out of the 'Toronto Newspaper War.' " *Media, Culture and Society* 23, no.5: 607–24.

Allen, Donna. 1994. "Women in Media, Women's Media: The Search for Linkages in North America." In *Women Empowering Communication*, ed. Margaret Gallagher and Lilia Quindoza-Santiago, 161–85. London: World Association for Christian Communication.

American Press Institute/Pew Center for Civic Journalism. 2002. "The Great Divide: Female Leadership in US Newsrooms." <www.americanpressinstitute.org/curtis/Great_Divide.pdf> (accessed 2 May 2006).

Antcliff, Valerie. 2005. "Broadcasting in the 1990s: Competition, Choice and Inequality?" *Media, Culture & Society* 27, no. 6: 841–59.

Asian Women's Resource Exchange (AWORC). 2001. The AWORC Research on the Use of Information and Communication Technologies by Women's Organisations in the Asia-Pacific Region." <www.aworc.org/went2001/tracks/joint/all-aworc-research.doc> (accessed 2 May 2006).

BBC News. 2002. "Afghan Lipstick Liberation." 17 October 2002. <http://news.bbc.co.uk/1/hi/world/south_asia/2336303.stm> (accessed 2 May 2006).

Byerly, Carolyn M. 2002. "Gender and the Political Economy of Newsmaking: A Case Study of Human Rights Coverage." In *Sex and Money: Feminism and Political Economy in the Media*, eds. Eileen R. Meehan and Ellen Riordan, 130–44. Minneapolis: University of Minnesota Press.

Byerly, Carolyn M and Karen Ross. 2006. *Women & Media: A Critical Introduction*. Oxford: Blackwell.

Calabrese, Andrew. 2005. "Casus Belli: Media and the Justification of the War in Iraq." *Television & New Media* 6, no. 2: 153–75.

Chambers, Deborah, Linda Steiner and Carole Fleming. 2004. *Women and Journalism*. London: Routledge.

Coulter, Nathalie, and Catherine Murray. 2001. "Watching the Watchers: Gender Justice and Co-regulation in the New Media Market Place." Report commissioned by MediaWatch, Toronto.

de Bruin, Marjan, and Karen Ross, eds. 2004. *Gender and Newsroom Cultures: Identities at Work*. Cresskill, NJ: Hampton Press.

Enteen, Jillana B. 2005. "Siam Remapped: Cyber-Interventions by Thai Women." *New Media & Society* 7, no. 4: 457–82.

Feminist Media Studies. 2002. "The Power of the Veil: Review Editors' Introduction." Vol. 2, no. 2: 267–72.

Feminist Media Studies. 2005. "Media Coverage of War." Vol. 2, no. 1: 127–56.

Fontaine, Mary. 2002. "A High-Tech Twist: ICT Access and the Gender Divide." *TechKnowLogia* 2, no. 2. www.techknowlogia.org/TKL_active_pages2/CurrentArticles/main.asp?IssueNumber=4&FileType=HTML&ArticleID=94 (accessed 2 May 2006).

Funredes. 2006. *Observatorio de la Diversidad Linguistica y Cultura en la Internet 2005*. Santo Domingo: Fundación Redes y Desarrollo (Funredes). www.funredes.org/lc/english/medidas/sintesis.htm (accessed 2 May 2006).

Gallagher, Margaret. 1995. "An Unfinished Story: Gender Patterns in Media Employment." Reports and Papers on Mass Communication 110. Paris: UNESCO.

———. 2001. *Gender Setting: New Agendas for Media Monitoring and Advocacy*. London: Zed Books.

———. 2003. "Feminist Media Perspectives." In *A Companion to Media Studies*, ed. Angharad N. Valdivia, 19–39. Oxford: Blackwell.

———. 2006. *Who Makes the News? Global Media Monitoring Project 2005*. London: World Association for Christian Communication.

Gender and Media Baseline Study. 2003. Windhoek/Johannesburg: Media Institute of Southern Africa/Gender Links.

Goga, Farhana. 2001. "Issues of Race and Gender in the Post-Apartheid South African Media Organizations, 1994-2000." In *Media, Democracy and Renewal in Southern Africa*, ed. Keyan Tomaselli and Hopeton Dunn, 209–29. Colorado Springs: International Academic Publishers.

Hamelink, Cees J. 2000. *The Ethics of Cyberspace*. London: Sage.

Hughes, Donna. 2000. "The Internet and Sex Industries: Partners in Global Sexual Exploitation." *Technology and Society Magazine* 19, no. 1 (2000): 35–42.

Human Rights Watch. 2002. "Taking Cover: Women in Post-Taliban Afghanistan." www.hrw.org/backgrounder/wrd/afghan-women-2k2.htm (accessed 2 May 2006).

International Freedom of Expression Exchange (IFEX). 2006. "Indonesia: 'Playboy' Magazine Sparks Violent Protests.'" *Communiqué* 15, no. 15. www.ifex.org/en/content/view/full/73908/ (accessed 2 May 2006).

International Labour Office (ILO). 2001. *World Employment Report 2001: Life at Work in the Information Society*. Geneva: International Labour Office.

Independent Communications Authority of South Africa (ICASA). 2003. *Code of Conduct for Broadcasters*. www.icasa.org.za/manager/ClientFiles/Documents/CODEGAZETTE.pdf (accessed 2 May 2006).

Jamieson, Kathleen Hall. 2001. *Progress or No Room at the Top? The Role of Women in Telecommunications, Broadcast, Cable and E-Companies*. Philadelphia: Annenberg Public Policy Center, University of Pennsylvania. www.annenbergpublicpolicycenter.org/04_info_society/women_leadership/telecom/2001_progress-report.pdf (accessed 2 May 2006).

Jiwani, Yasmin. 2005. " 'War Talk' Engendering Terror: Race, Gender and Representation in Canadian Print Media." *International Journal of Media and Cultural Politics* 1, no. 1: 15–21.

Joseph, Ammu. 2000. *Women in Journalism: Making News*. New Delhi: Konark.

Kim, Kyung-Hee. 2006. "Obstacles to the Success of Female Journalists in Korea." *Media, Culture & Society* 28, no. 1: 123–41.

Lemish, Dafna, ed. 2005. Special issue, "The Media Gendering of War." *Feminist Media Studies* 5, no. 3: 275–395.

Macdonald, Myra. 2006. "Muslim Women and the Veil: Problems of Image and Voice in Media Representations." *Feminist Media Studies* 6, no. 1: 7–23.

Magor, Maggie. 2002. "News Terrorism: Misogyny Exposed and the Easy Journalism of Conflict." *Feminist Media Studies* 2, no. 1: 141–44.

Mahtani, Minelle. 2005. "Gendered News Practices: Examining Experiences of Women Journalists in Different National Contexts." In *Journalism: Critical Issues*, ed. Stuart Allen, 299–310. Maidenhead, UK: Open University Press, 2005.

Mardzoeki, Faiza, and Max Lane. 2006. "Indonesia: Fight Broadens Against Anti-Women Laws." *Green Left Weekly*, 15 March. www.greenleft.org.au/back/2006/660/660p23.htm (accessed 2 May 2006).

Mattelart, Armand. 2003. "Realpolitik and Utopias of Universal Bonds: For a Critique of Technoglobalism." In *A Companion to Media Studies*, ed. Angharad N. Valdivia, 548–64. Oxford: Blackwell.

Media Monitoring Project. 1999. *A Snapshot Survey of Women's Representation in the South African Media at the End of the Millennium*. Study commissioned by Women's Media Watch, Media Monitoring Project, Johannesburg.

MediaWatch. 1995. *Women's Participation in the News: Global Media Monitoring Project*. Toronto: MediaWatch.

MediaWatch. 2000. Submission to the Canadian Radio-Television and Telecommunications Commission, CRTC-Corus Entertainment. Unpublished document.

Melin-Higgins, Margareta. 2004. "Coping with Journalism: Gendered Newsroom Culture." In *Gender and Newsroom Cultures: Identities at Work*, eds. Marjan de Bruin and Karen Ross, 195–220. Cresskill, NJ: Hampton Press.

Miller, David, ed. 2003. *Tell Me Lies: Propaganda and Media Distortion in the Attack on Iraq.* London: Pluto Press.

Mitra, Ananda. 2004. "Voices of the Marginalized on the Internet: Examples From a Website for Women of South Asia." *Journal of Communication* 54, no. 3: 492–510.

Mohanty, Chandra Talpade. 2003. *Feminism Without Borders: Decolonizing Theory, Practicing Solidarity.* Durham, NC: Duke University Press.

Morna, Colleen Lowe, and Zohra Khan, compilers. 2000. *Net Gains: African Women Take Stock of Information and Communication Technologies.* Research report commissioned by the Association of Progressive Communicators (APC)-Women-Africa and FEMNET.

Opoku-Mensah, Aida. 2004. "Hanging In There: Women, Gender and Newsroom Cultures in Africa." In *Gender and Newsroom Cultures: Identities at Work,* eds. Marjan de Bruin and Karen Ross, 105–17. Cresskill, NJ: Hampton Press.

Ó Siochrú, Sean. 2005. "Global Media Governance as a Potential Site of Civil Society Intervention." In *Democratizing Global Media: One World, Many Struggles,* eds. Robert A. Hackett and Yuezhi Zhao, 205–21. Lanham, MD: Rowman & Littlefield.

Parameswaran, Radhika E. 2003. "Resuscitating Feminist Audience Studies: Revisiting the Politics of Representation and Resistance." In *A Companion to Media Studies,* ed. Angharad N. Valdivia, 311–36. Oxford: Blackwell.

Paterson, Chris. 2005. "When Global Media Don't Play Ball: The Exportation of Coercion." *International Journal of Media and Cultural Politics* 1, no. 1: 53–58.

Peters, Bettina. 2001. "The Varied Pace of Women's Progress." *Nieman Reports* 55, no.4: 97–99.

Riordan, Ellen. 2004. "Feminist Theory and the Political Economy of Communication." In *Toward a Political Economy of Culture,* eds. Andrew Calabrese and Colin Sparks, 342–55. Lanham, MD: Rowman & Littlefield.

Shields, Vicki Rutledge. 2003. "The Less Space We Take the More Powerful We'll Be: How Advertising Uses Gender to Invert Signs of Empowerment and Social Equality." In *A Companion to Media Studies,* ed. Angharad N. Valdivia, 247–68. Oxford: Blackwell.

Siriyuvasak, Ubonrat. 1999. *A Thailand Country Report.* Report for Media and Gender Policy in a Global Age, Asian Network of Women in Communication/World Association for Christian Communication, Manipal/London.

Spears, George, and Kasia Seydegart, with Margaret Gallagher. 2000. *Who Makes the News? Global Media Monitoring Project 2000.* London: World Association for Christian Communication.

Sreberny, Annabelle. 2002. "Seeing Through the Veil: Regimes of Representation." *Feminist Media Studies* 2, no. 2: 270–72.

Stabile, Carole A., and Deepa Kumar. 2005. "Unveiling Imperialism: Media, Gender and the War on Afghanistan." *Media, Culture & Society* 27, no. 5: 765–82.

Stork, Joe, and Fred Abrahams. 2004. "Sidelined: Human Rights in Postwar Iraq." *Human Rights Report 2004.* www.hrw.org/wr2k4/6.htm#_Toc58744955 (accessed 2 May 2006).

Thompson, Margaret E., Katerina Anfossi Gómez, and María Suarez Todo. 2005. "Women's Alternative Internet Radio and Feminist Interactive Communications: Audience Perceptions of Feminist International Radio Endeavour (FIRE)." *Feminist Media Studies* 5, no. 2: 215–36.

Tielen, Ger, and Brian Groombridge. 2000. "The Impact of Globalization on the Images of Older Women." Report of a meeting organized by the American Association of Retired People (AARP), the Netherlands Platform Older People in Europe (NPOE), in association with the United Nations, New York, October 1999.

Tumber, Howard, and Jerry Palmer. 2004. *Media at War: The Iraq Crisis.* London: Sage.

Valdivia, Angharad N. 2000. *A Latina in the Land of Hollywood.* Tucson: University of Arizona Press.

van Zoonen, Liesbet. 2002. "Gendering the Internet: Claims, Controversies and Cultures." *European Journal of Communication* 17, no. 1: 5–23.

Wheeler, Deborah L. 2004. "Blessings and Curses: Women and the Internet Revolution in the Arab World." In *Women and Media in the Middle East: Power Through Self-Expression*, ed. Naomi Sakr, 138–61. London: I. B. Taurus.

Winegar, Jessica. 2005. "Of Chadors and Purple Fingers: U.S. Visual Media Coverage of the 2005 Iraqi Elections." *Feminist Media Studies* 5, no. 3: 391–95.

Youngs, Gillian. 2004. "Cyberspace: The New Feminist Frontier?" in *Women and Media: International Perspectives*, eds. Karen Ross and Carolyn M. Byerly, 185–208. Oxford: Blackwell.

Zhao, Yuezhi, and Robert A. Hackett. 2005. "Media Globalization, Media Democratization: Challenges, Issues, and Paradoxes." In *Democratizing Global Media: One World, Many Struggles*, eds. Robert A. Hackett and Yuezhi Zhao, 1–33. Lanham, MD: Rowman & Littlefield.

CHAPTER THREE

Public/Private:
The Hidden Dimension of
International Communication

Gillian Youngs

International communication (IC) has, like most social sciences, been predominantly constructed from a masculinist theoretical perspective. In simple terms this concentrates on the public domain, the worlds of mainstream politics (such as parliaments and other institutions, national and international) and economics (such as corporations, market structures, and policy processes impacting on them). Key areas of study in IC in this context include different national media systems and comparisons across them as well as transnational media processes and the major conglomerates shaping them. Policy is also of major significance at national, regional (European Union), and global levels, including in relation to regulatory frameworks, contrasting cultures of censorship or control on flows of information, data protection and copyright issues, and antiterrorist, security-oriented surveillance of data flows. The public domain of IC has similarities to that of international relations (IR) and its subfield of global political economy (GPE). It is a world of states and markets, and, in the case of IC, media processes related to them.

IC gives much less attention to the private domain (the home, family, and affective relations) and then usually in limited ways—for instance, consumption patterns and cultures related to different forms of media and new media. In other words, even when the private domain is included, it is usually in terms of the public domain, such as that of the market and its impacts. If the relation between public and private is addressed, it most often reflects such orientations.

We end up across IC literature, for all its diversity, with a particular picture of the world, one that feminist perspectives can contribute to transforming. These have central concern with public/private dynamics. This is quite a different starting point for analysis, reflected in varied ways across feminist analysis, including in media studies. It offers a different picture of the world, one that can be argued is more holistic because it takes into account in complex ways the impact of the public on the private and vice versa. This was relevant in the era of mass communication but is even more pertinent in the digital age, where interactive structures allowing processes and activities relating to production and consumption in both public and private are reshaping the daily existence of increasing numbers of people across the world. This is also a mobile age, where many public and private actions intermingle, either in public or private spaces, and where this occurs as much in relation to physical places as virtual spaces, and often on the move. Public/private dynamics are fundamental to new thinking about these digital times, and feminist perspectives have much to offer IC in meeting this challenge.

How do we transform international communication into a field that offers insights into the grounded realities of changing communications structures and processes and varied experiences of them? This is the question at the heart of this anthology and this chapter on the public/private. I begin by focusing on the question of transformation and the specific way in which I am using the term here. Then I move on to discuss why the relationship between public and private is core to critical analysis about the international sphere. Third, I link work on this area in feminist international relations to IC, and fourth, I consider how concrete developments from traditional mass media to new media press us toward conceptual revisionism to take full account of public/private dynamics.

Transformation and Ontology

Why is IC in need of transformation and how can this happen? I would argue that the most fundamental means of addressing this question is on the level of ontology. How do we view the world, how do we conceive of social reality, and to what extent have dominant (masculinist) framings of this reality been partial? How can we make it more complete, more insightful and meaningful? These are the kinds of questions we need to consider. When operating at the ontological level it is accepted that philosophical worldviews matter, that they influence profoundly what we can and cannot see and give causal significance to. When taking ontology seriously, there is recognition that claims about reality cannot be taken for granted, that reality cannot be simply assumed.

We need to interrogate how reality is being conceived and constructed. What are the perceptual frameworks that are impacting, shaping, and fashioning certain aspects as evident (real) and others as absent or not worthy of analytical attention (unreal or lacking in import). Ontological questioning saves us from traps that dominant paradigms may set for us at any time. For instance, such paradigms, through their status and influence over time, become accepted as given and thus tend to be unquestioned, or to locate any questioning as if it were outside reality, or of no significance. These paradigms gain the status of truth telling, however problematic, in part because they have held sway, endured, and influenced what is understood to be meaningful and real.

In a major way, the paradigm and the truth it offers, however partial, become fused over time, inseparable, so that the truth and the manner of perceiving it become inherently interdependent, bound in a deterministic trap that links one inevitably to the other. When the truth is sought, the dominant paradigm has the status as the only or prime way to reach it. This is a central part of explaining the power that the paradigm gains over time.

Transformation, as I am applying it, begins with a move away from this determinist binding of truth and dominant paradigm. It entails an analytical prizing apart of the seemingly inevitable connection between them and a new openness about alternative paradigms or paths to the truth about reality, alternative perspectives that might construct such truth quite differently, that might introduce new forms and patterns of causality and new questions about them. Such transformation is not sudden; it is incremental, and it is made up of multiple challenges to the dominant paradigm and a recognition that this paradigm stands in the way of understanding as much as it leads toward it. We cannot expect transformation to happen easily or quickly in such circumstances because the very ground that established truth stands on is being destabilized.

The kind of transformation that feminist critiques undertake of dominant masculinist paradigms can be viewed rather as a gradual chipping away at a huge stone wall until it finally crumbles (hopefully), and it is not a one-way process. Just as the wall gets chipped away, it is also continually rebuilt by renewed assertions of the dominant paradigm. And the pervasive acceptance and institutionalization of the dominant paradigm (in theory and practice) means that there are established and powerful conditions for its new bricks to be fashioned quickly and efficiently. After all, they represent a truth that is already widely known and accepted, largely taken for granted indeed, while the critical chipping away is achieved on the basis of challenges to such truth and acceptance, from a weak position outside of such truth.

The historically established sway of the dominant paradigm is key to its power to maintain its hold on the present and the future. Its enduring and rebuilding status makes it clear that truth claims do not possess equal status. Their power has to be fought for in conditions that are likely to be highly unequal. To achieve ontological transformation is most difficult, because it strikes to fundamental perceptions of what is real and meaningful in the first place. Social reality as it is generally known is being completely overturned. The familiar starting points for thinking about the world and how it works, who has influence within it and why, how this might change, what is possible or likely and what is not, are being removed. New starting points are being asserted.

Public/Private: Old and New Paradigms

It is important to start with the study of the dichotomy between public and private because it is where assumed and partial (public over private) masculinist views of the world are located and have been embedded as the beginning and end of social reality, and the sum total of its meanings and possibilities.

Masculinist ontologies, which have dominated historically in societies and their knowledge systems, have privileged the public over the private in multiple and highly complex interrelated ways. They have positioned the public as the prime sphere of social reality and power, action and meaning, and they have dualistically set it in opposition to the (inferior) private sphere. This ontological framing locates social reality and causality primarily in the public sphere. It fixes and bounds it there and inherently confines the private sphere to a realm outside of that social reality, one of relative nonexistence, nonmeaning, nonsignificance. The ontological process of positioning the public over the private, and the dualism of the construction, at one and the same time imbues the public with total power (conceptually and actually), while emptying the private of any such potency.

The strength of one relies on the weakness or insignificance of the other. To make the one powerful and present is to make the other weak and absent. This takes in places and spaces (physical, imaginary, and virtual), institutions and organizations, social processes and structures, relations and identities. The public/private binary impacts on all of them, and a masculinist paradigm of public over private inevitably feminizes all that is located on the wrong (weak) side of the public/private divide. So in general terms, men and masculine identities are primarily linked to public places and spaces, institutions and organizations, social processes and structures, and relations, while women and feminine identities are primarily associated with private settings and affiliations.

So while politics and the market as public realms have historically primarily been associated with men and masculine values and principles, the private (domestic) realm of the home and social reproduction, love and care, and the processes and identities linked to them have been primarily associated with women and feminine values. The private is constructed ontologically as inherently inferior to the public, and as this dualism is gendered, women and feminine identities and values are constructed as inherently inferior to masculine ones. Now it is worth pausing briefly to emphasize the use of *inherently* here, because it locks down the significance of this construction as operating at the ontological level. It is important to remind ourselves that when we are talking about this level we are talking about the meaning of reality.

So, ingrained in this opposition of masculine and feminine is a specific construction of social reality in human terms: one that locates that reality in gender difference. It is not just a case of thinking about the hierarchy of masculine over feminine, important as this is. It is also a case of thinking about the wider implication of defining social reality in terms of that hierarchy and the distinctions it is based on. Not only is social reality primarily located via this means in the realm of men and masculine identities and values, but it is also predicated on the pivotal binary between masculine and feminine. Masculinist social reality is predicated on the absence or otherness and ontological insignificance of all that is feminine.

It is useful to think about this in terms of public/private dynamics. This approach makes the exclusionary process operating through the binary opposition fundamental to how social reality is being conceived. The binary of public/private is matched and reinforced by a whole series of other matching definitional binaries—man/woman, subject/object, rational/affective, science/nature, and so on—which define masculine characteristics and values on one side of the binary and feminine ones on the other. It is not just that the masculine and feminine are different, and one has powerful social significance where the other does not; it is that this structure of difference is fundamental to the ontological construction of social reality.

Why talk in terms of dynamics? Because it highlights that there is always a process of exclusion through the binary; it is not static but always in process, because in order to define one side of it, there must be an assertion of the absence of the other side of it, even if that is implicit (as it will often be) rather than explicit. It is also possible to see via this means that gradations count; for example, the more masculine, the more powerful and socially real, the more feminine, the less powerful and socially real. These dynamics represent the backdrop to dominant masculinist constructions of social reality, whether they are overt or not. And the taken-for-granted nature of dominant paradigms means that they are more than likely to be covert rather than overt.

Another aspect of these public/private dynamics links to the "hidden" nature of the private. By constructing social reality as primarily located in the public, masculinist ontology, in a profound sense it contains the private within the public, making it at worst invisible and at best deeply subservient in terms of social meaning and causality. The private becomes a kind of residual sphere, supportive of social meaning rather than significantly instrumental in it in any grand sense. It is also useful to keep in mind my image of the wall when thinking about this point. For the public-private hierarchy needs to be understood as something that is constantly challenged or disrupted and reasserted. I am not saying that the private never appears in social discourse, including in policy processes, because of course it does. But when it does, the weight of masculinist ontology will bear down on it, and it will more often than not be articulated or put back in its subservient place.

The core feminist concept of patriarchy is key to understanding the concept of the private hidden within the public. The force of patriarchy is that it is maintained across both public and private. It is a holistic assertion of masculinist social power, and this facet of patriarchy sheds light on the residual nature of the private in social terms. If social power and meaning reside in the public, and this is defined in masculine terms, then the meaning of the private is logically defined through and in the terms of the public. This illustrates the incorporationist nature of masculinist meaning and power, and the means by which it is constantly asserted and reasserted across both the public and the private. While patriarchy has become a controversial concept for its overarching nature and lack of precision, among other things, it remains central to our understanding of the comprehensiveness of assertions of masculinist power, public and private.

Patriarchal influence is exerted as much in private as in public, as problems such as violence against women (VAW) show. For example, in the masculinist liberal construction of public and private, the private allows for some degree of individual freedom, expression, and association beyond the public (state) gaze or control, within certain limits. But the reluctance of the liberal state to interfere too much within the private (including the patriarchal family) has contributed to excesses of patriarchal power going unchallenged. VAW has been recognized as a global issue affecting all kinds of societies across the world and requiring increasing amounts of attention from state police and legal systems. VAW is an indication of gendered imbalances of power within the private as much as the public. Patriarchy is a concept that helps us to understand not only the practices and implications of that unequal power but also the importance of public/private dynamics for understanding gendered identities associated with it. Subordination of women occurs across the public and the private, and identity processes that objectify women and limit their sense of agency have both public and private dimensions.

Public and Private and the International

So, how do these questions of public and private map onto our thinking about the international? The first basic point is that it is a matter of epistemology, how we view the building of knowledge about the world and the processes we undertake to do this. The ontological framing of public over private discussed above represents a foundational constraint on knowledge-building in a field like IC. The terms of how that knowledge can be built have already been defined along these public-private lines, and this anthology is among the efforts to set out the degree to which this problem fails to be recognized, let alone taken into account in any deep way. We come again here to the taken-for-granted status of dominant paradigms and the difficulties of transformation. A number of useful points can be raised about masculinist framings of politics and the market, which lead toward a critical understanding of the limitations of dominant perspectives on the international in IC.

Politics and the market are both predominantly constructed and investigated in public-private masculinist terms. Therefore, the mainstream vision treats the private as generally contained within the public, ontologically speaking, and therefore of minimal if any (and then usually supportive or subservient) significance to explanations and understandings of social reality. Politics is generally defined as the realm of public institutions and processes, governments and other official and unofficial bodies, processes of voting and appointments, public pronouncements, and policy. In the study of communications, broadly speaking, the driving concept is the public sphere, which carries within it the ontological predispositions already discussed. The media are positioned within this public sphere concept, with distinctions being made between public service providers and commercial media players located in the market.

The state-based model of politics is reflected in the concept of the public sphere. Territorially defined and autonomous political entities—states—are configured as the key containers and shapers of politics, with public spheres manifest in quite different forms, depending on the range of political (democratic, authoritarian, and so on) forms and diverse media systems associated with them. The ideal notion of the public sphere is most closely associated with the so-called advanced democracies, where there is a high degree of individual and press freedom, minimal censorship, and an emphasis on the free flow of information. In such contexts, both public service and market media are seen to play complex roles in the flow of information and opinion from bottom up as well as top down.

IC has placed particular emphasis on the market, not least because of its focus on questions of cultural imperialism and the growth of a world media market dominated in recent history notably by U.S. players, but also others from the richest economies, and by English-language media. Mainstream IC perspectives largely follow the public-private construction of social reality, framing the market in broadly public terms and focusing on institutions, regulators and policymakers, policy processes, market actors (especially the major transnational media conglomerates), and a range of statistical data reflecting where power, wealth, and influence lie.

Clearly all of these aspects of politics and the market, as studied in IC, as well as many others not touched on, are important and influential. It is not my purpose to deny that. However, it is my purpose to discuss the partialities of the dominant ontological and epistemological perspectives, to chip away at that masculinist wall, and to posit that we consider more comprehensive and differently dynamic approaches than the public-private framework permits, or at least that we be open to the relevance of doing so. At this point it is useful to ask a big question: where are the women in the mainstream knowledge that IC builds as a field? The immediate response is, usually nowhere to be seen, thanks to the public-private hierarchy. This might be an overstatement, but it is certainly too often the case, and while feminist media studies are increasingly producing research, writing, and policy work that addresses the problem, such chipping away at the wall cannot be assumed automatically to lead to transformation. The dominant public-private paradigm continues to hold sway in practice as well as in theory, despite this critical work. Now I consider the issue of theory and practice in looking further at the international and how feminists have addressed it.

Public-Private in Theory and Practice

The public-private construction is a reflection of what is real in the world. Men do generally have more power in society than women (whatever different points of view we as individuals might have of that). They do dominate in politics and in the marketplace and hold the lion's share of the world's wealth and influence. Women are still in little evidence in boardrooms around the world and much less represented generally in national parliaments than men. Even though increasing numbers of individual women hold positions of leadership, they are still in the minority. Some readers may ask what this feminist fuss is all about. Whatever the ontological and epistemological constraints of dominant masculinist perspectives, they are fit for purpose. They do match the world as it is, although perhaps not as we might want it to be.

This last point is part of the interference feminist analysis frequently runs into. Because it is transformative, because it is often seen as dealing with what "ought" to be (that is, a more gender-equal world) rather than what is, it is accused of being fundamentally normative and thus of a markedly different status than mainstream theory, which is taken for granted to be dealing with what is. Part of the reason for the framing of the arguments in this chapter is to avoid this dismissal. The purpose of the remainder of the chapter is to try to offer some counterpoints and clarifications along these lines.

We should remember that theory is part of practice and therefore is implicated in it, not separate from it, as is sometimes assumed. Theory is generated out of practice and reproduces or works to change practice, and dominant theory should be interrogated for how it reflects real power structures. It is important to recognize that dominant masculinist paradigms are not just theory but are also in part a reflection of real power in the world. Masculinist paradigms reproduce in the main a masculinist view of the world, but this does not necessarily mean it is a complete or adequate view, and it does not necessarily mean that it is fit for purpose in any overall way.

It is bound to tell the masculinist story, to frame reality in masculine (public over private) terms, to articulate masculine power and agency, and to focus on what they assert and produce. Positioning feminist analysis as normative does not wipe away the partiality of masculinist perspectives in this regard. It does not answer the limitations of masculinist analysis—for instance, the significant way in which it frames men as subjects and women as objects (in fantasy as much as reality—see the Sarakakis and Shaukut chapter on pornography in this volume); its containment of the private within the public, resulting in a highly delineated, abstract, and in many ways static sense of public/private dynamics; and its limited interest in gender in relation to production and consumption.

Where are the women? And why has that question not come up more often and persistently in IC, let alone been addressed in diverse and extensive ways? Why is it taken for granted that it is valid to build knowledge about the world that is predominantly about men and in masculinist terms? And even if it is taken to be valid, why is there not more questioning about how this represents a highly partial and even distorted view of the world and what is happening within it? It is the ongoing assumptions of the public over private ontological and epistemological framings that counter such questions being raised, taken seriously in any grand way, and actively addressed.

Feminist IR and Spatial Politics

It is interesting, when thinking critically about IC in this way, to consider feminist work on the international in another area of the social sciences, international relations. Feminist IR has been a sphere of analysis that has not only prioritized the "where are the women?" question extensively, but has also confronted one of the hardest ontological and epistemological struggles in doing so. This is partly because the notion of the domestic has a double meaning in the study of IR from a feminist position. It refers to the domestic related to the private sphere, but it also refers to the notion of domestic "politics" when contrasted with foreign affairs, the latter being the prime concern of IR. In IR, women are doubly domesticated, as it were. They are contained within the public of domestic politics, which is dominated by men and masculinist values in the main, but women's lack of power and presence in this domestic sphere is much more exaggerated once we get to the realm of foreign affairs. So if women's presence and influence is highly restricted at the domestic level in practice, it is even more restricted in the realm of international politics, which historically has been predominantly an all-male preserve. There are signs of gender change, with figures such as the former UK prime minister Margaret Thatcher, the current U.S. secretary of state Condoleezza Rice, and Hillary Clinton as a contender for the Democratic nomination for president of the U.S. While these and other similar developments are significant, they remain the exception rather than the masculinist rule.

Feminist perspectives have shed diverse light on the gendered spatial politics of IR; much of this work has been conducted in relation to different processes of globalization, which emphasize cross-border and transnational patterns, focusing on the links between global and local and the need to transcend a purely state-centred orientation. Feminist IR and globalization studies have recognized the missing dimension of women, whether as activists in local and global movements for change; diplomatic or military wives or mothers; sex workers operating around military bases; assembly line operators and sweatshop workers of the global economy; women, especially in the South, carrying triple burdens of work in the home, subsistence farming, and the paid economy; migrant workers, including in domestic and sex work; girl soldiers; and trafficked women. What is often insufficiently recognized in wider IR circles is the deeper ontological and epistemological significance of this research.

Feminist research envisages a different kind of IR, one that it can be argued is more complete, particularly in terms of its dynamics, spatial and otherwise, because it does not abstract the public from the private and focus only on the former, and thus largely on the predominantly masculinist world of decision-making and influence, whether in politics, economics, or the military. Feminist IR presents a new ontology of both public and private, and crucially the interdependence of the two, and thus of gendered identities and processes operating across them.

IC and Public and Private in the New Media Age

While IC has suffered from the masculinist limitations of mainstream IR and much of social science, the feminist rationale for overturning the situation is perhaps even stronger than in IR. The nature of broadcasting (and now narrowcasting) and the diverse developments associated with digital developments are impacting in two major ways, which both relate to public/private social dynamics, whether we are thinking politically, economically, or culturally, or about social processes and structures or identities linked to them.

First, the ways in which media, especially radio and television, have crossed the public/private boundary are being deepened and transformed by digital mobile multimedia and their diverse interactive and networking functions. Being connected in the new social mode is via digital media, operating seamlessly across traditional public and private settings of production and consumption, with mobile devices integrating all forms of audiovisual and textual platforms for interaction. Virtual spaces, whether e-mail or social networking sites, cyber-malls, e-voting platforms, and so on, are every bit as important in the digital environment as more traditional physical spaces. It is not so much where you are physically that matters as whether you are digitally connected and the speed and facility with which that connection takes place. Public and private are defined virtually as much as physically, and the private occurs as much in the public as vice versa, whether we are thinking in the first instance of personal conversations on mobile phones in airports or on trains, or in the second instance of running a business or shopping from home. The multidimensionality of interfaces between virtual and physical spaces of public and private is at the heart of thinking about new definitions of the social and the interpersonal in the digital age, as well as the identities associated with it. Transnational connections can be as easy as those within national boundaries, so the rigidity of the national as a social container (for example, of political or market activity) is being increasingly challenged.

Whatever social boundaries are at issue, the public and private are intricately interwoven aspects in the digital era, reminding us, I would argue, of the potency of feminist analysis on public/private dynamics and its relevance to explanations and understandings of social structures and processes, including those associated with macro and micro changes. Feminist ontologies and epistemologies are among the most useful starting points when considering digital phenomena and their impact on large-scale political and market trends, as well as on the incremental everyday activities that contribute to them.

Masculinist ontological and epistemological predispositions to prioritize public over private are challenged by the contemporary conditions of the networked world, where it seems we need to think as much about the public in the private as the private in the public. This is a long way from abstract notions of them as discrete spheres. It configures a world of multiple and deeply interconnected spatialities, virtual and physical, private and institutional, interpersonal and international. It calls for new kinds of conceptual complexity about space and place. I hope that the relevant insights that feminist perspectives promise will not be overlooked yet again because of masculinist myopia. That would be a major missed opportunity, which reaches far beyond understandings of gendered processes. It relates rather to wider senses of the nature of the digital world and how it is being shaped and navigated, from the bottom up as well as the top down.

The implications of my points here are that IC is undergoing a major transformation in the digital era, one that builds on many developments in the age of mass communications but also goes far beyond them. This transformation is partly a matter of complex spatialities, physical and virtual, and who has access to them and how, whether we are thinking at the corporate, societal, or individual levels. Home and personal, market, leisure, and workspaces are overlapping in many ways, fusing the public and private as much as distinguishing them, and facilitating fluid interactions across them. The kinds of feminist ontological and epistemological perspectives discussed here contribute rich resources to new thinking about IC, now and in the future.

Some Relevant Readings

Enloe, Cynthia. *Bananas, Beaches and Bases: Making Feminist Sense of International Politics.* Berkeley: University of California Press, 1990 and 2001.

———. *The Morning After: Sexual Politics at the End of the Cold War.* Berkeley: University of California Press, 1993.

———. *The Curious Feminist: Searching for Women in a New Age of Empire.* Berkeley: University of California Press, 2004.

Gibson-Graham, Julie Katherine. *The End of Capitalism (As We Knew It): A Feminist Critique of Political Economy.* Oxford: Blackwell, 1996.

Harding, Sandra. *Is Science Multicultural? Postcolonialisms, Feminisms, and Epistemologies.* Bloomington: Indiana University Press, 1998.

Hooper, Charlotte. *Manly States: Masculinities, International Relations, and Gender Politics.* New York: Columbia University Press, 2000.

Kofman, Eleonore, and Gillian Youngs, eds. *Globalization: Theory and Practice.* London: Continuum, 1996 and 2003.

Marchand, Marianne H., and Anne Sisson Runyan, eds. *Gender and Global Restructuring: Sightings, Sites and Resistances.* London: Routledge, 2000.

Peterson, V. Spike. *A Critical Rewriting of Global Political Economy: Integrating Reproductive, Productive and Virtual Economies.* London: Routledge, 2003.

Pettman, Jan Jindy. *Worlding Women: A Feminist International Politics.* London: Routledge, 1996.

Ross, Karen, and Carolyn M. Byerly. *Women and Media: International Perspectives.* Oxford, Blackwell, 2004.

Sreberny, Annabelle, and Liesbet van Zoonen. *Gender, Politics and Communication.* Cresskill, NJ: Hampton Press, 2000.

Youngs, Gillian, ed. *Political Economy, Power and the Body: Global Perspectives.* London: Macmillan, 2000.

———. "Private Pain/Public Peace: Women's Rights as Human Rights and Amnesty International's Report on Violence Against Women." *Signs: Journal of Women in Culture and Society* 28, no. 4 (2003): 1209–29.

———. *Global Political Economy in the Information Age: Power and Inequality.* London: Routledge, 2007.

CHAPTER FOUR

Women, Participation, and Democracy in the Information Society

Ursula Huws

The very word *citizenship* carries with it a connotation of place, a "citizen" being, literally, the inhabitant of a city. Over the years the word has, of course, accumulated a number of associated meanings: a citizen is generally presumed to have a range of rights (for example, to political representation or to the protection of the law), freedoms (to travel at will, to work, or to purchase property), and responsibilities (to pay taxes, to send one's children to school, or to obey the law). The word has come to stand in for such concepts as participation, equality, and democracy. The fact that the concept of locality is deeply embedded in the word *citizen* suggests that it is also fundamental to our current understanding of these other, more apparently abstract words.

In Western thought, the concepts of citizenship, equality, and democracy are closely interlinked and can be traced back to a common source, in Athens in the fifth century BCE. Perhaps it is no accident that it was the same culture that also gave us, in its theater, the concept of the unity of time and space. The Greek city-state has been represented for centuries as the ideal model of democracy, with free and equal access for all citizens to decision making. Leaving aside, for the moment, the question of who was included and who excluded from this notion of citizenship, we can see that the sense of place is fundamental to this model. Entitlement to participate in the democratic process is circumscribed by geography; it is the inhabitants of the geographical entity of the city-state, precisely defined and bounded, who have the rights to citizenship. Those who are not defined as inhabitants of that specific city-state are explicitly excluded, although of course they may have the right to citizenship elsewhere.

In this model (which probably derives from a particular pattern of agriculture), the surface of the globe is carved up into a patchwork of entities, edge to edge, with borders that, although they may be contested, are clearly defined. And since it is not possible, in the traditional view, for any individual to be in more than one place at a time, the task of assigning people to their own patches is unproblematic. There is often also an underlying assumption that identities (racial, linguistic, or religious, for instance) map neatly onto these patches of soil. History is littered with blood-spattered instances where this has not been the case: where, for instance, a grid of national frontiers has been superimposed by imperial powers onto tribal or nomadic peoples whose traditions are not space-bound, or where some ethnic groups (such as Jews or Gypsies) have a dominant allegiance to a nongeographical identity.

Nevertheless, it seems possible to assert that the dominant models of democracy and participation are rooted both in a notion of place and, more specifically, in an assumption that some coincidence between space and time defines each individual's relationship to broader social structures. It is, above all, this identity of space and time that is challenged by the development of an "information society," a phrase which I am using, uncomfortably, to denote the changes in the organization of work and daily life which are facilitated by the new communication and information technologies which, in combination, are sometimes known as "telematics." These technologies permit a range of new developments that undermine the traditional model of democracy.

First, by delocalizing a range of economic and social activities, they make a nonsense of many traditional geographical boundaries, and with them a range of associated institutions, ranging from differential tax regimes to adages like Robert Frost's famous "good fences make good neighbors."

Second, they allow for shifting and multiple identities, enabling people to belong simultaneously to a number of different constituencies and thus weakening, if not invalidating, the notion of one person, one vote (which in turn rests critically on the notion that you can only be in one place at one time).

Third, and associated with this, they make it possible for individual identity to be concealed.

Fourth, they create new thresholds, in the form of access to the technology, imposing barriers to participation, which act like latter-day versions of the requirement to own property, which excluded all but the bourgeoisie from the right to vote in most Western "democracies" up to the early twentieth century.

To those seeking to maximize the participation of the widest number of people in the decision making that affects their lives, these threats to traditional forms of democracy may seem harmful. Let us not forget, however, that the systems currently in place are far from perfect, and it may well be that, even while they damage some forms of participation, these new developments may open up others, which could be empowering for groups that have been underrepresented in the past.

In this chapter I focus specifically on women's participation and representation. Before doing so, however, I would like to make the usual disclaimers about treating "women" as a unitary social category. A few general introductory points also need to be made about the limitations of the "information society."

Whose Information Society?

Much current discourse about the information society, knowledge-based economy, or weightless economy seems to assume that, as interlinked computers enter more and more areas of our lives, *all* activities will become delocalized, *all* products will become knowledge-intensive and weightless, and *all* relationships will become telemediated or "virtual." As I have written elsewhere (Huws 1999), the evidence points overwhelmingly to a global trend which consists predominantly not of decommodification but of commodification. Indeed, the world has never seen so much consumption of raw materials, so much material production of physical goods and services, so much energy spent in transporting goods from one spot to another on the earth's surface, and such a vast production of all-too-material waste. It seems likely that a high proportion of jobs will remain firmly rooted geographically to a given spot (be it a hospital, a school, a factory, or a supermarket) while others, albeit mobile, will require physical co-presence at predetermined places (whether this involves laying cables or laying tables, delivering goods or delivering babies, maintaining garden plants or maintaining power plants). It also seems likely that, despite the homogenizing effect of global cultures dominated by transnational corporations, the distinguishing features of individual places may well become more rather than less important as localities are pushed into competition with each other for niche positions in the new global markets. The decision, for instance, whether to arrange one's honeymoon in the Seychelles, Bali, or Barbados, or to get one's software developed in India, Russia, or Brazil, or to buy one's coffee from Nicaragua, Kenya, or Columbia may well hinge on quite small differences. The cumulative effect of such decisions, however, may have a dramatic impact on the livelihoods of local inhabitants.

Any discussion of democracy and participation must be based in an understanding that a substantial proportion—usually a majority—of the population in any given place will be economically dependent on activities that do not only involve the processing of information but also the processing or delivery of physical goods or services in real time and real space. These people, while they are carrying out these activities, will be anchored to particular, unduplicable physical locations. It is, however, one of the great ironies of our time that they will not necessarily be doing so in the places from which they originate. The globalization processes that have produced the new international division of information processing work have also coincided with major migrations of people around the world. Increasingly we find that the jobs with the most intensive requirements for physical copresence are also those most likely to be carried out by immigrants or refugees. Examples of these include domestic or industrial cleaners, child-care workers, low-skilled assembly workers, janitors and security guards, laborers on construction sites, sex workers, and service workers in hotels and fast-food chains.

A further general point that needs to be emphasized here is that participation in the information society requires a number of preconditions to be met. In order, for instance, to access the Internet it is necessary to

be able to read and write a global language (with a relative disadvantage if this is not English);

be able to use a range of software (with a relative disadvantage if this is not the latest Microsoft product or if you are using some means other than a mouse and keyboard to access it);

have access first to electricity, second to a telephone line with decent bandwidth, and third to a computer with a reasonably fast modem;

have sufficient leisure to browse the Internet;

have the personal ability to withstand the cultural onslaught of words and images which you may find shocking, aesthetically vulgar, blasphemous, racist, sexist, homophobic, or otherwise offensive.

At the risk of pointing out the obvious, it is necessary to demonstrate that none of these are distributed equally. Let us compare, for instance, the number of main telephone lines per 100 inhabitants of the population between countries. Table 4.1 shows the ten countries with the lowest teledensity and those with the highest.

Another indicator is cost. A local phone call in Armenia costs thirty-six times what it costs in Canada (at 18 U.S. cents, compared with 0.5 cent) while the cost of an annual subscription to a phone line represents only 1 percent of per capita GDP in the United States, but 20 percent in Madagascar or Tanzania and 39 percent in Egypt. It would clearly be ludicrous to suggest that the citizens of these countries have equal access to the information society.

In a world where national boundaries are increasingly transcended, it is necessary to bear in mind such differences between countries when considering differences within countries or regions.

Table 4.1. Main Telephone Lines per 100 Inhabitants

Location	Lowest Teledensity	Location	Highest Teledensity
Chad	0.15	Guernsey	98.77
Niger	0.17	Sweden	71.54
Cambodia/Central Africa Rep.	0.26	Switzerland	68.66
Rwanda	0.27	Germany	66.57
Afghanistan	0.33	Iceland	65.94
Guinea	0.34	Virgin Islands (US)	63.87
Uganda	0.35	Denmark	61.69
Congo/Madagascar	0.36	United States	60.60
Mozambique	0.37	Taiwan	59.80
Tanzania	0.39	St. Kitts and Nevis	59.26

Source: ITU data, 2005. www.itu.int/ITU-D/ict/statistics/index.html.

Let us now turn to a discussion of gender differences. In order to understand some of the historical forces that have shaped women's political participation and representation in the developed democracies, it is perhaps useful to begin by returning to the paradigmatic democracy of the Greek city-state in the fifth century BCE. This makes it instantly clear that the universalism implied by the concept of equal citizens making decisions on the principle of one person, one vote is a false one. The citizens who form the basic unit of this society are in fact a minority of the population, consisting only of men, and men who are not slaves. To the extent that women are represented at all in the formal decision-making process, this is an indirect representation, through the persons of their fathers, their husbands, or, if they are slaves, their owners.

Similarly, the "liberty, equality, and fraternity" of the French Revolution (although it inspired liberation movements among slaves and women) was limited in its scope to men. Indeed, Rousseau (its chief ideologue) was explicit in his view that women had been created for men's delight and that their role should be limited to that of nurturer and helpmeet to men (Rousseau 1993). The slow extension of the franchise that occurred during the nineteenth and early twentieth centuries in most countries extended to propertlyless men before it encompassed bourgeois women.

The formal vote is not, of course, the only means of participation in public decision making, nor has it been particularly effective in delivering economic or social goods in the past. It does, however, represent in a particularly visible form the value that is placed on women's contribution in any given society.

Women have managed to develop a large number of other forms of political practice, reflecting the different capacities in which they participate in society. The new information and communications technologies appear to threaten some of these. However, they also offer opportunities to develop inventive new

forms of organization, communication, and participation. Some of these contradictory developments will be explored in the rest of this chapter.

Public and Private Boundaries

One significant development has been a shift in the boundary between the
public and the private. In the past, in many cultures, the act of entering the
public space of the political hustings or meeting has in itself been extraordi-
narily difficult for women. Indeed, as Elaine Hobby (1988) shows in her study
of seventeenth-century English women writers, even the act of self-expression
involved in writing for a public audience was considered immodest and com-
promising to a woman's moral reputation. Her public political identity could
not be separated from her gender. In the nineteenth century, some women
(most famously, perhaps, the Brontë sisters, Georges Sand, and George Eliot)
assumed male pseudonyms in order to be taken seriously in print, although of
course only a small minority of relatively privileged women had the leisure,
the education, and the opportunity to write and be published.

Even on the Internet, women who present themselves as such can be sub-
jected to forms of intimidation, harassment, or even "virtual rape" (Brawn
1998). However, the Internet does offer the possibility for the first time for large
numbers of people to express themselves anonymously. When the only form of
communication is the digitized word, sound, or image, it is possible to assume
any identity. On the Internet one need in theory have neither a gender nor a
race: one need be neither beautiful nor ugly, neither thin nor fat, neither old nor
young, neither able-bodied nor disabled, neither bearing the accent of an expensive education nor speaking the argot of the ghetto; one can, in short, communicate as pure "mind," detached from any physical associations. That's the
theory. And there are large numbers of women, particularly women with dis-
abilities, shy women, and women from ethnic minorities, who will testify to the
newfound sense of empowerment they have achieved by using the Internet as a
means of communication, self-expression, and participation in public debates.
It must be remembered, however, that for each of these there are others who are
excluded from this form of participation: for instance, by lack of time, lack of
access to the technology, lack of money, or lack of appropriate skills. And even
for those who are included, assuming a false identity is hardly the best way to
claim attention. Indeed, by making women invisible, it could be seen as reinforcing the notion that the most authoritative voices are 'male.

A second and equally contradictory effect of the new technologies is to transform the economics of communication with a wide and geographically extended
audience. For those without direct access to the technology, a new barrier to
communication is imposed. A computer costs much more than a pencil and pa-

per, or a can of paint; it is much more difficult to learn to use a computer than it is to talk to other women at the village well or outside the local supermarket or school. However, once that first barrier has been crossed, it becomes very much cheaper to communicate globally. The Internet has become an effective and low-cost means of international information exchange and mobilization (for instance, through the French Cyberfemmes network[1]) and a powerful medium of publication (for instance in the Women's International Net,[2] a Web-based magazine which connects women in ninety-three countries, and Canada's Women'space, which is published both on the Web and in paper form).

Consumers, Citizens, and Work

How has this new potential impacted women's ability to engage practically in decision making? Here it is useful to distinguish between some of the different capacities in which women participate in public debate and decision making.

One important capacity is that of the consumer. In the past, one of the ways in which women played their most prominent part in organized, public political action was as consumers—for instance, organizing protests and boycotts over the price of food.[3] Here too the impact of the new technologies and the globalization of distribution that they enable have been highly contradictory. On the one hand, e-mail communication and the Internet have been used effectively as tools for organizing environmental consumer campaigns and boycotts.[4] On the other, the increasingly dispersed nature of retailing has made it much more difficult to target particular distributors. It is one thing for a group of customers living in the same community to organize a picket of a particular store; it is quite another for isolated individuals scattered over a wide area to protest to a call center or website from which they are ordering goods remotely.

A second capacity in which women have participated in social decision making has been as workers. Here too the traditional model has rested on the unity of time and space. To recruit and organize their membership, trade unions have generally relied on face-to-face methods of communication. In large workplaces like factories or offices, copresence at the worksite has made this relatively easy, although the task has become more difficult where the introduction of flexible working patterns has multiplied the forms of contract under which workers are employed and the shift-patterns that they work. It is not uncommon in large supermarkets in the UK, for instance, for some two hundred different shift patterns to be in operation simultaneously (Huws, Hurstfield, and Holtmaat 1989). In such a context, finding a time when the majority of the workforce can attend a meeting together may be well nigh impossible. There have always been some workers, many women among them, who have worked in dispersed or nomadic ways and for whom organization has been a greater challenge. And sometimes inventive means have been adopted to overcome the difficulties. One can point, for instance, to the Ahmedabad-based Self-Employed Women's Association, which now has a larger membership than any trade union in India and which organizes, among others, homeworkers and itinerant workers involved in such activities as rolling handmade cigarettes and incense sticks, collecting waste materials, sewing, and street vending. Homeworkers involved in manufacturing activities have also organized effectively in many other cities, including Toronto.[5] So too have domestic workers, notably in South Africa during the apartheid years. Such activities have usually been based in strong community networks, something that may become more difficult with the fracturing of local communities that accompanies economic migration and globalization.

The delocalization of work involving the processing of information is contradictory in its effects. On the one hand, it breaks up the traditional office, enabling work to be done at a distance, often in the home, by a remote workforce. On the other, it introduces new divisions of labor (often highly Tayloristic) and recombines and concentrates onto single sites tasks that may once have been scattered through a network of small branch offices or stores. The call center or specialist data entry function bears many of the hallmarks of the traditional factory: a large concentration of workers involved in repetitive, routinized tasks with highly monitored and stressful working conditions. There is considerable evidence that trade union organization is flourishing in such conditions (in one UK survey of call centers, over half were organized [Income Data Services 1998, compared with under a third across the economy as a whole[6]). Indeed, call center workers appear to be pioneering new forms of collective organization across national frontiers. One example of this was a joint agreement negotiated by trade unions in Canada, the United States, and Britain with Air Canada.

Evidence on the use of the Internet for worker organization is patchy. The Internet is clearly a useful tool for organizing solidarity action and has been used as such; the UK-based Labour Telematics Project was an early pioneering example, as were the associations of teleworkers or telecommuters that were set up in a number of European countries during the 1980s and 1990s.[7] Most trade unions in the developed world now have their own websites and many keep in touch with their members by e-mail. Little is known about the extent to which e-mail is used for lateral communication between groups of workers in different unions or different countries. However, Benner (2002) has documented the way in which new forms of worker organization (including "guilds" of high-tech workers) have emerged in Silicon Valley, facilitated by electronic communication.

There are a large number of websites aimed at home workers, many simply electronic versions of the dubious "get rich quick" advertisements traditionally found in local newspapers or taped to street lamps and aimed at the desperate.

Some commercial sites, however, have bulletin boards that are aimed at home-based workers. Some of these sites consciously target women. The iVillage work-at-home site,[8] for instance, adopts the patronizing style of a traditional women's magazine, placing chatty advice for "mompreneurs" about setting up a home-based business in among cheery hints about child care, weight loss, and keeping fit. While its heavily moderated message board may act as a source of social support for some isolated home-based workers, it can hardly be regarded as an active channel of participation.

Other, more subversive websites, run by workers themselves, appear to be emerging. Internet searches provide interesting clues that nascent organizations are beginning to engage in the sorts of dialogue that may well be precursors to more formal "virtual" trade union organizations. One example is Temp 24-7,[9] whose main purpose seems to be to enable temporary workers to share their frustrations with each other. Another site, Working Today, now the Freelancer's Union,[10] describes itself as "a national non-profit membership organization that promotes the interests of people who work independently—a diverse group that now makes up nearly 30% of the American labor force. Our members are free-lancers, independent contractors, temps, part-timers, contingent workers, and people working from home." The organization boasts 60,000 members and fifteen affiliated organizations and offers its members practical information about employment rights and wage rates, health insurance, and legal services. One of its affiliated organizations is the World Wide Web Artists Consortium,[11] which alongside its Internet-based special interest groups and e-mail discussion lists has started to offer that most nonvirtual of activities: the monthly meeting! I should emphasize, however, that my knowledge of these organizations is limited to what can be gleaned from their websites, and this illustrates perfectly what is perhaps the single greatest difficulty with virtual organizing: how do you know whether the other person is telling the truth? Even if you do know the organization, how do you know that the person you are dealing with is truly representative of it? Is the information you are receiving a genuine consensus of views or just the personal opinion of the group's resident nerd? Without some preexisting knowledge of one's communication partners, it is difficult to build the relationship of mutual trust that is a precondition for any effective joint initiative.

Another form of social engagement in which women have participated in the past has been the creation of prefigurative models for what Sheila Row-botham (1992) has called a "new moral world." Such initiatives move beyond the reactive or defensive strategies of protest, or the ticking of boxes on ballot forms, to the development of new social forms. These comprise an enormous range of projects, including cooperatives, credit unions, collective child care arrangements, alternative health projects, and the development of new, environmentally friendly products and services. They offer a collective vision of an

alternative way of living and, as such, contribute enormously to the shared political culture. There is no space in this short chapter to even begin to chronicle the many and varied forms these initiatives have taken, but the new technologies seem to have most to offer in this area, providing not just new means
of communicating but richer and more interactive ways of developing visions
and sharing them over time and space.

In the past, there have always been women who seized on whatever technology or means of communication was available and adapted it for their own
use. Sometimes in secret, sometimes in the course of their work, they learned
to read and write, to read Latin and Greek, to speak English, to use typewrit-
ers, telephones, addressographs, photocopiers, faxes, word processors, loud-
hailers, and tape recorders. In out-of-hours workplaces and basements and
around kitchen tables, they stapled and roneoed,[12] addressed and packed,
sewed banners, made placards, learned songs. The computer with its Internet
connection can be seen as a continuation of this process: a tool among many.
Like other tools, these reflect the priorities of their designers and have characteristics that distort the work processes of the users and, also like others,
they do not leave their users untouched. Just as the telephone created new
forms of vision-free intimacy, so e-mail generates another kind of interpersonal contact, a strange intimacy without touch or tone of voice, in which
misunderstandings can multiply.

These media also create enormous difficulties of prioritization, whereby remote events are constantly interrupting local ones in the competition for our
time and attention. We do not just need new intellectual and manual skills to
use them well, we also need new emotional skills. However, it is important not
to forget that these are just tools. While they have the potential to open up new
possibilities for communication and mental creativity, they cannot in and of
themselves change most of the material circumstances of our daily lives. The
body that sits at the keyboard, perhaps with aching neck muscles and sore
wrists, is still at the end of a day a physical body occupying real time and real
space, getting on with the business of digesting real food, circulating real blood,
and undergoing all the other processes, known and unknown to science, that
make up the act of living. This body may be hot or cold, hungry or overfed, tired
or energetic; it may be in a comfortable middle-class house or a shack tem-
porarily rigged up as a cybercafé; it may have children clinging to it, young men
attempting to patronize it, bosses waiting to be served by it. The surrounding
environment might be urban or rural. There might or might not be an uninter-
rupted supply of electricity, running water, sewerage; free primary schools; a
health center; or freedom to speak out politically. But whatever it is, it is located
somewhere. And, under present political conditions, that somewhere is where
participation and representation are needed.

The superimposition onto this physical patch of land of other overlapping geographies (of markets, languages, organizational cultures, trading pacts, finance capital, and political domination, to name but a few) enormously complicates this process of participation and representation. Because the local is increasingly shaped by the global, a global awareness and, sometimes, global campaigning and action may be required to intervene in the processes that determine its institutions and policies and the distribution of its resources. It seems unlikely, however, that local presence and local action can ever be dispensed with entirely. The trick will be to find new ways to use the new information and communications technologies, not to reinforce existing polarities but to reduce them, so they can become instruments of mutual support and solidarity among local communities of women.

Notes

This paper was originally written for and presented to the conference Citizens at the Crossroads: Whose Information Society? London, Ontario, Canada, October 22, 1999.

1. See Les Penelopes at www.penelopes.org (accessed 27 January 2007).
2. See www.womenspace.ca (accessed 27 January 2007).
3. Documented *inter alia*, by Sheila Rowbotham, for instance in *Women, Resistance and Revolution*, New York: Pantheon, 1973.
4. One example of this is the Clean Clothes Campaign, organized by women in the Netherlands and the UK in solidarity with garment workers in developing countries, documented in Ursula Huws, *Action Programmes for the Protection of Homeworkers: Ten Case-studies from Around the World*, Geneva: ILO, 1995.
5. Also described in Huws, *Action Programmes for the Protection of Homeworkers*.
6. Workplace Employee Relations Survey, Office of National Statistics, London, 1998.
7. In the UK, for instance, the Telecottage Association (TCA), www.tca.org.uk.
8. See http://home.ivillage.com (accessed 27 January 2007).
9. See www.temp24-7.com/LIVE/issue/current/home_frames.html (accessed 27 January 2007).
10. See www.freelancersunion.org (accessed 27 January 2007).
11. See http://wwwac.org (accessed 27 January 2007).
12. Before the days of cheap photocopying or do-it-yourself printing from a computer, the Roneo machine, or its chief rival, the Gestetner, was a staple piece of office equipment. Using a typewriter (without its inked ribbon) the text was typed into a stencil—a rather expensive item involving three sheets of paper attached at the top to a piece of card, with an elaborate pattern of holes designed to lock it to the machine. The uppermost layer of the stencil was an easily damaged layer of tissue paper in which the typewriter keys cut letter-shaped holes; behind it was a sheet of carbon paper; and behind that there was a sheet of paper, known as the flimsy, on which the carbon copy was recorded. Each page had to be typed on a separate stencil, and woe betide anyone who made a mistake. The only way to fix it was to paint a pink substance like nail varnish over the offending letters, wait for it to dry, reinsert it into the typewriter and type the correction over it, banging down very hard on the keys if it was a manual typewriter and typing over it twice if you had the modern luxury of an electric typewriter. The completed stencils (minus the two underlayers) were

then attached to the aforesaid Roneo (or Gestetner) machine, which had been previously filled with ink, and printed by turning a handle vigorously: one turn per copy. One stencil was good for around one hundred or two hundred printings, but the quality steadily deteriorated, looking more and more like some weird kind of code, as the centers progressively fell out of the o's, b's, d's, p's and q's. The printed sheets then had to be collated and stapled. Access to such a machine was beyond the means of most small women's groups and normally had to be negotiated with larger organizations or "borrowed" from one's daytime employer. It was obvious who had achieved such access from their ink-stained hands, well-developed biceps, and sometimes a lingering whiff of acetone.

References

Benner, Chris. 2002. *Work in the New Economy: Flexible Labor Markets in Silicon Valley.* Oxford: Blackwell.

Brawn, Anna Livia. 1998. "Women's Cultures on the Internet and the World Wide Web." In *Employment 2002: The Future for Women.* Federal Ministry for Women's Affairs and European Commission, Linz.

Hobby, Elaine. 1988. *Virtue of Necessity: English Women's Writing, 1649-1688.* London: Virago.

Huws, Ursula. 1999. "Material World: The Myth of the Weightless Economy." In *Socialist Register 1999*, eds. Leo Panitch and Colin Leys, xx. London: Merlin Press and New York: Monthly Review Press.

Huws, Ursula, Jennifer Hurstfield, and Rikki Holtmaat. 1989. *What Price Flexibility?: The Casualisation of Women's Employment.* London: Low Pay Unit.

Incomes Data Services. 1998. *Pay and conditions in call centres, 1998.* London: IDS Report no. 771.

Rousseau, Jean-Jacques. 1993. *Emile.* New York: Everyman.

Rowbotham, Sheila. 1992. *Women in Movement.* London and New York: Routledge.

PART TWO

GENDERING POLICY REGIMES

CHAPTER FIVE

The Expediency of Women

Alison Beale

In response to the technical-scientific and liberal-progressive claims of public policy, it is often argued, after Horkheimer, Foucault, and others, that governmentality rather than "outcomes" is what policy actually produces.[1] Given the well-documented ambiguities of the term, culture has been especially vulnerable to being deployed as a tool of governance directed at goals not obviously, or even in a generous interpretation, cultural. Cultural policy, since the neoliberal economics of the 1980s in particular, has been described as instrumental: "Instrumentalism justifies cultural policy most typically on economic grounds, and, to a lesser extent, social grounds as well, that is, grounds that are not specifically cultural."[2] As anthropologists of policy and of cultural institutions have also shown, policy can be a system of governance that is semiclosed, with its own opportunities for agency and its own discourses, rules, and rewards.[3] While the discussion that follows agrees substantially with these critiques, it should also be underscored that cultural policy should be looked at in a constructivist perspective. The identities of women, men, children, and ideas about gender relations, family norms, and sexualities are among the social norms affecting and affected by cultural policies and policy making. Research on cultural and communications policies has clearly demonstrated the interconnections between identity and its performance and policy.[4] Within the discourses of cultural policy, women have historically been a privileged, which is to say emphasized, signifier. In this chapter I am concerned with some recent elements of international cultural governance that deploy women and ideas and activities associated with women to formulate and implement cultural policies, conventions, and treaties. I argue that, considered in its ensemble, international cultural policy is deeply inflected by a gender consciousness but that this alone does not necessarily contribute to emancipation and equity.

Cultural policy is an interdisciplinary academic field with close ties to policy practitioners and the politics of culture. The issues addressed by academics in cultural policy emerged in anthropology, development studies, arts administration, cultural economics, urban planning, art history and museum studies, international relations, communications, cultural studies, and elsewhere. While the interdisciplinary field continues to expand, it has clearly been established, with all the institutional markers and recognition that implies. Dedicated journals such as the *International Journal of Cultural Policy* and the *Nordic Journal of Cultural Policy*, as well as research centers, networks, conferences, and an increasing number of publications have appeared since the 1980s.[5] Internationally the economic significance of the cultural industries[6] and the transformative allure of the "creative class"[7] in the "global city"[8] have contributed to the area's legitimation, to the funding of research, and to the creation of cultural policy units at all levels of government.

But what exactly is cultural policy, and why should feminists be concerned with it? We can map the field in a comparative and descriptive manner by contrasting the narrowly conceived national policies that confine the label *cultural* to the arts and heritage, with broader approaches that acknowledge linguistic, educational, and media policies as de facto cultural policies. These broader approaches have been especially meaningful to second-wave (and continuing) feminist communication policy scholarship in its concern with equity and equality of opportunity and with employment, media representation, and the cultural rights of women and children. Questions of inclusion, opportunity, and equity thus become features *of* culture, related to its characteristics and values, and not only sociological categories and concepts framing cultural practice and consumption. Continuing with this approach to cultural policy questions, feminist scholars have contributed significantly to studies of citizenship and social diversity, in addressing the sociocultural policies concerned with the boundaries of national and international multiculturalism, language, education, religion, and their constitutional foundations in the cultural rights of citizens and the cultural sovereignty of states.[9]

Given the growing attention to cities and to globalization in cultural policy, we must continually remind ourselves of the significance of the national framework for cultural policy and of the international support for national systems of cultural governance. Cultural policies contributing to nation building and nationalism from the eighteenth century on are familiar to cultural historians of the Euro-American world. It is important to acknowledge that they are also part of the contested "modernization" of much of the world in postcolonial, post-imperial, and now globalizing contexts.[10] National cultural policies have been supported by international human rights campaigns, nationalist governments, and development programs associated with cold war blocs, UNESCO (United Nations Educational Scientific and Cultural Organization) and the UNDP (United Nations Development Program), and the nonaligned movement, all of which have deployed women as teachers and administrators, while building on traditions in which the female is the bearer and symbol of national culture.

Beginning in the late 1980s, feminist research in international relations, cultural geography, and other fields addressing social relations in socially constructed spaces has added historical and theoretical depth to scholarship on cultural policy and cultural politics by addressing the political spaces—from the urban to the transnational—they are concerned with. This feminist scholarship is complementary to the analysis of the global city,[11] which revives (even in competing analyses of globalization) the ancient role of the city as the economic, cultural, and political hub of financial flows and human migration, settlement, and cultural encounters. Cities occupy a central conceptual and pragmatic role in cultural policy, but despite the crucial intellectual contributions of women scholars to the global city concept and to the analysis of women in globalized cultural production and in cultural diasporas,[12] feminist scholarship and gender-related analysis of the global city and the city as a fulcrum for cultural policy are marginalized in the most widely cited discussions of these concepts.

Furthest out in the spatial mapping of cultural policy, we find that to preserve the planetary ecosystem and mitigate global conflict, UNESCO and national governments argue that cultural policies are keys to the survival of the planet. The expansion of the mandate for cultural policy constructs cultural diversity on the ecological model of biodiversity. But the consequence of a sometimes well-intentioned connection between human cultures and the environment has been mixed. As this chapter discusses, critical feminist scholarship is beginning to engage with the widespread concept of women as the sources and embodiments of a *global cultural reserve*. The concept of culture as a reserve and the association of women with it may be emerging as among the most intransigent problems confronting feminist cultural activists and researchers today.

The New Popularity of Cultural Policy

In part because of the comprehensiveness of cultural policy (meaning both the multiple levels of governance through which it is addressed and the broadening range of cultural practices and issues it is concerned with) and in part because of the strategically significant and prestigious market and governance tools its practitioners have adopted (commodification, auditing, and surveillance), cultural policy may now be considered central rather than peripheral among public policies. However, this centrality does not take the form that proponents of culture have wanted. It certainly does not mean that culture in any intrinsic form[13] has achieved the status of international trade, or national security, though it is linked to these and other areas.[14] Instead, I suggest, cultural policy has achieved a level of acceptability because it has been identified globally as a source of value: it has adopted the tools linked to economic, technological, and ecological planning, and it has successfully been marketed by planners as a panacea for a range of social problems.

There are thus two problems with culture's new popularity as a medium for policy. One has been identified by cultural planners themselves. Having adopted many of the tools popular in public policy of the last decade, notably the audit and the branding exercise, some planners and the researchers who work alongside them are concerned about overstatements and misuses of these tools. There has been a modest backlash against the concept of the creative class and national branding exercises such as Cool Britannia. These highly popular marketing tools, near trademarks in themselves, have been revealed as methodologically limited and having played fast and loose with the economic indicators by which their success is measured. However, rather than abandon the cultural audit, or cultural accountancy, the search is on for social indicators and concepts, such as community well-being, to redefine them in less exclusively economic terms.[15] It is not evident, though, that in this process any more attention will be given to gender-based questions and research than before—and it may contribute to a new kind of problem.

The second problem has been exposed in George Yúdice's important book *The Expediency of Culture*, in which he argues that culture has become a resource or, after Heidegger, a "standing reserve."[16] Culture is expedient because it has become primarily (but not exclusively) "a resource for both sociopolitical and economic amelioration."[17] Culture as a resource is not only treated as such by commercial interests through commodification, copyright, and intellectual property,[18] which are supported by international trade and legal regimes. The opponents of cultural commodification, who would protect culture, or manage its economic exploitation in ways compatible with social justice, have created tools that are at risk of being complicit with the exploitation of culture. UNESCO's *Convention for the Safeguarding of Intangible Cultural Heritage* (2003) affirms the time-based, changeable nature of culture while requiring its tabulation and monitoring in national inventories. The UNESCO-sponsored Global Alliance for Cultural Diversity has similarly established a series of international lists intended to track an inventory of the globe's cultural diversity. In its own words, the Alliance "explores new ways to turn creativity in developing countries into sustainable cultural industries."[19] And as previously suggested, some recent attempts to refine planning methods in urban cultural policy have switched from claims based on the exponential value of the cultural dollar in the local economy to assessments of communities' cultural resources.[20] These examples of public-sector approaches to the cultural reserve show the extent to which policy makers at multiple levels buy into a virtually identical discourse and set of policy instruments and legal framework. As Bill Maurer and Gabrièle Schwab have argued,

> These complicated economic, legal and social changes are also transforming the very category of culture. As the concept itself comes under scrutiny in the anthropological and literary circles that for the greater part of the century made it their hallmark, culture is now increasingly recoded in proprietary terms. Collectivities and corporations battle over knowledges and practices that have been newly configured as potentially alienable and commodifiable cultural properties.[21]

Gender in International Cultural Policy

Women's participation in cultural governance and their interests as citizens, creators, and consumers are not acknowledged in policy forums, official sources, or academic publications. To point this out is of course to emphasize an *absence*. But my principal concern is with the nature of women's *presence*, and even omnipresence, in the cultural policy sphere. Inspired by Yúdice's *Expediency of Culture*, I suggest that "the expediency of women" gets at the way in which women in the biopolitical forms of our citizenship are now emphasized in cultural policies in order to achieve the general aims of a cultural security. As "culture" is emptied out by its instrumental address by policy regimes, while it remains a contested or multiple signifier to citizens, so women, as gendered beings and citizens, become the means to a set of ends. In cultural diversity and cultural security there is an unacknowledged omnipresence of women, through whom the expediency of culture is effected, and through whom the cultural reserve—in a parallel to the reserves of a diverse nature—is brought into play.

The concepts of biopower and biopolitics have been useful in getting at the way in which modes of surveillance and classification reaching into the conscious and biological lives of citizens (through classification for public health risks, biometric documents, and so on) and a pervasive culture of risk assessment contribute to a totalitarian form of governance whose objective is the security of the state itself.[22] Yet while the concepts can draw attention to the way in which difference is created and deployed to discriminate and to identify, especially post-9/11, the dangerous "other," they can also be used to erase gender as a critical category in the analysis of globalization. In her critique of Michael

Hardt and Antonio Negri's *Empire*,[23] Louise Yelin accuses them of a "partial" analysis, which manages to present a biopower at large in globalization that is unmarked by gender or by feminist politics. She says, "Occupying the space left vacant by *women* and *gender* is the Foucauldian concept of *biopower*, which 'refers to a situation in which what is directly at stake in power is the production and reproduction of life itself.' Hardt and Negri do not examine the ways that gender inflects—that it differently marks—consciousness, bodies and social relations more generally.[24] Yelin's critique is not alone in noting the lack of attention to gender in globalization theory and even in studies purporting to look at the transnationalization of production. In some respects this critique is an unfortunately necessary reprise of feminist interventions within the field of international relations and, more recently, security studies.[25] What is surprising is that the biopower concept has been deployed in so gender-blind a manner, when gender has provided a key classificatory system and discursive apparatus through which, in governance and especially in cultural policy, biopower has in fact been constructed.

Yet Foucault's concept of biopower is not more gender-blind than the accounts of modernity it critiques. Only a legalistic reading of human rights in European modernity would suggest that women have come to be rights-bearing citizens because the personhood of women is as fully recognized as that of men. The political rights of women in the binary schemes of modernity are historically secondary, and they are couched in a rhetoric of completion and complementarity. The citizenship of the second sex achieves closure of a process initiated in and idealized by male emancipation. To find an alternative sense of agency, we must look to antiracist and feminist political, psychoanalytic, and semiotic theory and contributions to anthropology. Feminist scholars have noted in the discussion around the public sphere and around state formation and nationalism that the suppression of forms of autonomy for women has been not incidental but essential to the formation of modern male citizenship. This sacrifice has become a permanent handicap and condition. When it comes to cultural rights, as a set of human rights, the same scheme applies. The invention of "women's rights" has occurred in a curious symbiosis with the enlargement of cultural governance by the nation-state—in earlier periods of the expansion of the welfare-state and in recent periods when cultural governance is turned over to instrumental and market-driven strategies.[26] In the hierarchy of rights, the dominant cultural rights *are* the rights of states. International law and international governance confirm the sovereignty of states regarding regulation and setting cultural priorities within their boundaries, and while there are strong contestations of this authority (such as the international movements advocating the rights of indigenous peoples), states continually recuperate their authority through their responsibility for monitoring the rights of minorities in international conventions. Geopolitics, race, and class differentiate women in the ways in which our cultural rights have been realized in these national frameworks. The histories of women's suffrage movements and of women's participation in anticolonial and worker struggles, as well as in peace movements such as the post–World War II antinuclear movement, provide many examples of the contingent and varied place of women's rights within national politics. But feminist researchers continue to have to point out the ways in which tropes of women as victims (of war, crime, and the criminal byproducts of globalization) play into a nationalist, patriarchal scheme of security and obfuscate the local particularities of women's agency.[27] This agency often includes, though it is not limited to, patterns in which primary education, public health, and child welfare (extensions of the domestic sphere); citizenship training, community volunteering, and moral and ethical training (sometimes in concert with religious education); and aesthetic expressions of national identity (extensions of the mother's moral example and decorum) become the basis for women's participation in public leadership, in certain occupations, in voluntary associations of citizens, and as artists.

The claims of women are often expressed not as the rights of individual, fully human citizens but in terms of culturally determined, limited citizenship roles. Current developments in cultural policy in both national and international frameworks have exacerbated this tendency. Furthermore there is evidence that the scope for politically based participation by women in the cultural sphere, under conditions and in frameworks linked to the nation-state, is giving way to a biologically based participation.

Women, Cultural Diversity, and Cultural Security

The move to a biopolitical citizenship for women comes from several directions, which can be traced to a common root. First, when we look at the discussion of cultural diversity in the UNESCO system, we can see that it has been closely tied to a cultural ecology modeled on and explained as parallel to the ecology of the natural environment. From the mid-1990s, key programs of UNESCO, including Cultural Diversity and Access to Information,[28] encouraged the view that cultural diversity was in the interest of all, in a model explicitly connected to the ecology of the biosphere. In its climb back to acceptability among leading capitalist countries following the failure of the New World Information and Communication Order initiative and the departure of the United States and Britain in 1984, UNESCO expanded its work on human rights by having them take the form of cultural rights within an irrefutable program of cultural diversity. There was something for everyone in this formulation. Cultural relativists and conservatives could be reassured that bad old one-size-fits-all modernization and related financial demands on first-world countries were out. Activists could find acknowledgment of the political initiative of women in their local communities and of the knowledge that people everywhere bring to understanding their own communities and environments. The 1996 report of the World Commission on Culture and Development, *Our Creative Diversity*, despite encompassing an almost impossibly broad set of interests and sources of expertise, is clear-sighted about the traps for advocates of women's rights in the encounters between cultures.[29] But as an advocacy document for human rights, it has a different weakness: its implication that the foundation for women's human rights is in various forms of potential *for others*—as a reserve of untapped creativity (in individual expression, knowledge, and politics and governance), as the possessors of knowledge (craft, healing, and the transformation of the natural environment into culture), and of course as the bearers of children. After this formulation, can both culture and women perhaps be considered expedient?

A 2006 issue of the *International Social Science Journal* on the theme of cultural diversity and biodiversity published a series of articles on cultures in places as "diverse" as northern Ontario, Canada; Finland; and northern Thailand, examining in detail the linked questions of the role of human cultures in preserving biodiversity.[30] These studies concern communities in which that cultural role (knowledge and practice) has become a political asset to the (usually) minority populations in question who often lack full citizenship rights within national boundaries. These studies (and many others that preceded them and that continue) demonstrate that the link between cultural diversity and biodiversity is not merely rhetorical. Because these studies and some of the projects they are concerned with (led by local citizens, NGOs, and governments) stress agency and the ways in which contemporary people in "traditional" environments can and often must use their link to biological potential wealth to achieve their own rights, they cannot be accused of collaborating with forced globalization-modernization or with sentimentalizing dying ways of life.

Yet the concern with collectivities can obscure the particular roles of gender in culture, and within cultures, of managing for diversity. By avoiding discussions of gender except sometimes in descriptive modalities, they make it difficult to use the complexity of gender concepts within cultures, a resource in itself, to enrich (as important feminist scholars have done[31]) our approach to urgent problems related to copyrighting knowledge and genetic material and to ascribing belonging and ownership to land and to elements of the natural environment.

UNESCO's pursuit of a global cultural ecology as the consensual and nonconfrontational basis for securing the lifeways and cultures of the world's less favored citizens has led to several international conventions on culture, including the Convention for Safeguarding Intangible Cultural Heritage.[32] The Convention on Intangible Heritage is a particularly important example for this chapter. It embodies the cultural reserve approach to international cultural policy and is explicit about the connection between cultural and biodiversities. Indeed, one of the six aspects of intangible culture the convention seeks to protect is "knowledge and practices concerning nature and the universe."[33] The convention also has an interesting history related to women. There was enough concern about the fact that some traditional cultural practices are not compatible with the Convention on the Elimination of All Forms of Discrimination against Women (CEDAW) for UNESCO to hold a special consultation related to women's rights in the preparation of the convention. In 2003 an expert group deliberated on issues such as the risks to women of the "cultural inventories" when women would not, without added legal protections, have their cultural ownership and practice recognized and validated. It is reflective of its diffidence over the rights of women, which a close reading of the report tends to suggest, that the expert group summarizes its consultation with a bewildering instruction that "any element of this [intangible] heritage that may seem to reflect gender inequality should be evaluated as part of a cultural canon which, as a whole, may transmit and preserve an overall gender balance."[34] In response we have the critical work of two UNESCO-based scholars who have undertaken to question the ultimate absence of a CEDAW framework from the Convention and, in addition, from the Universal Declaration on Cultural Diversity. They comment: "We have seen that feminists have been skeptical of international human rights instruments because most of these instruments were first drafted when there was a distinction between rights in the public sphere and those in the private sphere . . . Today we have special instruments that address women's rights in a holistic fashion. These instruments, and especially the women's convention CEDAW, should be referred to when new conventions are drafted and when they are implemented."[35]

From the World Decade on Cultural Development, which began in the mid-1980s, to the articulation of cultural rights in the recent conventions and declarations, there appears to be a movement toward the inclusion of women in gender-neutral language, in such a way as to not have to name them. It is hard to miss the strong association of women with natural and cultural reserves in some documents and reports versus an avoidance of naming women when it comes to cultural rights. The quiet restoration or reinvigoration of patriarchy through *security* in the years since 2001 may be partly responsible.

As this chapter has already noted, security was a prime concern of international cultural policy in the cold war years, and after. The terminology of security is also borrowed into cultural policy from urban planning, where practices of designing for the security of people in public spaces and their access to private commercial space have been critiqued as being fundamentally concerned with *differentiating* among and facilitating the surveillance of the population by authority. Among international agencies, we find that, from an emphasis on cultural diversity, in the years since 2001 cultural policy discourse has become equally if not more concerned with cultural security. The roots of cultural security, like diversity, are in an analogy that has turned out to be also a direct link between the cultural and the biological. The United Nations human security framework[36] extended the scope of risks to security beyond military force to include threats to the sociocultural integrity and physical survival of human populations. The framework attempted a paradigm shift, identifying risk-preventive measures of poverty eradication and capacity-building for self-governance. The related concept of cultural security began as a response to contemporary ethnic cleansing and genocides, acknowledging the global history of these forms of terror in many places such as the former Yugoslavia, Rwanda, and throughout the colonized world.

As has been the pattern before, the domestication of cultural policy from contexts of war and deprivation has meant that cultural security now has many applications in developed countries—although often in connection to the absorption of refugee and immigrant populations. In Europe, cultural security is the label given to projects of the European Commission, the Council of Europe, and national governments for a variety of projects designed to mitigate conflict between immigrants and native populations. Public forums, multicultural projects and celebrations, and the promotion of tolerance and antiracism are involved. We might term this security by means of culture.

However, cultural security has more recently been cited when community or national values are felt to be under attack and lines are being drawn in order to secure culture. In France, Denmark, the Netherlands, Italy, Quebec, and the UK, there are examples of a return to assimilationist policies. The media framing of these policies more often than not centers on confrontation over the wearing of the *hijab*. But this is not reflective of an interest in the cultural security of women. Rather, as Lisa McLaughlin, Katharine Sarikakis, Saskia Sassen, and other feminist scholars have shown, creating security for globalization means attendant roles for women as migrant labor and a minimizing of their participation in the governance of culture and communication.[37]

Conclusion

This chapter introduces some major themes and international frameworks for cultural policy in the early twenty-first century. It has argued that while the longstanding critique of governmentality in cultural policy is legitimate, it is not specific or gendered enough to get at the ideology and policy-enabled transformation of culture into a reserve, as George Yúdice has argued. The chapter has added to this analysis the suggestion that the human and cultural rights of women are profoundly enmeshed in this process, in that women continue to be valued biologically and in their capacity as indigenous experts on biodiversity and as a standing reserve of cultural agents and emblems. Recent attempts in international conventions to recognize the cultural rights of indigenous and disempowered people may be complicit in an expedient approach to women, and by adopting the tools of the cultural inventory may, perhaps unavoidably, bring culture yet more inexorably into association with commodification. The challenges for women's human rights and cultural rights in this context are compounded by a global security context in which a range of cultural and communication freedoms are compromised.[38]

Notes

1. Kian-Woon Kwok and Kee-Hong Low suggest that "it is instructive to understand cultural policy not just as an instrument of governing but more fundamentally, as both an instrument and manifestation of Foucault's notion of 'governmentality' or the particular form of rationality peculiar to state practices," in other words, as a way of thinking about what can be governed, how, and by whom. See page 159 in Kian-Woon Kwok and Kee-Hong Low, "Cultural Policy and the City-State: Singapore and the "New Asian Renaissance," in *Global Culture: Media, Arts, Policy and Globalization*, ed. Diana Crane, Nobuko Kawashima, and Ken'ichi Kawasaki, 149–68 (New York: Routledge, 2002).

2. Jim McGuigan, *Rethinking Cultural Policy* (Maidenhead, UK: Open University Press, 2004), 3.

3. See for example Cris Shore and Susan Wright, eds., *Anthropology and Policy: Critical Perspectives on Governance and Power* (New York: Routledge, 1997).

4. For discussions of performativity in cultural policy, see George Yúdice, *The Expediency of Culture: Uses of Culture in the Global Era* (Durham, NC: Duke University Press, 2003), especially chapters 1 and 2; and Alison Beale, "Gender and Transversal Cultural Policies," in *Global Media Policy in the New Millennium*, ed. Marc Raboy (Luton, UK: University of Luton Press, 2002), 199–214, and note 7, 211.

5. The Culture section of UNESCO's website provides information about its research and activities, as well as international treaties and programs. University-based research centers also provide links to cultural policy research networks around the globe. Two examples are the Centre of Expertise on Culture and Communities at Simon Fraser University, Vancouver (http://creativecity.ca/cecc/index.html) and the Centre for Cultural Policy Research at the University of Glasgow, Scotland (www.glu.uk/ccpr/).

6. UNESCO Institute for Statistics and UNESCO Sector for Culture, *International Flows of Selected Cultural Goods and Service, 1994–2003: Defining and capturing the flows of global cultural trade* (Montreal: UNESCO Institute for Statistics, 2003).

7. Richard Florida, *Cities and the Creative Class* (New York: Routledge, 1995).

8. Saskia Sassen, *The Global City: New York, London, Tokyo* (Princeton, NJ: Princeton University Press, 2001); Aihwa Ong, *Neoliberalism as Exception: Mutations in Citizenship and Sovereignty* (Durham, NC: Duke University Press, 2006).

9. Iris Marion Young, *Intersecting Voices: Dilemmas of Gender, Political Philosophy and Policy* (Princeton, NJ: Princeton University Press, 1997); Nancy Fraser and Axel Honneth, *Redistribution or Recognition: A Political-Philosophical Exchange* (New York: Verso, 2003).

10. Christine Keating, "Developmental Democracy and Its Inclusions: Globalization and the Transformation of Participation," *Signs: Journal of Women in Culture and Society* 29, no.2 (2003): 417–37.

11. Sassen, *Global City*.

12. Ong, *Neoliberalism as Exception*.

13. Chapter 1 of Yúdice's *Expedience of Culture* provides a clear discussion of the perils of treating culture as a reductive category and shows how anthropological relativism highlighting cultural difference has contributed to making difference available as a legitimation claim in politics. Jim McGuigan in *Rethinking Cultural Policy* provides an account of the expansion of "culture" in policy and argues for caution in the interest of preserving society and politics against the managerialism that has infected the treatment of culture (9–14).

14. Indeed, it is dispersed among them, which is one reason why ministries of culture and cultural budgets have not grown in proportion to the cultural policy hype. On the hierarchies of cultural policy, see Alison Beale, "Identifying a Policy Hierarchy: Communication Policy, Media Industries, and Globalization" in *Global Culture: Media, Arts, Policy and Globalization*, eds. Diana Crane, Nobuko Kawashima, and Ken'ichi Kawasaki (New York: Routledge, 2002), 78–104.

15. Elenanora Belfiore, "Auditing Culture: The Subsidized Cultural Sector in the New Public Management," *International Journal of Cultural Policy* 10, no.2 (2004):183–202; and Eleanora Belfiore and Oliver Bennett, *Rethinking the Social Impact of the Arts: A Critical-Historical Review*, Research Papers no. 9 (Warwick, UK: Centre for Cultural Policy Studies, University of Warwick, 2006).

16. Yúdice, *Expediency of Culture*, 26: "Heidegger identified technology as a way of understanding in which nature becomes a resource, a means to an end, or a 'standing reserve.' "

17. Yúdice, *Expediency of Culture*, 9.

18. For a discussion of how the balance of international trade in culture is heavily skewed against the least developed countries, see *International Flows of Selected Cultural Goods and Services*, UNESCO Institute for Statistics.

19. UNESCO Global Alliance for Cultural Diversity, http://portal.unesco.org/culture/en/ev .phpURL_ID=24468&URL_DO=DO_TOPIC&URL_SECTION=201.html (accessed 19 February 2007).

20. See cultural mapping and cultural planning "toolkits" at www.creativecity.ca.

21. Bill Maurer and Gabrièle Schwab, "Introduction: The Political and Psychic Economies of Accelerating Possession," in Bill Maurer and Gabrièle Schwab, eds., *Accelerating Possession: Global Future of Property and Personhood* (New York: Columbia University Press, 2006), 10.

22. Colleen Bell, "Surveillance Strategies and Populations at Risk: Biopolitical Governance in Canada's National Security Policy," *Security Dialogue* 37, no.2 (2006):147–65.

23. Michael Hardt and Antonio Negri, *Empire* (Cambridge, MA: Harvard University Press, 2000).

24. Louise Yelin, "Globalising Subjects," *Signs: Journal of Women in Culture and Society* 29, no.2 (2003):439–64.

25. Bell, "Surveillance Strategies," and Jacqui True and Michael Mintrom, "Transnational Networks and Policy Diffusion: The Case of Gender Mainstreaming," *International Studies Quarterly* 45, no.3 (2001):27–57.

26. Alison Beale, "Cultural Policy as a Technology of Gender," in Alison Beale and Annette Van Den Bosch, eds., *Ghosts in the Machine: Women and Cultural Policy in Canada and Australia* (Toronto: Garamond Press, 1998), 230–50.

27. Heidi Tinsman, "Gender and Citizenship: A Review of Recent Works," *Feminist Studies* 30, no. 1 (Spring 2004):200–10.

28. UNESCO and the Issue of Cultural Diversity, Review and Strategy 1946-2004 (Paris: UN-ESCO, 2004.)

29. World Commission on Culture and Development, Our Creative Diversity (Paris: UNESCO, 1996), 140–47.

30. International Social Science Journal 58, no. 187 (March 2006).

31. See Alejandro Lugo and Bill Maurer, eds., Gender Matters: Rereading Michelle Z. Rosaldo (Ann Arbor: University of Michigan Press, 2000); Marilyn Strathern, Property Substance and Effect: Anthropological Essays on Persons and Things (New Brunswick, NJ: Athlone Press, 1999); Marilyn Strathern, ed., Audit Cultures: Anthropological Studies in Accountability, Ethics and the Academy (New York: Routledge, 2000); and Marilyn Strathern, "Divided Origins and the Arithmetic of Ownership," in Maurer and Schwab, Accelerating Possession, 135–73.

32. Convention for the Safeguarding of the Intangible Cultural Heritage, www.unesco.org/culture/ich_convention (accessed 19 February 2007).

33. Valentine M. Moghadam and Manilee Bagheritari, "Cultures, Conventions and the Human Rights of Women: Examining the Convention for Safeguarding Intangible Cultural Heritage and the Declaration on Cultural Diversity," Social and Human Sciences Sector Papers in Women's Studies/Gender Research no.1 (Paris: UNESCO, 2005), 1.

34. Cited in Moghadam and Bagheritari, 6.

35. Moghadom and Bagheritari, 9.

36. United Nations Development Program, New Dimensions of Human Security: Human Development Report 1994 (New York: UNDP, 1994).

37. Katharine Sarikakis, "'Making' Security: Citizenship, Public Sphere and the Condition of Symbolic Annihilation" (Leeds, UK: University of Leeds Jean Monnet Centre of Excellence and Institute of Communication Studies, 2006); Lisa McLaughlin in this volume; and Saskia Sassen, Cities in a World Economy (Thousand Oaks, CA: Pine Forge Press, 2006), especially chapter 7, "Global Cities and Global Survival Circuits on the Mobility of Women as a Condition for Globalization."

38. McGuigan, Rethinking Cultural Policy, 142.

References

Beale, Alison. 1998. "Cultural Policy as a Technology of Gender. In Ghosts in the Machine:Women and Cultural Policy in Canada and Australia, eds. Alison Beale and Annette Van Den Bosch, 230–50. Toronto: Garamond Press.

———. 2002a. "Gender and Transversal Cultural Policies." In Global Media Policy in the New Millenium, ed. Marc Raboy, 199–214. Luton, UK: University of Luton Press.

———. 2002b. "Identifying a Policy Hierarchy: Commmunication Policy, Media Industries, and Globalization." In Global Culture: Media, Arts, Policy and Globalization, ed. Diana Crane, Nobuko Kawashima, and Ken'ichi Kawasaki, 149–68. New York: Routledge.

Belfiore, Eleanora. 2004. "Auditing Culture: The Subsidized Cultural Sector in the New Public Management." International Journal of Cultural Policy 10, no. 2:183–202.

Belfiore, Eleanora, and Oliver Bennett. 2006. Rethinking the Social Impact of the Arts: A Critical-Historical Review. Warwick, UK: Centre for Cultural Policy Studies, University of Warwick, Research Papers no. 9.

Bell, Colleen. 2006. "Surveillance Strategies and Populations at Risk: Biopolitical Governance in Canada's National Security Policy." Security Dialogue 37, no. 2:147–65.

Bennett, Tony. 1998. Culture: A Reformer's Science. London: Sage.

Cliché, Danielle, et al. 1998. *Women and Cultural Policies*. Bonn: European Research Institute for Comparative Cultural Policy and the Arts. www.unesco-sweden.org/Conference/Papers/Paper11.htm.

Coombe, Rosemary. 2001. "Preserving Cultural Diversity through the Preservation of Biological Diversity: Indigenous Peoples, Local Communities and the Role of Digital Technologies." In *Differing Diversities: Cultural Policy and Cultural Diversity*, ed. Tony Bennett, 169–200. Strasbourg: Council of Europe Publishing.

CRIS Campaign. 2005. *Assessing Communication Rights: A Handbook*. London: World Association for Christian Communication/Campaign for Communication Rights in the Information Society.

Florida, Richard. 1995. *Cities and the Creative Class*. New York: Routledge.

Fraser, Nancy, and Axel Honneth. 2003. *Redistribution or Recognition: A Political-Philosophical Exchange*. New York: Verso.

Hardt, Michael, and Antonio Negri. 2000. *Empire*. Cambridge, MA: Harvard University Press.

Hoogensen, Gunhild, and Kirsti StuvØy. 2006. "Gender, Resistance and Human Security." *Security Dialogue* 27, no. 2:207–28.

International Social Science Journal. 2006. Volume 58, no. 187 (March).

Keating, Christine. 2003. "Developmental Democracy and Its inclusions: Globalization and the Transformation of Participation." *Signs: Journal of Women in Culture and Society* 29, no. 2:417–37.

Kwok, Kian-Woon, and Kee-Hong Low. 2002. "Cultural Policy and the City-State: Singapore and the 'New Asian Renaissance.'" In *Global Culture: Media, Arts, Policy and Globalization*, ed. Diana Crane, Nobuko Kawashima, and Ken'ichi Kawasaki, 149–68. New York: Routledge.

Lugo, Alejandro, and Bill Maurer, eds. 2000. *Gender Matters: Rereading Michelle Z. Rosaldo*. Ann Arbor: University of Michigan Press.

Maurer, Bill, and Gabrièle Schwab. 2006."Introduction: The Political and Psychic Economies of Accelerating Possession." In *Accelerating Possession: Global Futures of Property and Personhood*, eds. Bill Maurer, and Gabrièle Schwab. New York: Columbia University Press.

———, eds. 2006. *Accelerating Possession: Global Futures of Property and Personhood*. New York: Columbia University Press.

McGuigan, Jim. 2004. *Rethinking Cultural Policy*. Maidenhead, UK: Open University Press.

Miller, Toby, and George Yùdice. 2002. *Cultural Policy*. London: Sage.

Moghadam, Valentine M., and Manilee Bagheritari. 2005. "Cultures, Conventions and the Human Rights of Women: Examining the Convention for Safeguarding Intangible Cultural Heritage and the Declaration on Cultural Diversity." Social and Human Sciences Sector Papers in Women's Studies/Gender Research, No.1. Paris: UNESCO.

Ong, Aihwa. 2006. *Neoloberalism as Exception: Mutations in Citizenship and Sovereignty*. Durham, NC: Duke University Press.

Raven-Roberts, Angela. 2001. "Human Security: A Gender Perspective." *Different Takes: A Publication of the Population Development Program at Hampshire College*, no. 14 (Fall): 1–3.

Sarikakis, Katherine. 2006. "'Making' Security: Citizenship, Public Sphere and the Condition of Symbolic Annihilation." Leeds, UK: University of Leeds Jean Monnet Centre of Excellence and Institute of Communication Studies.

Sassen, Saskia. 2001. *The Global City: New York, London, Tokyo*. Princeton, NJ: Princeton University Press.

———. 2006. *Cities in a World Economy*. Thousand Oaks, CA: Pine Forge Press.

Shore, Cris, and Susan Wright, eds. 1997. *Anthropology and Policy: Critical Perspectives on Governance and Power*. New York: Routledge.

Strathern, Marilyn. 1999. *Property, Substance and Effect: Anthropological Essays on Persons and Things*. New Brunswick, NJ: Athlone Press.

——, ed. 2000. *Audit Cultures: Anthropological Studies in Accountability, Ethics and the Academy.* London: Routledge.

——. 2006. "Divided Origins and the Arithmetic of Ownership." In *Accelerating Possession: Global Futures of Property and Personhood,* eds. Bill Maurer and Gabriele Schwab, 135–73. New York: Columbia University Press.

Tinsman, Heidi. 2004. "Gender and Citizenship: A Review of Recent Works. *Feminist Studies* 30, no.1:200–10.

True, Jacqui, and Michael Mintrom. 2001. "Transnational Networks and Policy Diffusion: The Case of Gender Mainstreaming. *International Studies Quarterly* 45, no. 3:27–57.

United Nations Commission on Human Security. 2003. *UN Commission on Human Security Final Report.* New York: United Nations.

United Nations Development Program. 1994. *New Dimensions of Human Security: Human Development Report 1994.* New York: UNDP.

UNESCO Division of Cultural Policies and Intercultural Dialogue. 2004. *UNESCO and the Issue of Cultural Diversity, Review and Strategy: 1946–2004.* Paris: UNESCO.

UNESCO Institute for Statistics and Sector for Culture. 2003. *International Flows of Selected Cultural Goods and Service, 1994–2003: Defining and capturing the flows of global cultural trade.* Montreal: UNESCO Institute for Statistics.

UNESCO. 2003. *Convention for the Safeguarding of the Intangible Cultural Heritage.* Paris: UNESCO. www.unesco.org/culture/ch_convention (accessed 19 February 2007).

World Commission on Culture and Development. 1996. *Our Creative Diversity.* Paris: UNESCO.

Yelin, Louise. 2003. "Globalizing Subjects." *Signs: Journal of Women in Culture and Society* 29, no.2:439–64.

Young, Iris Marion. 1997. *Intersecting Voices: Dilemmas of Gender, Political Philosophy and Policy.* Princeton, NJ: Princeton University Press.

Yúdice, George. 2003. *The Expediency of Culture: Uses of Culture in the Global Era.* Durham, NC: Duke University Press.

CHAPTER SIX

Gender-Sensitive Communication Policies for Women's Development: Issues and Challenges

Kiran Prasad

The women's international development movement has emerged to recognize the potential of women in government and public policy. Global communication policies have urged governments to provide support to women's development issues, including the use of information and communication technology (ICT) initiatives for international networking and the sharing of information. This chapter provides an analysis of the ways in which communication policy in the areas of broadcasting, telecommunications, and ICTs impact on women's development, against the backdrop of mainstream media, dominated by satellite television, which escape regulation and continue to reinforce stereotyped gender roles.

Communication for Women's Development and the Policy Gap

In the late 1950s, early communication theorists, including Wilbur Schramm (1964) and Daniel Lerner (1958), were convinced that the mass media could move developing countries beset by poverty, illiteracy, and poor infrastructure from traditional to modern ways of life. By the 1960s, UNESCO, the World Bank, and the International Monetary Fund began to focus on communication to promote modernization in the third world based on the experiences of the developed countries in Western Europe and the U.S. These early approaches failed, as modernization was equated with Westernization. Development was seen as a top-down process based on the mass media, which viewed as catalysts of change had limited reach. Moreover, these approaches did not take into account the complexities of culture and structures that could support change (Melkote and Steeves 2001). This led to the rise of alternative development models concerned not only with economic development but also with the goal to empower local communities to participate in development.

In the 1970s and 1980s countries including China, India, and Tanzania developed alternative development paradigms that recognized the use of cultural media to effectively meet communications efforts for development, particularly in rural areas. Alternative development communication widely used folk media that were seen as familiar, culturally sensitive, participatory, and cost-effective media to promote social change, adult literacy, population and health, women's issues, and rural development. Alternative development communications also included a gendered analysis of development programs to enable women's participation in health, environment, and rural development. Radio and television, largely state-controlled in the developing countries, were also envisaged as channels of information. The use of radio rural forums to discuss agricultural issues and television experiments like the Satellite Instructional Television Experiment (SITE), Kheda Communication Project (KCP), and Jhabua Development Communication Project (JDCP) in India, the Palapa Experiment in Indonesia, and prodevelopment soap operas on television in Mexico and India prompted several other developing countries like Kenya, Brazil, Thailand, Indonesia, Pakistan, and Bangladesh to adopt television as a communication strategy for development.

The existing situation in many developing countries is that ministries of agriculture, population and health, education, social welfare, forestry, environment, women's affairs, and rural development have their own development information and communication units. A national communication for development policy coordinating partnership efforts has yet to transpire in South Asia and Africa. But the lack of a communication policy framework in developing countries has not been perceived as a significant factor responsible for the failure of the mass media in furthering development.

It must be emphasized that, although many developed countries have clearly articulated and integrated communication policies, most developing countries do not have well-defined communication policies. If policies do exist, they are usually latent and disjointed. There may be general policies in the nature of desirable goals and principles, or they may be more specific and practically binding (Prasad 2002). The policy gaps on gender issues led to the organization of international conferences on gender and communication policy in Asia, Latin America, Anglophone Africa, the Caribbean, the Pacific, and the Middle East by the World Association for Christian Communication (WACC). During these conferences, Nevo (2000) observed that most countries did not provide self-regulatory guidelines, much less any national policies on gender issues in communication. Even when gender and communication policy or codes of practice exist, they are not always put to use in an everyday context (Pandian 1999). A meeting in Beijing in 2006 on gender policies in broadcasting organizations noted that all the staples of media coverage, such as conflicts and natural disasters, politics and economics, crime and punishment, involve and impact women, as do most other issues that the media need to cover, including poverty, the environment, culture, and health. Yet women's experiences and perspectives are largely missing from media coverage of such events and issues (Asia-Pacific Broadcasting Union 2006).

A survey from the Geneva-based World Economic Forum (2006) shows that full economic and political empowerment remain a distant dream for millions of women in much of the Western world, let alone in developing countries. The report also points out that no country has yet managed to eliminate the gender gap, but the Nordic European states—Sweden, Norway, Iceland, Denmark, and Finland—have succeeded best in narrowing it. Many developed countries that have high gender equality indexes (GEIs) with gender equality in basic capabilities such as life expectancy, educational attainment, and income have a low gender empowerment measure (GEM), which is a composite indicator of women's representation in parliaments, share of positions in managerial and professional levels, participation in the labor force, and share of national income. While high GEIs do not guarantee high GEM levels for women in developed countries including Japan, Ireland, France, the UK, and Spain, gender inequalities are more pronounced in the developing countries. It is estimated that 264 million (16 percent) of the world's poor will reside in South Asia by 2020 (Swaminathan 2001). In sub-Saharan Africa, over 400 million people (46 percent) live under the crushing burden of poverty (World Bank 2003). Of these, 25 to 33 percent of households in the world are headed by women whose families are the poorest—a phenomenon known as the feminization of poverty. It is often assumed that women's employment in the formal labor market will lead to better health and quality of life for women and their families. There is limited evidence to support that. Instead, as women gain presence in the formal labor market their relative pay remains substantially less than that of men, and they find themselves taking on multiple roles which in turn increase their workload while contributing little in additional rewards (Patel 2004).

In India, communication policies have been incorporated into national development policies, professional codes of ethics, and the constitution and operational rules of particular communication institutions based on self-regulation by journalists. But policies that address women and communication are practically nonexistent. In this context, communication policies are implemented as communication *strategies* to deal with the question of the development of women within the national planning processes (Prasad 2004a). Women were largely perceived as targets for welfare until the 1980s: the "family" rather than women continued to be the basic unit for intervention in providing housing and antipoverty benefits. It was only in the seventh five-year plan (1985–1990) that the concept of women's empowerment began to be considered as a development strategy. The overall objective of the ninth and tenth five-year plans (1997–2002; 2002–2007) has been women's empowerment, focusing on growth, equity, and participation of women, with the state governments and every department earmarking funds especially for women's development.

Moreover, the National Policy for the Empowerment of Women (2001) focuses on gender-sensitization measures through training personnel in the executive, legislative, and judicial wings of the state, with a special emphasis on policy and program framers, implementation and development agencies, law enforcement machinery and the judiciary, as well as nongovernmental organizations. The policy also aims to remove demeaning, degrading, and negative images of women and to use the mass media to portray images consistent with human dignity. It aims to involve private-sector partners and media networks to ensure equal access for women, particularly for ICTs. The policy encourages media to develop codes of conduct, professional guidelines, and other self-regulatory mechanisms to remove gender stereotypes and promote balanced gender portrayals. But this policy has had limited success. Women's empowerment faces an uphill battle from the mainstream media, satellite television in particular, in countries such as China, Malaysia, and Thailand, which continue to draw women into an image trap.

The Image Trap

Women in the developing countries of Asia and Africa find themselves in a "dichotomizing trap," where researchers and policy analysts envision them as either "traditional" or "modern." These images of women have reinforced simplistic ideas about the nature of society, the interpretation of the status of women, and prescriptions for their future (Williamson 2006). Many of these images flow from transnational media, mainly television. An important component of international mass communication is advertising, stemming from globalization of product markets and the internationalization of many advertising agencies. The mass media actively promote the image of a modern "new woman," as revealed by studies of women in advertising on satellite television in India (Prasad 2006), in China (Birch et al. 2001), and in Thailand (Biggins 2006). While mass media under Western cultural influences represent women as modern, they also depict them through the prism of deep-rooted traditional perceptions and expectations of women's roles in society and in families.

In the few extensive analyses of female imagery in the Arab states, Graham-Brown (1998) and Al-Mahadin (in this volume) argue that images of women may be used in conflicting ways: as symbols of progress or as symbols of continuity with the cultural past. In their analysis of women's magazines in Malaysia, Anuar and Manan (2006) find that postreform media increasingly target women as consumers for their buying power and link their professional success and economic power to the consumption of supposed "feminine" products. As Farganis (1994) observes, women have to deal with how modernization, the growth of production, and advertising promoting consumption affect personal autonomy.

In the Indian context, gender relations are determined by the complex interplay of power relations based on class, caste, ethnicity, and religion (Desai and Thakkar 2001). There is considerable variation in the social construction of gender in different parts of India, especially between the northern and southern regions (Prasad 2004a). Further, women's social class has a strong impact on their economic activities, access to agricultural land, employment opportunities, gender relations within the household, and intrahousehold resource distribution. While these complexities are seldom covered in the media, obstacles to the development of women in the global media are largely reported as rooted in the developing countries, not as outcomes of international development trends such as globalization and structural adjustment policies (SAPs). The most potent impacts of SAPs have been on mortality, girl's schooling, prenatal health care, and child nutrition, which had previously improved but has since deteriorated as government support in these areas has been withdrawn (Purewal 2001). This raises important questions about the extent to which international communication policies focusing on the mainstream media and new media are capable of reflecting the diversity and complexity of women's lives in a way that properly responds to current criticisms of gender activists. There are regulations governing radio and national television (Doordarshan), which state that women must not be portrayed in a manner that emphasizes passive, submissive qualities and that encourages them to play a subordinate role in the family and society. But these guidelines are widely flouted, especially in advertising. Women in television advertising are portrayed as obsessed with beauty; they are seen toiling away to improve their appearance, seeking every available cosmetic aid to catch the attention of men. In contrast, the world of business, banking, finance, and automobiles are the exclusive preserve of male models.

The Indian Broadcasting Federation (IBF) submitted a compendium of codes for satellite channels in 2003, ten years after satellite channels invaded Indian homes. The code looks into news, entertainment, films on television (films showing sex and nudity to be strictly scheduled after midnight), and radio, and it is binding on all satellite channels (Raman 2003). The IBF dropped fourteen liquor advertisements for not adhering to the advertising and program code. Strangely, despite several complaints about negative and obscene images of women on the big and small screen, the government declined to ban any television channel or film. In the absence of a comprehensive media policy in India, satellite television has grown to such an extent that today all television channels are oriented toward commercialization. Though national television in India began with the avowed goals of education, modernization, and development, the satellite television channels have damaged the cause of women's development by regressing to highly negative images of sexual objectification that impede women's empowerment (Prasad 2005). Mainstream communication policies have not addressed the pluralism of women's roles and images in the media; years of feminist grassroots activism has failed to influence the government and the media to significantly redress gender inequities. Even existing provisions that would ensure women's fair representation are not enforced because of obstacles posed by media profitability. Governments in developing countries such as India are concerned with other pressing development problems, including poverty, illiteracy, health, livelihood, and rural development; the privately owned media industry is largely left to regulate itself rather than be regulated through legislation. Further, the government controls its own national channels of radio and television and uses them for supporting development communications. However, most governments focus only on the direct benefits of state-owned media in development and rarely acknowledge the negative influences of privately owned media, including satellite television. Any attempt to monitor satellite television would need a strong partnership of public, private, and civic sectors for successful implementation of mainstream media policy. This combined pressure is clearly lacking in developing countries.

Media Policy and Women's Development: Access and Activism

In its nineteenth session (in Nairobi in 1976), UNESCO's priority was given to reducing the communication gap between developed and developing countries, with the aim of freer and more balanced international flows of information. It

Table 6.1. Radio and Television Access in 2001 (per 1,000 people)

Area	Radio	TV
South Asia	112	81
Sub-Saharan Africa	198	59
Middle East/North Africa	277	274
Europe/Central Asia	447	401

called for a review of the totality of communication problems in modern society. Even after three decades, media concentration and exposure continues to be greater in the developed countries because of better education and economic status.

World Bank (2003) statistics also show cable subscriptions per 4,000 people in 2001 as lowest at thirteen in sub-Saharan Africa, at thirty-five in the Middle East and North America, and at thirty-seven in South Asia. Access to the Internet is also lowest in the Middle East and North Africa, followed by sub-Saharan Africa and South Asia.

If media access in the developing world is among the lowest and women are among the most marginalized sections of the population, their media exposure is certainly low, and their role as participants or producers is even more limited. The World Plan of Action adopted by the World Conference of International Women's Year in 1975 called for the media to reflect the changing roles of both sexes and to employ women in greater numbers in decision making, professional, and creative capacities. Two decades later, the Beijing Platform for Action (BPFA) spelled out two strategic objectives aimed at promoting women's empowerment and development: (1) increase the participation and access of women to expression and decision making and through media and new technologies of communication, and (2) promote a balanced and nonstereotyped portrayal of women in the media (Tiongson 1999). Gender activists continue to raise the issue that the media do not mirror the real-world experiences of women in many developing countries.

Alternative communication strategies are attempting to break away from the "add women and stir" approach followed in the mass media of South Asia, Africa, and Latin America. Their focus is on dimensions of socialization and cultural discourse, representation and portrayal, self-identity and images, and breaking stereotypes to create a positive identity for women (Prasad 2005). In Asia, where nearly three-fifths of the world's population lives in diverse social, cultural, economic, and political settings, a growing number of women are creating and engaging various forms of media as an outcome of international policy efforts to advance women's empowerment and development. The Meena Communication Initiative in South Asia developed by UNICEF in 2002 and supported by the governments of Bangladesh, India, Pakistan, and Nepal, aims to change the perceptions and behavior that hamper the survival, protection, and development of female children in the region. The initiative involves production of multimedia packages to put across messages on gender, child rights, and education using the medium of popular entertainment. Conversely it has also been found that the media have the power to shut out and further make invisible women's agendas (Tiongson 1999). In Indonesia, women-oriented programs on TV discuss issues including domestic violence, sexual harassment, rape, and prostitution. But because of the sensationalism of these issues, these programs do not necessarily contribute to the empowerment of oppressed women (Mariani et al. 1998).

In countries where low literacy remains a substantial development barrier, radio is universally recognized as the most cost-effective mass medium for informing and entertaining a wide population. Radio programs aimed at women's development are broadcast in several countries—India, Indonesia, Mexico, sub-Saharan Africa, and the Dominican Republic. Radio can reach larger numbers of poor people because it is easily affordable and uses little electricity, which is both scarce and barely affordable for the poor. In spite of radio's inherent advantages, community radio practitioners were dismayed that the 2006 World Congress on Communication for Development ignored the salient role of community radio in empowering people and strengthening democracy (Kumar 2006).

Nonetheless, radio played a vital role in several developing countries even before governments opened the airwaves to the community. In India corporate houses could buy FM frequencies, but communities could not own and operate their own stations and were left with no choice but to buy airtime from existing All India Radio stations. International advocacy groups such as the World Association of Community Radio Broadcasters (AMARC), civil society organizations like the Community Radio Forum, and international development organizations including UNESCO and UNDP have over the past six years held several consultative meetings with the ministry to expand the eligibility criteria to include community-based organizations. This discrimination ended with the October 2006 policy that allows civil society organizations, NGOs, and women's self-help groups to apply for community radio licenses. One of the stated reasons for the government's objection to opening FM radio frequencies to the NGOs was the threat of insurgency, because India shares borders with Pakistan and Bangladesh. NGOs, many led by groups such as SEWA (Self-Employed Women's Association) and the thousands of self-help groups of women across the country, have been important partners with the government for the implementation of development programs. NGOs for decades have provided grassroots development work in capacity-building and mobilization, have been involved in several social movements, and have demanded the right to use media technologies to empower marginalized communities, including women, who have no access to the privately owned commercial media.

Even before the advent of this policy in India, projects involving women in community radio, such as "Our Voice" (Namma Dhwani) trained women in community broadcasting using a briefcase-size radio station (a portable production and transmission kit) provided by UNESCO in Budhikote village of Karnataka State. The themes of the thirty-minute program, aired on the local FM station AIR in 1998, included watershed management, girls' education, women's health, women's self-help, income-generating schemes, and the impact of literacy programs. The Namma Dhwani station has been in operation for eleven years and will receive a license to transmit under the new policy guidelines for community radio. Similarly, the Deccan Development Society (DDS) of Andhra Pradesh in South India has established a media center, and its Women Speak to Women project is carried out through community radio and video. The team has prepared two hundred hours of programming through four thousand women members of DDS. It is now awaiting approval from the government to switch on the transmitter, which has a radius of about thirty kilometers, covering nearly seventy villages.

Meanwhile, television is emerging as the most popular medium for a majority of illiterate women in developing countries. The Indian government's experiences of satellite communication for education and development during the Satellite Instructional Television Experiment (SITE) (1975–1976) and the Kheda Communication Project (1975–1991), which was awarded the UNESCO prize for rural communication effectiveness, led to the evolution of the Jhabua Development Communications project (JDCP), which focused on a predominantly tribal belt in one of the most backward regions in the country. The JDCP programs were produced by the villagers, with many acting or writing scripts for the series. These programs instilled widespread awareness regarding development, but social change requires wider community support systems and more time (DECU-ISRO 2000).

The Indian government has opened satellite-based communication systems under the aegis of the Indian Space Research Organization for education and training to the wider population, but it has been weak on regulating the portrayal of women on private satellite television, as have many governments in South Asia and Africa. In order to prohibit indecent representation of women, the Indian Parliament enacted the Indecent Representation of Women (Prohibition) Act of 1986. Under this Act, wide-ranging restrictions were imposed on content published or broadcast in the media. Introduced because of demands by women's groups and organizations for legislative action to curb the increasing exploitation of women by the media, the Act makes it an offense for any publication, writing, painting, or other medium to depict a woman or her body in an indecent or derogatory manner (Media Advocacy Group 1996). The National Commission for Women proposed amendments to the Act of 1986, and the Indecent Representation of Women (Prohibition) Amendment (of 1995) provides room for restriction on indecent advertisements in the print and broadcast media. The Committee on Portrayal of Women in Media (established in 1983) has representatives from thirteen women's organizations and is further divided into subcommittees, each of which is responsible for an in-depth study and critical analysis of specific media with reference to women's portrayal. The committee has conducted demonstrations against obscene billboards, has blackened obscene billboards, has staged massive protests against the screening of soft-porn films, and has presented memoranda to the prime minister and the information minister to review the portrayal of women in the media. A few media monitoring groups have been working actively to criticize sexism and obscenity in cinema, television, and print media. But none of these laws and efforts deters satellite television from stereotyping women. While national communication policies in broadcasting and telecommunications can provide women with greater access to information, fundamental inequities in gender relations present structural barriers that are difficult to surmount.

Human Rights and Violence against Women

The McBride Commission Report (1980) raised the issues of human rights violations and the equal rights of women, arguing that international communication policies should move toward a new world information and communication order to lower existing communication disparities and ensure that men and women are able to lead richer and more satisfying lives. According to Savitri Goonesekere, a member of the Monitoring Committee of CEDAW (quoted in Kannan 2003), NGOs in developing countries have raised awareness of these problems through foregrounding the human rights perspective to issues related to women and children, especially violence toward them. But the new communication order has had limited impact in Asian countries such as India and Thailand, where satellite television plays an important role in conditioning women to validate social norms in favor of patriarchal structures (Prasad 2006; Biggins 2006). The World Summit on the Information Society (WSIS) (2003–2005) did not consider these issues nor gendered digital disparities as dimensions of the overall global development divide. As Hamelink (2004) observes, the solution of the development divide has little to do with information, communication, or ICTs; it is rather a matter of lack of political will in a majority of nation-states. While women's development can be partially explained on these grounds, it ignores the unfair impact of globalization and SAP on women in developing countries.

Violence against women as embedded in patriarchal structures has been regarded as one of the key issues limiting women's development. A World Bank analysis of thirty-five studies from industrialized and developing countries shows that 25 to 50 percent of all women have suffered physical abuse by an intimate partner (Bunch 1997). In several countries of South Asia, violent practices against women are often recognized and defended as strands of culture (Prasad 2005) and form the storylines and plots of several popular soap operas on television. The United Nations Declaration on the Elimination of Violence

Against Women—which defines violence against women as "any act of gender-based violence that results in, or is likely to result in, physical, sexual, or psychological harm or suffering to women"—certainly provides scope for actions aimed at reducing or eliminating media violence in general and scenes of violence against women in particular. Satellite communication has weakened the control of national governments over a growing proportion of media messages and images and thus has given the debate on regulation and self-regulation new urgency. Only two countries—Canada and New Zealand—have taken a tougher stand on the portrayal of violence against women on national television (Racine 1995). The Canadian code prohibits any television program which "sanctions, promotes, or glamorizes any aspect of violence against women," and its Sex-Role Portrayal Code provides for greater diversity of roles and prohibits sexual exploitation and sexist language (Nevo 2000, Pandian 1999).

There is a need for international debate on reinterpretations of freedom of expression within the framework of women's human rights. With more communication channels under the control of fewer owners, there is a need to redefine this "freedom," taking full account of the contemporary global economic, information, and communication systems and of women's place within them. The report of the World Commission on Culture and Development (1995) provides a lead, with its proposals for "enhancing access, diversity and competition" in the international media system. The commission points out that the airwaves and space are part of a global commons—a collective asset that belongs to all humankind but which is at present used free of charge by those who possess resources and technology. Women have yet to benefit from the global commons. While Article 6 of the UNESCO Universal Declaration on Cultural Diversity (2001) calls for freedom of expression, media pluralism, and multilingualism; equal access to art and scientific and technological knowledge, including in digital form; and the possibility for all cultures to have access to the means of expression and dissemination as the guarantees of cultural diversity, most women in the developing countries have limited media access and gender justice in media portrayal.

ICTs and Policy Issues

While women continue to struggle against mainstream media, many see ICTs as a venue of communication for development. There are tangible examples of gender-sensitive policies in telecommunications which have set the framework for achieving desirable outcomes established by national policy, particularly with respect to universal access and affordability of services. Such policies have suited the needs of many rural women who may be homebound and have limited time for travel or limited income to incur travel costs. The Grameen phone project of the Grameen Bank in Bangladesh has enabled the borrowers, all women, to buy cellular phones in order to earn better income. Many rural women who are engaged in small-scale enterprises like poultry, farming, fisheries, livestock, and selling produce can find the current market rate through cellular phone service, thus eliminating the exploitation by middlemen (Amin 1998). The *theli* phone (shoulder-bag phone) initiated by SEWA (2003) in India, with tie-ups with the cellular and limited-mobility service providers and the handset manufacturers of the state, enabled five thousand members to buy mobile handsets as well as subscribe to the mobile services. The SEWA experience has also been shared internationally, resulting in similar models being set up, such as the Self-Employed Women's Union (SEWU) in Durban, South Africa, and the Women's Economic Empowerment Association (WEEA) in Yemen. SEWA in India has done outstanding work by training rural women in the production and use of video to generate income, disseminate new skills, and advocate policy changes. The self-help groups of women in Andhra Pradesh, India, are provided with mobile phones which have helped them to earn higher incomes by receiving more orders for their products and keeping in touch with the market demands and trends. The modest success of these telecommunications policies in Bangladesh and India have as a common aim the improvement of women's economic status through facilitating small businesses by the use of cellular mobile phones, particularly among women in rural areas. They have also aimed to enable the development of gender-aware universal access policies that stress public access points as an alternative to more capital-intensive choices (one line per home) and to ensure that the locations of public access points are gender-sensitive.

The World Bank emphasizes the need for development of content and technical support to developing countries and calls attention to connectivity issues, particularly connecting local communities to the international network. The latest Pew Global Attitudes Poll (2006) found substantially more people using a computer and going online in 2006 than in 2002. But there is a sharp divide between those in countries with high rates of Internet use in North America and Europe and those with less access to communication technologies. Men's use of computers exceeds that of women in fourteen out of the sixteen countries surveyed; only in Canada and Lebanon do the genders share the same amount of computer activity. Despite India's thriving computer-related industries, only 28 percent of men and 14 percent of women have access to a computer either at home or at work. Access to the Internet is largely facilitated in India by cybercafes that are found across the country, even in small towns.

This unequal access has resulted in "engendering ICTs" as a process of identifying and removing gender disparities in the access to and use of ICTs, as well as of adapting ICTs to the special needs, constraints, and opportunities of women (King and Mason 2001). Many NGOs find ICTs useful for networking and mobilizing support for women's issues. For instance, in South Africa, during the debate on reproductive rights and freedoms, a local women's network used e-mail mailing lists to present their views to the Parliament and to share information with a wide range of women in South Africa. This enhanced the NGO's ability to debate policy and also made it easier to consolidate and incorporate their views within the lobbying effort (Commonwealth Foundation 1997). The Women's Feature Service of the Inter Press Service gathers and disseminates news about women to more than eight hundred clients in eighty countries to influence public policy and development planning (Anand 1990). Its effectiveness was documented by Byerly (1990), who found that the service helped women in less-developed countries learn how to take an active role in their own progress.

Chandrasekhar (2006) suggests two routes by which technology can impact on the quality of life. Elite users, who use the technology to share information and analysis in crucial areas such as the environment, health, corporate practices, and labor conditions, can debate, develop, and contribute to creating international best practices in the relevant area. These can provide the basis for national policy and mobilization of public opinion nationally and internationally to change policy regimes. This is the top-down, trickle-down means for technology to influence human development. The other route is for technology to be diffused, leading to use and participation of the disadvantaged in the formulation and implementation of policies as well as to the direct provision of improved services that affect their lives. This is the more democratic face of technology and the most effective way to advance human development goals. Unfortunately the current extent and pattern of diffusion of technology in India is such that it is the first of these that dominates and is likely to continue to do so.

The Indian government's e-governance program with the Common Service Centres (CSCs) as its vehicle suggests that it wants to promote the second route. But to do so successfully there is a need for credible systems of gathering gender statistics about diffusion rates and use among women and other marginalized groups. For example, television exposure is substantially lower for women than for men, mainly due to women's preoccupation with household work. And TV viewing by male family members erodes women's ability to spend leisure time viewing TV. Similarly the social and cultural context of ICT use in India is a neglected research question (Prasad 2004b). According to gender advocates, there is considerable fragmentation of policy, combined with the approach that gender issues can be dealt with after "basic" problems have been solved, leading to the treatment of gender as a secondary or subcategory in policy documents (Chakravartty and Sarikakis 2006). There are also fundamental questions about how to effectively utilize development funds on a priority basis for education and basic needs that have a direct effect on women's lives, rather than incur huge expenses for projects whose benefits will scarcely trickle to them. As an example, the highly acclaimed Warana Wired Village Project covering seventy contiguous villages in Maharashtra in India cost $600,000; however, the costs of maintaining the technological infrastructure falls precipitously short of supply in all developing countries. Thus one must question whether the solution to the digital divide lies not in increasing access to hardware but to education that could change priorities, save money, and deliver better results (Chandrasekhar 2006).

Conclusion

The use of communication policies in development without rethinking structural and social inequities in gender relations renders women passive agents of projects conceived by developed countries; rarely are they transformed into active participants of the information age. Recent feminist analysis has shown that policy development is a long process and, given the extent of women's struggle in combating sexism in their lives, it requires continuous efforts in monitoring, research, awareness-raising, networking, advocacy, and lobbying (Nevo 2000). Developing communication policies focusing on economic development alone may not be a sufficient condition for women's empowerment in developing countries. Women's experiences and perspectives, missing from media coverage, need to be covered to bring about better understanding of how development programs involve and impact women. Media that give women in developing countries greater and easier access to information such as radio and telecommunications should be promoted on a priority basis, as they have demonstrated desirable development outcomes. Moreover, even when gender and communication policy or codes of practice exist, they are rarely enforced in the media. Activists need to think of ways in which policies can be better enforced to give a balanced and positive portrayal of women's roles and images. Communication policies can be successful if core issues of education, health care, and quality of life for women are addressed in national development communication policies. Media and gender issues are far from being resolved even in the developed countries, and women in the developed world continue to struggle to fit gender-sensitive communication policies in the larger context of national development.

References

Amin, Aasha Mehreen. 1998. "NCTs: Helping Hands for Women". In *Asian Women in Information Age: New Communication Technology, Democracy and Women*, ed. Ila Joshi, 7–14. Singapore: AMIC.

Anand, Anita. 1990. "Communication for Women in Development: The Experience of Inter Press Service." *Development* 2: 77–78.

Anuar, Mustafa K., and Shakila Manan. 2006. "Malaysian Women, Modernity and the Media: A Textual Analysis of Selected Women's Magazines in Malaysia." In *Women, Globalization and*

Mass Media: International Facets of Emancipation, ed. Kiran Prasad, 113–29. New Delhi: The Women Press.

Asia-Pacific Broadcasting Union. 2006. "Gendered Policies in Broadcasting Organizations." *ABU Weekly News Digest Week*, 24 November 2006. www.abu.org.my (accessed 25 November 2006).

Biggins, Ousa. 2006. "Cultural Imperialism and Thai Women's Portrayal on Mass Media." In *Women, Globalization and Mass Media: International Facets of Emancipation*, ed. Kiran Prasad, 95–112. New Delhi: The Women Press.

Birch, D., et al. 2001. *Asia Cultural Politics in the Global Age*. Crows Nest, Aust.: Allen Unwin.

Bryson, Valerie. 1999. *Feminist Debates: Issues of Theory and Political Practice*. London: MacMillan.

Bunch, Charlotte. 1997. "The Intolerable Status Quo: Violence Against Women and Girls." In *The Progress of Nations*. 41–48. New York: UNICEF.

Byerly, Carolyn M. 1990. "Taking a Stronger Hand: Women's Feature Services and the World News." *Development* 2: 79–85.

Chakravartty, Paula, and Katharine Sarikakis. 2006. *Media Policy and Globalization*. New York: Palgrave Macmillan.

Chandrasekhar, C. P. 2006. "India Is Online but Most Indians Are Not." *The Hindu*, September 25.

Commonwealth Foundation. 1997. "Communication Without Frontiers." *Common Path*, January.

DECU-ISRO. 2000. *The Direction: Jhabua Development Communications Project*. Ahmedabad: Indian Space Research Organization.

Desai, N., and U. Thakkar. 2001. *Women in Indian Society*. New Delhi: National Book Trust.

Farganis, Sondra. 1994. *Situating Feminism: From Thought to Action*. Thousand Oaks, CA: Sage.

Graham-Brown, Sarah. 1998. *Images of Women: The Portrayal of Women in Photography of the Middle East, 1860–1950*. London: Quartet Books.

Hamelink, Cees J. 2004. "Did WSIS Achieve Anything At All?" *Gazette* 66, nos. 3–4: 281–90.

Kannan, Ramya. 2003. "Role of Global Agencies Should Not Be Undermined." *The Hindu*, August 9.

King, Elizabeth M., and Andrew D. Mason. 2001. *Engendering Development*. World Bank Report. www.worldbank.org/devoutreach/spring01/article.asp?id=109 (accessed 4 February 2007).

Kumar, Rahul. 2006. "Communication Congress: Community Radio Left Out in the Cold?" *One World South Asia*, 27 October. http://southasia.oneworld.net/article/view/141619/1/2219 (accessed 16 November 2006).

Lerner, Daniel. 1958. *The Passing of Traditional Society: Modernizing the Middle East*. New York: Free Press.

Mariani, Ina Ratna, et al. 1998. "Hope for a New Future?" In *Asian Women in Information Age: New Communication Technology, Democracy and Women*, ed. Ila Joshi, 65–86. Singapore: AMIC.

McBride, Sean, et al. 1980. *Many Voices, One World*. Report by the International Commission for the Study of Communication Problems. Paris: UNESCO.

Media Advocacy Group. 1996. *A Brief Note on Indian Mass Media Laws*. New Delhi: Media Advocacy Group.

Melkote, Srinivas R., and H. Leslie Steeves. 2001. *Communication for Development in the Third World: Theory and Practice for Empowerment*. New Delhi: Sage.

National Policy for the Empowerment of Women. 2001. Department of Women and Child Development, Ministry of Human Resources Development. New Delhi: Government of India.

Nevo, Maria del. 2000. "Developing Gender Sensitive Communications Policies." www.wacc.org .uk/wacc/publications/media_development/archive/2000_3/developing_gender_sensitive_ communications_policies (accessed 20 October 2006).

Pandian, H. 1999. "Engendering Communication Policy: Key Issues in the International Women-and-Media Arena and Obstacles to Forging and Enforcing Policy." *Media, Culture and Society* 21: 459–80.

Patel, Vibhuti 2004. "Gender Budget: Media Concerns and Policy for India." In *Communication and Empowerment of Women: Strategies and Policy Insights from India*, ed. Kiran Prasad, 104–49. New Delhi: The Women Press.

Pew Global Attitudes Poll. 2006. "Truly a World Wide Web: Globe Going Digital." http://pewglobal.org/reports/pdf/251.pdf (accessed 9 January 2007).

Prasad, Kiran. 2002. "Media Policy for Developing Countries: The Indian Experience". In *Communication, Modernization and Social Development: Theory, Policy and Strategies*, eds. K. Mahadevan, Kiran Prasad, Ito Youchi, and Vijayan K. Pillai, 155–86. New Delhi: B.R. Publishing.

———, ed. 2004a. *Communication and Empowerment of Women: Strategies and Policy Insights from India*, vols. 1 & 2. New Delhi: The Women Press.

———, ed. 2004b. *Information and Communication Technology: Recasting Development*. New Delhi: B.R. Publishing.

———. 2005. "Women, Media and Society: Recasting Communication Policy." In *Women and Media: Challenging Feminist Discourse*, ed. Kiran Prasad, 1–18. New Delhi: The Women Press.

———. 2006. *Women, Globalization and Mass Media: International Facets of Emancipation*. New Delhi: The Women Press.

Purewal, Navtej. K. 2001. "New Roots for Rights: Women's Response to Population and Development Policies." In *Women Resist Globalization: Mobilizing for Livelihood and Rights*, eds. Sheila Rowbotham and Stephanie Linkogle, 96–117. London and New York: Zed Books.

Racine, Paul. 1995. "Converging Technologies, Converging Regulations." *InterMedia* 23, no. 5: 18–19.

Raman, Anuradha. 2003. "IBF Draws Up Do's and Dont's Code for Satellite Channels." *The New Indian Express*, January 17.

Schramm, Wilbur. 1964. *Mass Media and National Development: The Role of Information in the Developing Countries*. Stanford: Stanford University Press.

Self-Employed Women's Association (SEWA). 2003. www.sewa.org (accessed 9 November 2006).

Swaminathan, M.S. 2001. "Eliminating Hunger: A Challenge." *The Hindu*, October 7.

Tiongson, Mari Luz Quesada. 1999. *The State of Women and Media in Asia: An Overview*. Bangkok: ISIS International, Manila, for UN Economic and Social Commission for Asia and the Pacific (ESCAP).

UNESCO. 2001. "Universal Declaration on Cultural Diversity." http://unesdoc.unesco.org/images/0012/001271/127160m.pdf (accessed 16 November 2006).

UNICEF. 2002. "Meena Communication Initiative." http://gkaims.globalknowledge.org (accessed 2 November 2005).

UNICEF. 2003. *The State of the World's Children, 2003*. New York: Oxford University Press.

Williamson, David A. 2006. "The Promise of Change, the Persistence of Inequality: Development, Globalization, Mass Media and Women In Sub-Saharan Africa." In *Women, Globalization and Mass Media: International Facets of Emancipation*, ed. Kiran Prasad, 183–208. New Delhi: The Women Press.

World Bank. 2003. *2003 World Development Indicators*. Washington: The World Bank.

World Commission on Culture and Development. 1995. *Our Creative Diversity*. New York: United Nations/UNESCO.

World Economic Forum. 2006. "Women's Empowerment: Measuring the Global Gender Gap." www.weforum.org/en/initiatives/gcp/Gender%20Gap/index.htm (accessed 16 September 2006).

CHAPTER SEVEN

The Spectral Politics of Mobile Communication Technologies: Gender, Infrastructure, and International Policy

Barbara Crow and Kim Sawchuk

Cellular telephones have become one of the fastest-growing technologies in the last hundred years, and this proliferation has changed how people communicate in public and private around the globe (Townsend 2004). Cell phones[1] have been used for community economic development (Kamga 2006) and have become integral to new forms of community activism and social networking, from the emergence and waning of the "smart mob" (Rheingold 2002) to their use in e-campaigns for international human rights.

Cell phones are only one among a number of wireless communication devices that depend upon access to an invisible infrastructure known as spectrum. In this chapter, we discuss the politics of mobile communication technologies from an international policy perspective. We pay particular attention to the cellular telephone from within the larger issue of the distribution of and access to radio wave frequencies, otherwise known as spectrum allocation. In considering spectrum from the purview of international communication policy, and international communication policy from the purview of feminism, we take into account "gender sensitive infrastructure development" (Chakravartty 2006, 236). This position draws attention to the technical, political, and economic conditions that undergird everyday social practice of media consumption.

We argue, as feminist media scholars and activists, that it is crucial for both mainstream policy organizations and alternative organizations to consider gender within infrastructure development to ensure that spectrum as a public resource is fairly distributed and to open up the possibility for its use by those co-existing factions and forces, the subaltern counterpublics, who make up the wider political spectrum of that entity known as the public (Fraser 1993). Christian Sandvig (2006), for example, argues that access to the electromagnetic spectrum is one of the key foundations for development and democracy and that "those interested in development must act" (53). Yet Sandvig, like so many working in this area, rarely consider the politics of gender in their proclamations or their examples of organizations engaged in community media development and democracy.

Fraser's analysis of the conditions of democracy asserts that these subaltern counterpublics must exist, and that access to debate and deliberation are necessary to "ensure the dissemination of discourse into ever-widening spheres" (15). While crucial to our perspective, Fraser's view does not adequately account for the influence of media in this process (Sawchuk 2006). As the cell phone and Wi-Fi networks become more widespread, understanding the ownership and control of spectrum allocation takes on a new importance for feminists engaged in media democracy movements and social activism.

The Emergent Universe of
Wireless Mobile Communication Devices

Gow and Smith (2006) advise that "a firm grounding in basic technical terms and concepts is an important prerequisite for an informed, critical engagement with current and social issues in mobile, wireless communication" (2). This basic knowledge is particularly vital for feminists in an international context of policy making, where technical facility operates as a boundary issue, acting as a means of inclusion and exclusion in both mainstream and alternative organizations (Benston 1982, 1983; Hacker 1990). In order to comprehend what is at stake politically, feminists must understand what is at issue technologically.

Cellular phones are based on a networking system that communicates through cells rather than having one device that emits radio frequencies over a long distance. A cellular network is based on a number of low-powered transceivers serving shorter distances. As the cells cover smaller areas, the frequencies can be reused in other cells with less interference (Gow and Smith 2006, 149). Cell phones have a long history of technical development, represented as "generations." Each of these generations has been accompanied by a set of regulatory conditions and debates, nationally and internationally. With the rapid development of analog cellular phones, there was a need to develop one standard to allow the different devices to connect to one another. This standard addressed networking issues such as international roaming and channel structure and technical issues such as subjective speech quality, radio resources management, and anticipating user demands for new services. Rather than having devices that worked with one set of standards in one nation and having to have another device to work in another nation, a standard known as the global system for mobile communications (GSM), now operating in over two hundred countries, was developed. One of its key features is the subscriber identity module (SIM) card which allows users to transport their subscription information and phone book from one device to another.

This standard has largely supported what are known as 2G, or second-generation, cellular phone applications. 2G cell phones operate in a higher frequency range, allowing for faster networking, and employ different kinds of technology for smaller cell phone handsets. Currently we are in the midst of a 3G, or third generation, rollout of cellular devices and another technical standard, the universal mobile telecommunications system (UMTS), has been developed to facilitate the technical and network interoperability of these devices. What is important in this transition is that these phones are marketed and promoted as devices to transmit more than voice, but also rich media.

3G cell phones are capable of transmitting and streaming video and broadcasting (these require high-speed data transfer). While most operators and many governments cooperated in the development and commitment to the GSM standard, 3G phone developers and providers are not required to adhere to specific standards to facilitate interoperability. This means, for example, that users cannot watch mobile television in Spain on a device they bought in Denmark.

An emergent fourth generation of cellular phone refers to a phone that will offer the complete interoperability of all wireless devices. It will be packet based, which refers to how units of information "are routed between notes over data links shared with other traffic"[2] and will operate within one standard. Most of the phones currently in circulation are 2G and 3G phones, a distinction that is not only technical but connotes a different set of functionalities related to status.

Cellular phones and services have had a worldwide impact on communications, but the adoption of phones varies from nation to nation. The most recent mapping of the international use of cell phones clearly indicates that countries with poor landline service are the most likely to have higher rates of cell phone use.

In countries like Canada, where landlines are relatively inexpensive and the industry has been highly regulated (Winseck 1995), Canadians have been less keen to adopt cell phone use. Typically nations in Europe, Asia, and south of the equator have been the most ardent users of mobile telephony (see figure 7.1). While this is generally the case, there are exceptions, which points to the very real physical and material conditions that facilitate the uptake of cell

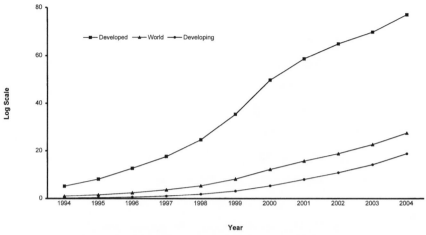

Figure 7.1. Cell Phone Ownership around the World (per 100 inhabitants)
Source: www.itu.int/ITU-D/ict/statistics/ict/graphs/mobile.jpg (2 February 2007).

phone technology. For example, Japan has had to continually rebuild its infrastructure as the result of earthquakes and volcanoes. Partly as a result of these climatic conditions, but also because of other cultural practices, wireless devices have been taken up in unprecedented numbers (over 100 percent ownership). In this context, wireless devices are more reliable in this landscape and less vulnerable to weather disasters.

While cell phones have become widespread, from a geopolitical perspective, the profits and ownership garnered from the research and development of cell phones are largely held by corporations situated in powerful Western nations (see figure 7.2).

The above data may seem to indicate that internationally the largest companies are located in developing nations, such as China. However, while Chinese and Japanese companies have a significant share of the international market, their investment is largely internal to their own countries.

As the most common and profitable mobile communication technology worldwide, cell phones are receiving ample academic attention from cultural and intercultural perspectives (Castells et al. 2006; Kavoori and Arceneaux 2006). Most of the social science research on cell phones has come from nations where the adoption of these devices has been swift, such as Finland and Sweden. However, research is beginning to emerge in the context of developing nations, such as a recent study of cell phone use in the Caribbean (Horst 2006; Horst and Miller 2006). Other research on regulation and infrastructure by Neto, Best, and Gillett (2005) demonstrates that there is a significant pressure for African nations to adopt commercial applications of cell phone services. They also demonstrate

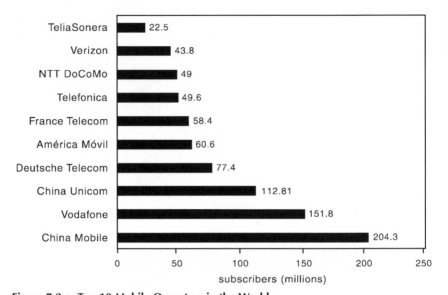

Figure 7.2.   Top 10 Mobile Operators in the World
Source: www.itu.int/osg/spu/newslog/December+2004+Top+Mobile+Operators+In+The+World.aspx (2 February 2007).

that the diversity of regulations have made it difficult for many of these nations to harness the significant possibilities of unlicensed spectrum.

Statistical research on the gendered use of mobile devices is scant. However, as we discuss later, the wide-scale adoption of cell phones does not mean that gender is not an issue. In the U.S., for example, men are more likely to use cell phones and to spend more money and time on them. This is not surprising, given two factors: cell phones have become part of the culture of paid work communications, and men generally still earn more than women. While numerous projects have facilitated cell phone activism, such as the *theli* phone initiated by SEWA and the Grameen phone in Bangladesh (see chapter 6), in some countries women's use of cell phones is associated with the sex trade industry. In these instances, women who use cell phones are discriminated against and discouraged from using this form of communication (Hafkin and Huyer 2006). There is clearly the need for more international and comparative work on these issues.

Other scholarship, from within the purview of cultural studies, examines the representations and practices of cell phone use from a gendered perspective including, for example, the creation of new icons and forms of linguistic shorthand by young Japanese girls—fomenting new collective formations, which Sandra Buckley (2007) has described as "thumb tribes"—which are pushing the development and design of phones and services (Ling 2004; Ito, Okabe, and Matsuda 2005). There is research on the creative ways young girls create content, subvert social conventions, and engage in fan cultures using their cell phones (Leung 2006). These studies indicate that women, as consumers and users of media technologies, negotiate these technologies in innovative ways which contribute to their development. Still other research examines how women are represented in cell phone advertising as socially skilled and as good communicators, while men are represented as alone and almost exclusively in work contexts (Rakow 1992; Shade 2007).

While there is a focus on intercultural, cross-cultural, and gendered practices and representations of the cell phone in recent academic literature, in terms of aggregate data on gender and cell phone use, gender, as a variable, seems to have fallen off the mainstream research agendas of the major telecommunications companies. Neither the ITU nor OECD has databases attending to gender and cell phone use. For example, in the recent ITU publication *Digital Life*, there were only three mentions of gender. Of these, one was about cross-gender representation online, and the other two were about how to protect women and children from online pornography. This is quite different from studies on the Internet; most of these studies made gender a variable (Norris 2002; Shade 2002; ITU 2006a; World Internet Project n.d.).

While mobile technologies have become synonymous with cellular or mobile phones, cell phones are only the most visibly and audibly pervasive component of the emergent assemblage of immersive mobile technologies. They can be best understood as part of a larger network of interoperable technologies that relay packets of information in bundles from one point to another point (Gow and Smith 2006). An analysis of mobile and wireless communications at a terrestrial level may include hybrid handheld entertainment and gaming platforms, such as the latest Nintendo platform, the Wii. Mobile and wireless telephony are also connected to multifunctional tools, such as PDAs (personal digital assistants). Many mobile devices are connected to one another, forming a tangled assemblage of both wired and wireless infrastructure, which is of major importance in the emergent development of the 4G cell phone. These devices are connected to a variety of base stations which have greater or lesser ranges. These area networks have relied on requirements, standards, and protocols to allow devices to connect with one another. These include PANS (personal area network systems) which allow devices in close proximity to connect to one another, such as Bluetooth and the files on your laptop; WANs (wide area network systems) which cover large areas, through connecting various LANs (land area network systems). These technologies and systems rely on the availability and licensing of a spectrum.

Making Spectrum Visible

Spectrum refers to the transmission and regulation of airwaves into frequencies. As Sandvig explains, the noun *spectrum* simply refers to a range, whether it be political or physical: "The spectrum used for communication is the range of electromagnetic radiation—the stuff that the familiar antennas of our cellular telephones are designed to send and receive" (2006, 51). The electromagnetic spectrum is organized by frequencies according to the length of the waves; waves, which carry communication signals, can be long or short.

Frequencies are allocated in bands, referring to services on an exclusive or shared basis (ITU 2004). There are also extensive regulations regarding service category (fixed service, mobile service), and service type (this describes types of transmissions and emissions).[3] While spectrum, like the air we breathe, seems to exist in unlimited quantities, it is a finite resource. From this fact arise a number of critical political questions that must be debated by all those who use spectrum: How should spectral frequency be allocated? For what purposes should we be using this shared resource? Who benefits from its sale and use? How is access ensured and is it enough? From a feminist perspective, we must consider how the technologies that use spectrum may create or disrupt existing relations of power. Further, how may an international policy regime that prioritizes the commercial use of the phones create obstacles to women's innovative uses of these technologies for political organizing?

As these research questions make evident, spectrum allocation, distribution, and regulation is a policy issue, nationally and internationally. Most nations have a government body setting and administering policies related to telecommunications. It is for these reasons that it is important to understand the organizational cultures of the ITU and the IEEE, two powerful players in the regulation of spectrum, as well as the potential contributions that a feminist understanding of politics and policy can make to the power dynamics within community-based activism.

At this point it is worth contemplating the wisdom of Chela Sandoval (2000), who argues that, in the struggle for emancipation, it is important for feminists to cultivate a "differential consciousness" that takes into account the need for political change in different contexts and conditions. As this perspective suggests, intervention is needed at state and policy levels. However, this does not preclude the kind of radical work to be undertaken within existing alternative organizations or forming organizations that have a completely separate agenda. Feminist political action must operate in tandem and advocate on multiple fronts.

Internationally two institutional bodies have played significant roles in shaping spectrum, the International Telecommunications Union (ITU) and the Institute of Electrical and Electronics Engineers (IEEE). The ITU, in particular, has been a critical player in setting out standards and policy recommendations on how to allocate spectrum. There are 191 member states of ITU. Member states determine representation on the ITU Council, with individuals appointed to the council. The ITU Council is made up of forty-six members from five different geographic regions, and they are elected by a conference with consideration of fair representation of the five regions: the Americas, Western Europe, Eastern Europe, Africa, and Asia and Australasia.

Currently all the elected members of the ITU leadership are men. Of the current ten representatives of the Office of the Secretary General, all but one have degrees related to engineering fields, with only one member having a degree in political science and law. This long-standing institution has played a critical role in brokering and negotiating telecommunications policy around the globe (Ó'Siochú, Girard, Mahan 2002).

The main objective of the ITU is to establish frequency allocations and regulatory procedures for the harmonious operation of global radio communication services and to ensure that these services do not interfere with competing signals and transmissions. Briefly, the politics of the distribution of this resource involves

first, the allocation of these blocks of frequencies for particular users (e.g., broadcasters, military, mobile operators, etc.) and second, the assignment of specific frequencies within the allocated blocks to different "licensees." Generally, licensees have the exclusive right to use the assigned frequencies to provide designated services. Typically, spectrum users are granted temporary licenses, even though renewal is often a formality. (ITU 2006b)

Standards governing the use of radio-frequency spectrum and the geostationary-satellite and non-geostationary-satellite orbits are determined at the World Radiocommunication Conference (WRC). Their meetings are based on an agenda determined by the ITU (ITU 2006b; ITU 2006c). There are two primary methods of purchasing these frequencies: through auctions and through "beauty contests" (a bit of terminology that reveals the highly gendered assumptions embedded in this technical universe). Auctions have tended to be the most popular way nations have sold spectrum allocation, and beauty contests are determined by which organization/individual/industry can demonstrate its capacity to best utilize spectrum allocation. Critics of the spectral auction raise concerns about governments generating revenue from licensing and the enormous capital required to bid for spectrum allocations. Critics of the beauty contest format worry whether government regulators have sufficient training to determine who has the best technical and business models (Xavier 2001).

What is clear is that these auctions and beauty contests are highly profitable events. In the last set of auctions for 3G licenses, in 2001, the auctions raised over 1.5 billion dollars. Costs for the spectrums ranged from 20 Euros per capita in Switzerland to 650 euros per capita in the United Kingdom (Klemperer 2004). This is hardly the cash reserve of most women's or feminist organizations. As well, it is unclear who profits from these auctions, and if the money garnered in different nations is being used to benefit its citizenry or is reinvested into public ventures.

Important to understand, particularly for feminists and other subaltern counter-public groups with limited financial resources, is this: there are two forms of spectrum. The largest part of spectrum, while licensed and regulated, is primarily limited to corporate control and being harnessed for profit because it is so expensive. A small proportion of spectrum is unlicensed, free, and available for public use. It is this portion of the spectrum that is primarily available to wireless technology activists and not-for-profit and community-based organizations. The unlicensed spectrum was first guaranteed by another international body that was key to the development of the wireless world of communication: the IEEE.

Established in 1963, the IEEE's main purpose is to advance the theory and application of electrotechnology and allied sciences, to serve as a catalyst for technological innovation, and to support the needs of its members through a wide variety of programs and services. Unlike the ITU, membership is "open to individuals who by education or experience give evidence of competence in an IEEE designated field of interest."[4] The designated fields are, in broad terms, engineering, computer science and information technology, physical sciences, biological and medical sciences, mathematics, technical communications, and related education, management, law, and policy. Recognizing that there are fewer women than men currently in the fields of engineering and computer science, in the last few years the IEEE has extended its membership to nonengineers. The IEEE also has a society on the "social implications of technology" and a publication dedicated to the nontechnical dimensions of their work; in 1996 they dedicated a theme issue to gender and the Internet. In other words, the IEEE has made an effort to expand diversity within its organization.

These two international bodies, the ITU and the IEEE, play a significant role in determining the uses and allocation of licensed and unlicensed spectrum. Membership in both of these international bodies, which determine public access to this important new resource, is highly divided by gender. This gendered division of labor is relevant in terms of the individuals who make the decisions regarding spectrum policy, connected as it is to the transference of the skill sets required to create, produce, and distribute spectrum. In this communication chain, women are positioned as users and consumers, not as innovators, owners, or creators. All the current executives of the ITU, for example, are men, with representation from developing countries. While, as feminist scholars and activists, we know that this issue is about more than numbers, this gender divide in both the IEEE and the ITU is an important exclusion to note, given their power to decide access to this increasingly valuable resource and their influence on its regulation worldwide.

Spectrum Policy Matters

In the last decade, there have been three promising developments with respect to global media advocacy and new media technologies. The first was the World Summit on the Information Society (WSIS) and its Gender Caucus in Geneva (in 2003) and Tunis (in 2005). Its involvement of governments, industry, and civil society, and its multistakeholder approach to policy, created significant international attention toward the widening global gaps to information and communication technologies (ICTs) (Chakravartty and Sarikakis 2006). The second is the widespread growth of community wireless networks (CWN) in North America. The third is cellular phone activist organizations, such as MobileActive, advocating and documenting global uses of the cell phone as an activist tool.

WSIS is a United Nations–driven initiative (Resolution 56/183, December 2001) that held two summits to address the foundations and the range of stakeholders in the development of the information society.[5] These summits were compelling for their unusual representation of developing nations and for the WSIS declaration of principles:. This declaration takes an important ideological stance, shifting notions of communication and constructing it as a human right. This fundamental shift acknowledges that communication skills, technologies, and infrastructure are critical to the healthy development of societies.

Despite these measures, there have been significant feminist criticisms of the WSIS process (Jensen 2005; McLaughlin and Pickard 2006; Sreberny 2005), which are germane for feminists working within both wireless community networks and in international mobile advocacy campaigns. Criticism is directed toward the emphasis in WSIS—and in other international organizations—on multistakeholder models of political participation, which do not acknowledge significant power differences between stakeholders when it comes to decision making. This model can be used to draw attention away from a social-justice perspective and the adoption of a liberal model of human rights. Feminist advocates have also criticized the WSIS process for its implicit market fundamentalism, where "pro-poor" interventions are consistently justified through pro-market solutions. Finally, feminist advocates from developing countries have consistently argued for the need to prioritize the productive capacities of ICTs over their consumption. For these reasons, a separate feminist caucus at WSIS addressed the gender divide in the global information society, in which "girls and women face universal disadvantage in terms of access, competence as well as social and economic mobility" (Chakravartty 2006, 256). However, while one might assume that the cell phone would be part of the discussion on the WSIS agenda, the term "information society" is largely Internet-based, a conceptualization of ICTs that does not consider the 4G specificities of mobile technologies and their increasing prevalence as a platform of media convergence.

Community wireless networks (CWNs) are committed to open-source software to create hotspot and mesh networks to provide free access to the Internet and the increasing number of Wi-Fi–enabled cell phones. They are also vocal advocates for the provision of more public access to spectrum allocation. The initiatives of CWNs have been successful largely in Western nations, such as Canada, the United States, and the U.K. Two U.S. national summits have been held, with an international summit scheduled for 2007 in Maryland. While intended to bring together activists from across the globe, because these summits have been held in the U.S., representation from developing nations has been limited. While there has been significant participation from women at these summits, even these activist events are not without their own gender hierarchies.

CWNs, not unlike the ITU and IEEE, have been driven mostly by men, both highly trained computer scientists and self-taught geeks, whose goals are to develop and deploy Wi-Fi networks in innovative ways (Powell 2007). The gendered differences in the use of community Wi-Fi and gender politics within these movements, including inadvertent exclusions in organizations that can result from the inappropriate use of sexualized language, have recently been discussed by Wi-Fi activists (Powell and Shade 2006). The importance of considering representation is evident if one looks as the gender breakdown of participants in the summits.[6] While there has been significant female participation in the development of ICTs at the policy level, the power dynamics within the field of alternative media bear an uncanny resemblance to the mainstream organizations previously discussed. The stories of women involved in CWNs also demonstrate how reliant these kinds of initiatives are on particular technical and political skill-sets, ones that many women in developing nations have not yet achieved. A persistent problem in ensuring the creation of an infrastructure that is gender-sensitive is the broader division of intellectual and activist labor. The technical arena is still largely dominated by males; the secretarial work is often assigned to females. There is a hierarchy of value in organizations where technology is center-stage: those who have an understanding of its functioning are given central space at summits and in decision making. Rodgers (2003,

26–39) explicates the implications of this politics of space, with respect to global activism on the Internet. As mobile phone and Wi-Fi activism gain importance, her analysis is critical to heed.

A third set of initiatives attempting to address the global politics of wireless telecommunications takes up the cell phone as a tool for e-advocacy and media activism. MobileActive.org is dedicated to using the mobile phone for civic actions and engagements, such as petitions and documenting human rights abuses. This site is a dynamic focal point for activism that uses the cell phone as a central organizing tool. It features a manifesto on the use of the cell phone as a communications device; it offers practical tips on how to use the cell phone for global rights campaigns; and it has opened up debate on why particular campaigns that used cell phones, such as the Amnesty International campaign to close Guantanomo Bay, failed. Importantly, it documents the work done by women's groups across the globe, including the UmNyango Project in South Africa which uses mobile phones to track and monitor domestic abuse, and the promotion of the mobile phone for microfinancing market activities in Bangladesh. As these examples illustrate, the cell phone is a potential tool for feminist organizing on a global level.

Unlike computer-based communication media, cell phone technologies, for the most part, do not require high literacy skills. Given global literacy divides, with a significant portion of illiterate peoples being women and children, cell phones can provide a modicum of access to telecommunications. In UNESCO's September 2005 Fact Sheet, it was reported that 771 million of the world's illiterate are women located mainly in nine countries, with 47 percent of this population living in the most populated nations of China and India (UNESCO 2005).

These initiatives represent important interventions and reveal the stakes and necessity for access to these technologies. However, the initiatives of groups such as MobileActive.org are restricted in terms of the technical challenges they pose to the major telephone companies who control cell phone usage, research, development, and access to services. Because cell phones run on proprietary software, users are unable to make modifications or develop or delete applications or codes and must instead rely on cell phone providers for their infrastructure (such as mobile phone towers) and service. This point is critical in the context of mobile technologies; all but one cell phone has open-source capacity: the Nokia Series 60 Platform, which, at approximately US$350, is one of the most expensive cell phones currently on the market.

The issue of proprietary software on cell phones may not be of concern to the average user. However, it is important to remember that many Internet developments, in particular innovations that have enhanced the Internet's many-to-many communications, such as trendy social networking applications like

YouTube and MySpace, have been the result of open-source practitioners. These innovations have increased various individuals' capacities to develop, create, produce, and disseminate content via text, sound, and images.

Conclusion

As more people around the world gain access to telephony, these devices have become a contested site of media convergence and investment for both political activists and industry stakeholders. Most of the widespread proliferation and use of these mobile devices is happening in the context of licensed spectrum—that part of the radio frequency that is owned and controlled by either private corporations or governments. As more and more devices become wireless, spectrum becomes more precious and indeed more valuable. Future research in this regard may address the privatization of spectrum; the lack of public sector accountability in key areas like access, pricing, and surveillance; and most importantly who benefits from spectrum auctioning.

As we have argued, it is crucial to make visible the invisible infrastructure that enables mediated forms of communications in our everyday lives. Key to this transformation is the acquisition of basic technical knowledge of what makes these devices operate and how spectrum works. A facility with this technical language acts as a boundary issue, delineating who is in and who is out of decision making at the policy level. This has a profound impact on gender politics in national and international organizations, from the mainstream international telecommunications regulators to the alternative, nonprofit Wi-Fi initiatives in diverse local communities. Both constituencies need to attend to the politics of representation in their organizations. The gendered distribution of labor and access to communication must stay an issue in media reform agendas.

The challenges for feminists navigating the media landscape of wireless mobile devices are manifold. Access and control of spectrum are regulated by occupations and organizations that tend to be gender-biased. Feminist activists, and other not-for-profit actors, tend to operate on a very small portion of the spectrum—the unlicensed part. For these reasons, feminist research and activism on wireless communications must not only look at the practices of innovative cellular use and questions of consumption. It is critical to advocate for attention to the gender implications of infrastructure development. Attention to organization and infrastructure is a vital component for the creation of the conditions for collective communicational self-determination for women. While it may not seem obvious at first, this implies an engagement with the technical dimensions of the cell phone and a critical interest in national and international policies of spectrum allocation.

Notes

Acknowledgments. We would like to thank Janice Leung for her research assistance, Leslie Regan Shade for her useful insights to strengthen this paper, and Katharine Sarikakis for her generous criticisms of an earlier draft.

1. We use the terms *cell phones*, *cellular phones*, and *mobile phones* interchangeably to refer to the same item.
2. See http://en.wikipedia.org/wiki/Packet_switching (accessed 7 February 2007).
3. There are a number of useful websites explaining spectrum. See Telecommunications Research Project, http://www.trp.hku.hk/e_learning/spectrum/section2.html; the ITU www.itu.int/osg/spu/ni/3G/resources/spectrum/index.html; and the ICTP-RADIONET Programme of Training and System Development on Networking and Radiocommunications, www.ictp.trieste.it/~radionet (accessed 7 February, 2007).
4. See www.ieee.org/web/societies/home/index.html (accessed 7 February, 2007).
5. See www.itu.int/wsis/docs/geneva/official/dop.html (7 February 2007).
6. See www.cuwireless.net/summit. Website listing of CWNs, www.toaster.net/wireless/community .html and http://wiki.personaltelco.net/index.cgi/WirelessCommunities (accessed 7 February 2007).

References

Aminuzzaman, Salahuddin, Harald Baldersheim, and Ishtiaq Jamil. 2003. "Talking Back! Empowerment and Mobile Phones in Rural Bangladesh: A Study of the Village Phone Scheme of Grameen Bank." *Contemporary South Asia* 12, no. 3: 327–48.

Benston, Margaret Lowe. 1982. "Feminism and the Critique of Scientific Method." In *Feminism in Canada*, eds. Angela Miles and Geraldine Finn, 47–66. Montreal: Black Rose Books.

———. 1983. "For Women, the Chips are Down." In *The Technological Woman: Interfacing with Tomorrow*, ed. Jan Zimmerman, 44–54. New York: Praeger.

Buckley, Sandra. In manuscript. "Intimate Strangers: The Keitai Culture of 'Belonging-without-being-with.' " In *Sampling the Spectrum: The Politics, Practices and Poetics of Mobile Communication*, eds. Barbara Crow, Kim Sawchuk, and Michael Longford.

Castells, Manuel, Mireia Fernandez-Ardevol, Jack Linchuan Qiu, and Araba Sey. 2006. *Mobile Communication and Society: A Global Perspective*. Cambridge: MIT Press.

Chakravartty, Paula. 2006. "Who Speaks for the Governed: World Summit on the Information Society, Civil Society and the Limits of Multistakeholderism." *Economic and Political Weekly* 41 (January 21): 250–57. www.people.umass.edu/pchakrav/documents/PChakravarty_epw.pdf? (accessed 7 February 2007).

———, and Katharine Sarikakis. 2006. *Globalization and Media Policy: History, Culture, Politics*. Palgrave Macmillan.

Fraser, Nancy. 1993. "Rethinking the Public Sphere: A Contribution to the Critique of Actually Existing Democracy." In *The Phantom Public Sphere*, ed. Bruce Robbins, 1–32. Minneapolis: University of Minnesota Press.

Gow, Gordon, and Richard Smith. 2006. *Mobile and Wireless Communications*. Maidenhead, UK and New York: Open University Press.

Hacker, Sally. 1990. *Doing It the Hard Way: Investigations of Gender and Technology*. Boston: Unwin Hyman.

Hafkin, Nancy, and Sophia Huyer, eds. 2006. *Cinderella or Cyberella?: Empowering Women in the Knowledge Society*. Bloomfield, CT: Kumarian Press.

Horst, Heather. 2006. "The Blessings and Burdens of Communication: Cell Phones in the Jamaican Transnational Social Field." *Global Networks: A Journal of Transnational Affairs* 6, no. 2: 142–60.

Horst, Heather, and Daniel Miller. 2006. *The Cell Phone: The Anthropology of Communication*. New York: Palgrave.

International Telecommunication Union (ITU). 2004. Overview, Radiocommunication Sector. www.itu.int/aboutitu/overview/o-r.html (accessed 7 February 2007).

———. 2006a. Gender Mainstreaming Strategy. www.itu.int/gender/about/ (accessed 8 February 2007).

———. 2006b. Overview, ITU Council. www.itu.int/council/index.html (accessed 7 February 2007).

———. 2006c. World Radiocommunication Conferences. www.itu.int/ITU-R/conferences/wrc/index.asp (accessed 7 February 2007).

Ito, Mizuko, Daisuke Okabe, and Misa Matsuda, eds. 2005. *Personal, Portable, Pedestrian: Mobile Phones in Japanese Life*. Cambridge: MIT Press.

Jensen, Heiki. 2005. "Gender Equality and the Multistakeholder Approach: WSIS as Best Practice." In *Visions in Process II of the World Summit of the Information Society*, eds. Olga Droussou and Heiki Jensen, 53–62. Berlin: Heinrich Boll Foundation. www.boell.de/downloads/medien/visions_in_process2.pdf (accessed 7 February 2007).

Kamga, Osée. 2006. "The Mobile Phone and Cultural Hybridization: Toward Reconceptualizing Uses in the Developing World." Paper prepared for the Canadian Communication Association Annual Conference/Colloque annuel de l'ACC, June 3, York University, Toronto.

Kavoori, Anandam P., and Noah Arceneaux, eds. 2006. *The Cell Phone Reader: Essays in Social Transformation*. New York: Peter Lang.

Klemperer, Paul. 2004. *Auctions: Theory and Practice*. New Jersey: Princeton University Press.

Leung, Janice. 2006. "Broadcast Your Fandom: An Analysis of Fan-Produced Concert Videos, Music-Fan Culture and YouTube.com." Unpublished paper, York University, Toronto.

Ling, Rich. 2004. *The Mobile Connection: The Cell Phone's Impact on Society*. San Francisco: Morgan Kaufmann.

McLaughlin, Lisa, and Victor Pickard. 2006. "What Is Bottom-Up About Global Internet Governance?" *Global Media and Communication* 1, no. 3: 357–73.

Neto, Isabel, Michael L. Best, and Sharon E. Gillett. 2005. "License-Exempt Wireless Policy: Results of an African Survey." *Information Technologies and International Development* 2, no. 3 (Spring): 73–90.

Norris, Pippa. 2002. *Digital Divide: Civic Engagement, Information Poverty, and the Internet Worldwide*. London: Cambridge University Press.

Ó'Siochú, Séan, and Bruce Girard, with Amy Mahan. 2002. *Global Media Governance: A Beginner's Guide*. Lanham, MD: Rowman and Littlefield.

Powell, Alison. 2007. "What Can I Say? (or, 'Île Sans Fil are Thieves and Liars'): Stories from the Heart of Participatory Research. *Wi: Journal of the Mobile Digital Commons Network* 1, no. 2. www.wi-not.ca (accessed 7 February 2007).

Powell, Alison, and Leslie Regan Shade. 2006. "Going Wi-Fi in Canada: Municipal and Community Initiatives." *Government Information Quarterly* 23, nos. 3–4: 381–403.

Rakow, Lana F. 1992. *Gender on the Line: Women, the Telephone, and Community Life*. Urbana: University of Illinois.

Rheingold, Howard. 2002. *Smart Mobs: The Next Social Revolution*. Cambridge, MA: Perseus.

Rodgers, Jayne. 2003. *Spatializing International Politics: Analyzing Activism on the Internet.* London: Routledge.

Sandoval, Chela. 2000. *Methodology of the Oppressed.* Minneapolis: University of Minnesota Press.

Sandvig, Christian. 2006. "Access to the Electromagnetic Spectrum Is a Foundation for Development." In *Media Matters: Perspectives on Advancing Governance and Development,* ed. Michael Harvey, 50–54. Paris: Internews.

Sawchuk, Kim. 2006. "Editorial: Public Matters." *Canadian Journal of Communication* 31, no. 2: 283–87.

Shade, Leslie Regan. 2002. *Gender and Community in the Social Construction of the Internet,* 179–89. New York: Peter Lang.

———. 2007. "Feminizing the Mobile: Gender Scripting of Mobiles in North America." *Continuum: Journal of Media and Cultural Studies* 21, no. 2.

Slater, Don, and Janet Kwami. 2005. "Embeddedness and Escape: Internet and Mobile Use as Poverty Reduction Strategies in Ghana." Working Paper No. 4, *ISRP Working Paper Series.* London: Information Society Research Group.

Sreberny, Annabelle. 2005. "Gender, Empowerment and Communication: Looking Backwards and Forwards." *International Social Science Journal* 57, no. 184: 285–300.

Townsend, Anthony. 2004. "Mobile Communications in the Twenty-first Century." In *Wireless World: Social and Interactional Aspects of the Mobile Age,* eds. Barry Brown, Nicola Green, and Richard Harper, 62–77. London: Springer-Verlag.

UNESCO Institute for Statistics. 2005. "International Literacy: Women Still Left Behind in Efforts to Achieve Global Literacy." Fact Sheet No. 6, September.

Winseck, Dwayne. 1995. "Power Shift? Towards a Political Economy of Canadian Telecommunications and Regulation." *Canadian Journal of Communications* 20, no. 1: 81–106.

World Internet Project. www.worldinternetproject.net (accessed 7 February 2007).

Xavier, Patrick. 2001. "Licensing of 3G Mobile." Briefing Paper, School of Business, Swinburne University of Technology. www.itu.int/osg/spu/ni/3G/workshop/presentations/xavier_1.pdf (accessed 1 May 2007).

CHAPTER EIGHT

The Global Structures and Cultures of Pornography: The Global Brothel

Katharine Sarikakis and Zeenia Shaukat

The pornography industry is a most successful global media industry: its products have a universal appeal; increasing demand fuels an innovative and intensified means of supply; its cost-effective production mode makes it versatile, tapping into new resources around the world; it addresses the needs and caters to the interests of a wide range of consumer groups; it is a fierce adopter of new technologies, has a most efficient distribution system, boasts staggering income figures and is increasingly gaining political clout in various regions across the world. The pornography industry has been studied and analyzed for over thirty years for its interindustrial links and its effects on its audiences. Its very nature has caused waves of regulatory intervention, which itself becomes the object of endless contestation across the world. Currently the universal culture and language of its products, combined with the industry's most sophisticated distribution methods, seem to have brought international authorities to a standstill, being unable and unconvinced about the best ways to tame this phenomenon. Yet it has not been considered a priority matter for study in international communication scholarship.

This chapter addresses questions that contemporary IC scholarship must tackle, further explore, and research. It looks at the pornography industry as a global medium which operates through networks and international distribution systems of the global media, impressively demonstrates a one-way flow of meanings and labor in terms of content control and production, and utilizes an almost universally understood language, despite its diverse and fragmented audiences around the globe. The chapter therefore argues that IC scholarship needs to urgently consider the modi operandi and the cultures and effects of the pornography industry in ways that identify and challenge its links to the state, its violation of human rights, and its gender inequity and exploitation, as well as its domination of patriarchal culture, which further colonizes public spaces and cultural attitudes and affects the ways that policy is perceived and implemented. IC scholarship can address the field much in the ways it has gazed at global media, but with the substantial benefit of three decades of enormous interdisciplinary feminist research on the subject. It also needs to look at the complex nexus of the production, consumption, and representation of pornography.

Money Makes the Porn Go 'Round: The International Political Economy of the Industry

The pornography industry—or "adult" industry as its producers prefer to call it—is estimated to be worth approximately $60 billion in 2007, or, put in a comparative context, equal to Hungary's foreign debt or Thailand's total sum of exports. The world leader in the pornography industry is the U.S., which spends $12 billion annually on porn—more than it spends on Hollywood and the same as on foreign aid. Each week, over two hundred films are produced, on the smallest possible budgets (Williams 2004). In 2002, porn films brought in nearly half as much as Hollywood's $9 billion at the box office, with 11,300 hard-core titles, 70 percent of them being produced in Los Angeles, compared to Hollywood's 470 film releases annually (Keegan 2003).

Australia appears to be the second revenue hub for the sector's A$1.5 billion (in 2002), with Queensland's A$16 million holding the lead, estimated to increase to A$35 million a year, given the recent legalization of X-rated material (Cassrels 2002; Dodd 2002), though Sydney, in New South Wales, is often described as the sex capital of the country and is home to an estimated 10,000 workers in the industry (Brace 2004). These figures make the pornography and sex industry in Australia second only to its tourism and pine products. Nevertheless this revenue comes from consuming—rather than producing—pornography. Perth-based AdultShop.com controls a major part of the legal adult media and products. AdultShop owns Axis, the country's biggest distribution outlet, which sells approximately 750,000 X-rated videos to customers on its mailing list; it also owns the Barbarella chain, as well as other smaller distribution outlets. The company is worth A$67.2 million (Dodd 2002). Italy, with its approximately A$1.5

billion pornography industry, is also a serious player, while Canada is seen as a favorable production location, due to its currency exchange rate and highly skilled workforce. As of 2004, there were more than twenty companies in the lower mainland of British Columbia producing porn movies, largely on commission for U.S. Internet companies (Williams 2004).

These figures are careful estimates, as precise information on the revenue of the industry is hard to come by. The industry is largely organized around networks, especially as far as the independent producers and companies are concerned, with more business opportunities being offered through the use of decentralized production and distribution technologies most successfully applied on the Internet. The rise of amateur websites claiming the exploits of small groups or one central character, as well as those encouraging the posting and publication of homemade movies and pictures, appear as independent enterprises, although there are links to each other that would indicate some form of commercial collaboration, if not coownership.

The Internet provides the illusion of anonymity (although Internet traffic can generally be traced back to servers and individual terminals), and it provides a forum for the exchange of information and access to peer-to-peer file exchange systems. However, it mainly offers instant gratification, also the main characteristic of consumer culture in the metropoles of the Western world. The porn industry has been quick to utilize the Internet as a new distributional technology of narrow/individual-casting. Indeed it has proved to be a continual innovator of technological adaptation and in particular of those technologies that are designed for practices of private consumption, as opposed to those involving mass and public viewings—the video versus film, and now computers or iPods. Its themes and its drive toward the lowest possible costs, as well as the need for flexible use of re/camcording technologies led producers to work their way through video first, and then digital media. The porn industry is said to account for the greatest growth of content on the Internet and to be driving the demand for broadband technology. It is estimated that there are currently over 15 million Web pages with pornographic content, while in 1999 there were estimated to be only 66,000 websites. In all, porn accounted for an astonishing 69 percent of the total pay-per-view Internet content market, thereby outpacing the news, sports, and video games market (Forgione 2005).

Despite this decentralized character of the sex industry, changes are taking place, such as increasing ownership concentration, growth of chains, and a shift toward large capital investment. Moreover, the boundary between pornographic material, understood as electronic and print images and words, and what is conventionally understood as prostitution—sex for money—is increasingly blurred. So are attempts to classify porn and distinguish violent and degrading content from simulated content. These characteristics point to an accelerated development of the pornography industry toward the production of content that addresses niche markets, creating and reinforcing demand for pornography in general and for certain forms more specifically. One of the strategies for the creation of new markets and therefore access to wider audiences is the cross-sectional operation of the industry. The intraindustrial collaboration with other global media industries signals not only the mainstreaming of pornography but also the recognition of a lucrative business model for bringing profits to the otherwise respectable media. The contractual agreements between porn portals and content providers of pornography and all main telecommunication operators across the globe are one aspect of this link. French operator Orange provides pornographic video clips on mobile phones from the company's wireless portal. As much as a quarter of all videos accessed from its portal are erotic—the equivalent of about 3,330 hours of viewing each month (Bryan-Low and Pringle 2005). The collaboration of Vivid (a major porn content provider) with Vodafone through the EroTrix games attracted 30,000 downloads in the first two months in Germany, Greece, and Portugal monthly traffic. PhoneErotica.com (a UK-based website) generates over 300 million hits per month (Tanner 2005). Playboy licenses pictures and videos to European mobile phone users. So well integrated is content provision and mobile use that there are predictions that $4 million will be spent on telephone downloads alone and that the numbers will grow with the improvement of mobile technology. Indeed, third-generation manufacturers count on pornography to drive the new media.

The industry's spread, however, is much broader. A prominent beneficiary is the hotel industry, with adult movies bringing over US$200 million through cable channels in the U.S.; 80 percent of in-room entertainment derives from consumption of pornography (J. Williams 2004; Devaney 2002). Behind them stand the respectable General Motors (with subsidiary DirecTV) and AT&T. Pornography is carried through cable channels, Internet service providers, and magazine distributors, while large chunks of the industry are maintained by media conglomerates that also own family-oriented channels. Pornographic images and messages are also routinely and increasingly included in women's magazines, advertising in public spaces,[1] daytime TV, and also in the press in a nearly ritualistic manner[2] (Itzin 1992). These profitable links to other media and culture industries have contributed to the acceptability of pornography, through the accessibility of the sexualization of the female self across a range of instances, contexts, and borders. The pornography industry utilizes the same avenues and largely follows the same routes for its survival and expansion. It is no different than any other industry.

Or is it?

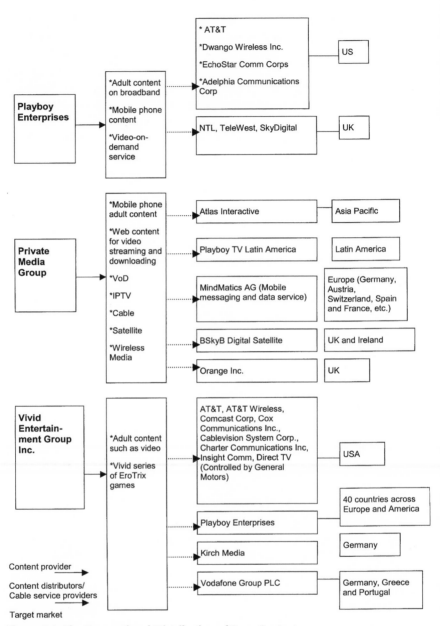

Figure 8.1. The Transnational Distribution of Porn Content
[Compiled from different sources]

Geographies, and Modes, of Production: The Demand-Supply-Demand Machine

Despite the newly respectable and often glamorous face of the porn industry and its successful cultural mainstreaming, the essence of the industry—its genre, representations, and mode of production—are deeply problematic. So too are its direct links with human trafficking and prostitution and the violation of human rights worldwide. It is often argued that the porn industry is one of the few industries where women have a privileged position—occupying "star" status and being rewarded better than men. But far from the glamorous show of conventions and advertising, laboring in the porn industry involves no protection from either trade unions or the state. The working conditions in the industry have not improved in the past three decades, as women's career spans become shorter, their income depends on the number of scenes they perform, there are no social or welfare benefits, such as sick pay or maternity leave, and there is no possibility for accessing state benefits, such as unemployment after the termination of a contract. True to the spirit of globalization, women, far from being the valued commodities of the industry, constitute the most flexible, replaceable, and unprotected workforce. Only a handful of leading actresses earn $100,000 a year; while most are paid $300 to $500 for a scene.

As we know from testimonies of producers and industry workers, the nature of these scenes also determine wages, popularity, and career, with actresses being classified according to their availability for different acts, which vary from conventionally understood sexual intercourse to scenes of violence and humiliation.[3] The lower the status of the woman's representation, the shorter her projected career track in the industry. The production of amateur or home videos has further lowered pay rates. The image of the innocent, fun-loving home video is shadowed by testimonies about the exploitation of women's images without their consent or knowledge.[4] The pictures, videos, and files live on long after the women are gone. The profits made throughout the life of the film never reach the laborer—whose pay is incomparable to revenues.

Technologies not only ease the consumption of pornography and its production: they are also used to further control women's bodies and impact upon the direction of extremity the industry is following. For example, the production of material that aims at portraying women as young, looking like the girl next door, and unsuspected—but deeply insatiable—becomes the inspiration for new generations of producers. Digital manipulation allows a variety of choices over the presentation of images, from the construction of images of underage girls from women, to the (comparatively) low-tech *retouche* of performers to resemble teenagers.[5] Companies create specific markets for young/teen-next-door images in a directed and systematic way. "This pursuit of the 'quality girl' not only reflected the GGW brand's name brand, what Leist called 'the ones you wouldn't expect to do it' but also influenced new amateurs hoping to become producers themselves" who, having the means of affordable and mobile technology, can achieve that easily (Mayer 2005). The recent move toward the use of high-definition technology polices women's bodies even further: producers, disturbed by the appearance of body marks (scars, cellulite, body imperfections), push women to undergo even more cosmetic surgery and tell them to "cut their carbs" (Richtel 2007). The financing of such undertakings, besides the emotional damage that the context of disapproval has on women in an industry that leaves nothing to imagination, creates further dependency on finding and sustaining work in the trade. The pursuit of images of unrealistic and infantilized female bodies is the norm.

New geographies for the production of porn are created, with outsourcing and the shifting of production to countries with more favourable economic conditions. According to reports, the Philippines has emerged as the major provider of pornographic materials, including photographs, films, and live sex acts. That country is also considered to be a leading source and producer of child pornography and cyberprostitution. The exploitation of workers is transferred into new territories, in particular in the countries of the former Soviet Union, with Hungary becoming the biggest center for pornography production in Europe, through its supply of women, surpassing "established" rivals such as Amsterdam and Copenhagen. Excruciating and humiliating acts are paid $200 or $300,[6] a third of the fees in 1988 (Anonymous 1998). Even the few available "stars" have seen a drop in their wages. A number of studies and a few serious and rarely available documentaries have exposed the labor conditions of women in the industry, showing how forced performance and rape are not occasional events but largely the norm among "respectable" porn conglomerates as well as among those companies considered "sick" or extreme by mainstream pornographers.[7] Evidence indicates that women are forced and coerced to participate in acts, pushed to their limits, and constantly pressured for more extreme performances. Moreover, the line between choice and force is becoming provocatively unclear.[8] Boyle argues that "such material is not *only* fantasy, but also a representation of sexual acts, authenticated by the signature shots of genitalia, penetration and ejaculation. This is significant not only in view of the varying conditions of production, but also in relation to the conventions of mainstream and pornographic sex and how these position consumers" (2000, 189). Conditions of crude abuse but also inherent pressure, through the use of indirect threats (of unemployment, unpopularity, insult, guilt feelings toward the production team) have little in common with the projected image of pornography as "fantasy" for the consumer and "choice" for the laborer. As Dworkin has poignantly observed: "Essential to this gratification on some level is the illusion that the women are not controlled by men but are acting freely" (1984, 136). Women working in the industry are more likely to be physically and mentally abused, held against their will, and threatened. Macrae (2003) argues that there is substantial evidence of women having been killed or murdered during shoots.

Furthermore, the links between pornography, trafficking, and prostitution are strong, contributing to a complex system of exploitation that fuels the global sex industry. The increasing use and growing accessibility of ICTs have paved the way for sophistication in these areas. Pimps, traffickers, stalkers, and users have adopted new technologies to further their abuse and exploitation (Hughes 2002). The global sex industry is a multibillion-dollar industry. According to an estimate in the *Economist,* the trafficking in women and girls, in particular for prostitution purposes, yields a staggering $20 billion (United Nations 1999). UNICEF estimates that some 2 million children, most of them girls, are exploited in the commercial sex trade annually.[9] The value of the global trade in women is estimated to be between $7 billion and $12 billion.[10] Overall, the mainstream sex industry claims one quarter of the 4 million people trafficked each year (Hughes 2000). Apart from being channelled into domestic prostitution, women and children are coerced into posing for pornography, which increasingly is trafficked internationally (Leifholdt 1999). Pornography is by far the most prevalent form of sexual exploitation in cyberspace (Umali 2005). With the collapse of the Soviet Union, Soviet republics including Ukraine, Belarus, Latvia, and Russia have emerged as major suppliers of women to be trafficked into the world. The Netherlands and Germany are the most popular destinations for trafficked women, due to their relaxed laws on prostitution. Trafficked women find themselves in a multiple trap, as they are forced to become part of the sex industry in their effort to migrate as economic immigrants (Hughes 2000).[11] The economics of trafficking has always been explained through the focus on the supply side in the sending countries. However, the complete equation can only be understood if factors on the demand side are also examined. An important factor is the organized crime network that finds trafficking and prostitution the most lucrative business opportunities, which expands to the control of pornography.[12]

Pornsocialization Cultures

The industry itself admits that porn is becoming grosser and more extreme. The use of amateurs—not well-established, well-known workers—not only drives production costs down but also gives a more authentic flair to the violence taking place in pornography: Scalisi, the owner of 21 Sextury Video explains: "Amateurs come across better on screen. Our customers feel that. Especially by women you can see it. They still feel strong pain."[13] The unlimited supply of images is pushing the normative threshold of acceptability lower, as it normalizes the depiction of violent behavior (Macrae 2003; Simonton 2004). There is evidence to suggest that most women in prostitution are involved in pornography at some point in their lives. The effects of their work are manifest in physical and emotional damage as well as in routine drug and alcohol abuse (Baldwin 1989; Gittler 1999; Farley 2003).

The content generated in the industry derives under sweatshop conditions, as far as women's rights, dignity, and safety are concerned. It is achieved through a dehumanizing process, accompanied by language and acts that expect women to perform tasks harmful to their physical health and damaging to their emotional balance, without the right to compensation or the power or means to improve their conditions. Despite the assumed consent and values of professionalism, largely based on the argument of pay and free choice when entering and working in the industry, the fundamentally individualistic focus on a worker's negotiating power is typical of neoliberal market ideology. Linked together with universal patriarchy, this sophisticated and versatile system of exploitation of women and children is driven by an increased demand for images that is further reinforced and maintained through popular culture.[14]

Meanwhile, the pornography consumer is becoming younger: children as young as nine years old are socialized through consumption of porn films, images, and lyrics. The link to popular culture, whether through the trivialization of consumption of pornographic material or through the colonization of public spaces and infiltration of children's fashion through sexualized images, is crucial to the shifting attitudes of young people: girls internalizing such norms[15] and boys in acting upon them. Pornography is available everywhere; the sexualization of women's and girl's bodies, indeed their disposability, is an everyday experience. But perhaps even more disturbing, violent pornography and its glorification leads to the enacting of scenes by young children and teenagers, as a way of socialization and connection to everyday experience. Child abuse and the grooming of children and young teenagers for sexual exploitation also takes place through pornography.[16] Among young people, porno rap (music with lyrics about rape, violent sex, and degradation of women) has become very popular, while porno rappers have become role models, propagating a way of life that feeds off the direct connection of images and texts and their translation into teenagers' actions.[17]

Pornography is imagery and textual representation of power relations and well-defined domination. "The primary domination/subordination dynamic eroticized in pornography is, of course, gender" (Jensen 2004). It is difficult to contest women's personal accounts and narratives that demonstrate the relationship between pornography and sexual violence (Macrae 2003). In one study, 73 percent of two hundred street prostitutes reported having been raped. Out of these, 24 percent reported that their rapists had made reference to pornography.[18] There have been a variety of arguments concerning the effects of consumption of pornography on men's sexual behavior. However, research methods are scarce that could provide conclusive data on a direct casual link between pornography and sexual violence in a traditional science model (Jensen 2004). For all its inherent flaws owing to difficulties with defining pornography, with measuring behavior, and with the artificiality of the laboratory setting, some relatively consistent findings indicate that exposure to violent pornography does increase, or is at least associated with, callousness toward women as well as an increased propensity to violence (Shaw 1999). Moreover, the consumption of violent pornography, similar to that of violent video games, requires a learning process. Violence is something one learns. It requires the desensitization of the consumer, and his or her emotional distancing from the humanity of the persons involved. Pornography is construed upon the fragmentation and deduction of the female body into parts. The impact of violence and force on real bodies (even if depicted in their parts) and on the large-scale and long-term understanding and interpretation of sexuality as violence is certainly a social question that cannot be answered through laboratory tests. In these terms, the cause-and-effect debate—as understood through the conventional ways of testing claims—is a misplaced attempt to guide policy making[19].

International Policy Regimes and the Disarticulation of Responsibility

While the pornography industry enjoys the luxury of having a global market ranging from the most socially conservative societies to the most liberal, it is not freed from challenges posed by its opponents. These range from totalitarian authorities and regimes to international organizations and religious groups. Feminist theory and activism have raised the issue of pornography as a matter of domination and power, for its derogatory approach toward and objectification of the female body and its long-term effects on the socialization of violence. This approach addresses women's rights to equality and life free from violence and objectification as human rights. The motivations of other actors do not necessarily focus on women's rights but rather on claims of morality problematized through sexual explicitness, promiscuity, or sexual expression.[20]

Interestingly, the industry too has developed ways to tackle these challenges, facilitated by its strong industrial foundations in countries like the U.S., its close relationship to politicians, and of course technology. Increasingly bureaucratization and a growth in business associations, lobbyists, and formal means of interacting with the state are the new strategies.[21] The industry's relationship to governments is entering a new era characterized by a culture of "business as usual," moving away from the stigma of filth, immorality, or illegality—an important cultural transformation (Brents and Hausbeck 1999). In Britain, for example, the news that the Labour Party has accepted funds and has been associated with a UK-based major pornography corporation (Richard Desmond's empire of porn magazines) was controversially met with endorsement by some Labour MPs.[22] Australian Left Labour consults with lobbyists from the sex industry on issues of human rights (Wu 2004). In other cases, governments have leased—intentionally or otherwise—their domain names for porn, such as Tuvalu (tv), the small African islands of Sao Tome and Principe, or the island of Niue (nu).

The dominant approaches of governments are centered around two axes: questions of decency and obscenity and harm to minors. The first kind of legislation is formulated in terms of morality (and immorality), is based on subjective interpretation of what constitutes obscene or indecent material, and is vague. Moreover, given the rapid pace with which the industry adapts and uses technologies as well as changing consumption habits, such laws are increasingly difficult to implement. The censorship of material on the basis of morality leaves vulnerable material addressed at marginalized sexualities—even when this material is neither degrading nor violent, such as home-erotic content. As Itzin explains, "Historically it has been used to censor art and literature, to suppress homosexuality and to control women's reproduction. In practice it protects pornography, permitting the increased production and circulation of . . . 'pornographic' pornography." In Canada and Ireland, such laws have been used to censor information on birth control and abortion, while in the UK such legislation has been used to tackle politically subversive literature (1992, 401, 408). In Britain, the law governing obscene publications is found principally in the Obscene Publications Act of 1959. Commercial dealings in obscene items or their possession is an offense. With or without a prosecution, the items can be seized under a magistrate's warrant and, after a hearing to determine whether they contravene the statute, can be forfeited.[23]

The second arm of legislation refers to the exposure or access of minors to pornographic material (predominantly as a matter of corruption) and in terms of actual minors being abused for the production of pornography.[24] Underlying these legislative responses is the conflictual discursive relationship between free speech and censorship. Although neither adequately or successfully provides a normative framework that can address the multifaceted issues raised by the production and consumption (and indeed culture) of pornography, as discussed here, they have dominated, and continue to do so, the legislative debate around pornography.[25] Moreover, legislation surrounding the context of the sex industry is also inadequate, further precipitating exploitation, human insecurity, and abuse, through trafficking, labor in the sex industry, and pornography.

For example, in the U.S., attempts by adult entertainers (exotic dancers) to claim labor rights have been defeated by the courts which "have become an active partner in the continuing financial exploitation of adult entertainers (namely exotic dancers) by legally classifying various types of stage entertainers as independent contractors, and thus denying these workers protection of the labor laws enacted for their benefit" (Wilmet 1999). In the Philippines, authorities are unable to arrest cybersex joints on grounds of prostitution, as these are valid only when sexual intercourse has taken place (Umali 2005). In many countries, women who are trafficked find the tides of law running against them due to their illegal status, which prevents them from using the law against their traffickers. In Germany, for instance, prostitution is legal for EU citizens, which means that trafficked women are doubly exploited, as they are both victims of trafficking and are outside the protection of the law (Hughes 2000). It is literally impossible to police websites that provide pornographic material and that sell women, because these operations take place through the use of legislative gaps and among several countries (Worden 2001).[26] Though prostitution itself is legal in Australia, the state requires brothels to be licensed. The laws vary from state to state, and the issue is highly contentious (Brace 2004). The federal Office of Film and Literature Classification (OFLC) acts as censorship authority for films, publications, the Internet, and computer games. In New Zealand, pornography comes under the Films, Videos and Publications Act of 1993.[27]

Although there is no concrete definition of pornography identified in legislation in Germany, German law makes a distinction between hardcore pornography embedded in violence or the sexual abuse of children and sexual acts between two people or simple pornography (which is yet to be defined). In German legal tradition, in the absence of a clear outline of law, formal commentaries are consulted to provide a nonbinding framework that courts seek as a guideline to act. Vague measures to define pornography are indicative of the tendency to frame the issue as a moral ill, rather than as a reflection of structural power relations in the society (Macrae 2003). This may be due to the lack of consensus within the women's movement, which gave the government an escape hatch for avoiding confronting the issue, combined with the position that family values, morality, and freedom of the press are perceived as paramount values.

In the EU context, pornography has been addressed as a product. The regulatory framework addressing the proliferation of pornographic material is the Television Without Frontiers Directive (89/552/EEC) (Council of European Communities 1989; Macrae 2003). This directive lays the onus of screening the appropriateness of broadcast on the country of origin rather than the recipient country, according to the principle of free movement of goods and services. In a 1979 case, the European court permitted member states to limit the importation of pornographic material, but in so doing it formally defined pornography as a commodity, rendering it subject to the same regulatory framework as any other community good (Macrae 2003). The TWF Directive subjects to additional reviews and barriers programs that "seriously impair the physical, mental or moral development of minors." Pornography and gratuitous violence come under this category. However, in the absence of a common definition of pornography, this article fails to regulate it. EU law is more concerned with the impact of pornographic material on minors than the use of such content among the adults in the region (Article 22), and it requires member states to take appropriate measures. Recent attempts at the EU level have been friendlier to the problem of gendered structural power and discrimination, shifting toward a legislative framework that incorporates principles of gender mainstreaming in policy. As Macrae (2003) rightly points out, this is due to the establishment of the European Women's Lobby (EWL) in 1990, the formal incorporation of the principles of gender equality and mainstreaming into the Amsterdam Treaty (1996), and the implementation of mainstreaming practices throughout the community following the 1995 Beijing Conference. Recently the issue of pornography has also received attention in the context of the fight against sexist advertising, and it got a further boost with recent initiatives addressing trafficking in women and its links with sexual exploitation.

In North America, the federal structure of the states means that regulation is regionally shaped. In the U.S., pornography is guided by First Amendment law. The Federal Communications Commission (FCC) regulates content that is broadcast as well as the content provided by wireless operators, but it does not have control over pay-per-view channels (Bryan-Low and Pringle 2005). There are currently no specific regulations governing adult content on mobile phones, but the U.S. industry itself is formulating guidelines to technologically prevent minors from accessing adult content and thus avoid government legislation. Canada's laws and regulations against pornography are thought to be stricter than those of the U.S. Some provinces sponsor film boards that censor movies. Canada's Charter of Rights and Freedoms seems to cover pornography, although the right to free speech largely continues to frame policy.[28]

The Indian government has attempted to address pornography on the Internet with the Information Technology Act (May 2000/July 2003). Websites promoting hatred, defamation, gambling, racism, violence, terrorism, pornography (including child porn), or violent sex risk being blocked or closed down. The decree says that barring access to such websites "may be equated to balanced flow of information and not censorship." Pornographic films in the form of B-grade cinema are present, but the Indecency Act is not thoroughly implemented, while pornography is increasingly becoming a common phenomenon.[29]

Table 8.1. Selected Legislation and Provisions on Pornography

Country	Legislation	Act
United Kingdom	Obscene Publications Act 1959	The law makes it an offense to publish, whether for gain or not, any content whose effect will tend to "deprave and corrupt" those likely to read, see, or hear the matter contained or embodied in it. This could include images of extreme sexual activity, such as bestiality, necrophilia, rape, or torture.[1]
Canada	Charter of Rights and Freedoms	The Charter has numerous civil and political rights enshrined in it. According to section 32, the Charter is binding on the federal government, the territories under its authority, and the provincial governments.
United States	First Amendment	Most pornography comes under the First Amendment that guarantees freedom of speech. The Supreme Court, in 1973, laid out the following "basic guidelines" for jurors in obscenity cases in its *Miller v. California* decision: <ul><li>Whether the average person, applying contemporary community standards, would find that the work, taken as a whole, appeals to prurient interests.</li><li>Whether the work depicts or describes, in a patently offensive way, sexual conduct specifically defined by the applicable state law.</li><li>Whether the work, taken as a whole, lacks serious literary, artistic, political, or scientific value.</li></ul> According to the court no individuals could be convicted of obscenity charges unless the materials depict "patently offensive hard core sexual conduct." This makes materials dealing with sex, including pornographic magazines, books, and movies, disqualified as legally obscene.[2]
Philippines	Republic Act 9208 or the Anti-Trafficking in Persons Act of 2003	Unlawful "to recruit, transport, transfer, harbor, provide, or receive a person by any means . . . for the purpose of prostitution, pornography, sexual exploitation, forced labor, slavery, involuntary servitude or debt bondage" (sec. 4a).[3] RA 9208 facilitates apprehending offenders who use the Internet to perpetuate pornographic acts. It mentions "information technology" among the possible means for disseminating pornography (sec. 3h), and "information technology and the Internet" among the venues for disseminating materials that promote trafficking (sec. 5c). RA 9208 facilitates apprehending offenders who use the Internet to perpetuate pornographic acts. It mentions "information technology" among the possible means for disseminating pornography (sec. 3h), and "information technology and the Internet" among the venues for disseminating materials that promote trafficking (sec. 5c).

(continued)

Table 8.1. *(Continued)*

Country	Legislation	Act
Germany	Section 184 of the Penal Code	The production, possession, distribution, and sale of pornography in Germany is currently regulated through section 184 of the Penal Code. Minors are protected through paragraphs 1 and 2 of section 184, which make it an offense to sell or otherwise make pornography materials available to minors under the age of 18. Individuals over 18 can access pornography except as limited by section 3. Pornographic images that contain violence, depict the sexual abuse of children, or show sexual acts between humans and animals are illegal to possess, produce, or handle.[4]
European Union	Broadcasting Directive (89/552/EEC; Council of European Communities 1989); Television Without Frontiers Directive	Article 22 of the Television Without Frontiers Directive states that member states may subject transmission that seriously impairs physical, mental, or moral development to additional reviews and/or barriers. The directive mentions programs that involve pornography or gratuitous violence.
Australia	Censorship Authority Office of Film and Literature Classification	The OFLC acts as a censorship authority for films, publications, the Internet, and computer games.
New Zealand	Films, Videos and Publications Act 1993	The Classification Office has the power to examine and classify a wide range of publications, including films, videos, computer games, books, magazines, T-shirts, and computer files. These publications may be classified as objectionable, restricted, or unrestricted. The term *objectionable*, defined in the act, addresses the question of whether the availability of a publication is likely to be injurious to the public good.[5]

Notes

1. Obscene Publications Act 1959 and 1964 www.iwf.org.uk/police/page.22.38.htm (19 February 2007).
2. David L. Hudson Jr., Pornography and Obscenity, www.firstamendmentcenter.org/speech/adultent/topic .aspx?topic=pornography (19 February 2007).
3. Umali, Violeda A., "The Cyber-trafficking of Filipino Girl-children: Weaknesses of Philippine Policies," *Asian Women* 20 (2005).
4. Macrae, Heather, "Morality, Censorship and Discrimination: Reframing the Pornography Debate in Germany and Europe," *Social Politics* 10, no 3 (Fall 2003).
5. Wilson, David, "Censorship in New Zealand: The Policy Challenges of New Technology," *Social Policy Journal of New Zealand* 19 (December 2002).

Conclusion

As we can see, the pornography industry presents scholars and activists with a number of issues: its international trading ties to mainstream media and industries as well as its network-based operation mode make it harder for policy-makers to intervene in a meaningful manner. The commercial interests from the circulation and consumption of porn are simply too high to ignore. Therefore the telecommunication industry resorts to self-regulation to avoid intervention and also to present an image of corporate social responsibility. Study of the industry raises serious questions regarding the treatment of women and children. It clearly operates a system of labor exploitation and violence that predominantly targets social strata of people with few resources. The question of class, globally, is interestingly intertwined with that of trauma and abuse, one that has not been developed in this chapter but which is, as evidence tells us, closely interlinked as a common factor among women working in pornography and the sex industry in general.[30]

Moreover, the problems of control over one's image and working conditions in this medium are exaggerated, due to the lack of a common regulatory framework that effectively addresses production, as well as due to the lack of the possibility for unionization among workers. The industry's international capability for incessant production and consumption demonstrate that policies oriented toward vague interpretations of acceptability levels and "community morals" are inadequate in addressing the problems because of the following factors: first, there is lack of coordination and cooperation at an international level. Most of the discussion in this chapter relates to the "pornification" of Western culture, although the objectification of the female body and its sexualization is taking place through different forms across the world, even in countries with very strict "community morals."[31] National policies alone cannot address the question of violence and abuse or the question of patriarchal cultures of representation when they are trapped between laws on obscenity and free speech. Moreover, national policy frameworks function only to the extent that an international regime focused on the protection of the human (what is known as human security) is in place.

Second, policies hardly ever address the mode of production and the working conditions of the industry. There is little possibility of change as long as the driving norm for policy becomes that of "free will," because consent and force become entangled in the same complex net of dependencies. Here the distinction between private (individual) and public is inherently problematic. Choice (to do pornography) is regarded a matter of private autonomy, as is its consumption (in one's own privacy). These dominant assumptions make it problematic to situate the worldwide phenomenon of exploitation in the public domain, when the whole cycle of pornography (especially amateur production and consumption) is understood as private.

Third, policies do not address these dependencies, either at the production site or for the long-term effects that the consumption of pornography has on society and future generations. Socialization through pornography increasingly becomes the only socialization for many youngsters, especially those from deprived backgrounds, though it is also a widespread practice among elites and male college students, who use it as a way to assert and confirm their masculinity.[32] We need a set of policies that are transnational in their foundational principles, that are organically coordinated to address the questions of violence, choice, sexuality, and citizenship at various levels throughout the formal educational system, and that also provide ways out for those in the industry. Moreover, such a set of policies should concentrate on the cycle of demand-supply-demand and should facilitate the possibility of self-governance for those in the trade. A major part of this project is tackling world female poverty.

Finally, the question of distribution and representation, which is currently the only one in place in most countries in the world, and which centers falsely around censorship, should become an integral part of media policy that recognizes the role of pornography in shaping consciousness, the same way it recognizes that media do affect human cultures or that ownership and control affect the ways in which certain voices are heard while whole social groups are silenced. International communication scholarship needs to take up this challenge and break its own silence.

Notes

1. For an example of such colonization see Jennifer Drew, "Organizing to Stop Sexual Violence in Media: Object's Work in the United Kingdom," *International Journal of Media and Cultural Politics* 3, no.1 (2005).

2. Also called, for example, the British "institution" of the *Sun's* Page Three.

3. The rate at which women's bodies are consumed and disposed of in the industry resembles probably only sweatshops: in the porn industry women experience a gradual decline from "acceptable" representations of sexual intercourse to those depicting extreme situations of physical violation, degradation, and harm within a period of twenty-four months.

4. Numerous sites profit from voyeuristic pictures of body parts taken from unsuspecting women; defamation is a problem, with videos circulating freely on the Internet—again without women's consent.

5. We are not addressing child pornography here, although it is clear that a large part of the industry works with assumptions/suggestions of borderline cases of children or teens or even uses real such cases. Child pornography expands into a debate on its own, but also the links of abuse and porn are more clear or evident to policy makers and the public, possibly due to the issue of free will and choice (lack of). We concentrate on the adult industry because abstract notions of fantasy and choice obscure the question of real, material, and emotional damage and social responsibility toward humanity.

6. "[Eastern European women] cost less and do more," an executive at Germany's Silwa production company explains (Anonymous 1998).

7. Numerous feminists and former workers have exposed the conditions dominating the porn industry; see a summary and recent testimony to Scottish Parliament at www.scottish.parliament.uk/business/committees/equal/index.htm and also at http://ics.leeds.ac.uk/papers/index.cfm?outfit=ks.

8. See, for example, the 2001 Channel 4 (UK) documentary "Hard Core."

9. UNICEF (United Nations Children's Fund), "*Factsheet: Commercial Sexual Exploitation*" at www.unicef.org/protection/files/sexex2.pdf (2005), cited in Jhappan 2005.

10. "UN Official Warns of Rise of New Slaves of Prostitutes," Xinhua, 21 September 1999, cited in Hughes 2000.

11. In Ukraine, for example, "marriage agencies" have emerged to contact women who are eager to travel abroad. Recruiters can be traffickers themselves or can work with them. They fix a woman with a man who may promise marriage at a later date. The man may use the woman himself for a short period of time, then coerce her into making pornography, and later sell her to the sex industry, or he may directly deliver the woman to a brothel. These women are mostly helpless and are unable to break the barriers, because usually their passports are confiscated by their traffickers, rendering them illegal emigrants in the host country.

12. See the work produced by Captive Daughters (www.captivedaughters.org) on aspects of demand in pornography and prostitution.

13. "Amateure kommen viel besser rüber. Das spüren unsere Kunden. Bei den Frauen, ich meine, da sieht man: Die haben noch richtige Schmerzen."

14. For an early defining account of pornographic popular culture, see Andrea Dworkin, *Intercourse* (New York: Free Press, 1987). Various studies also explore the sexualization of popular culture.

15. See, for example, Eisenstein 1998; Manning 2005; part 3 of Itzin's edited collection (1992).

16. Charities and NGO child protection centers and feminist organizations repeatedly point out the connection between production of pornography in general, and child pornography specifically, and its real harm on children. See also the *Guardian* 2004; Gallagher 2007; Wüllenweber 2007.

17. See Wüllenweber 2007 on the pornorappers Frauenartz and Sido in Germany; the lyrics of these "artists" are very clear: "The whore is the meat"; "Hey slut, spread your legs"; "We will fuck you until your lips break" (Frauenartzt). Another example is the new porn genre by Max Hardcore (producer of extreme, violent porn) who combines porn scenes to the music of the hardcore band 8mm Overdose, signaling the calculated but deeply disturbing marriage of popular culture and the youth scene with sexualized violence.

18. Gale Dines, Robert Jenson, and Ann Russo, *Pornography: The Consumption and Production of Inequality.* (New York: Routledge, 1998) cited in Macrae 2003.

19. See also Boyle 2000.

20. This way, any form of explicitness can be perceived as undesirable for religious groups, even educational documentary. Nevertheless, some of the early uses of pornography, although continuously misogynistic, were also construed as texts of political resistance to mores, political autarchy, and taboos. These forms of pornography, if still in existence, form neither the majority of circulated content nor the intentions of producers. Similarly, the argument of pornography as fantasy is nowadays rather overhauled—the industry increasingly does not feel the "need" to package its material in terms of fantasy, given the increasingly—and openly—violent character of sex depicted.

21. In Australia a vocal and aggressive pornography lobby group is the Eros Foundation, which is quick to respond to any government measures against the adult industry and is increasingly gaining political clout. It claims that voters resent government impingement on their sex lives.

The Adult Retailers' Association (TARA) is another body. TARA went to the extent of proposing legislative reform of the adult retail industry. In 2002 John Lark, founder of Australian *Hustler* magazine, mounted a constitutional challenge when his Brisbane-based adult product store Good Vibrations was charged with selling banned material after raids by Office of Fair Trading investigators in 2006. In the U.S. there are influential groups such as the Free Speech Coalition, a trade organization that represents nine hundred companies in the porn business, run by Bill Lyon, a former lobbyist for the defense industry. In the UK, ofwatch lobbies for the interest of adult entertainment sector. It claims to be "an independent organization that represents the interests of those who wish to see less censorship of UK subscription television services and who want to take more responsibility for their own viewing" (www.ofwatch.com).

22. Labour MP Glenda Jackson defended this relationship, making a market-centered argument, while Clare Short, also a Labour MP, tried a decade ago to introduce a law banning the objectification of women in the press (it was met with extreme hostility from the press, the adult industry, and her own party).

23. See Itzin 1992 for an excellent discussion on the normative and ideological foundations of obscenity in law.

24. The production and consumption of child pornography is not the focus of this work, although any such act is by definition abusive. Laws regarding child pornography vary, with some cases requiring the actual physical abuse of real children for the production of pornography while allowing the simulation of such material or its depiction through cartoons.

25. Thoroughly analytical works by MacKinnon (1989; 1994) and Itzin (1992) have explored the relationship between arguments for free speech in protecting the status quo in pornography, the limitation of the right vis a vis social responsibility, and the right to life, as well as the misrepresentation of controlling pornography as a single matter of censorship.

26. An example is the case of a website that was created by an American, filmed in Phnom Pehn, with Thai and Cambodian prostitutes and hosted on a server based in the U.S.

27. See Griffiths in this volume.

28. In the year 2003, then Canadian Justice Minister Martin Cauchon refused an outright ban on the possession of child pornography, for fear of violating the right to free expression under the Canadian Charter of Rights and Freedom.

29. See also Prasad in this volume.

30. See, for example, Melissa Farley, Isin Baral, Merab Kiremire, and Ufu Sezgin, "Prostitution in Five Countries: Violence and Post-Traumatic Stress Disorder," *Feminism & Psychology* 8, no.4 (1998): 405–26. www.prostitutionresearch.com/fempsy1.html; and Christine Overall, "What's Wrong with Prostitution? Evaluating Sex Work," *Signs* 17, no. 4 (1992): 705–24.

31. See Al-Mahadin in this volume.

32. See, for example, Rus Ervin Funk, "What does pornography say about me(n)? How I became an anti-pornography activist," in Christine Stark and Rebecca Whisnant, eds., *Not for Sale* (Melbourne: Spinifex, 2004).

References

Anonymous. 1998. "The Sex Industry: Giving the Customer What He Wants." *The Economist*, 346 (8055).

Baldwin, M. 1989. "Pornography and the Traffic in Women." *Yale Journal of Law and Feminism* 1 (1):111–55. Cited in Jensen 2004.

Boyle, Karen. 2000. "The Pornography Debates Beyond Cause and Effect." *Women's Studies International Forum* 23, no. 2:187–95.

Brace, Matthew. 2004. "Australian Scheme Is Political Hot Potato." *Times (London)*. July 17.

Brents, Barbara G., and Kathryn Hausbeck. 1999. "Bodies, Business and Politics: Corporate Mobilization and the Sex Industries." Paper prepared for the meeting of the American Sociological Association. www.unlv.edu/faculty/brents/research/ASA99Corpmob3.pdf (accessed 9 Feburary 2007).

Bryan-Low, Cassell, and David Pringle. 2005. "Sex Cells; Wireless Operators in Europe, Asia Find that Racy Cellphone Video Drives a Surge in Broadband Use." *Wall Street Journal*. May 12.

Cassrels, Deborah. 2002. "Press to Play." *Courier Mail (Queensland, Australia)*. June 29.

China Economic Quarterly. 2000. "Sex: China's New Growth Engine." http://asia.proquestreference.info/pqrasia (accessed 25 September 2005).

China Internet Information Center News. 2004. "700 Porn Websites Closed in 10 Days." http://asia.proquestreference.info/pqrasia (accessed 25 September 2005).

Council of European Communities. "Television without Frontiers" (TVWF) Directive. 2006. http://europa.eu/scadplus/leg/en/lvb/l24101.htm (accessed 20 August 2007).

"Cyber Pornography Case Registered with Delhi Police." 2005. *Times of India*. 26 October.

Devaney, Polly. 2002. "Pornography: The Rising Star of Corporate America." *Marketing Week*. November 28.

Dines, Gail, and Robert Jensen. 1998. "The Content of Mass Marketed Pornography." In *Pornography: The Production and Consumption of Inequality*, eds. Gail Dines, Robert Jensen, and Ann Russo. London: Routledge.

Dines, Gail, Robert Jensen, and Ann Russo, eds. 1998. *Pornography: The Production and Consumption of Inequality*. London: Routledge.

Dodd, Andrew. 2002. "Erotica's Bottom Line." *The Australian*. April 25.

Dworkin, Andrea. 1984. *Pornography: Men Possessing Women*. London: The Women's Press.

Eisenstein Zillah. 1998. *Global Obscenities: Patriarchy, Capitalism and the Lure of Cyberfantasy*. New York: New York University Press.

Farley, M., ed. 2003. *Prostitution, Trafficking, and Traumatic Stress*. Binghamton, NY: Haworth Press. Cited in Jensen 2004.

Forgione, Aldo. 2005. "The Good, The Bad, and The Ugly: The Frontiers of Internet Law." *Journal of Internet Law* 9, no. 1.

Gallagher, Bernard. "Internet Child Abuse: A Nuffield Foundation Study Casts Fresh Light on How Cases Should be Dealt With." www.communitycare.co.uk/Articles/2007/02/01/103129/internet-child-abuse-a-nuffield-foundation-study-casts-fresh-light-on-how-cases-should-be-dealt.html (accessed 9 Feburary 2007).

Gallagher, Leigh. 2003. "Holy Influence." *Forbes* 172, no. 12.

Galloni, Alessandra. 2001. "Clampdown on 'Porno-Chic' Ads Is Pushed by French Authorities." *Wall Street Journal*. October 25.

Gibson, Will. 2004. "Tangled Up in Blue." *Canadian Business* 88, no. 18 (September): 13–26.

Gittler, I. 1999. *Pornstar*. New York: Simon and Schuster.

Giving the customer what he wants. (The Sex Industry)(Cover Story)(Industry Overview). *Economist* (U.S.). February 14, 1998.

Gohring, Nancy. 2005. "Adult Content, U.K. Style." *Wireless Week*. September 15.

Hughes, Donna. 2000. "The 'Natasha' Trade: The Transnational Shadow Market Trafficking in Women." *Journal of International Affairs* 53, no. 2:1–18.

Hughes, Donna M. 2002. "The Use of New Communications and Information Technologies for Sexual Exploitation of Women and Children." *Hastings Women's Law Journal* 13:1.

The Guardian. 2004. "Internet Porn 'Increasing Child Abuse.' " January 12. http://society.guardian.co.uk/children/story/0,,1121332,00.html (accessed 16 February 2007).

Itzin, Catherine. 1992. *Pornography: Women, Violence and Civil Liberties*. Oxford and New York: Oxford University Press.

Jensen, Robert. 2004. "Pornography and Sexual Violence." St. Paul, MN: Minnesota Center Against Violence & Abuse, School of Social Work, University of Minnesota.

Jhappan, Radha. 2005. "Of Tsunamis and Child Sexual Exploitation: The Political Economy of Supply and Demand in the Sex Tourism and Trafficking Trades." *Asian Women* 20:137–74.

Keegan, Paul. 2003. "Prime-Time PORN." *Business 2.0* 4. no. 5:96.

Leifholdt, Dorchen. 1999. "The Position Paper of the Coalition Against Trafficking in Women." NGO Consultation with UN/IGOs on Trafficking in Persons, Prostitution and the Global Sex Industry, June 21–22.

MacKinnon, Catharine. 1989. *Toward a Feminist Theory of the State*. Cambridge, MA: Harvard University Press.

———. 1994. *Only Words*. London: HarperCollins.

———. 2005. "X Underrated." *Times Higher Education Supplement*, no.1692 (May 20):18.

Macrae, Heather. 2003. "Morality, Censorship and Discrimination: Reframing the Pornography Debate in Germany and Europe." *Social Politics* 10, no. 3:314–45.

Manning Jill. 2005. "The Impact of Internet Pornography on Marriage and the Family: A Review of the Research." Paper prepared for the Senate Subcommittee on the Constitution, Civil Rights and Property Rights, Committee on the Judiciary, Washington, D.C., August. www.heritage.org/Research/Family/upload/85273_1.pdf (accessed 3 January 2007).

Mayer, Vicki. 2005. "Soft-Core in TV Time: The Political Economy of a 'Cultural Trend.'" In *Critical Studies in Media Communication* 22 (October): 302–20.

Richtel, Matt. 2007. "X-rated Industry Finds High Definition Is Too Graphic." *Herald Tribune*. 22 January. www.iht.com/articles/2007/01/21/business/porn.php (accessed 3 February 2007).

Russell, Diana E. H., ed. 1993. *Making Violence Sexy: Feminist Views on Pornography*. Buckingham: Open University Press.

Shaw, Susan M. 1999. "Men's Leisure and Women's Lives: The Impact of Pornography on Women." *Leisure Studies* 18:197–212.

Simonton Ann. 2004. Ann Simonton interviews Carol Smith: Who are women in pornography? A conversation in *Not for Sale: Feminists Resisting Prostitution and Pornography*, eds. Christine Stark and Rebecca Whisnant. North Melbourne: Spinifex.

Tanner, John C. 2005. "3G: Naughty or Nice?" *Telecom Asia* 16, no. 1 (January): 4.

Umali, Violeda A. 2005. "The Cyber-trafficking of Filipino Girl-children: Weaknesses of Philippine Policies." *Asian Women* 20:175–206.

United Nations. 1999. NGO Consultation with UN/IGOs on Trafficking in Persons, Prostitution and the Global Sex Industry. "Trafficking and the Global Sex Industry: Need for Human Rights Framework," June 21–22.

Williams, Jessica. 2004. "Facts That Should Change the World." *New Statesman* 133, no. 4691: 15.

Williams, Linda. 2004. "Second Thoughts on Hard Core: American Obscenity Law and the Scapegoating of Deviance." In *More Dirty Looks: Gender Pornography and Power*, ed. Pamela Church Gibson, 165–75. London: BFI.

Wilmet, Holly. 1999. "Naked Feminism: The Unionization of the Adult Entertainment Industry." *Journal of Gender, Social Policy and the Law* 7:465–94.

Worden, Scott. 2001. "E-Trafficking." *Foreign Policy*, no. 123:92–94.

Wu, Joyce. 2004. "Left Labour in Bed with the Sex Industry." In *Not for Sale: Feminists Resisting Prostitution and Pornography*, eds. Christine Stark and Rebecca Whisnant, xx. North Melbourne: Spinifex.

Wüllenweber, Walter. 2007. "Sexuelle Verwahrlosung Voll Porno. " *Stern*. June 6. www.stern.de/politik/deutschland/581936.html?nv=ct_mt (accessed 16 February 2007).

Wyld, Ben. 2004. "Porn Link to Young Sex Offenders." *Sydney Morning Herald*. April 22. www.smh.com/au/articles/2004/04/21/1082530235683.html (accessed 16 February 2007).

PART THREE

MEDIATING MEANINGS, MEDIATING REGIMES OF POWER

CHAPTER NINE

Mediations of Domination:
Gendered Violence Within
and Across Borders

Yasmin Jiwani

The ability to narrate ourselves not from the first person alone, but from, say, the position of the third, or to receive an account delivered in the second, can actually work to expand our understanding of the forms that global power has taken.

—Judith Butler, *Precarious Life*[1]

In this statement, Butler makes a plea for hearing a narrative from multiple standpoints and thereby opening ourselves to a critical awareness of our interdependent and interconnected worlds. While she is referencing the post-9/11 context, a context marked by the declaration of a war on terror and the media's censorship of dissent, her remarks are equally applicable to our understanding of violence—across and within borders. But how the violence is defined, constructed, and shaped in its mediations across and within borders is crucial in influencing our response and calls for intervention. In this chapter, I focus on the mediations of violence as they occur in the Canadian context. I do so in an effort to destabilize the nationally projected image of Canada as a peaceable kingdom where minorities enjoy unencumbered rights and where different ethnicities reside in relative harmony. In the context of disrupting this inter/national imaginary, I pay particular attention to the intersecting and interlocking influences of race and gender in the lives of indigenous and racialized minority women who experience violence, both systemic and intimate. My central argument is that, in mediating these experiences of violence, the transnational imagery of culture plays a central role in how the dominant media frames gender and racializes violence against women of color and indigenous women. To this end, the dominant Western globalized media participate in the continued marginalization of indigenous women and women of color unless they demonstrate signs of assimilation—abdicating cultural allegiances in favor of the mythic liberation promised by Western notions of progress and equality.

On Transnational Links

Arjun Appudurai (1990) argues that media globalization facilitates the migration of images about other peoples, cultures, and nations. However, in the process of this migration, images change and national cultures get contorted, often to fit prevailing assumptions. Globalized media, as Herman and McChesney (1997) have noted, are controlled in large part by dominant multinationals, many of them situated and dominated by Western interests. This is not to suggest that these media overdetermine all images. Alternative media made possible by new technologies of communication do form a contesting base of knowledge. Nonetheless, new media, especially within diasporic contexts, remain subordinate and confined to small sectors of the population—a direct outcome and expression of audience fragmentation (Karim 1998; Naficy 1998). What is relevant here about media concentration and control is the circulation of images that reinforce and reproduce existing stereotypes. Sedef Arat-Koc (2002) provides a telling example when she recounts the history of the prominent Egyptian feminist Nawal El Sadaawi's book *The Hidden Face of Eve*. When initially published in Egypt, the book had a different title, but once it crossed the continents and was republished in England, the title and content changed to reflect prevailing preconceptions about Muslim women.[2] And Fatema Mernissi (2001), the renowned Moroccan sociologist, offers yet another account of how Western images of Muslim women in harems as depicted in Western art (such as travelogues and diaries) were engendered to fit prevailing conceptions of Eastern, exotic femininity—an idealized gendered Other that was passive, sexually available, and devoid of intellectual capacity.

In a revealing passage, Uma Narayan (1997) comments on how issues concerning violence become transformed once they cross borders:

> In thinking about issues of "violence against Third-World women" that "cross borders" into Western national contexts, it strikes me that phenomena that seem "Different," "Alien," and "Other" cross these borders with considerably more frequency than problems that seem "similar" to those that affect mainstream Western women. . . . It is difficult not to conclude that there is a premium on "Third-

World difference" that results in greater interest being accorded to those issues that seem strikingly "different" from those affecting mainstream Western women. (100)

Drawing from an intersectional framework, the greater purchase of Third World difference as emblematic of essentialized cultural differences serves a twofold function: it provides the media with fodder for a voyeuristic gaze that enables a strategic diversion and displacement of attention/concern for the issues confronting women living in Western societies in general, and it allows the media to offer a culturally encoded explanatory framework that makes "sense" of the violence that women of color and indigenous women face. In so doing, stereotypical representations are reproduced. The following sections demonstrate these points with particular reference to Canadian cases, though undoubtedly there are parallels between these case examples and others in the Western industrialized world.

Culturalizing Violence

Much has been written about the way in which the mass media portray violence against women (Meyers 1997; McLaughlin 1991). A common critique is how the media report violence that disinters it from its structural grounding as a widespread and pervasive phenomenon. Indeed, the World Health Organization's report on violence and health states, "Almost half the women who die due to homicide are killed by their current or former husbands or boyfriends, while in some countries it can be as high as 70 percent" (WHO 2002). Even in Canada, Statistics Canada reports that of all victims of crimes against the person in 2000, women accounted for the majority: 86 percent were victims of sexual assault; 78 percent were victims of criminal harassment, and 67 percent were victims of hostage taking/kidnapping or abduction.[3] Nevertheless, the gendered nature of violence against women is seldom explored in the dominant media, nor is there an attempt to situate it within a global framework of patriarchal power.

When the media do focus on violence against women of color, they most often invoke the banner of culture to explain such violence.[4] Sherene Razack defines this as a culturalization of violence and reasons that "culture becomes the framework used by white society to pre-empt both racism and sexism . . ." (1998, 60). But the problematic use of culture resides most clearly in its predominant and popular usage. In this regard, culture is used to refer to those aspects of an identity that are most clearly visible: clothes, songs, dances, and diet. In other words, a "boutique" notion of culture gains salience and acceptance (Fish 1997). The resulting concept of culture can most easily be mobilized toward engendering and solidifying regimes of difference—the signifying practices by which differences are understood and used strategically to distinguish not only between groups of people but to legitimize those differences in terms of allocation of resources and liabilities.

Such a boutique concept of culture then culturalizes violence by making it intelligible as a culturally enshrined practice—a tradition from a past that has been maintained and invoked in current practice. As Razack (1998) and Narayan (1997) among others have argued, the culturalization of violence plays a particular role. It draws upon colonial anthropological definitions of culture, which pivot on notions of essentialism and are mapped on a linear model of development, ranging from the primitive to the civilized, where the civilized stands for all that is Western, and the primitives constitute the rest of the world. This yardstick of development has served strategic functions of empire building through colonization and imperialism. The language of cultural distinctions has now become a principal technology by which difference is most readily understood and further legitimized or delegitimized in the interests of the powerful. These legitimations are then used to determine which kinds of violence will be rendered visible and regarded as deserving of attention and intervention and which can be dismissed, trivialized, or erased from the collective imagination (Collins 1998).

Thus, while infibulations, dowry-deaths, and child female infanticide are made visible—often as the defining features of entire groups of women's lives and experiences of violence—the violence of colonialism with its systematic breakdown of familial life, its devaluation of women's traditional roles, and its wholesale cultural genocide through the imposition of Christianity, mass appropriation of children, and seizure of lands is not considered violence in the popular stock of knowledge. Rather, it is dismissed as a sign of backwardness on the part of the colonizers and is used to legitimize genocide or to promote a "rescue" mission underpinned by a benevolent desire to save the colonized (Wynn Davies et al. 1993). The visibility accorded to one expression or manifestation of violence and the invisibility of the other are interlocked. One supports and depends on the other. Thus, as Razack (1998) points out, when a refugee claimant applies for status in Canada, she is most successful if she can invoke a colonial tale—that of the oppressed woman of color, in danger of "death by culture," where culture is constituted by those practices of violence that are seen to be peculiar and particular to the specific nationality or ethnicity to which the victim belongs (Nayaran 1997).

In contrast, Aboriginal women in Canada experience a multitude of different kinds of violence, ranging from exclusion from the dominant society, poverty and ghettoization in poorer urban areas and reserves, a heightened vulnerability to gendered and systemic violence, and a devaluation of their status as women and loss of the rights they once enjoyed in their cultures and nations.

This systemic and structural form of violence is negated. Instead, even its manifestations in the form of high suicide rates, high rates of addiction, and incarceration are erased of their sociohistorical significance. Rather, when rendered visible, these forms of violence are attributed to a people who cannot handle the pressures of living in a Western society—unable to cope, as it were—and to women as abject failures of the civilizing process. What needs to be underscored is how the sheer invisibility of this violence stands in stark contrast to the visibility of the stereotypical tropes of violence ascribed to women of color.

In examining how the dominant news media frame violence, two contemporary examples are salient: the first concerns the coverage of Muslim women in the aftermath of the events of September 11, 2001; the second concerns the coverage of missing and murdered Aboriginal women in Canada. I explore these issues with reference to the various ways that women from each of these groups are rendered visible and invisible and how the trope of culture explains away one kind of violence, while historical erasure works to delegitimize culture and thereby diminish the reality of another kind of violence. In describing these two mediatized tales, my aim is to underscore how certain women are positioned as "good" women and others as "bad" women. "Good" women are worth saving; "bad" women are beyond redemption.

Afghan Women Victims

The bombing of the twin towers of the World Trade Center and the Pentagon in 2001 galvanized an already escalating fear and demonization of Islam and all things considered Muslim. As Edward Said (1978) has noted in his influential work on orientalism, Muslim women have consistently been positioned as emblematic signifiers of the presumed oppressiveness of Islam (see also Yeğenoğlu 1998). In the aftermath of September 11, the *hijab* (head scarf) and the *burqa* (full body covering) became the most visible signs of this oppression and were the focal point of many national and international media debates. Yet the veil, according to Anouar Majid (1998), is a cultural symbol, not one advocated by Islam or the Quran. Nonetheless, as a sign the veil has played a strategic role in how particular Muslim (notably Afghani) women are represented in the Western media—as quintessential victims needing to be rescued by benevolent Western powers from barbaric Muslim men (Abu-Lughod 2002).[5]

This focus on the veil as a signifier of oppression effectively deflects attention from the reality of the Afghan women. Hirschkind and Mahmood (2002) have argued that under Taliban rule, only urban-based women were affected by the strictures on mobility, dress, and appearance. More poignantly, the focus on the veil deflects attention from the imposition of similar social codes and normative rules in Western societies. In her compelling analysis of the "obscene underside" of the American construction of the Taliban as evil, Mary Ann Franks (2003) underlines the similarities shared by both societies:

> There is no restriction under the law as to what a woman can wear in public, but a woman who wears "suggestive" clothing is often perceived as inviting sexual advances. These unwritten codes of violent subjugation of women in the West were explicitly written into the Law of the Taliban: whereas the Taliban hides the explicitly sexual aspect of this subjugation, and justifies its repressive dictums on the basis of "respect" for women, in the United States women are compelled to formulate their identities as ever-available sexual beings under the guise of "sexual liberation." (146)

I do not wish to suggest a kind of moral equivalence anchored on a mythical level playing field. The Taliban were/are just as ruthless. Among their ranks, they differentiated between "good" Muslim women, those fit to be mothers and socializing agents, and "bad" women, those whom they considered prostitutes and utilized for a growing traffic in women. My intent here, as Hirschkind and Mahmood (2002) argue, is to demonstrate the binary construction of the Muslim woman, a construction that corrals religion and cultural practice as pillars upholding the faulty logic of the West. This binary posits that "a Muslim woman can only be one of two things, either uncovered, and therefore liberated, or veiled, and thus still to some degree, subordinate" (352–53). Such a Western construction strategically negates any consideration of the material reality of Afghan women and can be ideologically harnessed to promote missions of rescue. Thus, the good woman/bad woman dichotomy prevails in both worldviews.

Western mediated constructions of Muslim women also rest on the complete erasure of the conditions governing women's lives. The trope of Islamic fundamentalism is then used as a paradigm to locate and analyze women's subordination under Islam (Hirschkind and Mahmood 2002). Writing more than a decade ago, Marnia Lazreg (1988) argues: "The overall effect of this paradigm is to deprive women of self-presence, of being. Because women are subsumed under religion presented in fundamental terms, they are inevitably seen as evolving in nonhistorical time. They have virtually no history. Any analysis of change is therefore foreclosed" (86; see also Yeğenoğlu 1998). That change may involve resistance, often through the voluntary adoption of the veil, is also foreclosed in such analysis; yet that is exactly what is transpiring in many parts of the Western world where Muslim women reside (Dwyer 1999; Hoodfar 1993). That the veil may be seen as a kind of "mobile home" affording women the anonymity they desire is also omitted from these accounts (Abu-Lughod 2002).

Further, the material reality of women's lives is effectively occluded in most Western mainstream media accounts. That Afghanistan has one of the highest infant mortality rates, is excessively embedded with landmines, and is heavily militarized as a result of previous interventions and occupations remains a hidden backdrop to the exploits of the international coalition that spurred the intervention in 2001 or to recent Canadian attempts to enforce "peace" in the region. Women's resistance movements within that region are also silenced, if not used to harness the construction of Muslim women as quintessential victims. The Revolutionary Association of the Women of Afghanistan (RAWA) had long warned against the violence inflicted by both the Taliban and the Northern Alliance (Moghadam 1999, 2001). Yet their warnings were given scant attention. Instead, the feminist majority in the U.S. quickly appropriated from their message the trope of victimization, launching an entire campaign around it, replete with postcards depicting a piece of the mesh commonly used in the burqa to shield the eyes of the wearer (Kolhatkar 2002; Hirschkind and Mahmood 2002). As Sonali Kolhatkar has stated, "The Afghan women of RAWA do not need to be 'liberated,' they simply need our moral and financial support to realize their vision" (29).

This brief sojourn concerning the situation of Muslim women highlights the erasure of context and the quick mobilization of the Islamic fundamentalist trope as an explanatory vehicle within the Western media. Within Canadian press accounts, this trope was harnessed with considerable ideological currency if not resonance (Karim 2000). Islam has become the culturalist explanation for a variety of different ills—ranging from the subordination of women to the emerging terrorist threat within the homeland. Yet, as many scholars of Islam have noted, there is considerable variation in the practice and interpretation of the faith. Despite this, the trope persists because it is easy, accessible, iconic, resonant with the historical context of orientalism, and ultimately a powerful strategic tool to contain the aspirations and manage the subordination of Muslims, reproducing in the process the binary on which the discourse of geopolitical manipulation and unequal power relations can be maintained.

One crucial way that this binary is maintained, and the ideological potency of the civilizational discourse pitting the West against the rest is accomplished, is through the contrast of Muslim women "over there" and those who are "over here." In previous research (Jiwani 2004, 2005) focusing on a textual examination of Canadian press coverage of the war in Afghanistan, I found that Afghan women were rarely quoted. In contrast, Muslim women living in the West were more likely to be interviewed and quoted directly. The overall impression left by these stories was that the West allows Muslim women to speak, whereas in Afghanistan they are silenced. However, all the Afghan or Muslim women who were quoted tended to articulate sentiments that fitted within prevailing conceptions of Afghanistan as a land of gendered oppression under Muslim rule. The brutality of Muslim men and particularly the Taliban was reiterated so frequently and repetitively that it seemed to become imprinted in the minds of both the columnists and the readers. It was not surprising then to read the words of Margaret Wente (2001), a popular columnist for the *Globe and Mail*, one of Canada's national dailies, when she penned the following:

> The women of Afghanistan are the most oppressed group of people in the world. Their country has been destroyed by wave on wave of war, and now they live under the tyranny of brutal misogynists. The Taliban believes that females are scarcely more than walking wombs, and they treat them worse than animals. If—when—the Taliban is overthrown, the women of Afghanistan will probably be better off. (A13)

This lack of agency and voice characteristic of representations of Afghan women carried over into other descriptions. For instance, even for those Muslim women living in the West whose words were quoted directly, their experiences of wearing the burqa or the veil were dismissed. Instead, in keeping with a sensibility akin to imperial feminism, reporters took it upon themselves to wear the burqa and experience firsthand their resulting feelings of oppression. As a reporter for the *Globe and Mail* wrote, "The burqa tells the world, 'Do not acknowledge that I am here.' But it is also a message for the woman who wears it: 'You are entitled to just this much physical space.'" (Nolen 2001, F8). And another, performing the same exercise, wrote, "The veil commands me to take my hands off my hips, round my shoulders and lower my chin. It persuades me to walk quickly with my arms at my side, staring down at the sidewalk" (McLaren 2001, L3). The use of the burqa as a disguise by reporters wishing to get past the Taliban was never raised as a point of comparison nor interrogated in any critical fashion.[6] This implies that it is all right for Western men or women to wear the burqa in order to penetrate "enemy" territory but not all right for those indigenous Others to wear such clothing.

In her insightful analysis of Muslim women, Cooke (2002) outlines "the four-stage gendered logic of empire." This logic, she argues,

> genders and separates subject peoples so that the men are the Other and the women are civilizable. To defend our universal civilization we must rescue the women. To rescue these women we must attack these men. These women will be rescued not because they are more "ours" than "theirs" but rather because they will have become more "ours" through the rescue mission. . . . In the Islamic context, the negative stereotyping of the religion as inherently misogynist provides ammunition for the attack on the uncivilized brown men. (468)

Thus, the victimhood of Afghan women remains a necessary foundation to resurrect these rescue myths and in the process Islam becomes the demonized religious/cultural force that needs to be dealt with effectively. But if the victim status of one group of women is to be ensured, then it must rest on a counter construction of other women who are not deemed to be victims per se but rather perpetrators of violence. This is apparent even in representations of Middle Eastern women that circulated in the *Globe and Mail* and the *National Post*, Canada's two national papers, over a two-week period following the events of September 11, 2001.[7] In both papers, a key story focused on Palestinian women celebrating in Ramallah and elsewhere upon hearing of the attacks in New York. Both papers reiterated the story. A journalist for the *Globe and Mail* wrote, "In Nablus, a town in the West Bank, 3,000 people poured into the streets, including a 48-year-old woman in a long, black dress who cried out in happiness: 'America is the head of the snake, America always stands by Israel in its war against us'" (Jimenez 2001). Palestinian women were constructed as the mothers of suicide bombers who actively perpetrated the conflict, and their lack of compassion for victims other than their families was described with resounding condemnation. Jessica Stern, identified as an expert from Harvard University, was quoted as stating, "Most of the mothers I interviewed . . . said they were happy to have donated their sons to jihad because their sons could help them in the next life, 'the real life'" (Brown 2001, F1).

In an insightful article on women suicide bombers, Mia Bloom (2005) observes that "anecdotal evidence suggests that many women bombers have been raped or sexually abused either by representatives of the state or by insurgents—thereby contributing to a sense of humiliation and powerlessness, made only worse by stigmatization within their own societies" (58). In neither paper was there any analysis of the conditions and the material reality affecting these women's lives, how in a sense they too were victims of the hegemonic patriarchal structures that operate within their own communities and in the dominant societies in which they reside.

Missing Aboriginal Women—Violence within Borders

If the trope of culture as a framework for the continued demonization of Islam, and as the explanatory framework that seals the victim status of Afghan women, is used to legitimize intervention through rescue and ultimately assimilation, then the case of missing Aboriginal women in Canada falls outside this purview—rendering them less as victims deserving rescue than as bodies that simply do not matter.

In the last two decades, more than five hundred Aboriginal women in Canada have gone missing, according to the Native Women's Association of Canada.[8] As I have argued elsewhere, if five hundred Canadian soldiers were missing in action, there would be a national uproar (Jiwani 2006). Part of the complacency that has greeted this issue has to do with the range of time over which many of Aboriginal women have disappeared. Most of it, however, has to do with the particular positioning of these women—as Aboriginal and in many cases as sex trade workers (Jiwani and Young 2006).

There have been several notable and insightful analyses of the conditions facing Aboriginal women in Canada (Lawrence 2002; Maracle 1996; Monture-Angus 1995; McIvor 1999). Amnesty International (2004) reported that Aboriginal women in Canada were identified as being at risk, particularly from sexual violence, addictions, suicidal ideation, and the like. However, rather than use these descriptions as essentialized traits of victimization, what needs to be underscored here is the history and legacy of colonization affecting their lived reality. These historical conditions seldom see the light of day in print media. Rather, the tendency of the media thus far has been to concentrate on issues of land claims and militancy, all the while emphasizing the "emotionality" and "lack of reason" of Aboriginal peoples (Harding 2006). That these land claims were and are predicated on a systemic dispossession of indigenous land by white settler societies is completely negated in contemporary media accounts (Harris 2004). Moreover, the actual victimization of Aboriginal women is seldom recognized as such— rather, more often than not, it is attributed to an inherent cultural deficiency— an inability to "fit into" white, middle-class society. What is most obviously missing in these accounts is the impact and influence of Christianity as a colonizing force resulting in the devaluation of Aboriginal women, their dispossession of land and rights, and their continued victimization by, if we are to use the parallel of the Islamic fundamentalist trope, white Christian settler societies.

In her analysis of the murder of Pamela George, a woman from the Salteaux nation, Sherene Razack (2002) points out that "newspaper records of the nineteenth century indicate that there was a conflation of Aboriginal women and prostitutes and an accompanying belief that when they encountered violence, Aboriginal women simply got what they deserved. Police seldom intervened, even when the victims' cries could be clearly heard" (130). Drawing on the historical analyses, Razack notes how Aboriginal women were used as sexual objects and that colonial officers would often withhold critical resources unless they were supplied with Aboriginal women to fulfil their sexual demands. In the same vein, Leacock's (1980) analysis of the Montagnais-Naskapi women of eastern Canada also demonstrates how historically their status was rendered subordinate to men once the Jesuit priests introduced monogamy, punishment of children, patriarchal power, and the segregation of sexes. And in line with the various technologies used to subordinate Aboriginal women, Lawrence (2003) recounts how the Canadian state regulated women's bodies so that if Aboriginal women married outside their nation, they were denied Indian status, whereas if a white woman married a native man, she would automatically be considered as belonging to the Indian nation. This strategy inferiorized the status of white women, such that those that were willing to marry Indians were themselves considered outside the pale of civilization. However demoted they were, white women still gained access to land and resources in Aboriginal communities. In contrast, thousands of Aboriginal women and their children were denuded of their Aboriginal heritage, membership in native nations, and most importantly, access to reserve land and housing. It was not until 1981, when the United Nations Human Rights Committee ruled in favor of Native women, that the Canadian government subsequently (in 1985) rescinded the offensive clause from the Indian Act.

The construction of the Aboriginal woman's body as expendable and without value is not new. Rather, it is the reproduction of this construction in contemporary reality and more particularly in mediated accounts that becomes the issue of contention. The erasure of Aboriginal women's bodies rests on the hypervisibility of other women—as with the women in Afghanistan, the two are interlocked. As with McLaughlin's (1991) description of the contrasting binary of the good woman/bad woman or the Madonna/whore, here too, one kind of victimized status assumes a moral legitimacy and urges a call for intervention, whereas the other is diluted of such moral victim status and thus intervention. It is the notion of *when* victimhood is granted as a status deserving of attention and intervention that is the problematic. Here, Aboriginal women's bodies are denied such legitimacy, and the cultural trope is either evacuated as an explanatory tool or delegitimized when it refers to Aboriginal cultures.

The case of the missing Aboriginal woman has recently commandeered some attention from the dominant print media. To some extent, this attention has been fueled by sympathetic reporters located in Vancouver, who subsequently investigated missing women from the Downtown Eastside area of the city. Press accounts estimate that sixty-seven women are missing from this area. More recently, media attention has been galvanized by the identification of an alleged serial killer, Robert William Pickton, who has now been charged with twenty-six counts of murder involving the missing women.

The media accounts pertaining to this case have been analyzed in some depth (Jiwani and Young 2006).[9] For the present analysis, what is noteworthy is how these publicly mediated accounts, circulated by the press, resulted in the minimization of the violence of everyday life experienced by Aboriginal women and also positioned them as "degenerate" Others. Three factors contribute to the diminished legitimacy of Aboriginal women as victims of violence. The first deals with the sign of Aboriginality—aboriginality as stigmata; the second point focuses on the devaluation and degenerate status of sex work and its slippage into Aboriginality; and the third aspect deals with the urban location of many of the missing women in Vancouver's Downtown Eastside, which invokes images of extreme poverty, drug dependency, and crime (Pratt 2005). My focus here is on the construction of Aboriginality as a sign invested with negative connotations—connotations that denude the legitimacy of Aboriginal women as victims of violence and that render them as degenerate bodies (Smith 2005).

Representations of Aboriginal women in popular media and folklore, not to mention in historical records, have positioned them as either "Indian princesses" or "repulsive lascivious squaws" (Portman and Herring 2001, 189). The mythical character of Pocahontas, the Indian princess who rescues a white man, clearly falls in the former category and has achieved iconic currency as a result of Disney's recasting of the tale. The "squaw" image, in contrast, is rooted in depictions of Aboriginal women engaged in drudgery and work. Based on her analysis of Euro-Canadian history and literature, Janice Acoose (1995, 44) observes that "the bad Indigenous woman or squaw (the shadowy lustful archetype) provided justification for imperialistic expansion and the subsequent explorers', fur traders', and Christian missionaries' specific agendas." What is of particular interest here is how the stereotypic image of the squaw became infused with images of available and easily exploited sexuality—a sexuality that was clearly deemed to be degenerate, opposed as it was to the venerated representations of the bourgeois white woman as virtuous and maternal. This contrasting binary resonates with McLaughlin's (1991) analysis of media narratives focusing on prostitution. Here the prostitute or sex worker becomes the "bad" woman, while the good woman remains the virtuous other. But, as McLaughlin elaborates, within "bad" women, there may be some parts worth saving. And this is where the rescue mission becomes paramount. Historically, through the efforts of missionaries and the "civilizing" intent of the State, the "good" aspects of Aboriginal women were seen as being worth saving in the interests of society, particularly through assimilation.

However, Aboriginality is a historically shifting construct—good when it demonstrates the benevolent aspects of the dominant society, bad when it is seen as making what are construed as unreasonable demands—like land claims—and when the civilizing mission has failed. It is not surprising then, as Harding (2006) concludes, that Aboriginal representations in the print media have by far been negative, constructed as they are around issues of land claims (read: unreasonable demands), the legacy of residential schools (read: failure of the civilizing mission), and excessive emotionality (read: childlike, militant, and uncontained). To this list, I would add criminality (as in drug addictions, violence, and sex trade work).

In focusing on the media coverage of the missing women, it becomes apparent that the sign of Aboriginal affiliation diminished the credibility of their victim status and therefore reduced the urgency for societal intervention and assistance. For one, in the case of the missing women from Vancouver's Downtown Eastside, Aboriginal women constituted thirty-nine of the sixty-seven women missing (Pratt 2005). Nevertheless, representations of missing women in the print media were overwhelmingly infused by references to Aboriginal healing ceremonies, memorials, and the like (Jiwani and Young 2006). More than that, Aboriginality was conflated with sex trade work and drug addiction, which the press condensed within the label of a "high-risk" lifestyle.[10] The implication is that the Aboriginal women who are missing put themselves at risk, rather than that they were put at risk by the social conditions and societal factors governing and shaping their lives. In contrast, indigenous activists such as Andrea Smith (2005) provide detailed accounts of how Aboriginal women are put at risk by sexual violence, forced sterilization, environmental racism, and confinement in boarding or residential schools.

That Aboriginality is regarded as a stigma and is viewed negatively, and that it lends to the erasure of Aboriginal women from public visibility, is evident in Pitman's (2002) analysis of an episode concerning the missing women on the heavily watched TV program *America's Most Wanted*. In recounting the case, the telecast erased the racial character of the missing women, inserting instead the body of a white woman as one of the missing. Such a move, on the part of the producers, reflects this "commonsensical" knowledge that inserting Aboriginal women into the frame would not give the issue of missing women the kind of public legitimacy that the producers desired. In other words, it would not be seen as relevant to the largely white and middle-class audience that was being hailed by the program. Inserting the frame of white women's vulnerability, Pitman argues, invoked "a long-standing morality tale," warning young white women to stay out of "bad neighbourhoods" (179).

Pitman's analysis is not only telling of how Aboriginal women get erased but it also underscores how "culture talk" is rarely if ever used to interrogate the contemporary conditions influencing Aboriginal women's lives. There is scarcely any mention of how Aboriginal bodies are rendered degenerate or why they do not matter. These aspects are simply taken for granted. And unlike the case of the Afghan women, whose oppression is indelibly linked to Islam, the Christianizing force that legitimized and subjugated Aboriginal women and that lent ideological force to their subject status is also not interrogated. The erasure of this cultural history is rendered all the more salient when we think about how Aboriginal peoples in Canada and the U.S. are continually required to "prove" the existence of their cultures when attempting to negotiate recognition and land claim disputes (Klein and Ackerman 1995). Culture talk, it would seem, is only acceptable under particular conditions.

Conclusion

Contrasting the two cases raises all kinds of polemical issues. My intent has been to draw attention to the circumstances and conditions wherein one group of women achieve the status of legitimized victims, demanding intervention and rescue, whereas another group of women are rendered invisible, their visibility only heightened within the frame of criminality and high-risk behavior.

Globalized media constituted by international oligopolies of power shape our mediascapes. They transfer images across distances, so that the plight of the Afghan women becomes not only newsworthy in the current context of the war on terror but also influences how we view and define violence. That the violence "out there" merits more attention, is given more credence, and is used to legitimize intervention, works hand in hand with the continued minimization and erasure of the violence that occurs "here" in the local context. Yet, the focus on Afghan women fits within the prevailing paradigm of Islam as a religion of gender oppression reproducing contemporary forms of orientalism. In contrast, the legacy of Christianity, and its attendant denigration of Aboriginal women's status, not to mention their sexual exploitation within residential schools and the like, is occluded within the local mediated landscape—a landscape similarly marked by the influence of a media monopoly. Structural violence then is erased from both these tales. Rather, the focus becomes one of singular pathological predators, as in the case of the missing women, or the obsessed Taliban, driven to extremes by Islam. In both cases, the only "good" women are those saved or rescued through the civilizing processes of Western imperialism, or in Butler's terms—the "forms that global power has taken."

Notes

Acknowledgment. This research was made possible by funding from the Social Sciences and Humanities Research Council of Canada (SSHRC).

1. Judith Butler, *Precarious Life: The Powers of Mourning and Violence.* London and New York: Verso, 2004, 8.

2. The title in Arabic, according to Arat-Koc (2002: 437), "literally meant 'the naked face of the Arab woman.'"

3. See the Fact Sheet on Violence Against Women in Canada, Status of Women Canada, www.swc-cfc.gc.ca/dates/dec6/facts_e.html (accessed 2 January 2007).

4. I draw a distinction here between native or indigenous women and nonnative women of color. The latter are immigrants or come from immigrant origins. By indigenous or native, I am referring to women who trace their origins to the native nations or traditions that were indigenous to Canada prior to colonial settlement and expansion. Naturally these categories are not watertight compartments; their very boundaries are blurred and constructed according to historical and contemporary factors. Many indigenous women are mixed race, for instance. However, it is their identification as native/indigenous that is the basis of the distinction.

5. The *hijab* and the *niqab* (full covering) have also been a source of contention among Muslim women and Western feminists.

6. See this account by Patrick Graham: "After shrouding us in blue burkas, the all-encompassing garment Afghan women are forced to wear outside their homes, and sneaking us past a police checkpoint, he [Mr. Khan] laughed and sang his way to the next post while we sweated away under the tent-like disguise." (2001).

7. A total of 108 stories in the *Globe and Mail* and 123 stories in the *National Post* were examined. The stories were culled on the basis of a key word search in the Factiva database of news print articles.

8. See Sisters in Spirit campaign: www.sistersinspirit.ca/engmissing.htm (May 2006).

9. Jiwani and Young examined 128 articles that appeared in the *Vancouver Sun* from 2002 to 2006.

10. See the *Globe and Mail*'s story on missing women in Edmonton, where the author mentions the term "high-risk lifestyles" in quotations—perhaps indicating that the source of the terminology was not hers but rather that of the police (K. Harding 2006).

References

Abu-Lughod, Lila. 2002. "Do Muslim Women Really Need Saving? Anthropological Reflections on Cultural Relativism and Its Others." *American Anthropologist* 104, no. 3:783–90.

Acoose, Janice. 1995. *ISKWEWAK–Kah' Ki Yaw Ni Wahkomakanak, Neither Indian Princesses nor Easy Squaws*. Toronto: Women's Press.

Amnesty International. 2004. "Stolen Sisters: A Human Rights Response to Discrimination and Violence against Indigenous Women in Canada." www.amnesty.ca/campaigns/resources/amr2000304.pdf (accessed June 2005).

Appadurai, Arjun. 1990. "Disjuncture and Difference in the Global Cultural Economy." *Theory, Culture & Society* 7:295–310.

Arat-Koc, Sedef. 2002. "Hot Potato: Imperial Wars or Benevolent Interventions? Reflections on 'Global Feminism' Post September 11th." *Atlantis* 26, no. 2:433–44.

Bloom, Mia. 2005. "Mother. Daughter. Sister. Bomber." *Bulletin of the Atomic Scientists* (November–December): 54–62.

Brown, Ian. 2001. Focus Special Report. *Toronto Globe and Mail*. September 22.

Butler, Judith. 2004. *Precarious Life, the Powers of Mourning and Violence*. London and New York: Verso.

Collins, Patricia Hill. 1998. "The Tie That Binds: Race, Gender and US Violence." *Ethnic and Racial Studies* 21, no. 5:917–38.

Cooke, Miriam. 2002. "Saving Brown Women." *Signs* 28, no. 1: 468–70.

Dwyer, Claire. 1999. "Veiled Meanings: Young British Muslim Women and the Negotiation of Differences." *Gender, Place and Culture* 6, no. 1: 5–26.

Fish, Stanley. 1997. "Boutique Multiculturalism, or Why Liberals Are Incapable of Thinking About Hate Speech." *Critical Inquiry* 23: 378–95.

Franks, Mary Ann. 2003. "Obscene Undersides: Women and Evil between the Taliban and the United States." *Hypatia: A Journal of Feminist Philosophy* 18, no. 1: 135–56.

Graham, Patrick. 2001. "Through the Peaks with Gun Runners in Pajamas: Post Reporter Enters Afghanistan by the Only Route Open." *National Post*. September 28.

Harding, Katherine. 2006. "The Edmonton Killings: Who Is Responsible for the Deaths of 15 Women?" *Toronto Globe and Mail*.

Harding, Robert. 2006. "Historical Representations of Aboriginal People in the Canadian News Media." *Discourse & Society* 17, no. 2:205–35.

Harris, Cole. 2004. "How Did Colonialism Dispossess? Comments from an Edge of Empire." *Annals of the Association of American Geographers* 94, no. 1:165–82.

Herman, Edward S., and Robert W. McChesney. 1997. "Alternatives to the Status Quo?" In *The Global Media: New Missionaries of Global Capitalism*, eds. Edward S. Herman and Robert W. McChesney, 189–205. Washington: Cassell.

Hirschkind, Charles, and Saba Mahmood. 2002. "Feminism, the Taliban, and the Politics of Counter-Insurgency." *Anthropological Quarterly* 75, no. 2:339–54.

Hoodfar, Homa. 1993. "The Veil in Their Minds and on Our Heads: The Persistence of Colonial Images of Muslim Women." *Resources for Feminist Research* 22, no. 3/4:5–18.

Jimenez, Marina. 2001. "Many Arabs celebrate; leaders decry attack: 'Bull's eye'." *National Post.* September 12.

Jiwani, Yasmin. 2004. "Gendering Terror: Representations of the Orientalized Body in Quebec's Post–September 11 English-Language Press." *Critique: Critical Middle Eastern Studies* 13, no. 3:265–91.

———. 2005. "War Talk—Engendering Terror: Race, Gender & Representation in Canadian Print Media." *International Journal of Media & Cultural Politics* 1, no. 1:15–21.

———. 2006. "How We See 'Missing Women.'" *The Tyee*, June 21. http://thetyee.ca/Views/2006/06/21/MissingWomen/ (accessed 28 January 2007).

Jiwani, Yasmin, and Mary Lynn Young. 2006. "Missing and Murdered Women: Reproducing Marginality in News Discourse." *Canadian Journal of Communication*, 31, no. 3:895–917.

Karim, H. Karim. 1998. "From Ethnic Media to Global Media: Transnational Communication Networks among Diasporic Communities." International Comparative Research Group, Strategic Research and Analysis, Canadian Heritage, June.

———. 2000. *Islamic Peril.* Montreal: Black Rose Books.

Klein, Laura F., and Lillian A. Ackerman, eds. 1995. *Women and Power in Native North America.* Norman and London: University of Oklahoma Press.

Kolhatkar, Sonali. 2002. "The Impact of US Intervention on Afghan Women's Studies." *Berkeley Women's Law Journal* 17:12–30.

Lawrence, Bonita. 2003. "Gender, Race, and the Regulation of Native Identity in Canada and the United States: An Overview." *Hypatia* 18, no. 2: 3–31.

Lawrence, Bonita. 2002. "Rewriting Histories of the Land: Colonization and Indigenous Resistance in Eastern Canada." In *Race, Space, and the Law: Unmapping a White Settler Society*, ed. Sherene H. Razack, 21–26. Toronto: Between the Lines.

Lazreg, Marnia. 1988. "The Perils of Writing as a Woman on Women in Algeria." *Feminist Studies* 14, no. 1:81–107.

Leacock, Eleanor. 1980. "Montagnais Women and the Jesuit Program for Colonization." In *Women and Colonization: Anthropological Perspectives*, eds. Mona Etienne and Eleanor Leacock, 25–42. New York: Praeger.

Majid, Anouar. 1998. "The Politics of Feminism in Islam." *Signs: Journal of Women in Culture and Society* 23, no. 2: 321–61.

Maracle, Lee. 1996. *I Am Woman: A Native Perspective on Sociology and Feminism.* Vancouver: Press Gang Publishers.

McIvor, Sharon Donna. 1999. "Self-Government and Aboriginal Women." In *Scratching the Surface, Canadian Anti-Racist Feminist Thought*, eds. Enakshi Dua and Angela Robertson, 167–86. Toronto: Women's Press.

McLaren, Leah. 2001. "Wearing the Hijab: Walking Straight with Your Arms at Your Side." *Toronto Globe and Mail.* October 27.

McLaughlin, Lisa. 1991. "Discourses of Prostitution/Discourses of Sexuality." *Critical Studies in Mass Communication* 8, no. 2:249–72.

Mernissi, Fatema. 2001. *Scheherazade Goes West.* New York: Washington Square Press.

Meyers, Marian. 1997. *News Coverage of Violence against Women: Engendering Blame.* Thousand Oaks: Sage.

Moghadam, Valentine. 2001. "Afghan Women and Transnational Feminism." *Middle East Women's Studies Review* xvi, no. 3/4: 1–12.

Moghadam, Valentine M. 1999. "Revolution, Religion, and Gender Politics: Iran and Afghanistan Compared." *Journal of Women's History* 10, no. 4:172–95.

Monture-Angus, Patricia. 1995. *Thunder in My Soul: A Mohawk Woman Speaks.* Halifax: Fernwood Publishing.

Naficy, Hamid. 1998. "Narrowcasting in Diaspora: Middle Eastern Television in Los Angeles." In *Living Color: Race and Television in the United States,* ed. Sasha Torres, 82–96. Durham and London: Duke University Press.

Narayan, Uma. 1997. *Dislocating Cultures/Identities, Traditions and Third World Feminism.* London and New York: Routledge.

Nolen, Stephanie. 2001. "Under the Cover of Darkness." *Toronto Globe and Mail.* November 10.

Pitman, Beverley A. 2002. "Re-Mediating the Spaces of Reality Television: *America's Most Wanted* and the Case of Vancouver's Missing Women." *Environment and Planning A* 34, no. 1:167–84.

Portman, Tarrell Awe Agahe, and Roger D. Herring. 2001. "Debunking the Pocahontas Paradox: The Need for a Humanistic Perspective." *Journal of Humanistic Counseling and Development* 40, no. 2:195–99.

Pratt, Geraldine. 2005. "Abandoned Women and Spaces of Exception." *Antipode* 37, no. 5:1052–78.

Razack, Sherene. 1998. *Looking White People in the Eye: Gender, Race, and Culture in Courtrooms and Classrooms.* Toronto: University of Toronto Press.

———. 2002. "Gendered Racial Violence and Spatialized Justice." In *Race, Space, and the Law: Unmapping a White Settler Society,* ed. Sherene H. Razack, 121–56. Toronto: Between the Lines.

Said, Edward W. 1978. *Orientalism.* New York: Vintage.

Smith, Andrea. 2005. *Conquest, Sexual Violence and American Indian Genocide.* Cambridge, MA: South End Press.

Wente, Margaret. 2001. "The Taliban's Forgotten War on Women." *Toronto Globe and Mail.* September 20.

World Health Organization. 2002. "First Ever Global Report on Violence and Health Released." www.who.int/mediacentre/news/releases/pr73/en/ (accessed 10 July 2006).

Wynn Davies, Merryl, Ashis Nandy, and Ziauddin Sardar. 1993. *Barbaric Others: A Manifesto on Western Racism.* London: Pluto Press.

Yeğenoğlu, Meyda. 1998. *Colonial Fantasies: Towards a Feminist Reading of Orientalism.* Cambridge and Melbourne: Cambridge University Press.

CHAPTER TEN

From Religious Fundamentalism to Pornography? The Female Body as Text in Arabic Song Videos

Salam Al-Mahadin

The Merriam-Webster online dictionary[1] offers the following list of compound nouns when the word *woman* is keyed in: fancy woman, kept woman, old woman. The first two are provided with the following synonyms: harlot, blowen, courtesan, emimondaine, demimonde, demirep, hetaera, kept woman, paphian, whore. "Old woman" is listed with the following synonyms: mother, ma, mam, mama (*or* mamma), mammy, mater, mom, mommy, mummy, old lady. Conversely, the word *man* occurs on its own as a noun that connotes anything from the human race to policeman, and as a compound noun in lexical items such as con man, confidence man, fighting man, hatchet man, and man-at-arms.

This linguistic articulation reflects the discursive space occupied by the socially constituted binary oppositions of man–woman. A cursory look reveals several processes at work. The lexical item *woman* does not exist independent of an adjectival referent. She is not an objective general term of reference to an object that exists autonomously. The signifier redeems its signified from the list of associations created between the two; woman cannot be "defined" without the terms *kept, fancy,* or *old,* which subsume women under two rigid dichotomies, the whore and the mother. Paradoxically *man* is not etymologically invested with a restrictive or dichotomizing economy of delineation. He is infinite, multiple, diverse, complex, and omnipresent. Man is the unmarked script in social texts, but woman is indelibly marked to connote a double form of subjectivity—the mother and the whore.

146

I have chosen this dictionary entry as a point of departure due to its simple but shocking implications, which often manifest themselves in the culture industry of the Arab World (Al-Mahadin 2003; Brennan 1993). Juxtaposition of disparate discursive realities may often reveal this linguistic anchorage of women's subjectivities. The medium of song videos is not the exception, as I aim to demonstrate in a careful consideration of this art form, which has swept many other popular genres aside to dominate the Arab entertainment scene.

In this chapter, I resort to the reductionist term "Arab societies" or the "Arab world." I claim it to be a form of reductionism for the sheer banality of claiming that the Arab world lends itself as a unified field of discursive practices. However, the songs at hand cater for a precise form of essentialized audiences (Fuss 1989), in effect producing what I refer to as a pan-Arabist entertainment industry. It is quite ironical that leftist pan-Arabism has been witnessing a resurgence in the consumerist arena following its mainstream political demise post-1967,[2] which paved the way for the rise of the right-wing Islamist parties.[3] In this chapter, I explore how the female body politic has been inscribed along these two paradoxical axes: highly visible in the media public sphere but invisible in the real/social/private sphere. There has been an explosion of body displays in music videos (known as video clips in the Arab world) without a concomitant shift in "body mores" in the lives of millions of Arab women. That body is legitimate to be gazed upon in media displays but remains elusive to the real/social/private gaze. I explore the political economy of the female body in Arab media and attempt to create a nexus between that form of media subjectivity and the political, social, religious, and economic realities of the Arab societies. Although an ambitious aim, I believe it is essential to pose some questions and draw links, even if the scope of this chapter does not allow for full analysis.

Inscribing Bodies

According to the Arab Advisors Research Group, there are currently thirty-two Arabic music channels[4] broadcasting on the Nilesat and Arabsat (the two satellite system providers that cater to the Arab region) out of a total two hundred free-to-air (FTA) satellite channels.[5] Arab FTAs have boomed dramatically over the last decade.[6] Close to 100 million Arab viewers, out of a total population of 300 million, now have access to satellite TV.[7] Although "Arab satellite television stations and some newspapers and their websites have started to provide avenues for knowledge acquisition and for freedom of expression and opinion that were previously unattainable" (UNDP 2004, 147–48), satellite TV and its contents have been a double-edged sword whose reality has been marred by an array of social, political, and economic considerations. The claim that satellite TV has contributed to increased freedom of expression may be true about the dozen or so news channels that offer Arab viewers reprieve from the one-sided reporting they endured when television channels were the domain of autocratic governments and establishments. Although the latter still exist, viewers are most likely to tune in to stations like Aljazeera or Al-Arabiyya, which they view as "objective" compared with either state-owned television channels (Aqtash, Seif, and Seif 2004; Miles 2005) or Western news satellite channels.[8] Some even argue that channels like Aljazeera are creating public spheres that promote liberalization and reform in the Arab world (Lynch 2006a). The impact of news channels, however, cannot be assessed in isolation from the equally popular entertainment channels, particularly music channels.

In February 2005, the *Economist* published an article on the impact of satellite TV on the Arab world. The writer argues that satellite TV "has not simply exposed their [Arab] people to extremes of behaviour, from stark pornography to fervid fundamentalism . . . Satellite television has created a sense of belonging to, and participation in, a kind of virtual Arab metropolis."[9] In one of the early articles on the implications of the Arab music industry, Freund argues that "this new world of Arab videos is a pan-Arab project" (2005). Several notions come into play in these comments. On the one hand, there is a clear juxtaposition between "pornography" and "fervid fundamentalism"; sexual space is created as the antithesis of religious fundamentalism, its counterdiscourse and the "other" block in a binary opposition. On the other hand, both remarks suggest that satellite TV is acting as a homogenizing sphere; the creation and commodification of cultural objects serve to merge the realm of Arab "experience." This begs the question: what objects (signifiers) have been reproduced and invested with unifying signification to engender a hyper-Arab identity (signified)? How does the latter signified act as a new signifier whose own signified attempts to transgress, destroy, and deconstruct the purported evils of religious fundamentalism? How does the interplay between all these signifiers and signifieds serve a political, social, and economic agenda? To address these questions, I start with the valorization and eroticizing of the female body in one of the most controversial media phenomena to emerge in recent years—the video clip.

The explosion in the number of Arabic music channels has made "Arab music the cornerstone of Arab entertainment" (Aziz 2004). The music industry currently churns out hundreds of new video clips every month, broadcast round the clock on thirty-two music channels. The industry is dominated by Saudi capital (Bakir 2004), with wealthy Arab Gulf markets the main targets for commercial endeavors and advertising, even by satellite channels not owned by Saudi businessmen (Lynch 2006b). Music channels rely heavily on TV interactivity services as sources of revenue, including phone-ins, downloading ring tones, requesting songs via SMS (short messaging system), and SMS messages viewers send which are then displayed on a bar on the screen.

Some Arabic music channels can have up to three bars of messages running simultaneously on the screen. I have tried to obtain figures about revenues from TV interactivity, but none of the satellite stations would release these numbers, mainly because they are not public companies but are owned by wealthy Gulf sheiks or Arab businessmen.[10] They are therefore under no obligation to reveal these figures to the public, including researchers. It is not difficult, however, to conclude, based on the cost of interactive services displayed on the screen and the nonstop flow of messages and phone-ins, that these figures run into billions of dollars. Rotana Audiovisual, based in Saudi Arabia and owned by Prince Walid Bin Talal of Saudi Arabia, was established in 1987 and currently dominates most of the music industry in the Arab World (Bakir 2004, 45). More than a hundred top artists have signed contracts with Rotana Audiovisual to produce their albums and video clips. The company also owns six satellite TV channels, five of which are dedicated to broadcasting video clips round the clock, in addition to musical programs.

Rotana's satellite channels have revolutionized the genre of the video clip, chiefly in their production and display of the female body. The Arab/Muslim woman's body, fraught with religious and social taboos that have traditionally banished it from the public gaze, is now seen swaying provocatively and erotically to the tunes of Arabic songs, as the female singer or as the love interest of the male singer. Although not all songs are about love or feature "semi-naked women gyrating to music" (Davies 2005), the majority of these video clips depict "a voluptuous female swinging her body back and forth in an atmosphere torrid with sex" (Khairy 2005). Countless articles have appeared in the Arab media criticizing "the pornography in video clips".[11] It is common for female singers to bare as much flesh as possible in these videos and for male singers to be surrounded by a group of seminaked female dancers. The emphasis on the female body is evident from the often incongruent dissected close-ups of various body parts. The body as spectacle often dominates and takes over from the lyrics, the music, and even the narrative of the video clip. As Mulvey (1975) demonstrates in her seminal paper on visual pleasure and narrative cinema, the woman functions as an erotic object for the characters within the screen story and an erotic object for the spectator. In this case, the female singer is the erotic object of her male hero (often played by a very handsome model), the erotic object of the male singer when she is the dancer, and also the erotic object of the spectator in both cases. Although Mulvey's work focuses on the manner in which the cinematic narrative produces the female subjectivity and sexuality, her observations can, to a limited extent, be applied to these video clips.

Screen representations and codifications of the female body, argues Mulvey, juxtapose the male viewer and the protagonist in a moment of identification geared toward the reconciliation of the ego-ideal of the viewer. Drawing upon

Lacan's mirror stage—where the child's own reflection in the mirror represents a perfect ideal he strives for—Mulvey argues that the male spectator/viewer perceives the male movie star as the perfect, complete, and "more powerful ideal ego conceived in the original moment of recognition" (1975, 8). The iconic value of the female body thus becomes one for both the protagonist and the male spectator. She is displayed for the gaze of the male—both within and outside the screen. Situating the female body within the annals of Freudian psychoanalysis, Mulvey mediates the signification of the body through phallic castration. The female figure evokes the castration complex; her lack of penis is the organizing principle, according to both Freud and Lacan, which provides the male entry into the symbolic order and the law of the father. Mulvey posits two avenues through which the male unconscious escapes phallic castration on the screen: the investigation and demystification of the woman's mystery and the fetishization of the female body through, for example, the creation of the cult of the female star. Both avenues secure control of the female body and alleviate castration anxieties. Cinematic representations of the female are an extension of the signifying process and discursive practices of patriarchal societies. By projecting the woman as a sexual object, she becomes the bearer of meaning constructed by the male gaze.

Uncovering patterns of signification on the screen can hardly be exhaustive without contextualizing modes of spectacle creation. Nor is it possible to generalize based on Mulvey's work on Hollywood movies. I propose, therefore, to expand the horizons of excessive spectatorial desire/sexuality, as evident in the video clips at hand, to include two more types of castration: hymenic castration and political castration. I will demonstrate the inevitability of sociopoliticizing the female body within the ideological constructs that drive both the screen spectacle and counter-spectacle of an assumed Arab reality. The discursive embeddedness of the female body resists the notion that there could be an overarching psychoanalytic narrative that reduces and resigns the situatedness of the body on the screen to the annals of patriarchal discourse. Mulvey's formulations about phallic castration, while beneficial, may obscure the subjectivity construction of the female body within other non-Western contexts where the female body is a constant site of different and various forms of struggle.

Polarizing the Female Body:
Hymenic and Political Castration

Screen representations of the female body in video clips have been controversial for the simple reason that they have "visiblized" hitherto invisible biospaces. To a large extent, the problematization of the sudden emergence of the female body as spectacle has been confined to traditional debates stemming from religious and moral considerations. In societies where the female body is expected to be veiled and hidden, the genre of the video clip has become the metonymy of moral depravity, explaining why video clips have been described as a new form of soft pornography which aims to destroy the social fiber of Arab societies. The debate has not gone further than accusing the video clip producers of attempting to enforce Western liberal values on traditional societies. Reading and hearing arguments advanced by opponents of this new genre, one cannot help but feel that video clips are isolated instances of consumerism where sex sells. These debates, moreover, exemplify the process of approaching the body of the female as a literal statement rather than questioning its iconographic and compositional signification through contextualization and, in this instance, polarization. Adopting Mulvey's phallic castration complex as a point of departure, I now explore the other two types of castration proposed above, hymenic castration and political castration, and their relationship to both the female and male subjectivities, rather than to the male ego-ideal. Before I note those differences, I emphasize that this is not a purely psychoanalytic approach to these forms of castration but rather a theorization about the female body as a discursive space and spectacle, as it relates to male-female symbiosis and power-relations, as evidenced by these video clips and their impact.

Prior to and during the emergence of the highly sexualized female body in video clips in the Arab world, that body was invested with many social and religious taboos, chief among them the circularity of honor. A woman's body is the repository of man's honor. Her hymen exists in a double bind: a metonym whose physical presence in the female body is essential for its extension as a metonym of male honor. She is the bearer of meaning insofar as her body (as sister, daughter, or wife) remains chaste and invisible except to those who have the legitimate right to gaze upon it. In this context, a women's virginity is a presence whose absence creates hymenic castration. The loss of her virginity signifies a loss of male honor. Women consist of three layered cores: the heart, the uterus, and the vagina, with an entrance to all three that should never be removed by anything but a legitimate gatekeeper. The female body is paradoxically visible and invisible: visible as a male self-qualifier but invisible as a woman self-signifier. The veil thus may gave the illusion of invisibility, but it functions as a stark, visible sign which imposes discursive boundaries to allay the anxiety of male hymenic castration. The most brutal form of hymenic castration are honor killings, where, with the loss of her virginity and the absence thereof, the whole body is deemed dispensable, discursively annihilated and thus physically removed in order for male honor to be present again. Hymenic castration can operate on a more disturbing level when a woman engages in illicit sexual activities, even if she is already divorced or widowed and by default had no hymen, or even if those activities did not lead to the loss of the hymen.

In this instance, the symbolism of the hymen loses it metonymic value and covers the whole expanse of the body; thus her morality is not physically invested in a hymen but in forms of conduct. The relationship between her body and her morality/hymen is enmeshed in an iconic relationship between signifier and signified. By default, her morality replaces her hymen as a metonym of male honor.

This complex semiotic matrix of the female body is represented in a *dispositif*,[12] which disciplines and governs her conduct within socially recognized schemata of knowledge. Epistemes codified in women's magazines, advertisements, commercials, TV dramas, school curricula, social mores, and institutionalized physical structures of segregations and veiling all articulate that matrix's grid of intelligibility. Video clips are a decisive break from these valorized representations of the female body. This is not to argue that women had not been previously represented in a manner similar to that in video clips, such as in some Egyptian movies, for example, nor does it suggest that all women in the Arab world are veiled and do not wear "revealing" items of clothing. What singles out and problematizes video clips as a major phenomenon, however, is their ubiquity, their situatedness within a new political economy of gender, and their transgression and apparent rupturing of the screen/public discursive boundaries of the female body. More important, they emerged at a time when political castration (the third type, which I discuss next) had eclipsed certain ideologies and rationalized new ones.

Political castration is at once a repressive and a productive form of power. In the Foucauldian sense, it has produced functionalities of power that have constructed gender relations along certain axes which cannot simply be reduced to the proverbial reference to patriarchy. In the repressive sense, political castration in the Arab world is reference to the absence of political freedoms. There are no electoral democracies in the Arab world (Karatnycky 1999). According to the *Arab Human Development Report of 2004* (AHDR), Arab people "are besieged in their own country, their takeoff is held back, their development is blocked and their nation is weakened" (UNDP 2004, iii). Civil liberties and political freedoms constitute the biggest area of deficiency. The authoritarian nature of Arab government and governmentality has been immune to the democratization processes that have engulfed other world regions since the 1970s (Dalacoura 2006). What is of concern to this chapter, however, are the parallels one can draw between the extreme polarity of the female body as spectacle in video clips (and regimes of truth surrounding that body in social contexts) and the similar polarity that exists between authoritarian regimes and emerging Islamic fundamentalist movements: in other words—the points of convergence between hymenic castration and political castration. It is therefore essential to address the virtual absence of left-wing politics in the Arab world, which I argue, underpins the discursive rather than the psychoanalytic manifestations of Eros (sex) and Thanatos (death) in both instances of castration.

Irrespective of local contextualized nuances, there has been a definite rise in right-wing Islamic movements and parties in the Arab world, especially following the 1967 war in which Israel occupied the West Bank of Palestine, the Sinai Desert in Egypt, and the Golan Heights in Syria. The war in effect made the Arab masses believe that leftist parties and politicians, especially secular Nasserite politics in Egypt, had not only failed to liberate lands occupied by Israel in 1948 but had lost even more lands in the 1967 war. Even prior to that, left-wing parties had taken a serious hammering in almost all monarchical Arab countries, who feared that secular ideologies like pan-Arabism, Baathism, Nasserism, Marxism, and Communism constituted serious threats to their frail legitimacy, which was the product of colonial division of the Arab world into smaller states in the aftermath of World War I. The 1970s and 1980s witnessed an Islamic renaissance, often with the blessing of some authoritarian states, either because the people shifted toward a right-wing form of politics in search of political inspiration or solace from harsh social and economic conditions brought about by the advent of capitalist market economies[13] (often for the economic benefit of the elitist few), or because Arab countries wished to ward off the threat of left-wing parties. In countries like Jordan, for example, the Muslim Brotherhood was allowed to flourish and carry out many projects of a social or religious nature, even after the declaration of martial law and the banning of all political parties in the late 1950s. The Jordanian establishment's symbiotic relationship with the Muslim Brotherhood was born out of both parties' desire not to see any secular Arab-nationalist movements secure a popular base. On a popular level, the Islamic revival was not deterred by some states cracking down on Islamic movements, as in Syria, Egypt, and Iraq. In the final analysis, the left took a back seat, while the right continued to rise, albeit in various popular and political forms in the Arab world. The lack of democratic reforms and the absence of political liberalizations impacted left-wing parties; they slowly disintegrated into either single-party authoritarian states like Syria and Iraq or disappeared completely from the political arena. The rise of "Muslim democracy" (Nasr 2005) through electoral politics in Islamic countries like Turkey, Iran, Malaysia, Bangladesh, and Indonesia should not be considered a trend that applies to the Arab world as well. Despite the success of some Islamic parties to legislative seats in Jordan and Egypt, for example, democracy was not consolidated to allow these legislative councils to wield any real power in those countries.

As Islamic ideologies slowly took root in the Arab world, a new form of Islamism was hurled into the limelight in the post-9/11 era of world order, namely, Islamic extremism, purportedly a cocktail of violence, terror, and suicide bombings. The era of terrorism as spectacle arrived, along with dialogical relations between terror and religion. The inescapable nature of this indissoluble link between Islam and violence is located in discursive practices in the aftermath of 9/11. Media spectacles and texts ingrained by means of repetition and ritualized narratives continuously conjured up the good versus evil dichotomy propagated by the U.S. administration. Making sense of 9/11 naturally required simplification and reductionism, in order for a mainstream audience to "comprehend" why such an atrocity occurred. As narratives legitimating retaliation circulated, a parallel sequence of signs created new sets of associations and binary oppositions: Islam versus freedom, Islam versus the West, Islam and violence versus the West and freedom, Islam, violence, self-sacrifice versus West, freedom, life. The spectacle, as Debord (2005) argues, often creates its own reality. The new reality was one where terrorism seemed to be on the rise to combat the feelings of resentment at U.S. epistemic and practical violence in the region. As millions watched their governments collaborate with the U.S. in the war against "terror," the occupation of Iraq, and the U.S.'s biased position vis-a-vis Israel, resentment grew along with trends leaning toward the right. The left has long been dead. In lieu of the left, a pseudo-liberal consumer culture has risen in the Arab world, at the same time as "terror" became reduced to "Islam" on the international canvas of simplification and reductionism. Although many debates, conferences, and books have been held and written to attempt to locate the roots of terrorism and arrive at a common definition, terrorism, in the mind of many, denotes death by violence but connotes Islam.

Suicide bombings have become the transcendent symbol of the ritualized violence of Islam. They have departed from their real object, which is the context of political disenchantment, oppression, repression, and U.S. foreign-policy bias, which determined self-sacrifice as the ultimate form of resistance. Self-annihilation or suicide bombings operate now as a self-contained narrative, juxtaposed within media discourse with U.S. ideals of "freedom, life and democracy." In their ultimate form, they are an absolute structured elucidation of evil in the good/evil binary opposition. The genealogy of the morality of suicide bombings is almost always absent. The immolation of both self and enemy exists in the vacuum of a decontextualized narrative. In this sense, Thanatos as a drive toward death to escape angst has been discursively encoded as a psychoneurotic trend rather than as a strategy of survival and resistance.[14] In the same schemata of knowledge, Eros, or the drive toward life, including its extreme forms of hedonism and sexual gratification, has been utilized by Arab mainstream media to palliate the impact of extreme fundamentalism. Arab satellite channels are either geared toward entertainment via the body of the female or steeped in religious discourse—an observation easily verified by quickly scanning the hundreds of channels currently available to Arab viewers (Atwan 2006). The Arab satellite entertainment industry serves a double purpose: to promote a pseudoliberal consumer culture, through which billions of dollars are reaped through commercials, SMS text messaging, phone-ins, and other interactive services, and to successfully utilize eroticism to sway a whole generation of youngsters to minimize resistance to authoritarianism and lack of political freedoms in the Arab world, while at the same time combating religious revival and some of its extreme forms.[15] The renowned Arab journalist Abdel Bari Atwan summarized this view on the occasion of World Press Freedom Day:

> The phenomenon of targeting the coming generations and stripping their identities will unfortunately increase because the oil revenues that are employed in this work are increasing day after day and month after month. The numbers indicate that more than $500B enter the Arabic treasuries (of the states) that produce oil, every year. And their explicit American instructions (are) to sink the markets with satellites channels, because this is the most influential means by which to brainwash the coming generations, cleansing from them any Arabic or Islamic trends which stick to dignity and moral codes and confront the humiliation and the project or domination project faced by the (Arab and Muslim) nation today. (Atwan 2006)

Atwan's remarks reflect the post-9/11 reality of the Arab entertainment industry with the aid of what he refers to as oil money and U.S. instructions. Whether this is entirely true or not, the fact remains that the entertainment industry is seen to be completely divorced from the political contingencies of the Arab world, unifying audiences within the confines of mindless escapism and apathy.

Public/Private Consumption of Bodies

The "government" of the female body in political and hymenic castration is dominated by the semiotic technologies of both Eros and Thanatos as discursive practices rather than psychoanalytic ones. The biopolitics that govern the conduct of the Arab woman disciplines the Eros and confines it to the private sphere to mitigate male honor/absence anxiety. The legitimating discourses of *femicide* act as interdictions, which produce female subjectivity along the axis of male honor through the constant threat of death. Some may argue that honor killings are quite rare in terms of actual official figures, but what concerns me is the disciplinary power of legitimating and codifying honor killings within both social and legal schemata. The latter schemata govern the lives and conduct of millions of Arab women. Thus, the normalizing judgment of the law of the hymenic castration acts within a machinery of power that manipulates the female body's elements, behavior, conduct, deportment, and value. The "docile" female body is its ultimate goal, hence the anatomo-politics in both social and media realities.

The incommensurable paradigms that have arisen with video clips should not, however, be seen as a rupture of the order of the female body nor as a fresh ethics of existence which resists the epistemes that govern that body. The Freedom House Report on women in the Middle East (2005) revealed that "a substantial deficit in women's rights exists in every country reviewed . . . and is reflected in practically every institution of society: the law, the criminal justice system, the economy, education, health care, and the media." The same findings were reported in the AHDR of 2005 (UNDP 2005). Rather than be viewed as a discontinuity or a suspension of disciplinary permanence, these video clips should be examined within the wider genealogy of politico-economic paradigms. It is just as essential to consider how pseudoliberal consumerism has been reconciled with schemata governing "docile" bodies through the channels of private versus public spheres to reinstitutionalize, perpetuate, and reproduce the same level of docility to avoid disrupting the social order of female subjectivity.

To illustrate this point, I consider one of the few academic studies on the image of the woman in Arabic video clips. Berenger and El-Nimr (2005) analyzed twenty-one video clips for the portrayal of women in terms of tight clothing, parts of the body revealed (shoulders, legs, cleavage, back, arms, navel), camera shots of various parts of the female body, makeup, facial movements (seductive smiles, winks, alluring pouts), types of dancing (belly dancing, movements of hips, waists, buttocks), and the female singer's interaction with male models (hugging, kissing, cuddling, touching). Presenting their findings in percentages, they conclude that video clips perpetuate stereotypes of women as sex symbols; the alluring and seductive depictions of women in video clips is geared solely toward profit making. The study is valuable for its deviations from generalizations about the "pornographic" nature of video clips toward a more systematic analysis, albeit content-based, of the portrayal of the female body in the clips. But these findings are not enough to elucidate how these depictions have been consolidated within existing schemata, in effect becoming collusive with dynamics of veiled bodies rather than discontinuous and rupturous of them.

To examine the politico-economic schemata that govern the production and consumption of those bodies, I divide both the public and private spheres of consumption into public-public, public-private, private-public, and private-private. The ubiquity of female bodies has extended to every public sphere of entertainment in the Arab world, but the explosion of bodies as a media spectacle has not been accompanied by a similar shift in social attitudes. The female space that has been publicized has also been fetishized, transforming those bodies into consumable products, ideal beauties, and spaces to be gazed upon but not mimicked in the social sphere. Thus the public image of those bodies is an invocation of the whore/mother dichotomy, whereby public bodies can be consumed as a fantasy, while the bodies of the sister, mother, daughter remain cloaked, veiled, and invisible in the public sphere. This is what is suggested by the terms public-public and public-private. Going back to Mulvey's formulation, phallic castration is replaced by hymenic castration, but the means of alleviating anxiety are different. In Mulvey's argument, fetishistic scopophilia—the fetishization of the female on the screen—alleviates the anxiety of phallic castration. The fetishization of the female body in Arab video clips, however, legitimates gazing at the female body as spectacle, through assigning her a definitive role within a clearly structured binary opposition. The screen "whore" is "othered" and displaced from the honor/absence anxiety. She exists in the realm of the spectacle, in the domain of the unreal, which does not transgress into the private sphere, except as an object to be enjoyed, desired, and gazed upon. The bodies of these women (sister, mother, daughter, wife) are not subject to the same displacement and should therefore remain invisible in the public sphere.

In the domain of the private sphere, two other subspheres may be discerned. The private-private is best exemplified in the relationship between the man and his wife, the legitimate body he is entitled to gaze upon. What has been most interesting about the rise of fetishized bodies on the screen is a similar rise in consumer trends that sell "real" women dreams of the ideal beauty through fashion, makeup, perfumes, and even plastic surgery.[16] Screen narratives are transferred into the private sphere, where they are legitimated and consumed.

Bodies are not deconstructed by the purported soft pornography of the screen but rather are reshaped by the annals of a new disciplinary branch of consumer culture that deconstructs the powers of the right, manufactures false consumption trends, and provides an outlet in societies generally characterized by sexual repression. Both nudity on the screen and the veil visibilize, discipline, and taxonomize; thus neither can claim to rupture and resist the other. Indeed, the symbiotic relationship between the two has been balanced out in a narrative that supports existing patriarchal regimes of truth, authoritarian systems of government, and a rising pseudoliberal consumer culture. Both fetishized screen bodies and veiled ones are parts of the field of the intelligible, where they are interrogated, problematized, and forced to signify. They both exist within the disciplinary and regulating schemata of discourse/knowledge, which may represent polarized codifications of the female body but can in reality be incorporated under the same political anatomy.

The last sphere, the private-public, is perhaps the one most neglected by researchers and one that remains outside the disciplinary regimes of truth that dominate the other three spheres. The private-public is that arena where the female body acts outside the intelligible, the known, the spoken-about, the discussed, the taxonomized, the controlled, and the disciplined. This is the arena where the body of the female is exposed to other females in the private sphere. Women's communities and rituals associated with them exhibit relationships to one's body and that of the others different from that of male communities. A striking example is that of sugaring, a ritual where two or more women engage in removing the excess body hair of, usually, a female customer. The naked body of the female customer lies outside the intelligible *dispositif* of the other three spheres. It is assigned new domains of self-recognition, self-definition, and self-actualization, not as a prediscursive body but rather as a self-signifying one. This explains why women are comfortable experiencing each other's bodies in ritualized communities but the same cannot be said about men. This is not to argue that the private-public is a return to a prediscursive transcendental *a priori* nature, but it is rather an arena where the body constructs itself and those of the others outside the sexualization dogma of intelligible disciplinary discourses. This may demonstrate why flaunting bodies on the screen cannot be examined as rupture and discontinuity of the veiled body. Resistance is not about developing new moments of sexuality in which the body is exhibited and exposed as spectacle, as has been done within the stifling confines of the intelligible consumer culture of the mass media. Resistance lies in reshaping the space that is feminine through the desexualization of body rituals in a moment where the *ethics of existence* are self-defined and self-constructed. The scope of this chapter does not allow for further elaboration of this argument, but I believe there is much that can be learned about the ritualized aspects of women's communities in the production of female subjectivity as a resisting entity.

This chapter has argued for the destabilization of the binaric dichotomizing trends that have posited depictions of female bodies in Arabic video clips as discontinuous and rupturous of veiled bodies. These trends have obscured the importance of situating the rise of the alluring female in video clips within a wider political anatomy, where patriarchal discourse is one of many discursive practices that govern the conduct and deportment of the female body. Admittedly the variables put forth by this chapter are wide in scope and complexity, but it is hoped that the argument will encourage a departure from the hitherto synechdochally limited paradigms of the female body. As a discursively malleable space, possibly even the most important biospace, the female body is the "exemplary problem" (Fuss 1989, 36–45) and an arena where ideological struggles have been mapped and fought in the Arab world. Thus the private and public corporeality of her body should be investigated as overlapping spheres of power within the knowledge and governmentality of both her subjectivity, that of her male-guardian, and the ethics of existence of both of them as citizens.

Notes

1. See www.m-w.com.

2. In 1967, Israel occupied the West Bank of Palestine after occupying the coastal areas of Palestine in 1948. Often referred to as *al- Nakba* (the catastrophe), the loss of the West Bank is considered a turning point in the history of the Arab region.

3. For more on the Islamic resurgence, see Yvonne Y. Haddad, John O. Voll, and John L. Esposito, *The Contemporary Islamic Revival: A Critical Survey and Bibliography* (New York: Greenwood Press, 1991); John L. Esposito, *Islam and Politics*, 3d ed. (Syracuse: Syracuse University Press, 1991); John L. Esposito, ed., *Islam in Asia: Religion, Politics and Society* (New York: Oxford University Press, 1987); James P. Piscatori, ed., *Islam in the Political Process* (New York: Cambridge University Press, 1983); and Nazih Ayubi, *Political Islam: Religion and Politics in the Arab World* (New York: Routledge, 1991).

4. Interview with Judeh Siwady, research analyst at Arab Advisors Group in Amman, Jordan, on 23 January 2006. See also Arab Advisors Group Newsletter, "The Arab World's Sat TV Boom Continues," July 14, 2005, www.arabadvisors.com/Pressers/presser-140705.htm (accessed 20 February 2006).

5. Arab Advisors Group Newsletter, "Pay TV Packages in the Arab world have an average cost of US $29 per Month," December 8, 2005. www.arabadvisors.com/Pressers/presser-081205.htm (accessed 22 February 2006).

6. Siwady, interview.

7. Siwady, interview. The figure varies dramatically between countries. In Saudi Arabia, for example, 89 percent of households have access to satellite TV, compared with 46 percent in Egypt and 5 percent in Somalia.

8. Arab Advisor Group, "Al Jazeera Viewers Base in Saudi Arabia is 5 Times Larger than the United States–Sponsored AlHurra's Audience." www.ameinfo.com/56546.html (accessed February 2006).

9. "The World Through Their Eyes," *Economist* 374, no. 8415 (February 2005): 23–25.

10. Siwady, interview.

11. "Arab Pop Video: 'Weapon of Singing Destruction'?" CBS 2003, wcbstv.com/entertainment/entertainment_story_296202634.html (accessed 10 September 2005); Bakir, "Repenting for the Sins"; Abdel Wahab M. Elmessiri, "Ruby and the Chequered Heart," *Al-Ahram Weekly*, http://weekly.ahram.org.eg/2005/734/feature.htm (accessed 9 September 2005).

12. *Dispositif* is a French word translated as "deployment" in English translations of Michel Foucault's books. The term refers to the network of practices and institutions that combine with epistemes (discourses operative in a context) to produce knowledge and webs of power relations.

13. Graham E. Fuller, *A Sense of Siege: The Geopolitics of Islam and the West* (New York: Westview Press, 1995); Thomas J. Butko, "Revelation or Revolution: A Gramascian Approach to the Rise of Political Islam," *British Journal of Middle Eastern Studies* 31, no. 1 (May 2004): 141–62; Carrie Rosefsky Wickham, *Mobilizing Islam* (New York: Columbia University Press, 2002).

14. Some have argued that Islam is inherently violent and evil rather than situate suicide bombings within a political context.

15. Atwan, "View from an Arab Newsroom"; Abdel Wahab Elmessiri, "Video Clips, Bodies and Globalisation," *Al-Ahram*, 8 April 2004, 20.

16. Hasan Hatrash, "Demand for Plastic Surgery on the Rise," *Arab News*, 7 May 2006, 5; Al-Jazeera, "Women and Fashion in Arab Societies" For Women Only, 13 June 2005, www.aljazeera.net/channel/archive/archive?ArchiveId=126885 (accessed 27 January 2007).

References

Al-Mahadin, Salam. 2003. "Gender Representations and Stereotypes in Cartoons: A Jordanian Case Study." *Feminist Media Studies* 3, no. 2:131–52.

Aqtash, Nashat A., Anna Seif, and Ahmed Seif. 2004. "Media Coverage of Palestinian Children and the Intifada." *International Communication Gazette* 29, no. 5:383–409.

Atwan, Abdel Bari. 2006. "View from an Arab Newsroom: Terrorising the Arab Media." *TBS Journal* 2006. www.tbsjournal.com/Atwan.html (accessed 10 July 2006)

Aziz, Moataz Abdul. 2004. "Arabic Music Videos and their Implications in the Realm of Arab Media." *Global Media Journal*. http://lass.calumet.purdue.edu/cca/gmj/fa04/graduatefa04/gmj-fa04grad-aziz.htm (accessed 22 August 2005).

Bakir, Mona. 2004. "Repenting for the Sins of Video Clips by Attending Religious Sessions." *Rose El Youssef* 78, no. 3975:43–48.

Berenger, Ralph D., and Dalia El Nimr. 2005. "Cultural Appropriateness of Music Video Clips in the Middle East." Paper prepared for the Association for Education in Journalism and Mass Communication, San Antonio, Texas, August.

Brennan, Teresa. 1993. *History After Lacan*. New York and London: Routledge.

Dalacoura, Katerina. 2006. "Islamist Terrorism and the Middle East Democratic Deficit: Political Exclusion, Repression and Causes of Extremism." *Democratisation* 13, no. 3:508–25.

Davies, Humphrey. 2005. "Video Venom Must Stop!" *TBS Journal* 2005. www.tbsjournal.com/Archives/Spring05/davies.html (accessed 20 March 2006).

Debord, Guy. 2005. *Society of the Spectacle*, trans. Ken Knabb. London: Rebel Press.

Freedom House. 2005. *Report on Women in the Middle East 2005*. www.freedomhouse.org (accessed 25 May 2006).

Freund, Charles P. 2003. "Look Who Is Rocking the Casbash: The Revolutionary Implications of Arab Music Videos." *Reasononline*. www.reason.com/0306/cr.cf.look.shtml (accessed 1 March 2005).

Fuss, Diana. 1989. *Essentially Speaking: Feminism, Nature and Difference*. New York: Routledge.

Karatnycky, Adrian. 1999. "The Decline of Illiberal Democracy." *Journal of Democracy* 10, no. 1:112–25.

Khairy, Amina. 2005. "Arabic Video Clips Flirt with Desires of Egyptian Youth." *TBS Journal*. www.tbsjournal.com/Archives/Spring05/khairy.html (accessed 21 March 2006).

Lynch, Marc. 2006a. *Voices of the New Arab Public: Iraq, Al Jazeera and Middle East Politics Today*. New York: Columbia University Press.

———. 2006b. " 'Reality Is Not Enough': The Politics of Arab Reality TV." *TBS Journal*. www.tbsjournal.com/Archives/Spring05/lynch.html (accessed 20 March 2006b).

Miles, Hugh. 2005. *Al Jazeera: How Arab TV News Challenges America*. New York: Grove Press.

Mulvey, Laura. 1975. "Visual Pleasure and Narrative Cinema." *Screen* 16, no. 3:6–18.

Nasr, Vali. 2005. "The Rise of 'Muslim Democracy'." *Journal of Democracy* 16, no. 2:13–27.

United Nations Development Programme. 2004. *The Arab Human Development Report 2004: Towards Freedom in the Arab World*. New York: United Nations Publications.

CHAPTER ELEVEN

Female Faces in the Millennium Development Goals: Reflections in the Mirrors of Media

Nancy Van Leuven, C. Anthony Giffard,
Sheryl Cunningham, and Danielle Newton

We are on a journey—a journey for equality, development and peace for all women everywhere in the interest of humanity. . . . The challenge we face in 2005 and beyond is to turn these lofty words into deeds.

—Thoraya A. Obaid[1]

Women are everywhere in the communication of international relief and development. No longer the "other" in the dust-wash of poverty, they are now the known. We see them in photographs of the poorest of the poor in Africa, and they appear in the latest headlines about the race to "save" that continent. We hear the stern voices of United Nations spokespeople, expounding the reality of doom. We listen to television ads or news reports of the well-meaning privileged who aim to make poverty history. We are inundated with the dire statistics of an impoverished continent whose mothers are choking on its dirt: today, most of the absolute poor are women, living on less than one dollar a day; two thirds of the world's illiterate are female, over 584 million women; and a woman living in sub-Saharan Africa has a one in 16 chance of dying in pregnancy, compared to a one in 3,700 risk for a North American woman (UNFPA 2005).

A combination of methods is essential for the study of artifacts such as mass media texts in our work toward solving feminist concerns about scholarship. For instance, qualitative methods enhance data through in-depth reading, comparative methods are sensitive to complex issues of diversity, and quantitative methods can condense data and study relationships among variables (Ragin 1994, 76–93, 132–66). Yet feminist methodology is much more than scholarship related to but separate from race and class; it is also the acknowledgment of lived experience that often becomes a talisman for social change (Fonow and Cook 2005). Since the feminist wave of the 1970s, feminists have attempted to intervene in social science research, even though feminist discourse is marginal to mainstream debates (Khan 2005). Harding and Norberg (2005, 209) contend that "these theorists and researchers have argued that conventional standards for 'good research' discriminate against or empower specific social groups no less than do the policies of legal, economic, military, educational, welfare, and health-care institutions; in fact, these standards actually enable the practices of these institutions."

Because feminist research is focused on justice for women, scholarship must address the challenge of what constitutes knowledge and the knowledge base without trivializing cultural symbols. Feminist methods also question the usefulness of "using the master's tools to dismantle the master's house" (Lorde 1984), an understatement for the problem of researchers striving for both objectivity and social change. For instance, a comprehensive research design is concerned with how texts organize power, how texts present organizational practices, and how texts act socially to organize knowledge by inscribing lived experiences into textual forms (Fair 1996, 3). Plus, keeping the current debate about unequal news flows in mind, it is important to consider how Northern empirical studies might also include indigenous knowledge apart from an imperialist paradigm (Mohanty 2004, 33–37, 231–38.).

Despite multiple audiences for our work, we must build an argument that examines how notions of ideology or hegemony operate in discussions of agency; for instance, are newspaper producers or marginalized media consumers seen as having agency or as being agents in the communication process? Or are news media participants merely hegemonic dupes, simply reproducing the strategies of elites without the transparency assumed in media systems? In this chapter we suggest that media consumers are not necessarily cultural dupes, but that representations of women in news do emphasize certain meanings over others and that, in this case, media producers make a troubling distinction between woman and mother.

These are crucial considerations, but how does information reach a global audience? Consider how news agencies, as custodians of facts and as global storytellers, represent international development issues, specifically those concerning women. We begin by summarizing the United Nations' Millennium Development Goals (MDGs) as an unprecedented global pact that builds upon other international agreements and considering how each goal relates to women. Next, we review media's role in today's global environment, including how producers help construct world opinion through issue framing. We then summarize how news agencies, as the wholesalers of news, operate to disseminate information throughout the world and why five specific news agencies were selected for this study. By placing this analysis within a human-rights framework, we argue that media producers routinely overlook issues of women's empowerment and equality, especially issues such as reproductive and sexual rights, which are at the heart of development.

The Millennium Development Goals and Women

The eight Millennium Development Goals were described by then UN Secretary General Kofi Annan as "an unprecedented promise by world leaders to address, as a single package, peace, security, development, human rights and fundamental freedoms" (UN 2005). These goals offer a precious chance for global agendas to be framed in a common language and with transparent benchmarks to gauge how countries are progressing. They are also reinforced by previous agreements, such as the Fourth World Conference on Women (in Beijing). And, because all UN members are involved, it is a closely watched process to see which states will attain their targets and which are falling short, especially in areas of gender inequality and violence against women.

The first seven goals focus on reducing poverty in all its forms—including disparities in education, health, and environmental sustainability—while the eighth prescribes how to achieve the first seven through economic and other growth policies. Specifically, the goals are (1) Eradicate extreme poverty and hunger; (2) Achieve universal primary education; (3) Promote gender equality and empower women; (4) Reduce child mortality; (5) Improve maternal health; (6) Combat HIV/AIDS, malaria, and other diseases; (7) Ensure environmental sustainability; and (8) Develop a global partnership for development (UN 2005; Population Action 2005).

In this chapter, we expand upon previous media studies that illustrate how gender and power form the subtext of media discourse surrounding international development. This research also builds upon previous studies of news coverage about women, including several that conclude that news coverage in developing countries is most often gender-based discourse, with women positioned as a theoretical focus of maternal, sexual, or reproductive terms (WMSC 2001). As global mechanisms of change, the MDGs are perceived by some as a switch to including women as decision makers instead of an embrace of traditionally patriarchal approaches, which construct culturally victimized "others" requiring "help" (Wilkins 2005). Such emphasis on "empowerment" of women is a recognized development theory, which advocates self-reliance to ensure equity, with "women's subordination seen as a problem not only of men but also of colonial and neo-colonial oppression" (Moser 1993, 56–57). Considering the highly publicized UN commitment to women's rights, it is logical to study frames within coverage of the MDGs because of their inclusion of rights and equality agendas generally held by feminists (Terkildsen and Schnell 1997). And, because the UN declares that every goal is directly related to women's rights, it is also important to analyze news frames as agents of socialization, including issues that contest or support constructions of culture and gender (Gill 2004). That is, less than ten years before the MDG target date of 2015, how do media frame the goals in terms of the marginalization or empowerment of women?

Traditional Media in Today's Developing World

As communicators have long known, people form opinions and make decisions based on their received information. And there are many actors involved in the process of providing information, ranging from those who make the news to those who report it, as well as those who determine how that information is distributed. As chief providers of shortcuts to information, media producers are central actors, framing such transnational human issues as poverty, education, and health for the global public. Media framing is defined as "selecting and highlighting some facets of events or issues, and making connections among them so as to promote a particular interpretation, evaluation, and/or solution" (Entman 2004, 4–7). News media thus guide opinions and judgments by emphasizing certain facts of issues, especially since many have no firsthand experience with global issues such as abject poverty (Lind and Salo 2005). And because the perspectives of reporters who compile and write the stories continually shift, how they construct frames also bends and shapes what global citizens learn and believe about our world (Jamieson and Waldman 2003, 77–98). Current research questions whether increasingly corporate media are shaping society's attitudes toward the male point of view (MediaChannel 2006). Not only does media-generated information influence public opinion, but it also plays a significant role in how elite decision makers approach a particular policy or project (Robinson 2002, 37). How media present news is crucial because their ability to present both "broad" and "deep" news may influence certain powerful individuals as well as collective worldwide opinion, with proven links between what individuals believe and what is embedded within their political and cultural societies (World Values Surveys 2004).

According to UN official Hilary Benn, media play an enormous role in influencing international development as well as our personal beliefs, being the "mirror we hold up to ourselves—that has an enormously powerful part to play in helping to make this happen, both in what we call 'the North', and in 'the

South' where so many people bear the brunt of poverty" (Benn 2004). This role is partially played by news agencies, which supply many newspapers and TV and radio stations with the same stories, effectively spreading reports into new areas. Local outlets pull the stories for local distribution, meaning that one story may be picked up throughout the world, often reaching an announcer for community radio or other local outlets. And, with more people hearing the same message over several forms of media, news agencies can help create an echo effect which strengthens information circuits and also magnifies the privileging of specific information.

In addition, news agencies provide a crucial filter in today's informational overload (Read 2001). They represent "communication appropriate to the informational and relational needs of the state, capital, and civic society in modernity" (Boyd-Barrett 1977). According to a former editor for the *New York Times*, news agencies "unquestioningly distribute the greatest share of news about what is taking place in the developing world" (Altschull 1985, 35).

Several recent studies demonstrate the role and benefits of media in promoting social change. New technologies allow news agencies to reach the public directly through online databases, thus bringing development news out of official offices and into homes and libraries around the world (Hancock 2000). And, according to a recent economic report, vulnerable citizens such as the poor and hungry fare better in states with higher levels of media development; specifically, a 1.1 percent increase in newspaper circulation results in a 2.4 percent increase in public food distribution and a 5.5 percent increase in relief expenditures for natural disasters (Besley and Burgess 2002). What is often missing in scholarly analyses is a combination of methods to study representations of oppressed populations; in addition to looking at what information is carried in the media, it is also crucial not to presuppose that people act on those messages.

As an instrument of development, mediated information helps uncover corruption and mismanagement, as in the case of one government campaign in Uganda that enlisted parents (primarily mothers) and teachers in helping ferret out why public funds were not received by intended schools. Not only did public access to information help anticorruption efforts, but the newspaper outlets greatly enhanced local education efforts for boys and girls (Reinikka and Svensson 2004). This example of tying media's interest in development to specific issues is increasingly addressed by resources devoted to this field, including the collaborative Communication Initiative's website of facts, links, and resources about the impact of communication on the MDGs (Communication Initiative 2006). With media as a foremost microphone for the voices in support of globalization, and possibly for those who dissent, the outlets and audiences have grown throughout the globe and warrant attention (Anheier, Glasius, and Kaldor 2005, 251–56).

Several studies, which can be broadly described as various types of textual analysis, show that women, particularly feminist women, have had a rather antagonistic relationship with the press, as they are often framed in stereotypical or trivial ways (Ashley and Olson 1998; Kahn and Goldenberg 1991, 112; Meyers 2004). However, women are also gaining ground as agents in news media coverage (Costain and Fraizer 2000). A textual analysis of the framing of news reports relating to women and MDGs reinforces some of these findings in terms of agency for women, but also in terms of trivialization and stereotypical representations. Taking previous findings into account, Lind and Salo (2005) offer a comprehensive study of a framing of women in media to date and are able to show the predominance of the following frames about women in news coverage:

inattention/neglect (the lack of coverage about women's issues)
personalization and trivialization (attention to personal attributes which trivializes people, such as women's marital status and references to children and babies)
victimization (references to weakness and vulnerability)
agency (reflections of strength, leadership, power)
blurring the focus (focusing on self/individual woman rather than social transformation)

We use the above framing categories to ascertain the representations of women in media coverage of the MDGs, but we are also expanding upon a previous quantitative, computerized content analysis of how global news agencies cover the MDGs (Giffard and Van Leuven 2005).[2] That media study displays a pronounced lack of coverage for goals 2, 3, and 5, demonstrating that the MDGs most directly relating to women's gender-specific roles and well-being are at the bottom of the ladder of media priorities. In addition, nearly 80 percent of all people named in the stories are male, pointing to the absence of female voices in the mass media and thus affirming the symbolic annihilation of women (Rhode 1997). Using men as sources is also the product of journalistic norms, as reporters prefer to source governmental leaders (Entman 2004). Governmental leaders are overwhelmingly male in many countries. Different media coverage of men and women can hinder women's access to the public sphere and requires scholars to gain a better understanding of news-gathering routines as well as what might improve relationships between women and media (Kahn and Goldenberg 1991). In terms of how news agencies frame information for specific cultures, voices of the North (Associated Press and Agence France-Presse) are starkly different from those of the South (Panapress and Xinhua), an important media fact for those comparing global discussions. That is, the MDGs are reported mostly within local contexts, with developed Northern-based agencies focusing on more elite issues of administration and spectatorship of the United Nations and United States, while media in developing countries concentrate on people, places, and themes of human rights and poverty. While such quantitative data tell us what newspapers choose to say, it is important to determine how it is said. A previous content analysis, for instance, explicitly shows that mothers and women are less likely to appear in coverage because most news agencies concentrate on goal 8, which deals with development and financial issues (Giffard and Van Leuven 2005). When they are in the news, then, how are goals for women presented? Are women entitled to strength and gender equality, as stated in MDG 3? Or are women's overall struggles ignored in favor of what media deem more relevant male-influenced contexts?

How Women Are Mirrored in the Media

To examine how women are framed by these news agencies, we coded all stories from the five news agencies to determine how the words *women* and *mother* are used in newspaper reports. Measurements of such framings of women are important, to see if media coverage reflects whether the role of women is altered from being primarily childbearers to being empowered decision makers. For example, as the life spans of women are lengthened to extend beyond the growth of their children, are mothers linked to more general issues such as careers and individual expression? To compare how news agencies presented women, we examined coverage in three ways: the number of stories mentioning women/mothers, the number of times each of the words was mentioned, and a final textual analysis to determine the contexts of those mentions.

Table 11.1 notes that the majority of stories about women and MDGs are published by the non-Northern news agencies, specifically Inter Press Service (IPS), Panapress (PANA), and Xinhua. Certain characteristics of each agency reveal distinct trends of coverage, which become clearer after a contextual analysis. We studied how each word is used within Lind and Salo's (2005) previously mentioned framing model, with the word *women* linked to the MDGs within these contexts: inattention/neglect, personalization/trivialization, victimization, agency, and blurring the focus. Within each news agency, the word *women* or

Table 11.1. Mentions of the Words *Women* and *Mothers,* by Agency

	Agence France Press	Associated Press	Inter Press Service	Panapress	Xinhua
Number of stories	260	297	422	476	716
Mentions of women/woman	127/17	50/14	1051/48	111/11	305/13
Mentions of mother	8	28	98	44	40

woman is or is not linked to the MDGs within such topics and frames, as indicated in these examples:

Within the *frame of inattention/neglect* (which signifies a lack of coverage about women's issues), according to the Associated Press (AP), a UN report suggests that while China seeks to project an image of itself as a rapidly modernizing society—it even plans to send a woman into space—women in fact are disadvantaged from cradle to grave.

Not one agency presented obvious examples of the *frame of personalization/ trivialization*, the attention to personal attributes that trivializes people, such as women's marital status and references to children and babies.

The *frame of victimization* (references to weakness and vulnerability), however, was a major focus, with the AP reporting that the head of the African Development Banks stated that women and girls are still responsible for onerous chores such as fetching water, greatly curtailing their school attendance. IPS reported statements by the Russian Association of Crisis Centers that more than fifty thousand Russian women are beaten by their husbands or partners every hour, a number vastly under the figures of public agencies. And PANA quoted a WHO official who stated that widespread political instability, armed conflicts, and the pandemic of HIV-AIDS have reduced the ability of the African woman to cope with daily life.

The *frame of agency* (reflections of strength, leadership, power) was flush with new agency interest. For example, the AP reported that more than two hundred African women leaders and rights activists called for the continent's governments to stop paying billions of dollars in external debt and instead spend the money on languishing social programs. IPS reported statements by the International Planned Parenthood Federation that contraception is the missing link for women in the Millennium Development Goals. PANA reported that the president of Nigeria called for the empowerment of women by supporting their engagement in fish processing and trade as well as the promotion of biodiversity and sustainable environment through responsible fishing. Xinhua quoted Chinese President Hu Jintao as stating that women are playing an irreplaceable role in promoting world peace and common development. Further, Xinhua reported that the WHO chief pronounced the health of mothers and children as key to solving wider economic, social, and developmental challenges, saying that mothers and children are a foundation of societies, and that when a mother or child dies, that foundation crumbles.

The *frame of blurring the focus* (focusing on an individual woman rather than social transformation) was a darling of the Associated Press. AP published a story in which a woman, Makhubela, pauses to comfort her friend and neighbor, a twenty-nine-year-old African mother of five slowly dying of AIDS, saying that every night she "prays to God that we could just be like normal people."

The above examples reveal the use of *woman* in multiple contexts which include economic, political, and social targets of the MDGs. Feminists might refer to such comprehensive use of terminology as a symptom of unequal discourse, in that not all inclusions of women are tied to female-only issues, thus opening the MDGs and other global initiatives to portrayals of equal progress for all people.

Finally, to compare constructions of women as mothers, we analyzed each story for how *mother* is used in context. Do media producers adjust the rhetoric of women when choosing to acknowledge a person as childbearer, and does coverage of mothers differ from the coverage of women? *Mother* was or was not referenced within these frames:

Not one news agency presented obvious examples of the *frame of inattention/ neglect.*

Within the *frame of personalization/trivialization*, IPS stood out, reporting Cambodia's First Lady stroking the head of her infant son, and a sixteen-year-old Cuban girl undergoing multiple abortions because of her aversion to condoms.

The AP and IPS put the *frame of victimization* at the forefront, with AP reporting that nineteen-year-old Urideia from Sao Paolo, Brazil, described how she was left by her mother, rejected by her father, raised by her grandmother, and rejected for college because she lived in a *favela* slum. IPS, for its part, reported on the death of a baby girl in Uruguay who died of malnutrition when her mother fed her only the water in which she boiled the pumpkin that she fed to the rest of her children.

Not one news agency presented obvious examples of the *frame of agency*.

The *frame of blurring the focus* found voice with the AP, which reported that expectant Asian mothers are often offered sympathy when they tell acquaintances that they are expecting a girl. Additionally, IPS reported on a Nicaraguan twenty-six-year-old mother who was taken as the wife of a day laborer at the age of fourteen and has never attended school or learned to read or write.

So, how are women represented in the media covering international development? Most of the five news agencies, especially AFP, mention women primarily in contexts of MDG compliance reports and mothers in terms of HIV/AIDS and maternal death rates. Xinhua's high rate of inclusions is due to coverage of World Health Day, titled "Making Every Mother and Child Count." It is also valuable to measure the absence of females in media coverage; for instance, women are not framed at all in terms of personalization/trivialization, whereas mothers are not presented in frames of inattention/neglect or agency. While the general population of women are thus not enmeshed with personal details such as martial status, the subgroup of mothers are not viewed as reflecting strength, leadership, or power.

In terms of contrasting North/South perspectives, Xinhua's views of Chinese progress in promoting women's issues clash with how AP perceives China. While AP presents China as a male-oriented society that ignores the realities of oppression, Xinhua echoes elite leaders, who declare that the country is making great strides toward gender equality and women's development.

In comparison, IPS discusses women and the MDGs much more than the other news agencies, displaying through both quantitative and qualitative analyses a significantly higher coverage of global objectives as seen through local perspectives. After noting the differences between IPS and the other four news agencies, we analyzed each agency's website for obvious links to either the MDGs or women. We discovered that IPS maintains not only a thematic page of "independent reporting on how the MDGs are influencing policy decisions and whether they are making a difference on the ground" (2006a) but also a separate site about women's issues with this foregrounding statement:

> It has become increasingly obvious that a future without poverty, hunger, AIDS and illiteracy depends on the empowerment of women—especially in developing regions where they produce most of the food but own almost none of the land, and many women lack even basic human rights. Ten years after governments promised equality—and ten years before a key deadline to lift at least half the world's poorest people out of misery—women and men together are asking what must be done to make the voices of this silenced majority finally heard. (IPS 2006b)

Perhaps the most significant finding about IPS is that it includes independent reporting, meaning that the views of bloggers from the recent World Social Forum and UN elites are presented.

Finally, how are mothers represented? The above textual samples indicate a tendency of news media to focus on *women* as an identification of a population, as opposed to *mother*, which is often used to describe individuals as vulnerable victims and trivialized nurturers. Mothers are covered primarily in terms of bodies; women are also seen as sharing in the plight of poverty, lack of education, and mortality. This study reveals that media are clearly focused on the marital and personal descriptions of mothers; however, women are less often framed in a trivialized fashion and are more likely to be portrayed within frames of agency and collective focus than are mothers.

Conclusion

Quantitatively, women's issues do get into the news—but they remain embedded in patriarchal hierarchy, especially in terms of framing. In other words, female leaders and MDGs explicitly focused on women are less likely to be covered.

Women are also positioned within social or economic frames rather than in terms of empowerment (MDG 3), meaning that development issues are more likely to receive coverage within frames of poverty and maternity than gender equity. Thus, as synergistic systems that figure prominently in the privileging of voices, these news agencies enable global dialogues that focus far more on men than women. And, when women are discussed, they are rarely linked to human rights issues in larger development agendas.

We argue that global media studies should be acknowledged as crucial allies to development efforts for several reasons. First, international coverage of women makes issues more "real" to those who may not otherwise be concerned about worldwide poverty or human rights; for instance, a journalistic focus on the MDGs allows media to show intimate geopolitical connections between superpowers and lives of ordinary people. We are thus urged to move past what Graham Huggan describes as "the post-colonial exotic," with cultures frozen in time and then restored to life through circuits of consumption and development (Gregory 2004, 10).

Second, initiatives such as the MDGs challenge traditional presumptions of the hierarchy of power in decision making. By reinforcing the concept that women are globally entitled to certain rights, media producers may help nations, NGOs, funders, and other decision makers to define and measure their work as it pertains to women. MDG measurements, for example, shine a spotlight on gender equity, such as the publicized finding that discrimination against girls and women in India "remains pervasive, reflected in the systematic under-allocation of food and education to women and girls within households" (UNDP 2005, 63–94). Acknowledgments of such disparities may help improve the stability in developing countries as transparency increases.

Finally, as influential framers of information, media can track deep-rooted changes in worldviews as measured by public opinion. As seen in World Value Surveys, development is viewed as essential in achieving longer life spans, good governance, and well-being. Such information would be valuable in projecting credible information to elites as well as those far away yet receptive to information. In terms of feminist agendas, attention to the MDGs could reenergize rhetoric to focus on women in issues of violence, consumption, and procreating. Of course, it is to be expected that greater emphasis on reproductive and sexual health care will make it easier to achieve four specific MDGs: gender equality, reducing child mortality, improving maternal health, and combating HIV/AIDS (UNFPA 2005). However, media's discourse does not often acknowledge the shared visions of other cultures, so the Northern rhetoric—which often emphasizes women in developing countries as absent or "other"– is the most prevalent. In addition, analyses of how women are portrayed as individuals as well as how they are described collectively by media may open up gender-equal cultural spaces with women's concerns more central (Mosse 2005, 150–51).

Of course, media is bound by strict markets or state constraints, which do not foster the growth of democracy and social change. Likewise, news media coverage only presents forms of what exists; in this case, MDG coverage concentrates primarily on the exact goals, without exploring what is missing. There is little attention to universal human rights in the MDG coverage because women's empowerment is sought primarily for ripple effects, such as equality, that will solve market inefficiencies and subsequent reductions in birth rates. The MDGs do not include international human rights laws as tools to achieve development. And, given that the MDGs lack a mechanism to measure participation by civil society, how can media cover equality when the Gender Empowerment Measure and Gender Development Index are not included as blueprints for women's empowerment? Before we see improvements in media coverage, we must formalize issues at the core of women's development, such as reproductive and sexual rights, as well as security.

What visionary perspective is essential for this new path? Vision, according to Donna Haraway, is always culturally performed and produced. It is also provisional and partial, making the lens of globalization a blurred perspective that needs to be cleared before smooth passage (1992). That is, even though power (including media's) may claim to view "others" and their spaces as transparent, such hegemonic visions are also constructions of invisibility.

This chapter demonstrates how this invisibility occurs in media's practice to link women explicitly to poverty (the MDG it does cover) or to focus more substantially on those MDGs that explicitly cover "female" issues—gender equality and maternal health. As observed by Diane Elson, a member of the MDG task force for goal 3, practitioners of feminist development economics look through a "gender lens," making visible what is routinely hidden. And disaggregating by sex, such as the data obtained for this study, is necessary but not sufficient. Gender, like race, is a constructed system of social power determined by biological differences (2004).

While scholars continue to explore a link between women's issues and media, attention is drawn to new possibilities emerging from combinations of methodologies recognizing human rights and gender equality to achieve development. In *Waiting for the Barbarians*, J. M. Coetzee writes, "The new men of Empire are the ones who believe in fresh starts, new chapters, new pages; I struggle on with the old story, hoping that before it is finished, it will reveal to me why it was that I thought it worth the trouble" (1982, 24). For the MDGs to achieve fresh starts, media must create women in new framings, answering the question of why the goals matter and why they are worth the trouble.

Notes

1. Thoraya A. Obaid, Executive Director, United Nations Population Fund, address to the Commission on the Status of Women, marking the ten-year review of the Beijing Conference and Platform for Action, March 7, 2005.

2. To sample global media, we searched the Lexis/Nexis database for MDG coverage by news agencies, producing a ranking of the top news agencies in terms of extensive reporting between January 1, 2004, and September 15, 2005. This time span is bracketed by two significant events—the World Social Forum in 2004, which brought together the voices of social activists, and the UN Summit in 2005, which affirmed the commitment of developed nations to fund the MDGs. Including perspectives of both developed and developing countries, the five selected news agencies and their headquarters are Agence-France Presse (France); Associated Press (United States); Inter Press Service (Italy); Panapress (Senegal); and Xinhua (China).

References

Altschull, J. Herbert. 1985. *Agents of Power: The Media and Public Policy*. White Plains, NY: Longman.

Anheier, Helmut, Marlies Glasius, and Mary Kaldor. 2005. *Global Civil Society 2004/5*. London: Sage.

Ashley, Laura, and Beth Olson. 1998. "Constructing Reality: Print Media's Framing of the Women's Movement, 1966 to 1988." *Journalism and Mass Communication Quarterly* 75, no. 2:263–77.

Benn, Hilary. 2004. Presentation to the BBC-World Service Trust/DFID Conference, November 24. www.dfid.gov.uk/news/files/speeches/sp-hilarymedia24nov04.pdf (accessed 1 January 2007).

Besley, Timothy, and Robin Burgess. 2002. "Political Economy of Government Responsiveness: Theory and Evidence from India." *The Quarterly Journal of Economics* 117, no. 4:1–31. www.wcfia.harvard.edu/seminars/pegroup/BesleyBu.pdf (accessed 1 January 2007).

Boyd-Barrett, Oliver. 1977. "Media Imperialism: Towards an International Framework for the Analysis of Media Systems." In *Mass Communication and Society*, eds. J. Michael Curran, Michael Gurevitch, and J. Woollacott, 174–79. London: Edward Arnold.

Coetzee, J. M. 1982. *Waiting for the Barbarians*. New York: Penguin.

Communication Initiative. 2006. "Millennium Development Goals Impact." www.comminit.com/mdgs.html (accessed 1 January 2007).

Costain, Anne, and Heather Fraizer. 2000. "Media Portrayal of 'Second Wave' Feminist Groups." In *Deliberation, Democracy, and the Media*, eds. Simone Chambers and Anne Costain, 155–74. Lanham, MD: Rowman & Littlefield.

Elson, Diane. 2004. "The Millennium Development Goals: A Feminist Development Economics Perspective." www.iss.nl/news/dies2004.pdf (accessed 12 February 2007).

Entman, Robert. 2004. *Projections of Power: Framing News, Public Opinion, and U.S. Foreign Policy*. Chicago: University of Chicago Press.

Fair, Jo Ellen. 1996. "The Body Politic, The Bodies of Women, and the Politics of Famine in U.S. Television Coverage of Famine in the Horn of Africa." *Journalism and Mass Communication Monographs* 158:1–41.

Fonow, Mary Margaret, and Judith A. Cook. 2005. "Feminist Methodology: New Applications in the Academy and Public Policy." *Signs: Journal of Women in Culture and Society* 30, no. 4:2211–36.

Giffard, C. Anthony, and Nancy Van Leuven. 2005. *Five Views of Development: How News Agencies Cover the Millennium Development Goals*. Inter Press Service. http://ipsnews.net/new_focus/ devdeadline/MDGsgiff05.pdf (accessed 1 January 2007).

Gill, Sonia. 2004. "Marginalization of Women in the Media." *UN Chronicle* 40, no. 4:38.

Gregory, Derek. 2004. *The Colonial Present*. Oxford: Blackwell.

Hancock, Alan. 2000. "UNESCO's Contributions to Communication, Culture and Development." In *Walking on the Other Side of the Information Highway: Communication, Culture and Development in the 21st Century*, ed. Jan Servaes, 61–73. Penang, Malaysia: Southbound.

Haraway, Donna. 1992. "Situated Knowledges: The Science Question in Feminism and the Privilege of Partial Perspective." In *Simians, Cyborgs and Women: The Reinvention of Nature*, 9. London: Routledge.

Harding, Sandra, and Kathryn Norberg. 2005. "New Feminist Approaches to Social Science Methodologies: An Introduction." *Signs: Journal of Women in Culture and Society* 30, no. 4:2009–16.

Inter Press Service. 2006a. "Development Deadline 2015: Millennium Development Goals." http://ipsnews.net/new_focus/devdeadline/index.asp (accessed 1 January 2007).

———. "Women Leading the Way." 2006b. http://ipsnews.net/new_focus/women/index.asp (1 January 2007).

Jamieson, Kathleen Hall, and Paul Waldman. 2003. *The Press Effect: Politicians, Journalists, and the Stories that Shape the Political World*. New York: Oxford University Press.

Kahn, Kim Fridkin, and Edie N. Goldenberg. 1991. "The Media: Obstacle or Ally of Feminists?" *The Annals of the American Academy of Political and Social Science* 515:104–13.

Khan, Shahnaz. 2005. "Reconfiguring the Native Informant: Positionality in the Global Age." *Signs: Journal of Women in Culture and Society* 30, no. 4:2017–36.

Lind, Rebecca Ann, and C. Salo. 2005. "The Framing of Feminists and Feminism in News and Public Affairs Programs in U.S. Electronic Media." *Journal of Communication*. 52, no.1:211–12.

Lorde, Audre. 1984. "The Master's Tools Will Never Dismantle the Master's House." In *Sister Outsider*, 110–14. Berkeley: Crossing Press.

MediaChannel. 2006. www.mediachannel.org (accessed 1 January 2007).

Meyers, Marian. 2004. "African American Women and Violence: Gender, Race, and Class in the News." *Critical Studies in Media Communication* 21:95–118.

Mohanty, Chandra. 2004. *Feminism without Borders: Decolonizing Theory, Practicing Solidarity*. Durham: Duke University Press.

Moser, Caroline. 1993. *Gender Planning and Development: Theory, Practice and Training*. London: Routledge.

Mosse, David. 2005. *Cultivating Development*. London: Pluto Press.

Population Action International. 2005. "How Access to Sexual & Reproductive Health Services Is Key to the MDGs." www.populationaction.org/resources/facsheets/FS31_MDGs_FINAL.pdf (accessed 1 January 2007).

Ragin, Charles C. 1994. *Constructing Social Research*. Thousand Oaks, CA: Pine Forge Press.

Read, Donald. 2001. "Newspapers, Politics, and Public Opinion." *English Historical Review* 114:136.

Reinikka, Ritva, and Jakob Svensson. 2004. "Power of Information: Evidence from a Newspaper Campaign to Reduce Capture." Washington, D.C.: World Bank Institute. http://econ.worldbank.org/external/default/main?pagePK=64165259&theSitePK=469372&piPK=64165421&menuPK=64166093&entityID=000012009_20040326142036 (accessed 1 January 2007).

Rhode, Deborah L. 1997. "Media Images/Feminist Issues." In *Feminism, Media and the Law*, eds. M.A. Fineman and M.T. McCluskey, 8–21. New York: Oxford University Press.

Robinson, Piers. 2002. The CNN Effect: The Myth of News, Foreign Policy and Intervention. London: Routledge.

Terkildsen, Nayda, and Frauke Schnell. 1997. "How Media Frames Move Public Opinion: An Analysis of the Women's Movement." Political Research Quarterly 50:879–900.

United Nations (UN). 2005. "The UN Millennium Development Goals." www.un.org/millennium goals (accessed 1 January 2007).

United Nations Development Program (UNDP). 2005. Investing in Development: A Practical Plan to Achieve the Millennium Development Goals. London: Earthscan.

United Nations Population Fund (UNFPA). 2005. "Summary of Gender Equality." www.unfpa .org/gender/beijing10/ (accessed January 1 2007).

Wilkins, Karen. G. 2005. "Valuing Women." Association for Women's Rights in Development. www.awid.org/members/reports.php?id=25 (accessed 1 January 2007).

Women and Media for Social Change (WMSC). 2001. "Overlapping Agendas, Different Priorities: The Global Alternative Report on Section J of the Beijing Platform for Action." www .womenaction.org/women_medioa/eng/1index.html (accessed 1 January 2007).

World Values Surveys. 2004. www.worldvaluessurvey.org/news/index.html (accessed 1 January 2007).

CHAPTER TWELVE

Deadly Synergies: Gender Inequality, HIV/AIDS, and the Media

Patricia A. Made

The Acquired Immune Deficiency Syndrome (AIDS) pandemic has been news now for more than twenty years. Telling the same story for such a long period of time has tested the values that the media uses to determine what is newsworthy, who makes news, and what remains on the news agenda long after the story is no longer "new."

AIDS should continue to be a compelling story that captures the realities of millions of women, men, girls, and boys who are infected and affected, for the simple reason that worldwide, 5 million people contract HIV every year, and 3 million are dying of AIDS-related illnesses—90 percent of them in developing countries (Cowley 2006).

Internationally, social scientists have agreed that AIDS is more than a biomedical problem. The social constructionist approach to the problem of AIDS takes account of prevailing public depictions of the disease, their interaction with current social structures, and their impact on individual experience, public views, and policy formulation[1] (Strebel 1997, 109).

There have been several discourses in the public and media domains since the pandemic emerged some twenty-five years ago. The political construction of AIDS and the official AIDS information framing the dominant discourse has fallen into four categories, which construct AIDS as (a) a homosexual affliction, (b) a sexually transmitted disease, (c) an affliction of IV drug users, and (d) a scientific/medical problem (Kistenberg 2003). While these categories reflect the dominant HIV/AIDS discourse in Western societies, they also have been points of reference for the discourse on HIV/AIDS in Africa and other parts of the world.

The first three categories, which have been dominant themes in the media's coverage of the pandemic, have been the basis for the stigmatization of those living with HIV/AIDS, as well as those seen as most vulnerable to infection. The dominant discourse has reinforced the link between AIDS and sex by continuously referring to AIDS as a sexually transmitted disease. This linkage has provided many moralists with ammunition to use against persons with AIDS (Kistenberg 2003, 14). This is particularly true in sub-Saharan Africa, where HIV is mainly transmitted through heterosexual relationships.

The London-based Panos Institute says, in *Missing the Message? 20 Years of Learning from HIV/AIDS* (2003), that the media is critical for stimulating public debate and dialogue and for challenging the kind of long-established social norms that prevent more widespread changes in behavior.

Gender inequality, well documented as one of the primary allies that fuel the spread of HIV, is among the traditional social norms in many societies worldwide that needs to be challenged by the media in its reporting on the pandemic. This is because women and girls continue to be at the epicenter of the AIDS pandemic. Women now represent half of all people living with HIV, including nearly 60 percent in Africa. In parts of Africa and the Caribbean, young women aged fifteen to twenty-four are up to six times more likely to be HIV-infected than are young men (UN Declaration of Commitment 2006).

Drawing on constructionist understandings, feminist work on gendered power relations and the political economy of sexual relations has articulated the problems women face in the prevention of AIDS. From this perspective, patriarchy is seen to exert substantial though inconsistent control over women in ways that have direct implications for their protection from HIV infection. Safe sex options (condoms, abstinence, and monogamy) reflect acceptance of a male sex drive that women must counter and also represent attempts to reexert control over female sexuality (Strebel 1997, 110–11). Married women, for example, cannot abstain from sex, or insist that their husbands use a condom during sexual intercourse, or demand their husband's fidelity (UN Declaration on Commitment 2006). Worldwide, 80 percent of women newly infected with HIV are practicing monogamy within a marriage or a long-term relationship, shattering the myth that marriage is a natural refuge for AIDS (Gates 2006). Feminists argue that AIDS needs alternative and more emancipatory responses. These include fundamental changes in power relations between men and women, as well as different notions of sexuality (Holland et al 1990; Juhasz 1990; Kippax et al 1990; Strebel 1997, 110–11).

The media has a critical role to play in (re)shaping the different notions of sexuality and in challenging the gender power relations, cultural beliefs, and gender norms, values, and practices that make women vulnerable to HIV and put men at risk. This is especially the case in the media's news coverage of the HIV/AIDS pandemic, because news accounts contribute decisively to the discursive construction of reality by creating, supporting, or refuting cultural beliefs and practices (Vavrus 2002, 14).[2]

In southern Africa, a region where, according to UNAIDS (The Joint United Nations Programme on HIV/AIDS), the pandemic continues to strengthen and take a major toll on the political, economic, and social fabric of countries such as Botswana, Lesotho, Namibia, South Africa, Swaziland, and Zimbabwe (six countries where HIV infection levels among pregnant women is 20 percent or higher) the print and broadcast media continue to vacillate between putting the spotlight on women's rights violations, gender inequalities, gender violence, increasing levels of poverty among women and girls, and harmful traditional and social practices that make women and girls vulnerable to HIV, while at the same time fostering traditional gender norms and notions of masculinity and femininity that underpin patriarchy. What is needed in the media's reporting on the AIDS pandemic is a fundamental shift to create media news narratives that are more grounded in the context of the roots of the pandemic—gender discrimination and human rights violations. Reporting on the gender dimensions of the AIDS pandemic provides the media throughout southern Africa with the lens to not only question the patriarchal hegemony embedded in all political, economic, and social structures and institutions in the countries of the region, but to also begin to interrogate how this hegemony defines and influences the media's own news values, media processes, and newsroom cultures.

Roles and News Values: What Makes the Media Tick?

What role the media can realistically play in the fight against the AIDS pandemic and gender inequality in southern Africa continues to be a hotly debated issue within the region's media; and this is still a fertile field for research.

All countries in southern Africa are signatories to the Convention on the Elimination of All Forms of Discrimination Against Women (CEDAW), the 1995 Beijing Platform for Action (media was one of the twelve "critical areas of concern"), among other international conventions, declarations, and commitments that not only uphold gender equality and women's rights as key principles of democratic societies, but which also include measures and actions to guarantee and achieve gender justice. The region also has its own 1997 Southern African Development Community (SADC) Declaration on Gender and

Development, with an addendum in 1998 on the Elimination of All Forms of Violence against Women. Southern African countries also have signed the Women's Protocol of the African Charter on Human and Peoples Rights.

Countries in the region also have put their stamp on a number of declarations: the Millennium Development Goals (MDGs), which include targets on gender equality (goal 3), reducing poverty (goal 1), and the AIDS pandemic (goal 6), among others; the 2001 and 2006 declarations of the UN General Assembly Special Session on HIV/AIDS (UNGASS), both of which draw clear links between gender inequality and women's and girls' vulnerability to HIV; the SADC Declaration on HIV/AIDS; and the Abuja Declaration on HIV and AIDS, tuberculosis and other related infectious diseases, among others. Many of these regional and international declarations and platforms for action underscore the role of the media. But to play a more effective and transformative role in the fight against AIDS and gender inequality, the media has to be challenged through advocacy, research, and internal introspection to examine the news narratives they produce daily. The media also has to be challenged to reexamine the political economy that makes it tick.

Worldwide, there is growing concentration of media into the hands of those with power, money, and an understanding of the influence that media can wield in the global, regional, and national political and economic spaces. The media can and do shape how we see the world—who is good, who is bad, who is important and in control, and who are victims, powerless, and not in control. Media corporations serve to consolidate the wealth and power of white, mostly United States–based, wealthy male owners. By the mid-1990s, the United Nations put the telecommunications industries at the top of the revenue hierarchy, with most of those companies being U.S.-based (Byerly 2004, 227). In southern Africa, the media is owned, controlled, and dominated by black males, and the media's news values and norms often veer toward wealth and power within the countries of the region as opposed to marginalized groups.

Carolyn Byerly (2004) argues that the extent to which any mainstream print or broadcast medium today serves the public's interests or fosters a marketplace where diverse ideas compete is open to serious question. As the carriers of corporate financial data, as well as government news, entertainment, and advertising, the news (and, I should add, entertainment) media have been central to creating and normalizing the global economy. For women, sexual minorities, and others historically marginalized, this concentration of wealth and power has intensified the challenge to open up access to their voices, concerns, and analyses. The news media will remain an important site of struggle for truly free speech.

The media construct particular views of the world, and through continuous interactions with these views, we mold and shape our own perspectives and orientations toward reality (Vavrus 2002, 2). This process of representation demands that media texts, including news texts, both generate and respond to the myriad material and symbolic dimensions of the "real world." In other words, the material and the symbolic are mutually constitutive. The media's contribution to this process, however, is not especially comprehensive or inclusive of a diversity of views and voices—this point too is widely accepted by many academics and news workers.

Although women are more than half of the world's population, they are not the decision makers in the news media, nor are their voices and perspectives key to shaping the "realities" we see, read, and hear about daily. Women's marginalization in the media has been consistently documented through the Global Media Monitoring Project (GMMP), a tool through which women (and men) can scrutinize the media in a systematic way and can document gender bias and exclusion. The GMMP provides a set of straightforward quantitative measures of media content which can be universally used and which provide useful research data and documentation for lobbying and advocacy work (Gallagher 2001). The GMMP is coordinated by the World Association for Christian Communications (WACC) and is an outcome of the 1994 Women Empowering Communications conference in Bangkok. The projects took place in 1995, 2000, and in 2005.

The 2005 GMMP, in which seventy-eight countries took part in monitoring the news for one day, found that while women constitute 52 percent of the world's population, they comprise only 21 percent of the people featured in the news; men are the majority of the news subjects in all story topics; 86 percent of all people featured in news stories as spokespeople are men; and men also make up 83 percent of all experts. The 2005 GMMP also found that gender equality is not considered newsworthy. Ninety-six percent of news stories worldwide did not highlight issues of gender equality or inequality, and the stories that did highlight gender equality or inequality only comprised 4 percent of the news stories (GMMP 2005).

Countries in southern Africa were among the seventy-eight countries that participated in the 2005 GMMP, and in 2002, Gender Links, a South-African-based NGO that promotes gender equality in and through the media, and the Media Institute of Southern Africa (MISA), a regional network that seeks to foster a free, independent and diverse media, coordinated a landmark study on gender in the editorial content of the southern African media.

The study in which twelve countries participated (Seychelles later did the same research), covered a total of 25,110 news items printed and broadcast in September 2002. One of the significant findings was that women's views and voices are grossly underrepresented in the media. Women make up 52 percent of the region's population, but constituted only 17 percent of the known news sources. The study also found that older women (over age forty-nine) are virtually invisible; that gender equality is hardly considered newsworthy (gender-specific news items accounted for a mere 2 percent of the total, and about half of these were on gender violence); that women are least well represented in the print media (they constituted only 22 percent of those who wrote news stories); and women media practitioners predominate in the areas considered "soft beats" (not often having strong news angles), such as health, media, and entertainment, among others (MISA 2003).

This marginalization of women's voices and perspectives, and their low representation as newsmakers, is a cause for concern when the media are viewed as texts that never simply mirror or reflect "reality" but instead construct hegemonic definitions of what should be accepted as "reality." Feminists have redeployed the notion of hegemony in order to argue that most of us cannot see how patriarchal ideology is being actively made to appear as nonideological, objective, neutral, and nongendered (Carter and Steiner 2004, 2). This argument is a direct challenge to the media's claim that they only reflect or mirror the gender realities in society in objective and neutral reporting.

The media's reporting on the AIDS pandemic in southern Africa has also played a role in constructing hegemonic definitions of what realities are important or not important in terms of news about the pandemic's impact on southern African nations and their peoples. The media in southern Africa continue to cover AIDS twenty-five years into the pandemic as if it is nongendered, and the links between patriarchal norms and values, gender inequalities, and the devastatingly high HIV prevalence throughout the region remains a news story still to be told.

The Hidden Gender Realities in
HIV/AIDS Coverage in Southern Africa

Media reporting on HIV/AIDS in southern Africa continues to hide the gender dimensions of the pandemic. Issues of gender justice are largely reported as news with no links or connections to the HIV/AIDS pandemic, while a large majority of the reporting on HIV/AIDS is gender-blind. Gender-blind reporting fails to illustrate how gender inequalities impact on the lives of women and girls in all sectors, and it fails to access the voices and perspectives of women as credible and newsworthy sources. This type of reporting also results in editorial content that tends to make women almost invisible in comparison to the realities they live and face each and every day.

"Symbolic annihilation," the term used by mass communication scholars George Gerbner (1978) and Gaye Tuchman (1979) to describe the claim that powerful groups in society suppress the less powerful by marginalizing them to such an extent that they are rendered virtually invisible as a representable group, applies to the media's reporting in the region of many issues, including the AIDS pandemic. In other words, stories on HIV/AIDS effectively erase women's presence in various ways.

Recognizing this gap in the media's response to the AIDS pandemic in its coverage and its own newsroom editorial and workplace policies, the Southern African Editors Forum (SAEF) and several civil society partners have embarked on an initiative to improve coverage of HIV and AIDS and gender in the region's media. As part of the Media Action Plan (MAP) on HIV and AIDS and Gender program, 132 media houses in eleven countries were monitored for fifteen days in October and November 2005, resulting in an analysis of 37,001 media texts from the print and broadcast media. This study found, among other findings, that the gender dimensions of the AIDS pandemic do not receive sufficient coverage.

Gender is not well integrated into HIV and AIDS coverage, much of which was classified in the study as either gender-blind or unclear. For example, the subtopics that examined gender power relations, prevention of mother-to-child transmission (PMTCT), gender-based violence, the role of men and boys, cross-generational sex, cultural practices, and sex work, all significant drivers of the epidemic in the region, received less than 5 percent of coverage. And the finding that the topic of care, which has a major bearing on women's lives, comprised only 13 percent of the coverage signals that this is still regarded as a marginal issue in the media (MMP 2006, 8).

One of the most subtle ways of erasing women's presence is the absence of their voices and perspectives as sources in media articles on the AIDS pandemic. The HIV and AIDS and Gender Baseline study found that, during the period of study, women comprised 39 percent of the sources on the pandemic, while 61 percent of the sources were men. But as the regional report on the study states, in the context of a regional epidemic in which women are at a higher risk of HIV infection, bear the burden of caring for the sick and orphaned, and continue to suffer the inequalities imposed upon them by a patriarchal society, there is still scope for improving the gender balance in sources (MMP 2006, 22). One way a gender analysis in and through the media can be achieved is through the simple process of looking at women's worlds through their eyes, and of hearing problems and solutions described in their voices.[3]

When women's voices are accessed by the media on HIV/AIDS, however, a large majority of these stories deal with the issue of home-based care, a situation whereby the care of people living with HIV/AIDS is done by family members at home, the majority of whom are women and girls. The 2005 HIV and AIDS and Gender Baseline Study found that men's views and voices dominate in most HIV and AIDS topics, except care, where women comprised 52 percent of the sources. The capturing of women's voices and their portrayal in the roles of care givers and nurturers in the HIV/AIDS pandemic, while depicting their day-to-day reality, also reinforces the gender stereotype of women's perceived role in society, even when they are greatly affected by the HIV/AIDS pandemic in many other profound ways. About 10 percent of the items monitored in the 2005 MAP study were regarded as perpetuating stereotypes (MMP 2006, 33).

Missing Links, Missing Stories in the Media

One of the most invisible stories on the gender dimensions of HIV/AIDS is women's and girl's increased vulnerability due to gender-based violence. Violence and HIV are mutually reinforcing. Violence can lead to infection, either directly through the act of rape, or indirectly by predisposing women to risk-taking behavior later in life (UNAIDS 2004). Also, because women are often the first to be tested because of their access to prenatal services, they are the first to know their status and may become the targets of violence by their spouses and partners, who fail to take responsibility for the spread of the virus and deny their own status. Violence against women in general, except in crime and court reporting or sensational stories involving prominent persons, and the link between violence and HIV/AIDS specifically, are not topics of consistent, in-depth, or investigative news coverage.

The bulk of the general coverage on the AIDS pandemic in the region focused on policy, politics, and government (51 percent) and statistics and research (33 percent). Poverty, which has major implications for the vulnerability of women to HIV infection, received only 7 percent of coverage in the region (MMP 2006, 27). As Cynthia Carter and Linda Steiner (2004, 5) state in their introduction to *Critical Readings: Media and Gender*, while the media have unquestionably contributed to the (re)production of sexist norms, values, and beliefs, the same media can play an important role in highlighting the effects of sexism and gender inequalities on the lives of women and girls.

The media throughout southern Africa do reflect the reality that women and girls continue to bear the burden of care in the HIV/AIDS pandemic because of gender inequalities and patriarchal norms and values that box women into the care economy, and articles have appeared on sexual violence against women and girls that has resulted in HIV infection or violence against women perpetrated by their partners or others because of the woman's HIV status. But at the same time, the media fail to interrogate why women and girls continue to carry the heavy care load, continue to be far more likely than men to be infected with HIV, and continue to be the targets of gender-based violence. And the media does not question the issue of access to care for women themselves—who ultimately takes care of the women caregivers who are often ill themselves?

Making the Links for Better Coverage

Given the impact of HIV/AIDS on all sectors of society and on the economic and social development of the area, almost every story in the media in southern Africa can have an HIV/AIDS component, and gender should be mainstreamed into these stories. The high prevalence rates in countries in the region and the impact the pandemic has had and continues to have on national development warrants far more media coverage than the mere 3 percent of the 37,001 news items monitored regionally in the MAP study. Media researchers and communications scholars have documented and illustrated how the media is not a neutral bystander in any society, but an institution that can and does play a major role in shaping public discourse and influencing policy.

Policy makers in southern Africa are aware of the need to mainstream gender into HIV/AIDS policies and programs and of the importance of mainstreaming HIV/AIDS into gender laws, policies, and programs, as illustrated by the international and regional conventions, declarations, and commitments signed. But this awareness often does not translate into effective and concrete action for several reasons.

One reason is that often policy and decision makers themselves lack vital and key data on the gender dimensions of the pandemic, and they do not through their own channels of communication access the voices and perspectives of women and girls. The media's failure to capture these voices and perspectives in their coverage of the pandemic, and their failure to increase the quantity of coverage of the gender dimensions of HIV/AIDS, therefore help to keep invisible the economic, social, and gender inequalities that fuel the spread of HIV and that need to be tackled in multisectoral policies and programs.

Also, the media do not hold policy and decision makers accountable to issues of gender equality, giving this a low priority in their coverage and defense of political, economic, and social rights in the country. Instances of violence against women, which increase their risk of HIV infection, for example, are not covered by the media as rights violations which call for more stringent laws, policies, programs, and actions to protect women and girls. Instead they are treated as isolated incidents, crimes of passion, or extraordinary acts that need not be part of public discourse.

By ignoring the gender dimensions of the HIV/AIDS story, the media do not play the pivotal role that they could in the fight against HIV. By not challenging the gender inequalities that continue to keep women and girls in lower political, economic, and social statuses, thereby making them vulnerable to HIV infection, the media do not help to build a public discourse on the links between gender and HIV/AIDS, which could be influential in changing the course of both gender and HIV/AIDS policy.

A media that continues to foster gender inequalities through its representation and portrayal of women and girls in news narratives, or that ignores the millions of people who die of AIDS-related illnesses one by one each day, becomes an ally of the virus, which has become deeply rooted in societies where poverty, gender inequalities, and human rights violations join forces with HIV to distort women's and girls' lives in both public and private spheres.

Mainstreaming gender in media coverage of the AIDS pandemic in the region requires that journalists more actively seek out and include the voices and perspectives of women, as well as men, in their reporting. It requires that they search for and use data disaggregated by sex to illustrate how women, men, girls, and boys are affected differently by many policies and developments due to the gender power relations within both the public and private spaces in society. It requires the conscious use of language that does not promote gender stereotypes and discrimination against women. And it requires an analysis through the voices and perspectives of women and men "experts," the affected and the infected, and appropriate background information and data that add depth and context to stories to provide a gender analysis of the HIV/AIDS pandemic.

One of the key functions of the media in any society is to question, to seek answers to why, despite the guarantees of equal rights, equal opportunity, and equal access for all, segments of a society are still unable to exercise their rights because of discrimination based on sex, HIV status, race, ethnicity, and so forth. The larger proportion of women and young girls infected and vulnerable to HIV infection, the shifting of the burden of care onto the shoulders of women and girls, among other gender disparities highlighted within the AIDS pandemic, provide numerous opportunities for the media to dig beneath the surface, to question, analyze, and explore what should be done in the form of laws, policies, and other changes to protect women's and girl's fundamental right to life.

Notes

1. Strebel (1997). See also Sander L. Gilman, *Disease and Representation: Images of Illness from Madness to AIDS* (Ithaca, NY: Cornell University Press, 1988); Susan Sontag, *AIDS and Its Metaphors* (New York: Farrar Strauss Giroux, 1988); and Paula Treichler, *How to Have Theory in an Epidemic: Cultural Chronicles of AIDS* (Durham. NC: Duke University Press, 1999).

2. Vavrus (2002) also cites the work here of Lana Rakow and Kimberlie Kranich, "Women as Sign in Television News," *Journal of Communication 4, no.1,* 1991; and Caryl Rivers, *Slick Spins and Fractured Facts: How Cultural Myths Distort the News* (New York: Columbia University Press, 1996).

3. Paula Donovan, "Gender, Human Rights and HIV/AIDS," address to the Inter Press Service (IPS) global news agency Support Group, Media and NGO Roundtable, 25–26 September 2001.

References

Byerly, Carolyn. 2004. "Shifting Sites: Feminist, Gay and Lesbian News Activism in the U.S. Context in Gender and Newsroom Cultures." In *Identities at Work*, eds. Marjan de Bruin and Karen Ross. Cresskill, NJ: Hampton Press.

Carter, Cynthia, and Linda Steiner. 2004. Introd. to *Critical Readings: Media and Gender*, eds. Cynthia Carter and Linda Steiner. Maidenhead, UK: Open University Press.

Cowley, Geoffrey. 2006. "The Life of a Virus Hunter." *Newsweek*. May 15.

Gallagher, Margaret. 2001. *Gender Setting: New Agendas for Media Monitoring and Advocacy*. London: ZED and WACC.

Gates, Melinda French. 2006. "What Women Really Need." *Newsweek*. May 15.

Gerbner, George. 1978. "The Dynamics of Cultural Resistance." In *Hearth and Home: Images of Women in the Mass Media*, eds. Gaye Tuchman, Arlene Kaplan Daniels, and James Walker Benet, 46–50. Oxford: Oxford University Press.

Global Media Monitoring Project (GMMP) 2005. 2005. London: World Association for Christian Communication.

Holland, Janet, Caroline Ramazanoglu, Sue Scott, Sue Sharpe, and Rachel Thomson. 1990. "Sex, Gender and Power: Young Women's Sexuality in the Shadow of AIDS." *Sociology of Health & Illness* 12, no. 3:336–50.

Juhaz, Alexandra. 1990. "The Continued Threat: Women in Mainstream AIDS Documentary." *Journal of Sex Research* 27, no. 1:25–47.

Kippax, Susan, June Crawford, Cathy Waldby, and Pam Benton. 1990. "Women Negotiating Heterosex: Implications for AIDS Prevention." *Women's Studies International Forum* 13:533–42.

Kistenberg, Cindy. 2003. "The Voice of Reason? A Political Construction of AIDS in Media-Mediated AIDS." In *Media-Mediated AIDS*, ed. Linda K. Fuller, 11–22. Cresskill, NJ: Hampton Press.

Levell, Ann, Amanda Kottler, Erica Burman, and Ian Parter, eds. 1997. *Culture, Power and Difference: Discourse Analysis in South Africa*. London: Zed Books, and Capetown: University of Cape Town Press.

Media Institute of Southern Africa (MISA) and Gender Links. 2003. "Women and Men Make the News, Gender and Media Baseline Study, Southern African Regional Overview." Windhoek, Namibia: MISA.

Media Monitoring Project (MMP). 2006. "HIV and AIDS and Gender Baseline Study, Regional Report." Johannesburg: Gender Links and Media Monitoring Project.

Morna Colleen Lowe, ed. 2006. *Who Makes the News? Mirror on the Southern African Findings of the Global Media Monitoring Project (GMMP), 2005*. Johannesburg, South Africa: Gender Links.

Panos Institute. 2003. *Missing the Message? 20 Years of Learning from HIV/AIDS*. London: Panos Institute.

Population Reference Bureau. 2000. *Conveying Concerns: Media Coverage of Women and HIV/AIDS*, Women's Edition. Washington, D.C.: Population Reference Bureau.

Sayagues, Mercedes. 2006. "Writing for Our Lives, How the Maisha Yetu Project Changed Health Coverage in Africa." Washington, D.C.: International Women's Media Foundation.

Strebel, Anna. 1997. "Putting Discourse Analysis to Work in AIDS Prevention." In *Culture, Power and Difference: Discourse Analysis in South Africa*, eds. Ann Levell, Amanda Kottler, Erica Burman, and Ian Parter, 109–121. London: Zed Books, and Capetown: University of Cape Town Press.

Tuchman, Gaye. 1979. "Women's Depiction by the Mass Media." *Signs: Journal of Women in Culture and Society* 4, no. 3:528–42.

UNAIDS (Joint United Nations Programme on HIV/AIDS). 2004. "Facing the Future Together: Report of the Secretary General's Task Force on Women, Girls and HIV/AIDS in Southern Africa." www.unicef.org/publications/index_22222.html (accessed 7 May 2007).

"United Nations Declaration of Commitment on HIV/AIDS: Five Years Later." 2006. Report of the Secretary General, March 24. ata.unaids.org/pub/Report/2006/20060324_SGReport_GA_ A60737_en.pdf (accessed 7 May 2007).

Vavrus, Mary Douglas. 2002. *Postfeminist News, Political Women in Media Culture*. New York: State University of New York Press.

CHAPTER THIRTEEN

Online News:
Setting New Gender Agendas?

Jayne Rodgers

Historically, news has been seen as a male-dominated phenomenon, economically, technologically, and culturally. Women were, and some continue to be, sidelined into "soft" reporting areas, such as education and social affairs. Male reporters have traditionally dominated the "hard" and more important news areas, such as security, defense, and international relations. Women as subjects of news have also been less visible than men, with the focus on elite affairs sidelining political and economic issues that fall outside the realm of high politics. These structural imbalances have a significant impact on the ways news is constructed and on its characteristics.

Women in the news are more than twice as likely to be portrayed as victims than men; men are far more likely to be consulted as experts, while women are more often used to offer personal opinions or speak as observers; men's voices dominate in hard news subjects; and, though comprising 52 percent of the world's population, women make up only 21 percent of the people featured in news stories (Gallagher 2005).[1] Moreover, media ownership by women is miniscule and, where women are majority owners, the media involved are usually small-scale, localized enterprises (Byerly 2006). Women's ownership of global media—if defined as large-scale, international operations—is virtually nonexistent.

Feminist studies of technology have long identified concerns associated with the masculinization of technologies and the ways gender is positioned within dominant technological frameworks.[2] When extending technology studies to the Internet, questions of access, infrastructure, and underrepresentation of women—as users, developers, and content providers—become key. Feminist scholars have been pivotal in identifying multiple digital divides, noting that the "haves" and "have-nots" cannot easily be distinguished by relative wealth alone (Lebert 2003).

As news moves online and becomes a key venture for independent and commercial newsmakers, questions about the gendering of news need to be revisited. With majority male media ownership and news agendas that strongly favor corporate and conservative interests (Pozner 2005), interactive technologies appear to provide new opportunities for women to influence online content and for feminist thinking to have an impact upon news agendas. As a global technology, through which mainstream and alternative media increasingly converge, analysis of the gendering of news available to Internet users needs to be undertaken. This chapter explores the concept of news as a gendered product in the Internet era and examines the growth of independent online media. It seeks to address the question of whether this apparently liberal "free" and "open" technology replicates structural divisions, and the gendered assumptions and undercurrents of mainstream, corporate media, and whether emerging media contribute to the dissolution of gendered news. Perhaps most important, does the Internet as media offer opportunities for more gender-neutral forms of news?

In addressing these issues, this chapter considers three key areas: first, the growth of online news in recent years—Internet users are increasingly turning toward the Internet for information and to share content; the growing interest of media corporations in the Internet, alongside the swell of citizen journalism, has wrought interesting variations in how news is perceived and conceived; finally the chapter assesses the best opportunities for feminists to influence news content and agendas, concluding with notes on advocacy to effect change.

Feminist news sites as a separate entity are not analyzed in this chapter; they already understand feminist politics (see the chapter appendix below). What is of interest here is an examination of how organizations that have demonstrated little or no awareness of gender issues in developing their news agendas have responded to the fluidity of information exchange online.

Mainstream, Alternatives, and Online News

Feminist analysis of the gendering of media has been widespread if, unsurprisingly, somewhat marginalized. The growth of the Internet has facilitated the development of new forms of independent media. Wide-ranging commentary on current affairs is provided by contributors to independent news sites, blogs, and podcasts, supplying a counterpoint to the perspectives promoted by the major media conglomerates. These sites, many originally intended to provide an alternative to the mainstream, now operate on a global scale, often with regional reporting. These new media actors have become a powerful voice in the reporting of events, changing the ways in which news stories are broken. Internet history is now littered with examples of how nonmainstream actors have used the Internet and mobile media to generate content and, ultimately, influence the ways news is constructed. The first and perhaps best known of these, the breaking of the Clinton/Lewinsky story online by drudgereport.com, set a precedent in challenging the monopoly of mainstream media on agenda setting and information provision. This early example of nonjournalists forcing news stories onto media agendas was the first in a now-common model of seeming symbiosis between formerly separate spheres: the private world of bloggers joined the public world of corporate media and, as relationships between the two have slowly mutated, their bond has now been cemented.

In two other cases, noncorporate agents—as individuals and as organized "alternative" media—demonstrated how information from sources other than mainstream media could play an important role in shaping news output, by providing information from the scenes of often distant events. In the case of the Asian tsunami of December 2004, on-the-spot photographs, text messages, videos, Internet postings, and blogs demonstrated clearly how individuals could contribute to the content and construction of news, generating links between mainstream media, nonprofit organizations, disaster relief agencies, and the wider Internet community (Outing 2004).

The London bombings of July 2005 demonstrated another way in which nonjournalists have become involved in the development of news stories. Photographs, videos, e-mails, calls, and text messages from members of the public at the four bomb sites were central to the content of mainstream news reporting of these events. On the day of the bombings, the BBC website received more than 20,000 e-mails, 1,000 photographs, and 20 videos, from eyewitnesses and from people concerned about the impact of the blasts. At the same time, high volumes of content were generated by individual contributors on both the online encyclopedia Wikipedia and the image site Flickr.

Following the hanging of Saddam Hussein in December 2006, "unofficial" video shot with a cell phone appeared on the Internet and on Al-Jazeera within twenty-four hours. Immediately after the peace rally in Washington, D.C., on 27 January 2007, over a hundred videos were posted on the YouTube site. These examples—and the list grows longer daily—are illustrative of the ways in which nonjournalists have influenced the shaping of news content in recent years. They are important, as they indicate gaps in our knowledge regarding the construction of online news and, of particular relevance to this chapter, the gendering thereof.

Although much has been written about the growth of online independent media, much of the work on this topic to date has tended to reify the form and concept, focusing specifically on comparisons between mainstream, corporate-owned media and its independent, online counterpart. Little feminist insight into the gendering of print and broadcast news appears to have filtered into analysis of online news. On the contrary, "alternative" news online (generally analyzed as separate to and separable from mainstream media), has often been portrayed as a gender-neutral form of media output, with emphasis placed on the virtues of the technology and little attention given to the social, cultural, and economic environment in which it functions (Brun 2005).

Independent news online has generally been positioned as part of the broader movement of "alternative" media. While many online news sites deliberately focus on alternatives to mainstream output, the mere fact of online existence and independence from corporate ownership does not constitute "alternative" media. While alternative media comprises a wide range of activities, from online literacy campaigns to hacking to public access programs, these are broadly understood to "offer fundamentally different messages and images to those of the mainstream" (Fenton 2006).

The merging of new and old media has led to broad similarities in the content and style of both public, corporate and private, noncorporate media. Analysis of citizen journalism[3] and unofficial news sourcing makes the explicit assumption that these news forms are inherently good things. This may be true; for many, it seems self-evident that challenges to the dominance of corporate media should be welcomed.

To position noncorporate media as the natural antidote to global conglomerates implies, however, that alternatives to the mainstream operate in a social vacuum. It is time to theorize the dynamics of online news, with particular reference to the gendering of access and content. Here it is useful to outline the key developments and core characteristics of independent online news. There are three main dimensions to the development of this form of news: technological change, economic activity online and off, and audience reception of Internet content.

The technological dimension is perhaps the most readily understood, its effects being measurable, visible, and often fairly dramatic. Before the Internet, producing nonmainstream media was difficult because alternative papers were costly to produce, generally suffered from poor distribution networks, and were often of an inferior quality to publications from commercial organizations (both aesthetically and content-wise).

The Internet provides several valuable features to alternative media producers, notably low production costs with high distribution potential, high production values (potentially equivalent to mainstream media), low-cost archiving facilities (extending the availability of publications indefinitely), and access to global audiences (Rodgers 2003, 95). For those seeking to pursue the tradition of independent journalism (Atton 2002; Downing 2001), the Internet has removed barriers—technical, financial, and distributive—inherent to offline publishing. This is not to suggest that this is media without problems, as audiences still need to be found, copy written, and websites produced and maintained.

The economic dimensions of Internet activity are manifold and complex. Mergers and acquisitions, the phenomenal growth of Internet advertising, and the sale of goods online alongside free offerings, contribute complex variables to a still little-understood marketing tool. In their early incarnations, many independent news sites saw their main objective as countering the output of mainstream media, as a small number of large media corporations, often perceived as biased toward the interests of political authorities and business elites, dominated media economics for more than two decades.

The liberalization and deregulation of markets in the 1980s created a "fiercely competitive environment where high investment costs necessitate access to overseas markets to produce the required returns" (Rodgers and Davison 2005, 60). In this competitive environment, the need to conglomerate increased, given the huge costs of entry into global markets. Media concentration has been widely debated, mainly regarding the demerits of a lack of pluralism in ownership and output. Doyle (2002, 11) has highlighted the potential sociopolitical and cultural implications of media concentration and the economic implications of allowing such large-scale operations. Within large-scale mergers and takeovers, profit generation through the creation of media synergies is crucial. Consequently the major media organizations seek to ensure that they own not only the means of production but also the means of promotion, merchandising, distribution, and redistribution. Although mainstream media organizations were slow to adopt or adapt to the Internet, this changed swiftly as the technology began to reach a wider audience and opportunities to generate revenue through sales and advertising became more obvious. As a result, online media is now another synergetic tool.

The notion of the Internet as an alternative to mainstream media has been tested with the increasing number of mergers and acquisitions transforming independent sites into global corporate phenomena. Partnerships include News Corporation's purchase of MySpace, a social networking site, for US$580 million in July 2005.[4] In October 2005 eBay, the Internet auction site, bought Skype, the dominant—and at the time of purchase largely free—Internet telephone service, for US$2.6 billion.[5] In 2005 Google, the world's biggest search engine, invested US$1 billion in America Online, a flagging offshoot of the Time Warner empire, in return for a 5 percent stake in the company. In 2006, in the largest of a long string of other investments, Google purchased YouTube, a video-sharing site established in May 2005, for US$1.65 billion.[6] In November 2006 Yahoo! announced a strategic partnership with 150 daily newspapers in the U.S., "in another step towards creating the most comprehensive advertising network in the online industry."[7] Microsoft, in the meantime, steadily bought other Internet, software, and media companies, acquiring over eighty between 1994 and 2006.[8]

Major Internet media corporations are now entrenched, with the profit motive solidly positioned in their business models. This is the environment in which online independent media now operates, a setting starkly different from the pioneering days of "alternative" information provision online. In this respect, the audience reception of content is intrinsically linked to the technological and economic changes witnessed on the Internet. Audiences are now in a much stronger position to post news stories online. At the same time, the news sites with the most traffic are corporately owned or controlled. While many sites hold onto independence, the major media organizations—with the Internet now being seen as part of the stable of media assets by the corporations themselves—are strongly positioned to influence news agendas online.

From a feminist perspective, these changes are significant because they signal a growing commodification of news online and offline. Commodification places constraints on journalistic content, as the need to attract and retain advertising revenue becomes prioritized (McNair 2003, 58). The status quo—uncontroversial content that does not offend advertisers and draws in revenue—is transferred by mainstream organizations to the online arena. At the same time, however, Internet users may have opportunities to disrupt the status quo in ways that broadcast and print media have never permitted. In theory, the technology allows this. In practice, some mechanisms may prove more useful than others to those seeking to adjust news agendas.

Multiple Models of Online News

The ways in which independent online news has evolved and its rapid expansion has raised two issues of particular significance: exclusionary practices that have evolved through the design (or lack thereof) of the organizational structure, and the potential replications of gender exclusions that have long been broader societal norms.

The convergence of technologies—particularly the ease of video streaming and podcasting—has led to a proliferation of news sites, with the definition of "news" becoming ever broader. The extensively modified concept of news values originating from the work of Galtung and Ruge (1981) must now be revised. As the *Washington Post* puts it, "News is no longer a lecture. It's a dialogue, a conversation, a fast-and-furious exchange among the millions around the globe who choose to know."[9]

News online spans a vast range of subjects, far broader than print and broadcast news have typically addressed, and the priorities of different websites permit alternative framings of both subjects and stories. It is here where the independent or alternative nature of some news sites is most evident. While the large commercial news sites seem to draw from a variety of news sources, the majority of stories originate with sources dominant in mainstream media. For example, Google News appears to offer thousands of interpretations of a single story, but items from the major agencies—Reuters, Associated Press (AP), and Agence France-Presse (AFP)—and the major mainstream sites—CNN and the BBC—heavily dominate agendas. Cross-media ownership—where media organizations own print, radio, television and Internet news outlets—compounds the narrow scope of online content, with the same stories distributed and syndicated across multiple networks.

By way of illustration, consider that of the top twenty online news sites in the U.S. in October 2006, only one of the companies listed was dedicated exclusively to news provision.[10] That company, the AP, is a not-for-profit news cooperative and one of the world's largest news agencies. Its board of directors includes executives from the world's leading media organizations, none of which is exclusively a news provider. Changes may be taking place in the news industry, but it seems that the funnel model of top-down news provision is still operational in the interactive era.

For Downey and Fenton (2003), the current state of media ownership has created a situation where "horizontal communication between citizens is increasingly replaced by vertical communication between mass media . . . and consumers" (186). Many argue that the content of much mass media output, and of journalism in particular, has been dumbed down, partly to meet the needs of media corporations, to prevent offense to advertisers, and to suit the mobile lifestyles of Western consumers. For Davis (2003), "investigative, contextualized journalism and coverage of complex debates and policy-making . . . [has] made way for scandal, 'infotainment,' personality-led news and public relations material" (671). Despite the economic shifts in media industries, the concept of dumbing down does have its detractors.[11]

Whichever perspective is taken, it was this arena—of corporate monoliths, with their news operations only one of a range of profit-generating divisions—that the new players entered. These new players—"ordinary" people—have used the Internet to affect, substantially but largely without design, the nature of news provision. On the early independent news sites, the technology was seen as a powerful mechanism for providing alternatives to the output of corporately owned publications, publishing stories that would not appear in mainstream media, written in ways that challenged some of the traditions of conventional journalism. Dan Gillmor (2004), a journalist and long-time advocate of the Internet, suggested that

> the ability of anyone to make the news will give new voice to people who've felt voiceless—and whose words we need to hear. They are showing all of us—citizen, journalist, newsmaker—new ways of talking, of learning (xviii).

This invocation of the freedom of expression that the Internet could offer echoes early feminist reflections on the technology's promise, as noted by Simone Murray in chapter 17 of this volume. While Murray later critiques the notion of female emancipation, Youngs (2003) highlights the concept of boundaries that contain and constrain women: "There is an understanding that boundaries of many kinds shape the processes by which knowledges are developed and established, understood and communicated. These boundaries are physical, organizational and symbolic" (55).

As the Internet continues to grow, these boundaries become increasingly evident online. The vast, unknowable expanse called cyberspace has firm demarcations. There is gatekeeping, and there are multiple constraints on women's influence on and inclusion in the development of the social, economic, and political orders of the Internet.

Despite this—or perhaps because the boundaries become ever more evident—there are ways in which the evolving discourse of the Internet can be shaped. Citizen journalism is the key component of online independent media although, given the changes noted previously, there are now multiple factors that come into play when determining what constitutes "alternative" media. While format, focus, and content may differ, there is an identifiable common objective for many of the independent online news sites: to create a mechanism for raising the profile of issues generally not covered by, or perceived to be subject to biased coverage by, media owned by the major conglomerates. This concept is applicable to both profit-making and nonprofit sites operating, in principle at least, outside the mainstream.

If a key motivation for many social movements is to create a mechanism for raising the profile of issues that operate outside of mainstream political thought, actors operating in this area are positioning Internet technology as a key tool in activist practice and for raising awareness.[12] Seeking to use the lack of corporate or institutional barriers to publication to best effect, independent online news can look like and compete with mainstream output; it does not, however, have to sound like it or reflect its agendas.

The commercialization of Internet news has led to a hybrid model for some sites that aim to be commercial and profit-generating, while encouraging citizen journalism and alternative voices. OhmyNews, a Korean website that now publishes a popular international version in English, is seen as the standard-bearer for this form of professional plus citizen journalism (Outing 2004). While nonprofessionals submit the bulk of content (around 70 percent), editors employed by the site prepare the articles for online publication. While the emphasis is certainly on citizen journalism and nonmainstream publishing, the site is also profitable, with income of US$6 million in 2005, plus an investment of US$11 million from Softbank in 2006 (Gannes 2006).

Two of the most prominent independent online news sites were formed on the basis of a more overtly ideological reading of mainstream media. AlterNet is a nonprofit offshoot of the Independent Media Institute, with a management structure, a team of paid staff, and fund-raising mechanisms that include the sale of stories and acceptance of grants from foundations. One of the most successful left-leaning political websites, averaging 1.7 million visitors each month, AlterNet sees its goal as inspiring citizen discussion, action, and advocacy, while challenging "the ability of the right-wing media apparatus to dominate public discourse at the expense of liberal and progressive values."[13]

With its nonprofit status and professional editorial team, AlterNet might best be seen as a professional-plus-political model for online journalism. The bulk of its content is written by its own team of journalists, though the organization uses much reader-generated content[14] and engages readers in two-way communication. AlterNet is not a citizen journalism space; rather, it is a news site with a nonmainstream agenda, where the reporting is heavily influenced by both the political stance of the organization and by readership input.

Outside the hybrid professional-plus-citizen (such as OhmyNews) and professional-plus-political (such as AlterNet) models, stands Indymedia, a loose collective of local news sites operating under a global organizational framework. Formed in Seattle in November 1999, the project was originally conceived as a short-term, one-off venture that covered protests against the World Trade Organization meetings taking place in the city. This first Indymedia website received an estimated 1.5 million hits during the protests (Hyde 2005). The main reason for this high volume of traffic was the eyewitness reports and on-the-ground video footage providing evidence of police actions which the mainstream media either did not have access to or chose not to report. Specifically the Seattle Indymedia site (or, to use the organization's terminology, Independent Media Center, or IMC) had access to footage of police using rubber bullets during the protests. This footage was uploaded and accessible online at the same time as denials of such actions were being made in televised press conferences. This generated a huge amount of publicity for Indymedia—not least because news networks changed their output in response to the website.

Indymedia differs from the other organizations examined so far in that it "provides a public forum for independent journalists and media organizations to post their own articles about myriad issues but doesn't determine what issues those independent journalists cover."[15] Indymedia is staffed entirely by volunteers and accepts no funding apart from individual donations. The sites—in all continents, numbering over 150 in November 2006[16]—are all locally managed, though there are no central offices. Any individual can start an IMC, once sanctioned by the Indymedia global group (another collective of volunteers), and any individual can post to the sites. Indymedia has no editorial policy, other than not to edit: if you post, you will be published.

Filling the Gender Gaps

With the new models of news construction and distribution, it could be assumed that opportunities for feminist influence of news content have increased. Some structures of online news offer greater potential than others, however. While the technology permits interaction, dialogue, and a flexible approach to news provision, real and symbolic barriers to access remain. Where it is in the interest of news providers to permit or promote feminist agendas, the potential exists for this to happen. There is a need, though, for active engagement on the part of both news organizations and feminists as commentators and content providers to effect such change.

Commercial, mainstream media owned and operated by major corporations offers little comfort to analysts who predicted that the Internet would herald a new, more egalitarian news order. Although they have slowly embraced Internet technologies, the top-down structure of agenda setting and old media priorities prevail on the websites of large media corporations. Individuals can contribute to news stories, through "have your say" links, blogs, and podcasts. The Internet is only just becoming a potentially profitable venture for large companies—note that they need to achieve returns on their heavy investments and find ways of acquiring predictable revenues from advertising. For these reasons, and in spite of appearances to the contrary, their approach to Internet economics is cautious at best.

Moreover, although women have made some headway in broadcast and print media, none of the major commercial news divisions online demonstrates a commitment to addressing, or even acknowledging, the gendered constituents and construction of news. There are few, if any, spaces for feminist news, stories, or priorities on the major news sites. The Internet may prove instrumental in influencing the gendered construction of news over time; it is, after all, a relatively new technology in a commercial environment that is adapting slowly to broader social change. Changes in the working environment for women as journalists, editors, and producers have, however, been long-fought-for and hard-won, and as long as economic imperatives allow media companies to treat gender as a marketing demographic, it is likely that they will continue to do so.

Neither the professional-plus-citizen sites nor the professional-plus-political sites offer a commitment to addressing gender concerns. That said, input from nonprofessionals, coupled with the active endeavors of such sites to use stories not included in mainstream media, have already influenced the shape and style of online news and, more broadly, other media. The main contribution this form of media makes to feminism is to blur the boundaries of news making, positioning citizens and their interests within news agendas. This shift in focus—from the elite to the everyday—has trickled down from sites like this into mainstream news production, with citizen journalism sites making use of available interactive technology long before the major media organizations did. AlterNet does include feminist blogs occasionally and does cover "feminist" news stories. These are not highlighted as such (for example, there are no separate headers and the items are not foregrounded), though it could be argued that this positions feminist news as an ordinary, rather than an extraordinary, feature of the information environment.

Of the online news models considered here, only Indymedia demonstrates a commitment to addressing gender issues, first through its organizational structure, and second through its content. Following criticism from women within the network, the organization has recognized that there are two main areas where gender exclusions occur. One is around the amount of time that needs to be dedicated to involvement with the sites, particularly in their startup stage. In previous interviews on online activism, a number of Indymedia volunteers commented that the constant demands of participation are onerous for many women. As Sara Platon put it, "There are tensions between male and female participation. Being a part of an editorial collective often means being accessible twenty-four hours a day"[17] (see also Platon and Deuze 2003). Terms such as *burnout* and *exhaustion* surfaced repeatedly, particularly with respect to establishing new centers.

Indymedia is often praised for its proprietary software which provides a space for open publishing. Criticisms have arisen among female volunteers, though, regarding the "ownership" of the network by techies. One interviewee suggested that there is a "cliqueiness" to the tech side of Indymedia, saying that the mainly young men who run it are largely unaware of gender/technology considerations and often speak in exclusionary, jargonistic terms.[18] Pickard (2006) notes that a "prevailing problem is power asymmetries within the network . . . and lingering traditional hierarchies dominated by white North American men" (334). The IMC global group is seeking to address these issues through the

ImcWomyn space, a discussion forum by and for women regarding their role within the organization.[19]

There is room for the inclusion of feminist voices in online media; needed first are strategies to make these heard. Indeed, the Internet can offer opportunities that mainstream media cannot and will not provide. Alongside structural imbalance in news media is a negative influence on public debate, which "is further skewed by an institutional bias toward the perspectives of corporate spokespeople and away from the voices of women, people of color, and other public interest representatives" (Pozner 2005). This dual and self-replicating bias does not necessarily need to be transferred to the online environment. While alternative news media will play an important function in shifting the focus away from corporate concerns, feminists too—as organizations and individuals—will need to take an active role.

Conclusion

That Internet technology historically has been designed along gendered lines is well known and, for many, no longer acceptable. As the numbers of women training in information technology grow, so too does the potential for influencing Internet content and, by extension, the ways that news is constructed. Projects such as the APC Women's Networking Support Project,[20] UNESCO's Gender and ICTs program,[21] and thousands operating at local, national, and international levels are designed to help women redress the skills balance in the use of information technology.

Male domination of the Internet is not a given. While it is evident from the discussion above that feminist influence of online news is still limited, some of the prominent tools of Internet content development are increasingly being adopted and adapted by women. For example, in a wide-reaching analysis of blog activity, Burton (2005) notes that a significant majority of bloggers are women under age thirty (68.1 percent female to 31.9 percent male). This encouraging statistic implies that barriers—physical, organizational, and symbolic—can be shifted, sometimes unexpectedly and almost imperceptibly. The significance of women bloggers lies in the fact that this is the most innovative area of online news, disrupting both traditional form and content. For Paul (2005), blogging and forums "promise to bring in a new wave of communication linkage between reporters and their audiences." While the majority of online news comes from wire copy, blogs and discussions on news forums provide original content and, with this, opportunities to shape agendas.

Youngs (2003, 62) has stressed the importance of recognizing the silences that position women. There are differing possibilities for influencing the discourse of online news, promoting gender as a category of interest and concern in news agendas, and using the Internet to challenge the potential of big voices to drown out smaller ones.

The most compelling possibility would be to subvert mainstream media from within. This is particularly applicable to the professional-plus-citizen journalism sites, whose increasing advertising revenues suggest at least the potential for growing influence. If a story has already been written for feminist media, why not copy it to OhmyNews, AlterNet, and others—sites that actively seek stories that do not reflect mainstream news agendas? The major commercial sites also provide some opportunities to comment and respond to stories, so, if CNN asks "what do you think?" perhaps it is time for more feminists to tell them. Finally, although the majority of blogs are posted by females, there is an imbalance in our understanding of who dominates this field. This is not a technological realm dominated by white males; it is a female-friendly technology based on networking and sharing information and ideas. Maybe feminist blogs should be shared a little more widely.

Pozner (2005) identifies a number of ways in which feminists, as media players, can confront news bias. Her suggestions include turning the corporate media monologue into a dialogue, countering misrepresentations and attacks, correcting the record, exposing biased framing, challenging double standards, and supporting groups that debunk media bias and amplify public interest voices. Any of these approaches may have an impact on gender bias online and, importantly, none are too onerous and all can be done without undue pressure on anyone to change the world alone.

In spite of the best efforts of major media organizations, the Internet is an arena where patriarchal power structures are yet to be embedded. Online news is one area where feminist influence can become apparent. Given the number of female bloggers, professional and citizen journalists, and, increasingly, technicians and software designers, it is evident that women possess the tools to promote a gender-aware approach to news online. It would be a shame if the opportunity were wasted.

Appendix: Feminist News Sites

Feminist Campus
www.feministcampus.org/know/news/
The world's largest prochoice student network.

Feminist Majority Foundation
www.feminist.org/news/
Founded in 1987, dedicated to women's equality, reproductive health, and nonviolence.

Feministing
www.feministing.com/
Provides a platform for young women to speak on issues that affect their lives and futures.

Ms. Magazine
www.msmagazine.com/news/news/asp
"More than a Magazine—A Movement," founded in 1971 and now part of the Feminist Majority Foundation.

National Organization for Women
www.now.org
Founded in 1966, the largest organization of feminist activists in the United States.

Protofeministimiehet
www/profeministimiehet.net/en/aggregator/categories
Helskinki-based profeminist group, founded in 1999.

Said It Feminist News
www.said it.org/
Feminist news, culture, and politics.

Women's eNews
www.womensenews.org/
Covers issues of concern to women and provides women's perspectives on public policy.

Women's Wire
http//womenswire.net.intro.htm
International women's news site, funded by a grant from UNICEF.

World Pulse Magazine
http://worldpulsemagazine.com/
Addresses the underrepresentation of women and children in international news media.

Notes

Acknowledgments. Thanks to Sherri Harnden, Devin Therriott-Orr, Sara Platon, Tony Harcup, Chris Atton, Geoffrey Gurd, and other interviewees and e-mail correspondents who have chosen to remain anonymous.

1. The most comprehensive report to date on global news and gender was conducted in 2005 by Gallagher (2005). See also Benton Foundation, "Does Bigger Media Equal Better Media—Four

Academic Studies of Media Ownership in the United States," October 2006, www.benton.org/ Benton_files/MediaOwnershipReportfinal.pdf (accessed 30 January 2007); Jayne Rodgers, "Icons and Invisibility: Gender, Myth and 9/11," in *War and the Media*, ed. Daya Thussu and Des Freedman, 200–12 (London: Sage, 2004); Karen Ross, "Women at Work: Journalism as En-gendered Practice," *Journalism Studies* 2, no. 4 (2001):531–44; Annabelle Sreberny and Liesbet van Zoonen, *Gender, Politics and Communication* (Cresskill, NJ: Hampton Press, 2000).

2. See the following for early, influential writings on gender and technology: Cynthia Cockburn, *Brothers: Male Dominance and Technological Change* (London: Pluto Press, 1981); Cynthia Cockburn and Susan Ormrod, *Gender and Technology in the Making* (London: Sage, 1993); Saskia Everts, *Gender & Technology—Empowering Women, Engendering Development* (London: Zed Books, 1998); Keith Grint and Rosalind Gill, *The Gender-Technology Relation—Contemporary Theory and Research* (London: Taylor & Francis, 1995); and Judy Wajcman, *Feminism Confronts Technology* (Cambridge: Polity, 1991).

3. "Citizen" or "grassroots" journalism can be defined as "the collecting and publication of timely, unique, nonfiction information by individuals without formal journalism training or professional affiliation." See Robert Niles, "A Glossary of Online News Terms," *USC Annenberg Online Journalism Review*, www.ojr.org/ojr/wiki/glossary/ (accessed 29 January 2007).

4. For background and analysis, see Patricia Sellers, "MySpace Cowboys," *CNN Money 2006* http://money.cnn.com/magazines/fortune/fortune_archive/2006/09/04/8384727/index.htm (accessed 27 November 2006).

5. For background and analysis, see Rob Hof, "Why ebay is Buying Skype," *Business Week*, 12 September 2005, www.businessweek.com/the_thread/techbeat/archives/2005/09/why_ebay_is_buy.html (accessed 27 November 2006).

6. See Google corporate information, www.google.com/corporate/history.html#2006 (accessed 27 November 2006); Bob Garfield, "The YouTube Effect," *Wired* magazine, December 2006, 222–26.

7. Hearst Corporation, "Yahoo! forms strategic partnership with Hearst and consortium of more than 1500 newspapers across the US," www.hearst.com/news/press_112006.html (accessed 29 November 2006).

8. See Microsoft Investor Relations—Acquisitions, www.microsoft.com/msft/acquisitions/history .mspx#EV (accessed 27 November 2006).

9. Washington Post/Newsweek Interactive, www.washingtonpost.com/wp-adv/mediacenter/ html/about_welcome.htm (accessed 29 November 2006).

10. CyberJournalist.net, "Top News Sites for October," www.cyberjournalist.net/news/ 003878.php (accessed 29 November 2006).

11. McNair (2003) argues that the thesis "represents an imposition of relatively arbitrary taste distinctions on the journalistic arena, and the application of traditional mass culture theory, developed in the very different social and political conditions of the pre–World War Two era, to circumstances in which it no longer has much relevance."

12. Whether the forms of online news considered here constitute a social movement is open to debate. They certainly demonstrate many characteristics of social movements, but their scope and remits are too broad to be considered as a unifying objective. This is a topic too complex to engage in here but should be subject to further research.

13. "The Case for AlterNet," http://alternet.org/about/ (accessed 28 November 2006).

14. "Case for Alternet."

15. Indymedia FAQs, https://docs.indymedia.org/view/Global/FrequentlyAskedQuestionEn#post (accessed 28 November 2006).

16. Indymedia FAQs.

17. Sara Platon, e-mail correspondence with author, 16 March 2004. Sara has been involved with the Indymedia network as both a contributor and an academic.

18. Sara Platon, e-mail correspondence, 16 March 2004.

19. Indymedia Documentation Project, 2006, https://docs.indymedia.org/view/Global/ImcWomyn (accessed 26 November 2006).

20. APC Women's Networking Support Project, www.apcwomen.org/eng_index.shtml (accessed 7 January 2007).

21. http://portal.unesco.org/ci/en/ev.php-URL_ID=1475&URL_DO=DO_TOPIC&URL_SECTION=20.html (accessed 7 January 2007).

References

Atton, Chris. 2002. *Alternative Media*. London: Sage.

Brun, Axel. 2005. *Gatewatching: Collaborative Online News Production*. New York: Peter Lang.

Burton, Kevin. 2005. "Balancing Acts." Perseus Weblog Survey. www.perseus.com/blogsurvey/blogsurvey.html (accessed 26 November 2006).

Byerly, Carolyn M. 2006. "Questioning Media Access: Analysis of Women and Minority FCC Ownership Data." In *Does Bigger Media Equal Better Media—Four Academic Studies of Media Ownership in the United States*. www.benton.org/benton_files/MediaOwnershipReportfinal.pdf (accessed 30 January 2007).

Davis, Aeron. 2003. "Whither Mass Media and Power? Evidence for a Critical Elite Theory Alternative." *Media, Culture & Society* 25:671.

Downey, John, and Natalie Fenton. 2003. "New Media, Counter Publicity and the Public Sphere." *New Media and Society* 5, no. 2:185–202.

Downing, John. 2001. *Radical Media: Rebellious Communications and Social Movements*. London: Sage.

Doyle, Gillian. 2002. *Media Economics*. London: Sage.

Fenton, Natalie. 2006. "Another World Is Possible." *Global Media and Communication* 2, no. 3:355–67.

Gallagher, Margaret. 2005. "Who Makes the News? Global Report 2005." Global Media Monitoring Project. www.whomakesthenews.org/who_makes_the_news/report_2005 (accessed 22 December 2006).

Galtung, Johan, and Marie Holmboe Ruge. 1981. "Structuring and Selecting News." In *The Manufacture of News*, eds. Stanley Cohen and Jock Young, 62. London: Constable.

Gannes, Liz. 2006. "*OhmyNews* Bags Softbank Millions—Red Herring." March 13. http://english.ohmynews.com/articleview/article_view.asp?article_class=8&no=153109&rel_no=2#Ohmynews:%20Voices%20From%20the%20Street-Business%20Week (accessed 28 November 2006).

Gillmor, Dan. 2004. *We the Media: Grassroots Journalism by the People for the People*. Sebastopol, CA.: O'Reilly Media.

Hyde, Gene. 2005. "Independent Media Centers: Cyber-Subversion and the Alternative Press." *First Monday* 7, no. 4. www.firstmonday.org/issues/issue7_4/hyde/ (accessed 28 November 2006).

Lebert, Joanne. 2003. "Wiring Human Rights Activism: Amnesty International and the Challenges of Information and Communication Technologies. In *Cyberactivism: Online Activism in Theory and Practice*, eds. Martha McCaughey and Michael D. Ayers, 209–32. New York: Routledge.

McNair, Brian. 2003. *News and Journalism in the UK*, 4th ed. London: Routledge.

Outing, Steve. 2004. "Taking Tsunami Coverage into Their Own Hands." Poynter Organization. www.poynter.org/content/content_view.asp?id=76520 (accessed 20 December 2006).

Paul, Nora. 2005. "New News Retrospective: Is Online News Reaching its Potential?" USC Annenberg Online Journalism Review. www.ojr.org/ojr/stories/050324paul/ (accessed 29 December 2006).

Pickard, Victor W. 2006. "United Yet Autonomous: Indymedia and the Struggle to Sustain a Radical Democratic Network." *Media, Culture & Society* 28, no. 3:315–36.

Platon, Sara, and Mark Deuze. 2003. "Indymedia Journalism: A Radical Way of Making, Selecting and Sharing News?" *Journalism* 4, no.3:336–55.

Pozner, Jennifer L. 2005. "Reclaiming the Media for a Progressive Feminist Future." *Media Development*, no 3. www.wacc.org.uk/wacc/publications/media_development/2005_3/reclaiming_the_media_for_a_progressive_feminist_future (accessed 30 January 2007).

Rodgers, Jayne. 2003. *Spatializing International Politics: Analysing Activism on the Internet*. London: Routledge.

Rodgers, Jayne, and Annette Davison. 2005. "Sounds Complicated? Music, Film and Media Synergies." In *Resounding International Relations: On Music, Culture, and Politics*, ed. M.I. Franklin, 53–70. New York: Palgrave/Macmillan.

Youngs, Gillian. 2003. "Virtual Voices: Real Lives." In *women@Internet: Creating New Cultures in Cyberspace*, ed. Wendy Harcourt, 55–68. New York: Zed Books.

PART FOUR

LABORING INTERNATIONAL COMMUNICATION

CHAPTER FOURTEEN

Convergences: Elements of a Feminist Political Economy of Labor and Communication

Vincent Mosco, Catherine McKercher, and Andrew Stevens

This chapter examines four interrelated perspectives on a feminist political economy of labor and communication organized around responses to the converging worlds of work and home. In the process, it draws into the orbit of communication studies an area of research, feminism, that is typically left on the borders of the field by taking up a topic, labor, that is itself typically sequestered on the margins (for an exception, see Balka and Smith, 2000). The chapter aims to demonstrate the value of bringing together feminist and political-economic ways of thinking about labor in the broadly defined communication arena. All four perspectives take seriously the need to build connections between political-economic and feminist research, and they recognize the importance of the communication, information, and knowledge sphere as a substantive base for exploring that relationship. The chapter also maintains that it is not possible to fully comprehend the relationship of gender to the workplace without understanding the relationship of the workplace to the home. Finally, the chapter suggests that a feminist analysis is a crucial component of research on labor because, as Zillah Eisenstein (1998) argues, global capitalism thrives on a transnational sexual division of labor.

The first perspective identifies home and work as separate categories of analysis but draws on political-economic and labor theory to understand domestic labor. The home is a nexus for the reproduction and maintenance of labor power, and gender is an inseparable element of this reality, since traditionally it is women who do the housework. A feminist analysis of domestic work under capitalism offers a useful starting point for this perspective, one that recognizes the complex structures of work, home, and gender relations (Gerstein 1973; Rubin 1975). Furthermore, this approach uses the language of wage labor and the market, particularly the processes of commodification and decommodification, to make sense of what has historically been women's unpaid work. This perspective adds fresh dimensions to understanding the function of household labor in capitalism, particularly the forms of women's exploitation, and uncovers grounds for feminist resistance.

Much of this scholarship originated in feminist technology studies. Cowan (1983), studying a series of innovations that amounted to an industrial revolution in the home in the early twentieth century, found that new technologies like electricity and indoor plumbing brought about significant changes in the labor process of the household. Servants—mainly women who were paid for their labor—disappeared from middle-class homes. The number of tasks for which the unpaid housewife was responsible increased as the work became more generalized. In the factory, industrialization and scientific management led to a specialization of work that divided it into discrete tasks. This was not the case in the home. And while the labor process in the factory tended to reduce the emotional content of men's work, the industrial revolution in the home had the opposite effect on women. Advertisers in popular women's magazines used guilt and embarrassment to prod women into adopting higher standards of cleanliness and household organization, thus creating markets for new cleaning products and housewares.

Ursula Huws has recently applied this perspective to the sphere of communication and information technology. In *The Making of a Cybertariat* (2003), Huws builds on the growing body of literature on women, work, and the home with over two decades of research to challenge some of the truisms that limit understanding in the field. One of the most fundamental views is that technology saves work time in the home and therefore frees women to enter the world of wage labor. There is no doubt that electrification and gas power distribution, which made possible the numerous appliances that fill most homes in the developed world, cut substantially the amount of time it takes to complete certain tasks. But as Huws documents, these devices create time commitments of their own and contribute to the expansion of needs and desires that take up time in new ways. Considerable energy is now invested in the purchase and upkeep of appliances and in a culture that fills time with the need to make the best use of them. Purchasing the right stove and fridge with just the right customized features, including the new "smart" appliances, is a significant component of creating and running a modern household. Even more significant in eroding the "labor-saving device" thesis is the proliferation of new and time-consuming ways to use home technologies. With the right appliances, everyone can—and, more importantly, everyone should—become a master chef, as well as an expert in home decorating, design, and maintenance. These jobs take time, usually the time considered saved by the devices themselves.

In essence, this perspective suggests that capitalism commodifies the home by enforcing the notion that the value of domestic work depends on the value of the products and services that fill the home. The list of appliances considered indispensable for a quality home now includes the full range of communication and information technologies—cable and satellite-delivered television, high-speed Internet services, multiple wired and wireless telephones, high-end video and sound systems, digital cameras, and all of the customized add-ons that are considered essential to realize the full potential of these devices and services. The all-electric home promoted by the General Electric Company in the 1950s appeared futuristic, but it barely hinted at the range of communication, information, and entertainment systems that would fill households fifty years later. It also neglected to note that operating and managing all of these new systems would require substantial labor commitments in terms of both time and skill.

The expansion of capitalism into the home has not, however, resulted in any substantial advance in bringing household work into the orbit of wage labor. In essence, capitalism expands its presence in the household by generating new technologies and the new needs they help to create. But it stops short of paying those who work on them for their labor. And although men have become increasingly involved in areas like communication technology management, women are still largely responsible for much of the household management process. It is women, therefore, whose exploitation in the home is deepened. Research on time spent on household management indicates that men enjoy at least thirty minutes more free time per day than women (Mattingly and Bianchi 2003). Furthermore, because the modern household requires major investments in technology and services, there are strong pressures to turn unpaid household labor into paid labor, either in the home or outside it.

In essence, what start out as conceptually separate arenas, home and workplace, turn into zones of mutual constitution, as the need for wage labor to maintain the home grows. To compensate, women (and men) whose household labor goes unrewarded in the wage system are bringing wage labor into the home or going out into the traditional workplace. The only alternative is mobilizing the labor power of unwaged household laborers, and efforts in this area have not been particularly successful. Nevertheless, Huws maintains, labor organizations and feminist social movements need to make this a priority because the growth of what amounts to labor-creating devices in the home will only deepen the problem of unwaged household labor in the future. Moreover, some analysts demonstrate that the expansion of women's unpaid labor is merely symptomatic of a deeper extension of labor into the consumer realm, as those who purchase goods and services increasingly contribute to the labor required to supply them. This so-called voluntary labor means that, among many other things, we now pump our own gas, clear our own tables in fast food restaurants, dial our own telephone calls, assemble our own furniture from Ikea, and find our own groceries in supermarkets (Fox 2002).

Communication scholars can contribute to deepening our understanding of the area with research that documents the nature of unpaid work in the home. And because an increasing amount of housework is spent on old and new media, this increasingly falls into the realm of our expertise. Years ago, the political economist of communication Dallas Smythe established a groundwork for this kind of research by documenting the extent of audience labor in the home through the sale of people's attention to advertisers. Smythe (1977) calculated the capital that families invested in providing the equipment—at the time it was radio and television receivers—and the money required to keep them operating, and also calculated the value of the time that audiences spent delivering their attention to advertisers of the programs they listened to and watched. In Smythe's view, unwaged audience labor propelled the commercial broadcasting system. Meehan (Meehan and Riordan 2002) has built on this work to examine the commodification of audiences through the broadcast ratings services and has extended it by constructing an important bridge between Smythe's political-economic analysis and feminist research. Drawing on this work and expanding its conceptual grounding with the work of Huws and others could lead us to calculate the wage bill for uncompensated household labor. Combine this with the absence of many of the benefits that typically accompany waged work, including health insurance, safety regulations, disability and pension plans, and so forth, and one would come up with a large sum which would serve as one index of the enormous gap between what labor and other social movements have achieved and what is left to be done.

If the first perspective focuses on the penetration of capitalism into the home and how it profits from unwaged or free labor, the second concentrates on the expansion of the workplace into the home, making the latter the site for traditionally waged labor. Furthermore, the contemporary incarnation of global capitalism creates a multiplicity of roles for women, as wives, housekeepers, child rearers, *and* as low-paid workers (Eisenstein 1998). One especially valuable exemplar, particularly for students of communication and information technology, is the work of Pellow and Park, whose book *The Silicon Valley of Dreams* (2002) documents the expansion into the home of the high-tech industry, which relies on low-wage (and often immigrant) female labor to carry out basic assembly work. In this view, home work is not the domestic labor of the unpaid homemaker but the wage labor of women with few alternatives than to turn their homes into an extension of a factory or a call center (Head 2003).

There is nothing new about home work, including industry reliance on newly arrived legal or illegal immigrants. Decades ago the U.S. textile industry was heavily dependent on home work. After the Second World War, the U.S. government banned industrial home work in seven industries—including women's apparel, embroideries, handkerchief manufacturing, jewelry manufacturing, and knitted outerwear—in response to evidence that minimum wage and child labor laws were routinely being violated. Most of the bans were lifted in 1989, with the exception of women's apparel and "unsafe" jewelry production (Edwards and Field-Hendrey 2002, 172). What makes the work that Pellow and Park describe particularly interesting is that it is an important dimension of what is arguably the most strategically important industry in the world, one that promises a new grounding for work—information rich, environmentally sound, and likely to lead from traditional capitalism to a "friction-free" (Gates 1996), postindustrial, or networked capitalist society. But for those working at the bottom of the network society food chain, there are forms of exploitation that turn the home into a site of production.

According to Pellow and Park, literally thousands of immigrants, including many Cambodian, Korean, Vietnamese, Latina, and Filipina women, work on production jobs out of their homes in Silicon Valley. They make cables, circuit boards, and other computer components, working mainly in their kitchens, though bedrooms, bathrooms, garages, and living rooms are also popular. They routinely work with acids, lead, and solders, a chemical mix essential to construct modern communication infrastructures. Because they are paid at piece rates as low as a penny per component, it is not unusual for them to get their extended family of children and grandparents to help out. These women work long hours under the constant threat of dismissal. Health problems are common, ranging from neck and back pain through eye strain and sleep deprivation to respiratory disorders, problem pregnancies, and the inevitable serious health disorders like cancer brought about by long-term exposure to toxic chemicals.

In recent years, communication scholars have turned their attention to new media, including the worldwide spread of the Internet, cellular phones, and other computer communication systems. As a result, much of the attention in the home work field has gone to white-collar workers who do contract jobs writing software and managing websites (Barley and Kunda 2004). Furthermore, a number of scholars have looked at how these technologies have enabled women to do their paid work from home (Tremblay, Paquet, and Najem 2006). Some have suggested that, rather than allowing women to improve the balance between the demands of work and family, telework increases the strains (Menzies

1997; Duxbury and Higgins 2001). The use of new media in home work is an important development, but scholars have not probed deeply enough into the core of the production process that makes these technologies possible. As a result, very little work addresses the role of home work in building the information infrastructure. Given that the vast majority of home workers are women, this area should be of particular concern to those interested in a feminist analysis of communication and information technologies. Moreover, this research need not only focus on the admittedly significant problem of exploitation. One of the more remarkable stories to come out of Silicon Valley and other centers of information technology production in the developed and developing world is the growth of resistance to exploitation, particularly through the formation of unions, labor associations; and community-based social movements to bring change to the industry (Louie 2001; Smith, Sonnenfeld, and Pellow 2006).

The third perspective sees the erosion of both categories as home and work become so interpenetrated that they lose what independent value remains. Best exemplified in the work of the autonomist theorists, this perspective focuses on the emancipatory potential of new technologies and the accompanying rise of a knowledge-worker class. From this point of view, the home and the traditional workplace both become places of work and play, mutually constituted and a fundamental challenge to capitalist efforts to reduce all activity to wage labor. Building on a long tradition of Italian social theory, Hardt and Negri gave this autonomist perspective wide circulation in their book *Empire* (2000). A central pillar of this work is a belief in the rise of immaterial labor, or what some scholars call knowledge work (Huws 2006).

The development of immaterial labor has provoked widespread debate, but general agreement has emerged in key areas. First, a number of service- and knowledge-based occupations have been recognized as having a full range of health hazards (eye strain, back pain, stress, physical and mental health disorders, and so forth), including clerical jobs staffed largely by women. This reality certainly conflicts with the traditional image of office work as clean, safe, and healthful (Cassedy and Nussbaum 1983). There is also consensus that a shift from manufacturing to knowledge work has occurred in developed societies and is beginning to occur in some emerging economies as well. While there is recognition that knowledge is a crucial basis for manufacturing and agricultural work, the difference today is that an increasing amount of work is taken up with the production and distribution of information, communication, and knowledge. Furthermore, there is agreement that a dynamic process of deskilling, upskilling, and reskilling is taking place in the occupational hierarchy. At different times and in different sectors, one or another of these processes dominates, though the labor process, most concur, cannot be reduced to the singularity of one process (Brint 2001; Powell and Snellman 2004). What is often neglected, however, is the degree to which women workers may suffer the most, experiencing deskilling, labor intensification, and at the same time being pushed into jobs that constitute the peripheral labor market (Wigfield 2001), such as those located in the temporary help industries and other precarious sectors (Vosko 2000; 2006).

In today's new boundaryless workplace, workers are promised employability rather than long-term jobs, differential salaries pegged to market rates rather than wages tied to length of service, and networking opportunities rather than promotion opportunities (Stone 2004). And as Sweeney and Nussbaum (1989) concluded in the late 1980s, business policies are creating and destroying jobs at an accelerated pace, disrupting individual careers and communities overnight. Of course, such trends have had different impacts on men and women, thus the significance of a gender dimension when analyzing the consequences of corporate globalization and outsourcing.

Autonomist scholars have argued that the digital economy differs from one based on manufacturing because it requires a qualitatively different kind of work, one that demands a great deal of skill and creativity. This makes it much more difficult to manage and control (Terranova 2000; 2004). As such, these scholars have sought to uncover the transformational and liberatory potential of these new forms of work. From Terranova's perspective and that of other autonomists like Lazzarato (1997), it is very difficult to capture or routinize this type of creative labor. Such work can take place, and often does, virtually anywhere, from the traditional workplace to the home, and even in the substitutes for both, such as wireless-enabled coffee shops. But it bears the mark of none of these places and, in the process, challenges traditional notions of all of them. It is neither workplace work nor home work but represents, as the autonomists like to put it, the creation of the "social factory," or the transition of work processes from the factory to society. With an increasingly mobile workforce, work and play have become increasingly placeless—a situation that calls into question the nature of both work and home. Nevertheless, there is evidence to suggest that knowledge workers who perform their work at home and elsewhere are still subject to the managerial gaze through sophisticated networks of surveillance and screening techniques (Felstead, Walters, and Jewson 2005; Halford and Leonard 2006). While there are limitations on how far deskilling and routinization can go, management practice and theory (Davenport 2005) have attempted to bring knowledge work into the sphere of managerial control.

The idea that computer technology can support liberation movements as well as the march of capital has been introduced to communication studies primarily through the work of Nick Dyer-Witheford (1999), but this perspective has found less resonance in the feminist literature. One notable exception is the work of Mariarosa Dalla Costa on women and labor (Dalla Costa and Dalla Costa 1999). This is surprising in one sense because questioning fundamental, especially industrial, categories is certainly a pillar of feminist perspectives. However, it is clear that many of the jobs the autonomists describe are occupied by young men who work in the software firms, creating videogames or the latest online advertising. The autonomous perspective is less applicable, at least for now, to women who work in the knowledge industries. Their jobs, at the low end of hardware production or in rapidly growing service fields like call center work, are more easily subject to scientific management. In this respect, a feminist reading of autonomist theory applied to the contemporary workplace would see its value primarily in pointing to a gender divide in the kinds of work performed in the digital economy. It is the boys working on the toys who fit the autonomist vision of immaterial labor smashing traditional categories (Kline, Dyer-Witheford, and de Peuter 2003). Meanwhile, the girls are still working in a painfully material world, a world that promises flexibility but delivers precariousness, and that, for many, offers little more than what Leah Vosko (2000) calls "halfway houses for housewives." The autonomist vision holds out the potential for another world. Realizing that vision is a prodigious, if not impossible, task.

The final perspective draws on Mosco and McKercher's current research project and takes up responses from workers' organizations to the changing configuration of home and work. In essence, it focuses on the workplace, whether in the traditional factory or office or in the home, but from the perspective of trade unions and those social movements that are attempting to deal with the crisis in organized labor.

In recent years, the communication arena has seen the rise of large, integrated trade unions that bring together workers from across the converging communication sector. These efforts strengthen organized labor, particularly against conglomerate corporations. Nevertheless, although these unions are committed to equity, they tend to be dominated by men, not just in terms of hierarchy but in organizational culture as well. At the same time, declines in traditional union membership and the notorious difficulty of organizing workers in the information technology sector have prompted the rise of labor associations or social movements formed to defend the rights of workers by drawing into the movement people who cannot (or will not) join a traditional trade union. This section concludes by examining how both groups—traditional labor unions and nontraditional workers' organizations—address the needs and desires of their female membership.

Organized labor in Canada and the U.S. has been facing a crisis for a number of years. In both countries, union density, or the percentage of wage and salary workers who are union members, has declined substantially in the past two decades, even though the real numbers have increased. In the U.S., the overall percentage of unionized workers in 2003 sat at 12.9 percent, a startling figure when compared to the high of 20.1 percent in 1983 (U.S. Bureau of Labor Statistics 2006). The situation is marginally better in Canada, where in 2005 30.7 percent of workers were union members, an increase from 30.4 percent in 2004 (Bédard 2005). Interestingly, education, training, and library occupations, all of which include a large percentage of women members, had the highest unionization rates in 2004, at about 37 percent. This raises the tantalizing question of whether women knowledge workers might represent the cutting edge of a revival in trade unionism.

Nevertheless, there is general agreement among scholars and trade unionists that workers in the knowledge economy face serious problems. Two strategies stand out for doing something to rectify the problem. The first has seen established trade unions in the United States and Canada pursue mergers with other unions in hopes of mobilizing and concentrating resources. The second is the creation of worker associations or worker movements that operate outside the collective bargaining system.

In the United States, a range of media unions—the International Typographical Union (ITU), the Newspaper Guild, and the National Association of Broadcast Employees and Technicians (NABET)—have joined the Communications Workers of America (CWA). As a model convergent union—as the CWA likes to call itself, "the union for the information age"—the CWA represents 700,000 workers employed in telecommunications, broadcasting, cable TV, newspaper and wire service journalism, publishing, electronics, and general manufacturing, as well as airline customer service, government service, health care, education, and other fields. In Canada, the 150,000-member Communications, Energy and Paperworkers Union (CEP) has pursued a similar strategy. Its members work in pulp and paper mills, telephone and telecommunications companies, newspapers, radio, and television. They are also employed as graphic artists, hotel workers, computer programmers, truck drivers, and nurses. The diversity of the membership in these converged unions in the United States and Canada is also embodied in gender diversity. Predominantly female occupations, like telephone operator or newspaper clerical worker, are now a central part of largely male unions that include computer programmers and pulp and paper workers.

To a degree, the unions see convergence as defensive, or as a way of protecting their members against the increasing power of bigger and more concentrated employers. But significantly, they also see labor convergence as an attempt to take advantage of synergies brought about by growing convergence in the nature of their work (Bahr 1998). Since they represent workers who are increasingly involved in producing for a converging electronic information services arena, they see improved opportunities for organizing and bargaining.

In essence, converging technologies and converging companies have led workers to come together across the knowledge industry into converged labor unions (McKercher 2002).

At the same time, deconvergence has been occurring within labor organizations. For instance, the Service Employees International Union (SEIU) threatened to pull out of the AFL-CIO unless the federation permitted significant new mergers and made other organizational changes aimed at reversing the slide in union density. One of the demands presented by SEIU was to increase funding for grassroots organizing. The 1.8-million-member SEIU was a major force in the federation: not only was it the fastest-growing union in the AFL-CIO, it was the most diverse. Fifty-six percent of its members are women and 40 percent are people of color (SEIU 2005). In July 2005, the SEIU pulled out of the AFL-CIO to pursue a different model of unionism than that practiced by the AFL-CIO at the time. Six other unions, including the powerful Teamsters union, followed suit and joined with the SEIU to create a new labor federation, Change to Win. At its founding convention that September, the group chose Anna Burger as chair, making her the first woman to serve as leader of a major labor federation in the U.S. It also pledged the most aggressive organizing campaign in fifty years. Whether the group will succeed remains to be seen, but what is clear is that at the highest levels of organized labor in the United States, there is widespread dissatisfaction and a belief that labor convergence—larger but leaner unions, organized by industry or the economic sector, and committed to grassroots organizing—may be one of the major tools to address the crisis in trade unionism.

It is uncertain just how far the urge to merge and the creation of a new labor federation with an aggressive organizing campaign will take North American trade unions. Certainly, these developments contain echoes of the ideals behind the One Big Union movement, made popular in the nineteenth century by the Knights of Labor and the Industrial Workers of the World. Both the Knights and the Wobblies resisted the notion of exclusive craft unionism, pursued an agenda of social reform, and fought to bring into the labor movement groups that the craft unions excluded—including women and African Americans. In addition, the creation of Change to Win resonates with the debates over industrial unionism that led to the establishment and subsequent success of the CIO in the 1930s.

Trade union convergence is not without its opponents, however. Critics argue that it increases centralization and bureaucracy, which could mean a growing distance between the (predominantly male) leadership and women rank-and-file members. Women account for about 40 percent of union members in the U.S. and close to 50 percent in Canada (Granville 1999; Akyeampong 2004). In October 2005, the forty-six-member executive council of the AFL-

CIO had thirty-seven men. Women fare a bit better in the Canadian Labor Congress, holding about one-third of the positions on the federation's executive council. Joyce Nonde, the first female vice-president of UNI-Africa (Union Network International), remarked that it is difficult to implement policies specifically oriented toward women if union structures and responsibilities do not make such initiatives a priority (UNI 2004).

Supporters of trade union convergence argue that it gives unions greater clout in collective bargaining, which holds the potential for preserving and extending the so-called union wage premium—the difference between what a unionized and nonunionized worker earns when all other factors are constant—now averaging about 15 percent in Canada. But union membership is especially significant for women, since unions play a major role in closing the wage gap. Nonunion women make about 76.5 percent as much as nonunion men. Union women, by contrast, make 91 percent as much as union men, and a whopping 39 percent more than nonunion women (Jackson 2003, 7–9). Therefore, the stronger the union movement, supporters argue, the better it is for women workers.

Moreover, supporters of convergence argue that mergers allow unions to be more involved in social and political activities. Unions that address such issues provide venues for a multitude of oppressed groups to operate collectively, offering spaces for emancipation and empowerment through direct involvement in the process of change (Egan, Gardner, and Persad 1988). For example, in 2006 the CEP won its fourteen-year pay equity battle against Bell Canada, in a case brought on behalf of its women workers. Only a strong union could possibly afford to continue such an action against Canada's largest and arguably most powerful conglomerate. Moreover, one of the advantages of a converged union is its ability to rise above the narrow interests of some of its members. For instance, the CEP has fully supported the Kyoto accord to reduce greenhouse gas emissions, has been extensively involved in the antiglobalization movement (see Swift 2003), and has worked to build better protections for workers against workplace surveillance through collective bargaining agreements (Kiss and Mosco 2005).

Nevertheless, it is uncertain whether converged unions are genuinely bringing together different kinds of workers in the knowledge, information, and communication sectors, such as print or broadcast reporters and telephone operators, or whether they are merely federations of what are, in effect, dissimilar labor organizations representing dissimilar employees. This is particularly significant for women, because the merged unions are typically led not just by men, but by men from merger partners that historically were led by male workers. For convergence to genuinely benefit women workers, real integration is essential.

In the early 1980s, Ellen Cassedy and Karen Nussbaum recognized unionizing as a means for women to overcome class and gender inequalities in the workplace, notably sexual harassment and discrimination. Their influential 9 to 5: The Working Woman's Guide to Office Survival (1983) charted the multiple challenges facing women in the office and offered hope that collective organizing and knowledge of fundamental legal rights in the workplace could provide a sense of empowerment. Today the National Association of Working Women is committed to making the same gains for women and sets its sights on social justice unionism, not only economic gains. Social movement unionism has taken a crucial global step within the Union Network International, a Swiss-based organization formed in 2000 from a merger of four union federations spanning commerce, finance, telecommunications, and media. With over 15 million members in 150 countries, UNI has the potential to foster internationalism like no other labor organization.

In many ways, UNI takes up a similar torch as 9 to 5 by tackling the problems faced by women worldwide, in and out of the workplace: poverty, segregated career paths, discrimination, HIV/AIDS, and the traffic in women for sexual and labor exploitation. UNI recognizes that women workers are among those most likely to suffer from the negative impacts of globalization. Occupations dominated by women in the telecommunications, finance, graphical, and other services industries are increasingly being cut, contracted out, or outsourced to lower-wage countries or regions (UNI 2005c). UNI World Women's President Barbara Easterling has set a clear trajectory for women in the union movement: "It is women who are the vanguard of a new worldwide labor movement, one that has equality and justice at its core . . . one that is global in its outlook . . . creative in its strategies . . . and tenacious in its tactics" (UNI 2006). The 2005 World's Women Conference in Chicago supported an action program that put emphasis on organizing women into unions that are working in the formal and informal economy, in customer services, and in countries receiving outsourced work (UNI 2005b). Some months before, French telecom unions jointly signed an agreement determined to pressure telecommunications companies to reduce the imbalances between men and women in that industry (UNI 2005a).

Since its conception, UNI and some affiliate locals have been addressing inequalities between men and women in the workforce. As a UNI statement entitled "Women and the Information Society" points out, working women are to be found in lower-paid jobs at the bottom of the occupational scale in almost every sector, such as call handling, electronics assembly plants, teleworking, data entry, and customer service centers (UNI 2003). Devoid of job security, income security, and social protections, workers in these occupations are certainly in need of organizing. Importantly, structural changes and union democracy can offer equity-seeking groups and workers in precarious employment greater opportunities to participate fully in the movement (Gupta 2006).

A second response to the crisis in North American labor has been the formation of worker associations or worker movements that provide tangible and intangible benefits without formally negotiating collective agreements. These have been especially prominent in the high-tech sector, where union organizing has been especially difficult. Worker associations are also more prominent among part-time permanent workers and especially among contract employees, who are difficult to organize because they typically work for an employment agency that has a contract with high-tech companies, rather than being employed directly by the corporation. They have grown up in places like Silicon Valley in California, where fully 40 percent of workers are employed in non-standard ways, and in Microsoft's territory in the Pacific Northwest. Microsoft gave rise to the term "permatemp," or permanent temporary worker, someone who works full-time but on hourly contracts that contain practically no benefits or overtime pay (Brophy 2006). Among the goals of these associations are portable benefits for a highly mobile workforce, lifelong training, job placement, assistance to individual workers, dissemination of information to workers, and health care plans for workers who are not eligible for employer-paid benefits.

The Washington Alliance of Technical Workers (WashTech), an offshoot of the CWA, was formed in the Seattle high-tech industry by disgruntled Microsoft permatemps. It is the leading example of a worker association in the knowledge sector. WashTech includes programmers, editors, Web designers, systems analysts, proofers, testers, and engineers who aim to win higher pay, health benefits, vacations, access to retirement plans, discounted stock options, and workplace training. Drawing on the skills of its members, WashTech found a secret Microsoft database on employee performance containing information that it made available to its members. It also found contract documents dating back to 2001 cementing deals to outsource high-end software architecture to Indian firms that the company hoped to keep secret. WashTech has been successful at Microsoft, helped by its association with research advocacy groups such as the Center for a Changing Workforce and its online site, Techsunite.org, which provides information and online organizing for high-tech workers. WashTech's major victory was a court-ordered award of back pay and benefits for permatemps that Microsoft categorized as temporary workers in order to deny them the salary and benefits that permanent workers enjoyed. (van Jaarsveld 2004; Brophy 2006). Today WashTech is especially involved in fighting the outsourcing of tech jobs to places like India and China and has been successful in convincing some state legislators to stop outsourcing government tech work.

Worker associations are also increasingly prominent among content producers, whose ranks are more heavily composed of women. The advocacy group Working Today—representing independent workers like freelancers, consultants, and temps who are based in the area of New York known during the high-tech boom as Silicon Alley—has been particularly successful in providing basic health insurance to members. The Graphic Artists Guild represents Web creators, illustrators, and designers who come together to improve working conditions and intervene in the policy process dealing with copyright, taxation, and other important policy issues.

Finally, the AFL-CIO has been successful in building a new, community-level organization known as Working America, signing up close to a million members across the United States in less than a year and a half. Working America members agree to pay an annual fee and pledge to cooperate with unions in political and legislative campaigns. The organization reaches into the home, targeting nonunion members and retirees. In addition to traditional door-to-door canvassing, it signs up members online. It is especially noteworthy that its founding director is Karen Nussbaum, one of the founders of the National Association of Worker Women. According to Nussbaum, "Working America has found a way to harness the power of workers who do not have a union on the job in the fight for better social and economic policies, and corporate and political accountability." The goal is to encourage activism and, eventually, a progressive majority in the U.S. (Nussbaum 2005).

Supporters of worker associations see these groups as a new form of unionism that makes use of new technology to reach workers, particularly women, who have little experience with unions (Greene and Kirton 2003). These associations are also a way of bringing into the labor movement people who, for whatever reason, do not necessarily want to be part of a trade union. They also represent a recognition that in a world of accelerating mobility, formal collective agreements do not mean as much as they once did. Critics see the new associations as providing little hope for the future. Because they are by and large not directly involved in collective bargaining, worker associations offer few if any guarantees for wages and working conditions. Where supporters see worker associations as a start toward rebuilding the labor movement, or perhaps even as a revival of the social movement unionism of earlier years which brought about significant reforms and a step toward providing genuine representation and leadership roles for women, critics see them as little more than a false hope for female workers.

This chapter has offered four perspectives on the intersection of feminism and political economy and the intersection of home and work. It has argued that the communication, information, and knowledge arenas offer a substantive base for exploring the relationships among political-economic and feminist research. It also has attempted to bring attention to a topic—labor—that has for too long been seen as marginal to the discipline. In doing so, it has mapped a terrain for communication scholars and has called on them to broaden the traditional concerns of the field. Whichever of these perspectives one might find more appealing, and that would very much depend on the questions one is asking, it is time to abandon the barriers that have separated feminism and political economy, work and home, labor and consumption.

Note

Acknowledgments. This chapter was completed with the assistance of a grant from the Social Sciences and Humanities Research Council to examine trade unions and convergence in the communications industry. We would like to thank the research assistants for the trade unions project: Enda Brophy, Chris Bodnar, David Lavin, and Laura Glithero.

References

Akyeampong, Ernest. 2004. "The Union Movement in Transition." *Perspectives on Labor and Income* 5, no. 8. Ottawa: Statistics Canada.

Bahr, Morton. 1998. *From the Telegraph to the Internet.* Washington: National Press Books.

Balka, Ellen, and Richard Smith, eds. 2000. *Women, Work, and Computerization.* Boston: Kluwer.

Barley, Stephen R., and Gideon Kunda. 2004. *Gurus, Hired Guns, and Warm Bodies: Itinerant Experts in a Knowledge Economy.* Princeton, NJ: Princeton University Press.

Bédard, M. E. 2005. *Union Membership in Canada.* Ottawa: Human Resources and Skills Development Canada, Labor Program.

Brint, Steven. 2001. "Professionals and the 'Knowledge Economy': Rethinking the Theory of Postindustrial Society." *Current Sociology* 49, no. 4:101–32.

Brophy, Enda. 2006. "System Error: Labour Precarity and Collective Organizing at Microsoft." *Canadian Journal of Communication* 31, no. 3:619–38.

Cassedy, Ellen, and Karen Nussbaum. 1983. *9 to 5: The Working Woman's Guide to Office Survival.* New York: Penguin.

Cowan, Ruth Schwartz. 1983. *More Work for Mother: The Ironies of Household Technology from the Open Hearth to the Microwave.* New York: Basic Books.

Dalla Costa, Mariarosa, and Giovanna Dalla Costa, eds. 1999. *Women, Development, and Labor of Reproduction: Struggles and Movements.* Trenton, NJ: Africa World Press.

Davenport, Thomas. 2005. *Thinking for a Living.* Boston: Harvard Business School Press.

Duxbury, Linda, and Chris Higgins. 2001. *Work-Life Balance in the New Millennium: Where Are We? Where Do We Need to Go?* Ottawa: Canadian Policy Research Network.

Dyer-Witheford, Nick. 1999. *Cyber-Marx: Cycles and Circuits of Struggle in High Technology Capitalism.* Urbana and Chicago: University of Illinois Press.

Edwards, Linda N., and Elizabeth Field-Hendrey. 2002. "Home-based Work and Women's Labor Force Decisions." *Journal of Labor Economics* 20, no. 1:170–200.

Egan, Carolyn, Linda Lee Gardner, and Judy Vashti Persad. 1988. "The Politics of Transformation: Struggles with Race, Class, and Sexuality in the March 8th Coalition." In *Social Movements/Social Change: The Politics and Practice of Organizing*, eds. Frank Cunningham, Sue Findlay, Marlene Kadar, Alan Lennon, and Ed Silva, 20– 47. Toronto: Between the Lines.

Eisenstein, Zillah. 1998. *Global Obscenities: Patriarchy, Capitalism, and the Lure of Cyberfantasy.* New York: New York University Press.

Felstead, Alan, Sally Walters, and Nick Jewson. 2005. *Changing Places of Work.* London: Palgrave.

Fox, Nichols. 2002. *Against the Machine: The Hidden Luddite Tradition in Literature, Art and Individual Lives.* Washington, D.C.: Island Press.

Gates, Bill, with Nathan Myhrvold and Peter Rinearson. 1996. *The Road Ahead.* New York: Penguin.

Gerstein, Ira. 1973. "Domestic Work and Capitalism." *Radical America* 7, vol. 4:101–28.

Granville, Suzanne. 1999. "Women Workers and the New Economy." Presentation to a conference on American Labor and the New Economy, Washington, D.C., 22 January 1999. www.newecon .org/womenwork_sg.html (accessed 13 October 2005).

Greene, Anne-marie, and Gill Kirton. 2003. "Possibilities for Remote Participation in Trade Unions: Mobilizing Women Activists." *Industrial Relations Journal* 34, no.4:319–33.

Gupta, Tania Das. 2006. "Racism/Anti-Racism, Precarious Employment, and Unions." In *Precarious Employment: Understanding Labor Market Insecurity in Canada,* ed. Leah Vosko, 318–34. Montreal and Kingston: McGill-Queen's University Press.

Halford, Susan, and Pauline Leonard. 2006. *Negotiating Gendered Identities at Work: Place, Space and Time.* London: Palgrave.

Hardt, Michael, and Antonio Negri. 2000. *Empire.* Cambridge, MA: Harvard University Press.

Head, Simon. 2003. *The New Ruthless Economy: Work and Power in the Digital Age.* Oxford: Century Foundation/Oxford University Press.

Huws, Ursula. 2003. *The Making of a Cybertariat: Virtual Work in a Real World.* New York: Monthly Review Press.

———, ed. 2006. *The Transformation of Work in a Global Knowledge Economy.* Leuven: Katholieke Universiteit Leuven.

Jackson, Andrew. 2003. "In Solidarity: The Union Advantage." *Research Paper No. 27.* Ottawa: Canadian Labor Congress.

Kiss, Simon, and Vincent Mosco. 2005. "Negotiating Electronic Surveillance in the Workplace: A Study of Collective Agreements in Canada." *Canadian Journal of Communication* 30, no. 4:549–64.

Kline, Stephen, Nick Dyer-Witheford, and Greg de Peuter. 2003. *Digital Play.* Montreal and Kingston: McGill-Queen's Press.

Lazzarato, Maurizio. 1997. *Lavoro Immateriale: Forme di Vita e Produzione di Soggettività.* Verona: Ombre Corte.

Louie, Miriam Ching Yoon. 2001. *Sweatshop Warriors: Immigrant Women Workers Take on the Global Economy.* Cambridge, MA: South End Press.

Mattingly, Marybeth J., and Suzanne M. Bianchi. 2003. "Gender Differences in the Quantity and Quality of Free Time: The U.S. Experience." *Social Forces* 81, no. 3:999–1030.

McKercher, Catherine. 2002. *Newsworkers Unite: Labor, Convergence and North American Newspapers.* Lanham, MD: Rowman and Littlefield.

Meehan, Eileen, and Ellen Riordan, eds. 2002. *Sex and Money: Feminism and Political Economy in the Media.* Minneapolis: University of Minnesota Press.

Menzies, Heather. 1997. "Telework, Shadow Work: The Privatization of Work in the New Digital Economy." *Studies in Political Economy* 53:103–24.

Nussbaum, Karen. 2005. Letter to the editor of Labor Talk, *The Labor Educator.* 1 June. www.laboreducator.org.karnuss.htm (accessed 12 October 2005).

Pellow, David Naguib, and Lisa Sun Hee Park. 2002. *The Silicon Valley of Dreams: Environmental Injustice, Immigrant Workers, and the High-Tech Global Economy.* New York: New York University Press.

Powell, Walter W., and Kaisa Snellman. 2004. "The Knowledge Economy." *Annual Review of Sociology* 30:199–220.

Rubin, Gayle. 1975. "The Traffic in Women: Notes on the 'Political Economy' of Sex". In *Toward an Anthropology of Women,* ed. Rayna R. Reiter, 157–210. New York: Monthly Review Press.

Service Employees International Union. 2005. "Who We Are: Fast Facts." www.seiu.org/who/ fast%5Ffacts (accessed 13 October 2005).

Smith, Ted, David A. Sonnenfeld, and David Naguib Pellow, eds. 2006. *Challenging the Chip: Labor Rights and Environmental Justice in the Global Electronics Industry*. Philadelphia: Temple University Press.

Smythe, Dallas W. 1977. "Communications: Blindspot of Western Marxism." *Canadian Journal of Political and Social Theory* 1, no. 3:1–27.

Stone, Katherine V.W. 2004. *From Widgets to Digits: Employment Regulation for the Changing Workplace*. Cambridge: Cambridge University Press.

Sweeney, John J., and Karen Nussbaum. 1989. *Solutions for the New Work Force: Policies for a New Social Contract*. Washington: Seven Locks Press.

Swift, Jamie. 2003. *Walking the Union Walk*. Ottawa: Communications Energy and Paperworkers Union of Canada.

Terranova, Tiziana. 2000. "Free Labor: Producing Culture for the Digital Economy." *Social Text* 18, no. 2:33–58.

———. 2004. *Network Culture: Politics for the Information Age*. London: Pluto.

Tremblay, Diane-Gabrielle, Renaud Paquet, and Elmustapha Najem. 2006. "Telework: A Way to Balance Work and Family or an Increase in Work-Family Conflict?" *Canadian Journal of Communication* 31, no. 3:715–31.

UNI (Union Network International). 2003. "Women and the Information Society." www.union-network.org/uniwomen.nsf/9548462b9349db27c125681100260673/931flc9c544705e1c1256ce700 32481a?OpenDocument (accessed 14 November 2006).

UNI. 2004. "Culture, Union Constitutions Impeding Women." www.union-network.org/uniwomen.nsf/9548462b9349db27c125681100260673/1e7c50fla4909ee7c1256f03003abbab? OpenDocument (accessed 14 November 2006).

UNI. 2005a. "For Gender Equality to Become a Reality in French Telecommunications Companies." www.union-network.org/uniwomen.nsf/9548462b9349db27c125681100260673/ 7d5794698403ff79c12570ad002cf071?OpenDocument (accessed 14 November 2006).

UNI. 2005b. "Stepping Up Fight for Equality and to End Discrimination." www.union-network.org/uniwomen.nsf/9548462b9349db27c125681100260673/f921b944c9c7769ac125706 5004d6196?OpenDocument (accessed 14 November 2006).

UNI. 2005c. "Conclusions and Action Points," *Women's Work: Organizing for the Future*. 2d UNI World Women's Conference. www.union-network.org/uniwomen.nsf/70c3d04c5f60c73cc12568 00001e3b89/f5f195318b8cdee0c125708c00304e73/$FILE/E-%20Conclusions.pdf. (accessed 28 April 2007).

UNI. 2006. "Message from Barbara Easterling, UNI World Women's President." www.union-network.org/uniwomen.nsf/9548462b9349db27c125681100260673/c563d0246aedda6cc125712 a0051bc76?OpenDocument (accessed 14 November 2006).

U.S. Bureau of Labor Statistics. 2006. *Union Members in 2005*. Washington, D.C.: Bureau of Labor Statistics.

van Jaarsveld, Danielle D. 2004. "Collective Representation Among High-Tech Workers at Microsoft and Beyond: Lessons from WashTech/CWA." *Industrial Relations* 43, no. 2:364–85.

Vosko, Leah. 2000. *Temporary Work: The Gendered Rise of a Precarious Employment Relationship*. Toronto: University of Toronto Press.

———. 2006. "Precarious Employment: Towards an Improved Understanding of Labor Market Insecurity." In *Precarious Employment: Understanding Labor Market Insecurity in Canada*, ed. Leah Vosko, 3–39. Montreal & Kingston: McGill-Queen's University Press.

Wigfield, Andrea. 2001. *Post-Fordism, Gender and Work*. Aldershot, UK: Ashgate.

CHAPTER FIFTEEN

Women, Information Work, and the Corporatization of Development

Lisa McLaughlin

The recent United Nations World Summit on the Information Society (WSIS) had as one of its major themes the notion that the information age offers great opportunities for enhancing human potential and increasing social rewards. In many respects, the discourse associating information and communication technology (ICT) for development with "the emancipation of the human being" (WSIS 2003) reflects the voices of gender equality advocates who have been instrumental in reorienting development discourse away from approaches that measure progress through macroeconomic indicators alone and toward an understanding that forms of human and social development focused on well-being and fulfillment are important ends in themselves. A key assumption shared among many gender and development (GAD) experts is that, largely because of patriarchal biases, policies and practices in the area of information and communication technology for development often are gender-blind, gender-insensitive, and/or gender-neutral in tenor. By contrast, in this chapter, I attempt to illustrate that, far from being inattentive to various forms of women's inequalities and potentialities, current ICT development policies and practices routinely exhibit a form of gender awareness narrowly focused on defining and targeting women as information workers. In this sense, my position is aligned with that outlined by Elson and Pearson over twenty-five years ago:

We do not accept that the problem is one of women being left out of the development process. Rather it is precisely the relations through which women are "integrated" into the development process that need to be problematized and investigated. For such relations may well be part of the *problem*, rather than part of the *solution*. (1981, 87)

There is nothing inherently wrong with information work, although the concept tends to cluster together a number of occupations that have little in common except that they involve making and using new technologies (F. Webster 1994). However, there is a problem when the provision of jobs becomes the most important element in integrating women into the development process and the panacea for overcoming gender subordination (Elson and Pearson 1981). Additionally, it is cause for concern when mainstream gender and development policies and practices focus on "unleashing" individual women's entrepreneurial energies and mainstreaming women into corporate-led, public-private partnership initiatives instead of confronting structural inequalities that establish women as the preferred laborers in the lowest ranks of occupations associated with new technologies.

As Wilkins (1999) describes, from the beginning of the UN Decade for Women in 1975, development attention toward women has increased, while women's conditions have declined in respect to poverty, illiteracy, and access to health services and education (46). Attention to women most often occurs through social marketing projects, in which women are classified as consumers, purchasers of products and services: "It appears that the Decade for Women has been replaced by a 'Decade of Privatization' for USAID [the United States Agency for International Development], as social-marketing projects, closely associated with the private sector attempt to capture a middle-SES, consumer audience with the ability to purchase products and services" (62). Considering the importance of purchasing power, treating women as technology users and workers should go hand-in-hand with identifying them as consumers. Yet, in the field of international communication, as with the field of communication overall, scant attention has been paid to labor. Labor, as McKercher and Mosco (2006, 493) write, "remains a blindspot of western communication studies."

Although issues of consumer protection, needs, and access to ICTs featured significantly throughout the WSIS, I maintain that the role of women as information workers was a more pronounced, though largely overlooked, preoccupation of the summit. At a time when trends toward the corporatization of development prevail within most governmental and multilateral institutions, the solution to integrating women into the information society becomes one of assimilating them as information workers. The example of the WSIS and the public-private partnerships forged throughout the process illustrate that approaches to gender and development have become integrated into the corporatization of development. Ostensibly, information technology corporations make partnership agreements with the UN, various governments, and nongovernmental organizations (NGOs) and provide funding in order to address inequalities associated with the "digital divide." As I suggest, what is troubling about this phenomenon is that it reflects the growing role of corporations in framing and setting the development agenda, thus providing the private sector with an influential role in constructing a vision for future-oriented social change.

Developing the "Flexible Woman" of the Information Economy

Among the areas included within the sweeping terrain known as international communication, few consistently present more thorny, multifaceted, and often dispiriting issues than does the area of development communication. As with the larger field, development communication has proceeded through a number of stages marking concerns cutting across theory, research, and practice, none constituting a paradigm shift in the sense of displacing a prior trend (Wilkins and Mody 2001, 386). Approaches to international communications and development have shifted from those advocating the use of communication and information for modernization purposes, to critiques based in cultural imperialism and dependency theories, to the recognition of cultural pluralism, and finally to what Annabelle Sreberny-Mohammadi (1991, 122), in recognition of the relationship and tensions between the global and the local, refers to as "the global in the local, the local in the global." Although identifiable trends, these should not be understood in isolation from one another or in the sense of an evolution; rather, they have tended to reflect new conceptualizations based on dominant modes of development thinking and practice, and, as such, they emerge in dialogue with other approaches judged to be inadequate by development scholars and practitioners.

Given their founding in economic development theory, it is not surprising that, within international development research in general, the prevailing approaches have arisen from developmentalist and dependency theories oriented to understanding and remedying disparities in quantity of information and quality of communications among so-called third world underdeveloped countries and first world developed countries. The distinction among the latter conventionally has been determined by virtue of levels of industrialization and economic growth within a country. Each theory considers media and communications to be forces for economic growth and thus important factors in differentiating among countries in respect to levels of development (Kavoori 2006, 50–51). Dating from the 1950s and 1960s, developmental theories and practices have had a progressivist orientation toward helping "underdeveloped" countries "catch up" with "developed" countries. Underlying such models is a hierarchy of development in which ideal-typical models, drawn mostly from examples of U.S. political-economic superiority, are exported to the third world, with media playing a central role in helping to create a favorable climate in which change might lead to modernization (Melkote and Steeves 2001, 215; see also Prasad, this volume). Dependency theory, in turn, offers the critique that the economic prowess of Western countries, and primarily the U.S., is not indicative of the preeminence of the free market but rather of the degree to which powerful interests are served when third world countries never catch up and rather remain in a state of dependent development. Cultural dependency follows from economic dependency with "the informational and cultural sector [having] ascended the last prominent place on the commanding heights of the economy" (Schiller 1996, 2).

When women and development emerged as a concern in the 1970s, largely due to the influence of economist Ester Boserup, its main focus was on integrating women into forms of productive labor that facilitate capitalist economic development. Criticisms of this approach have provoked a greater awareness of the need to attend more to matters of social equality, respect for local cultures and cultural diversity, appreciation for the importance of quality of life, and the provision for everyone to have the opportunity to reach her or his full potential as an individual and member of society (Benería 2003, 17). Omvedt and Kelkar (1995), for example, suggest that enhancing access to information technology should amount to more than increasing women's individual skills and capacities so that they can participate in the production system of outsourcing, subcontracting, and networking; rather, the goal should be to approach technology development as a way of enhancing women's agency and political-economic empowerment.

The invocation of a schism between economic and social development can serve strategic purposes, particularly within the context of events such as the WSIS, where civil society stakeholders routinely countered the notion of a knowledge economy or information economy by noting how these overwhelmed a sense of a knowledge society or information society during the proceedings (see, for example, Gurumurthy 2004). This strategy can be effective in the short term, in the midst of battles between stakeholders with differing agendas. It is also important, however, to recognize that neoliberalism is not only a set of economic policies; it is a political philosophy with a normative foundation, a set of ethics, and a social vision. Specifically, this vision is one in which society benefits through market competition because the latter is the most efficient means for justly distributing scarce resources, ensuring economic well-being, and empowering individuals (Mittelman 2000, 74; Habermas 2001).

This meritocratic social vision, in which those who succeed in the market rise to the top and those who fail to do so are left behind, is carried through in the work of Manuel Castells. As described by Castells (1996, 17), the current economy features an "informational mode of development" in which "the source of productivity lies in the technology of knowledge generation, information processing, and symbol communication." The category of "informational labor"—the "self-programmable," networked, adept, high-skilled, and well-educated worker in the knowledge economy—offers great rewards for those who are able to develop in tandem with a flexible global economy. "Generic labor, by contrast, is exchangeable and disposable, and co-exists in the same circuits with machines and unskilled labor from around the world" (Castells 2000, 12). Castells recognizes that there exists a structural divide between informational and generic labor, with a concomitant increase in social exclusion, inequality, and division; the response to these circumstances, however, must be for generic labor to assume the flexibility required in a global context of informational capitalism.

The "new" capitalist economy features a feminization of paid labor, which in Castells's conception means that " 'flexible woman' gradually replac[es] the 'organization man' as the harbinger of the new type of worker" (2000, 12). He offers the stark generalization that "new social relationships of production translate into a good fit between the 'flexible woman' (forced to flexibly cope with her multiple roles) and the network enterprise" (20), surmising that, by helping to challenge patriarchy, new social relationships of production lead to new gendered social relationships. Patriarchy falls into crisis not only because of the massive influx of women into informational labor but also because of the mobilization of feminism as a political movement, the latter of which is thought to be one of several networked struggles based in identity and the forging of new identities (1997).

Castells's conception fits with a number of contributions to the literature on cosmopolitan democracy, in that it takes the feminist movement (or movements) as its muse without seeming to grasp the diversity of women's experiences and social contexts, to understand the contradictions and conflicts within feminism, or indeed to have sufficient familiarity with the feminist scholarship in which these are detailed. There is no question but that some of the world's women have benefited economically from new job opportunities in ICT, in addition to enjoying the waning of patriarchal relations in the home. However, many more women are clustered within the category of numerically flexible, low-skilled, and casual and subcontracted laborers, who are stereotyped as docile and often forced into compliance because they lack the social status and job and income security that would provide them with the resources to resist occupational subordination (Robins and Webster 1989; Matthews 2003; McLaughlin and Johnson forthcoming).

From the International Labor Organization (ILO) to the United Nations Conference on Trade and Development (UNCTAD), it is recognized that women tend to predominate in service sectors involving routinized, low-skilled labor and limited technical training. Men are far more likely to have access to the better-paying, higher-skilled jobs in the ICT service sector, such as those in software development or programming. The fast-growing retail and financial services industries have become increasingly feminized, and within these sectors women generally are employed in the lower-status occupations (which are usually defined as less-skilled) where work is often temporary and poorly remunerated (J. Webster 1996; 2000). Even more women endure employment insecurity as laborers in the informal economy or in low-wage telework, call center work, and electronics assembly. The latter, although it does not qualify as informational labor, does occupy a capital-intensive place in the information economy (see Ng 1997). Since the 1970s, the manufacture of electronics and computer components have been among the goods most outsourced to the developing world by the U.S. and other industrialized countries, with women targeted in particular for employment in this labor-intensive, low-waged, and often hazardous work (Lim 1978; Elson and Pearson 1981; Hossfeld 2001; Matthews 2003). The stratification of labor by gender, race, and nation is especially intense in electronics manufacturing, where cultural and political forms of oppression, such as managers' stereotyping of Asian women as nimble-fingered and compliant, serve to obfuscate economic exploitation (Sussman 1998; Hossfeld 2001). As Hossfeld has described, immigrant women in Silicon Valley often internalize patriarchal ideology more readily than they do racist assumptions, viewing technology work as "unfeminine" as well as "unwifely" if one earns more than one's spouse (43).

Kelkar and Nathan (2002, 439) observe that "while the new information technologies in manufacturing, services and communications have great promise in terms of dissolving old bases of discrimination, such as heavy and light work, the potential of these technologies for decentralized and more humane development, with participatory political structures, has yet to be realized because of continuing patriarchal relations and the domination of accumulation over development goals." At the same time, feminist approaches often are described as sharing an avowed commitment to a "decentralized, multifaceted, and bottom-up effort to find alternative models" for development (Benería 2003, 16). No doubt, a combination of patriarchy and an overriding orientation to capitalist accumulation create great obstacles to moving from commitment to practice. However, as a number of feminists have argued, gender advocates often hinder their own avowed agenda of changing social relations; that is, the more that they are formally included at the table where decisions are being made under the auspices of the United Nations, the less obviated is their status as members of a transnational advocacy group working to establish a "globalization-from-below" by redirecting the focus of economic and social development from a neoliberal agenda to questions of justice and equality.

The influence of NGOs has grown enormously, in large part through their participation in UN-sponsored meetings. But, as an increasing number of feminist scholars have observed, no matter how progressive may be the agenda of an NGO, the price of access to bureaucratic structures is the distancing of insiders from their outsider constituencies (Alvarez 1998, 192). Now, after decades of "gender mainstreaming" within the UN, feminists have begun to recognize that, overall, the integration of women with the organization has had the effect of empowering not women but bureaucracies that have signed on to resolutions that declare gender integration to be their goal (Staudt 1997, 7).[1] As Jain (2000) has noted, although women have made great strides in gaining access to the structures of the UN in order to influence policy, it sometimes appears as though "lobbying for a conference document becomes the consuming energy."

Hawkesworth offers an acute analysis of how NGOs conducting gender advocacy "manifest tendencies toward privatization" and therefore become compromised through their insinuation with neoliberalism:

[NGOs are] both crucial vehicles for the advancement of certain women's interests under resurgent capitalism and as an effect of the dismantling of welfare state structures, and as such complicit in the delegitimation of social rights and the privatization of women. In their mode of operation and in the unintended consequences of their action, NGOs affirm entrepreneurial individualism as a privileged mode of political agency and displace participatory politics. (2001, 232)

In the following section, I focus on the World Summit on the Information Society as an example of a multistakeholder event that promised to offer heterogeneous, multilayered governance arrangements through the substantive participation of nonstate actors. In practice, the multistakeholderism of the WSIS served a legitimating function for what in fact is the privatization of global governance, aiding the extension of private authority over global media governance by multinational corporations, private business associations, and international institutions with neoliberal agendas (Cutler 2003). The privatization of global governance, I suggest, is a necessary component of the corporatization of development, one in which women become important actors in the legitimation of ICT development policies and practices.

The Summit of Solutions

The World Summit on the Information Society (WSIS) officially surfaced in January of 2002 in the form of a United Nations General Assembly resolution advocating a collaborative effort in which representatives of governments, international institutions, civil society, and the private sector would arrive at "a common vision and understanding of the information society." The International Telecommunication Union (ITU), as the UN agency overseeing the WSIS, inaugurated the first (Geneva 2003) phase of the summit with words proffering that its "open process" and "new dialogue" among stakeholders would become a model for the "new governance in the Information Society" (WSIS 2003). The WSIS was imagined to succeed in "establishing the foundation of an equitable information society, one that respects cultural diversity and provides opportunities for all." This would be the Summit of Solutions, announced ITU Secretary-General Yoshio Utsumi nearly three years later, as the WSIS proceeded to its second and final phase, held in Tunis, Tunisia, in 2005. The WSIS was promised to guide efforts to close "the digital divide": providing access to information and communication technologies (ICTs) to "all the world's inhabitants," "giving a voice" to them, and "bring[ing] them to the attention of national and even global markets" (Utsumi 2005).

Official statements and documents produced throughout the WSIS—notably the Declaration of Principles and Plan of Action—made clear that this was the summit of market-based solutions. Perhaps more precisely, the WSIS was the summit of network solutions, if the term "network solution" can be drawn from the marketing rhetoric of commercial entities in information technology sectors, where it is used to describe technological applications and competencies meant to effectively meet the needs of business. The summit's objective to close the "digital divide," in and of itself, is expressive of a quick-fix, technocratic approach, in which ICTs become the solutions to complex problems. As Wajcman (2002, 349) has observed, "Rhetoric about the 'digital divide,' that between the information rich and the information poor, serves to camouflage pre-existing patterns of social and class inequality." Within the terms of the digital divide, women's social subordination is to be remedied by offering empowerment through "capacity building" and opportunity through ICT skills training.

UN Secretary-General Kofi Annan's pre-WSIS invocation to Silicon Valley industry leaders is illustrative of the approach to technology that dominated the summit. His "Challenge to Silicon Valley" recommends investment in "both ethics and economics": "The new economy can only be productive and sustainable if it spreads worldwide and responds to the needs and demands of all people" (2002). Both the "knowledge economy" and the "information economy" have become placeholders for an "information society" grounded in a predilection toward neoliberal economic orthodoxies coupled with an instrumentalist approach toward human development or social well-being. As an unfinished concept, the information society all the more easily could be assimilated to a neoliberal ideology promoting the notion that economic development is best achieved through the smooth functioning of the market system, so long as the latter is protected as much as possible from the interferences of social and political institutions (Gurumurthy and Singh 2005, 4).

Civil society participants attempted to counter this technocratic, market-led approach with an alternative declaration, "Shaping Information Societies for Human Needs" (Civil Society Geneva Declaration 2003). No radical document, this declaration represents a "one foot in, one foot out" strategy, striving to include a number of constituencies and concerns that were not addressed in the official documents but avoiding confrontation to the extent that there is no analysis of the neoliberal paradigm which provides the framework for attention to ICT for development (FIRE 2003). At most, the 2003 Civil Society declaration insinuates that social justice approaches to development are more important than the market-driven mechanisms advocated by most governments and the private sector. The 2005 (Tunis) Civil Society statement, "Much More Could Have Been Achieved," is more direct in addressing the failures of the WSIS to consider development approaches other than those which depend upon the largesse of the private sector in offering public-private partnership initiatives and investing in ICT for development. According to the statement, "The Tunis phase in particular, which was presented as the 'summit of solutions,' did not provide concrete achievements to meaningfully address development priorities" (Civil Society Tunis Declaration 2005, 4).

I do not take issue with the general outline of the criticisms stated in these WSIS Civil Society documents. Nevertheless, it is important to press forward with an analysis that seeks to redirect the focus from "development priorities" as a taken-for-granted category to questions pertaining to how specific development priorities may be interpreted based on the solutions that result from how development itself is defined and approached in the first place. The latter are not merely outcomes but rather are reflective of various problem definitions and agendas, some of which are helped along via the participation of civil society participants whose actions, intentional or not, may lend legitimacy to processes of global governance over which more powerful actors prevail. What solutions emerge within a context in which predominant development priorities mostly are established prior to collaborations and struggles among those with a stake in the outcome of a process meant to overcome the "digital divide"? If it is supposed that all persons are to be included in the "information society," *how* are they to be integrated within the dominant framework for constructing this imaginary?

One solution is to invoke cosmopolitan notions of democratic inclusion through the reanimation of an aging policy scheme known as corporatism, a form of governance that seeks to create cooperative agreements among a limited set of conflicting social groups as a strategy for promoting social integration and stability within capitalist economies. Within economic policy making, corporatist approaches act as a bargaining mechanism between the state and leaders of organized interest groups defined in class categories. Labor unions and business associations become the state's key partners in this effort to promote class collaboration and ward off class conflicts that might otherwise challenge national economic interests.

As the influence of civil society organizations has grown throughout the various 1990s UN-sponsored meetings, corporatism takes on new relevance as a policy arrangement intended to meet the challenge posed by new political actors exercising authority within institutions of global governance. With the erosion of the influence of labor unions and the increasing power of groups promoting so-called postindustrial themes such as environmental protection, consumer rights, and women's rights, corporatist states have created bargaining arrangements with the new interest groups as well. Global neocorporatism, despite diverging from traditional corporatism in some significant ways, is serving a similar purpose in offering the UN a mechanism for responding to NGO challenges to international institutions and transnational corporations by promoting cooperative arrangements among international organizations, business, and civil society. As with traditional corporatism, this approach is intended to defuse radical opposition by coopting more moderate groups (Dryzek 2000; Ottaway 2001).

The WSIS offers a clear illustration that, although multistakeholder arrangements may promise pluralistic dialogue, neocorporatist policy concertation tends to both begin and end with the passive—and occasionally active—exclusion of groups that threaten neoliberal economic imperatives (McLaughlin and Pickard 2005).[2] As an example, although two gender advocacy groups —the Gender Caucus and the Gender Strategies Working Group (GSWG)— were active during phase one of the summit, by the time that phase two was underway, only the Gender Caucus remained. A key difference between the two groups was that, despite its formal inclusion within the civil society stakeholder group, the Gender Caucus represented an alliance among representatives of national governments, civil society and nongovernmental organizations, the private sector, and the United Nations system. Several participants in the GSWG, as George (2004) describes, were troubled by the prospect of participating in a sort of gender advocacy that "was very much a case of settling for the lowest common denominator—one that the CEO of Hewlett Packard and an NGO worker from the South could agree to."[3] Although some members of the GSWG associated with the Gender Caucus during the second phase, several simply de-linked from the summit.

Ottaway (2001) maintains that civil society organizations have forced global neocorporatism upon the UN and the private sector through their demands to represent causes on behalf of larger constituencies. And still, she suggests, the UN remains the head of the body politic because, as a quasi-state, it has the task of coordinating and reconciling the interests of the three sectors, which include the state, the market, and civil society. In contrast, I would argue that, within today's tripartite forms of policy concertation, the market has become the head of the body politic (McLaughlin and Pickard 2005). This is exemplified by the march of the WSIS toward a conclusion in which the Global Alliance for Information and Communication Technology for Development (GAID), headed by Intel board chairman Craig Barrett and focused on creating synergies between the private sector and international financial institutions for purposes of forming large partnership initiatives, was envisioned as the best model for overcoming the digital divide.

Within the UN system and its member states, the corporatization of development now is the overriding solution to the problem of overcoming the digital divide. Private-sector investment has become a substitute for funding previously provided by national and international development agencies. As I suggest below, within the context of the WSIS, the corporatization of development became most apparent through the creation of public-private partnerships meant to offer access to, and training in, information technologies, with women as a principal target of these development initiatives.

Partners in the Corporatization of ICT for Development

On December 12, 2003, as the first phase of the WSIS was coming to a discordant end, the ITU circulated a news release announcing that the summit had "closed on an optimistic note of consensus and commitment," with the forging of numerous public-private agreements between various governments, the United Nations Development Program, the ITU, and corporations, which included information technology giants Hewlett-Packard and Cisco Systems (ITU 2003). Such partnerships, above all else, confirm that the process of the corporatization of development is well under way. Donor countries increasingly are unwilling to provide public financing for development, while underfunded national and international development agencies often are unable to do so. Spurred on by Kofi Annan's support for a voluntary and unmonitored Global Compact with the private sector, by the end of the 1990s, a number of corporations have been willing to step into the breach as a way of exhibiting global corporate citizenship. Corporations are not willing to step into just any breach but rather prefer to invest in projects undertaken in countries where there exist new markets, cheap sources of labor, and new sites for capitalist accumulation; the result is the spatial extension of commodification (in the form of products and services) into developing countries and regions and the incursion of market relations into ever more areas of peoples' lives (Huws 2006).

Technology, computer, and electronics companies are prominent among the entities that work in partnership with the UN on development initiatives. Most of their corporate citizenship efforts focus on supporting technical training in new media applications and hardware manufacturing. For a variety of reasons—and perhaps most notably because of the existence of a gendered digital divide—several of the technology corporations that have developed partnership arrangements with the UN and various governments focus their efforts on gender initiatives that include creating Internet training centers and providing curricula meant to teach women how to assemble, use, and maintain information hardware and software for network systems. Among these, none has been so prolific as Cisco Systems, the dominant player among networking hardware manufacturers (specializing in routers).[4] Internationally, Cisco Systems's projects mostly have been devoted to Gender and Least Developed Countries Initiatives. Practically speaking, this means that students, especially female students, in the global south are enrolled into the Cisco Networking Academy Program (CNAP), a two-year program in which students are trained to design, build, and maintain computer networks. Since the CNAP was initiated in the U.S. in 1997, Cisco Systems has spread its academies throughout much of the world, with programs in more than 160 countries; 11,911 academies worldwide, and over 1,569,931 students trained since 1997. According to Cisco Systems, there are over 500,000 students enrolled in its academies at this time. The CNAP is offered through high schools, technical schools, colleges and universities, and community organizations.[5]

The stated purpose of the Least Developed Countries Initiative (LDCI) is to enhance technology skills development and to empower countries to accelerate progress, attain sustainable development, and fully integrate into the world economy. The Gender Initiative is intended to "increase female participation in the Internet economy." The United Nations Development Fund for Women (UNIFEM) has been a key partner in this effort, although the ITU is also a significant partner due, in part, to its ongoing relationships with both Cisco Systems and UNIFEM. The two most prominent events related to the Gender Initiative both occurred in 2002: the establishment of the first women-oriented Cisco learning academy and Internet training center in the Department of Women and Gender Studies (DWGS) at Makerere University in Kampala, Uganda; and the Achieving E-Quality in the IT Sector program, launched in Jordan. The goal of the DWGS program is to increase the number of women in the IT workforce and to integrate them into decision-making positions (ITU 2002). This is consistent with the Achieving E-Quality in the IT Sector program, in which IT training is supplemented with what UNIFEM describes as "soft skills" training, meant to improve women's self-presentation and communication skills, which along with IT skills are "the necessary market-required skills" (APC 2003).

It is not surprising that the motives of Cisco Systems and other corporations that enjoy partnerships with the UN are not entirely altruistic. Corporations have a variety of reasons for seeking partnerships: partnerships allow corporations to influence policy making through the UN system, to emphasize private-sector solutions as the only feasible responses to development problems, to counter the influence of nongovernmental organizations, to place their issues at the top of the UN agenda, and to promote their own products at UN events and through various partnership initiatives (Paine 2000). One reason for creating the CNAP was to increase the number of skilled information technology workers in order to meet industry demand. Offering the CNAP worldwide helps to alleviate the networking skills shortage and allows companies to lower salaries and labor costs.

My purpose here is not to unveil a conspiracy but to suggest that the corporation, its personnel, and its partners may be ideologically committed to a socioeconomic vision in which the market truly is capable of offering a just distribution of social goods. It is imperative to take into account the social vision of neoliberalism if one is to explore the promises offered by its advocates and to discredit them when appropriate. Few efforts have been made to monitor or evaluate Cisco/UN partnership initiatives. Most Cisco-supported reports present glowing accounts of its efforts and successes in the area of corporate social responsibility, a handful of testimonials from CNAP instructors and students who have completed the CNAP certification, and a few best practices cases offered on the Cisco website. Cisco Systems neglects to address the breadth and depth of women's IT education, the classroom environment, the numbers of students who are gaining meaningful experiences to allow them to enter the labor market as well as participate as active citizens, the number of graduates who have secured employment that allows for self-determination, and the conditions in which individuals work once they have secured employment.

Conclusion

Public-private partnerships produce "flexible women" as a solution to three development problems: the need to empower women, the need to overcome the digital divide, and the need to finance poverty reduction strategies. Yet market-based approaches to development generate their own problems, by maintaining old forms of class segmentation and social control while creating new ones and subordinating the needs and interests of those who suffer the most injustices to the changing needs of industry. Although it may be suggested that the new information economy offers women more choices than they have enjoyed in the past, it is important to note that, particularly in the case of poorer women in the global south, one dimension of inequality is the great extent to which women routinely have been denied choices in comparison to men (Kabeer 1999). Perhaps it is time to adopt a new definition of the flexible woman, in which *flexibility* refers to the capacity to move beyond the range of choices currently offered within the context of the corporatization of development.

Notes

Acknowledgments. I am grateful for research funding offered through the Hampton Fund for International Faculty Initiatives and the University of Queensland Grant for International Collaborative Research. Many thanks to Isis International-Manila (and particularly to Susanna George), as well as to the UQ Centre for Critical and Cultural Studies, for providing spaces that allowed me to conduct the research that informs this chapter.

1. "Gender mainstreaming means that women and men have equitable access to, and benefit from society's resources, opportunities and rewards and equal participation in influencing what is valued and in shaping directions and decisions" (Gibb 2001, 7).

2. The expression "policy concertation," although used minimally in the United States, is used routinely in European discussions of corporatism. Traditionally it refers to the process of establishing arrangements among government, capital (the private sector), and labor (trade unions) for purposes of tripartite bargaining intended to lead to agreement on matters of policy (Berger and Compston 2002).

3. Susanna George, then executive director of Isis International-Manila, was the chair of the GSWG. She should be credited here for offering the expression "corporatization of development."

4. See McLaughlin (2005) for a more detailed analysis of Cisco Systems/UN initiatives.

5. Background information regarding Cisco Systems partnerships has been accessed from the corporation's website, www.cisco.com, unless otherwise suggested.

References

Alvarez, Sonia E. 1998. "Latin American Feminisms 'Go Global': Trends of the 1990s and Challenges for the New Millennium." In *Cultures of Politics, Politics of Culture: Revisioning Latin American Social Movements*, eds. Sonia Alvarez, Evelina Dagnino, and Arturo Escobar, 293–324. New York: Routledge.

Annan, Kofi. 2002. "Kofi Annan's Challenge to Silicon Valley," November 5. www.unicttaskforce.org/sg_challenge.html (accessed 4 March 2003).

Association for Progressive Communications (APC) Women's Networking Support Program. 2003. "2003 Gender and ICT Awards: Outstanding Multistakeholder Initiatives." www.genderawards.net/winners/2003/finalists/gr_multi_full.shtml?cmd%5B274%5D=i-277-b8396a4e1c835 e4ebc9bc89c74d0f32b (accessed 14 March 2004).

Bener a, Lourdes. 2003. *Gender, Development, and Globalization: Economics as if All People Mattered.* New York: Routledge.

Berger, Stefan, and Hugh Compston, eds. 2002. *Policy Concertation and Social Partnership in Western Europe: Lessons for the Twenty-first Century.* Oxford: Berghahn Books.

Castells, Manuel. 1996. *The Information Age: Economy, Society and Culture.* Oxford: Blackwell.

———. 1997. *Power of Identity: The Information Age: Economy, Society, and Culture.* Cambridge, MA: Blackwell.

———. 2000. "Materials for an Exploratory Theory of the Network Society." *British Journal of Sociology* 51, no.1:5–24.

Civil Society Geneva Declaration. 2003. "Shaping Information Societies for Human Needs." www.itu.int/wsis/documents/doc_multi.asp?lang=en?&id=1179%7C1208 (accessed 13 December 2003).

Civil Society Tunis Declaration. 2005. "Much More Could Have Been Achieved." www.itu.int/wsis/documents/listing-all.asp?lang=en?&c_event=s%7C2&c_type=all%7C (accessed 28 December 2005).

Cutler, Claire. 2003. *Private Power and Global Authority: International Merchant Law in the Global Political Economy.* Cambridge, UK: Cambridge University Press.

Dryzek, John. 2000. *Deliberative Democracy and Beyond: Liberals, Critics, Contestations.* Oxford: Oxford University Press.

Elson, Diane, and Ruth Pearson. 1981. "'Nimble Fingers Make Cheap Workers': An Analysis of Women's Employment in Third World Export Manufacturing." *Feminist Review* 7:87–107.

Feminist Interactive Radio Endeavor (FIRE). 2003. "Neoliberal Context Missing from Official and Civil Society Documents." World Summit on the Information Society. December. www.fire.or.cr/dic03/notas/eng/wsis_ing6.htm (accessed 15 January 2004).

George, Susanna. 2004. "Mainstreaming Gender as Strategy: A Critique from a Reluctant Gender Advocate." *Women in Action,* no. 1. www.isiswomen.org.wia.wia1-04/susanna.htm (accessed 1 December 2004).

Gibb, Heather. 2001. *Gender Mainstreaming: Good Practices from the Asia-Pacific Region.* The North-South Institute/L'Institut Nord-Sud. www.nsi-ins.ca/english/ pdf/Gibb_Gender_Mainstreaming.pdf (accessed 12 September 2006).

Gurumurthy, Anita. 2004. "Knowledge Economy: Does It Come with a Knowledge Society?" *Women in Action,* no. 2. www.isiswomen.org/pub/wia/wia1-04/anita2.htm (accessed 20 January 2006).

Gurumurthy, Anita, and Parminder Jeet Singh. 2005. *Political Economy of the Information Society: A Southern View.* Montevideo, Uruguay: Instituto del Tercer Mundo. http://wsispapers.choike.org/papers/eng/itfc_political_economy_is.pdf (accessed 10 February 2006).

Habermas, Jürgen. 2001. *The Postnational Constellation: Political Essays.* Trans. and ed. Max Pensky. Cambridge, MA: MIT Press.

Hawkesworth, Mary E. 2001. "Democratization: Reflections on Gendered Dislocations in the Public Sphere." In *Gender, Globalization, and Democratization,* eds. Rita Mae Kelly, Jane H. Bayes, Mary E. Hawkesworth, and Brigitte Young, 223–36. Boulder, CO: Rowman and Littlefield.

Hossfeld, Karen. 2001. "Their Logic Against Them: Contradictions in Sex, Race and Class on the Silicon Valley Shop Floor." In *Technicolor: Race, Technology and Everyday Life,* eds. Alondra Nelson and Thuy Linh N. Tu, 34–63. New York: New York University Press.

Huws, Ursula. 2006. "Begging and Bragging: The Self and the Commodification of Intellectual Activity." Inaugural Professorial Lecture, Working Lives Research Institute, London Metropolitan University, June 7. www.asah09.dsl.pipex.com/uhinaugural.pdf (accessed 30 November 2006).

International Telecommunication Union (ITU). 2002. "Launch of the First Women-Oriented ITU Internet Training Centre at Makerere University." www.itu.int/wsis/geneva/newsroom/press_releases/wsisclosing.html (accessed 4 August 2003).

International Telecommunication Union (ITU). 2003. "Global Information Summit Spurs Solidarity, Alliances But Hard Work, Action Ahead." www.itu.int/wsis/geneva/newsroom/press_releases/wsisclosing.html (accessed 12 December 2003).

Jain, Devaki. 2000. "What Have We Not Done? Where Have We Gone Wrong?" Presentation to the Conference on Nongovernmental Organizations. June 3. www.womenaction.org/ungass/devaki.html (accessed 14 July 2002).

Kabeer, Naila. 1999. "The Conditions and Consequences of Choice: Reflections on the Measurement of Women's Empowerment." UNRISD Paper no. 108. Geneva: United Nations Research Institute for Social Development.

Kavoori, Anandan P. 2006. "Thinking through Contra-flows: Perspectives from Post-Colonial and Transnational Cultural Studies." In Media on the Move: Global Flow and Contra-flow, ed. Daya K. Thussu, 49–64. London: Routledge.

Kelkar, Govind, and Dev Nathan. 2002. "Gender Relations and Technological Change in Asia." Current Sociology 50:427–41.

Lim, Linda. 1978. "Women Workers in Multinational Corporations: The Case of the Electronics Industry in Malaysia and Singapore." Michigan Occasional Papers no. 9. Ann Arbor, MI: Women's Studies Program, University of Michigan.

Matthews, Glenna. 2003. Silicon Valley, Women, and the California Dream: Gender, Class and Opportunity in the Twentieth Century. Stanford, CA: Stanford University Press.

McKercher, Catherine, and Vincent Mosco. 2006. "The Labouring of Communication." Canadian Journal of Communication 31, no. 3:493–97.

McLaughlin, Lisa. 2005. "Cisco Systems, the United Nations, and the Corporatization of Development." In The Incommunicado Reader: Information and Communication Technology for Everybody Else, eds. Geert Lovink and Soenke Zehles, 50–63. Amsterdam: Institute for Network Cultures.

McLaughlin, Lisa, and Helen Johnson. Forthcoming. "Women and Knowledge Work in the Asia-Pacific: Complicating Technological Empowerment." In Knowledge Workers in the Information Age, eds. Catherine McKercher and Vincent Mosco. Lanham, MA: Lexington Books.

McLaughlin, Lisa, and Victor Pickard. 2005. "What is Bottom-up About Global Internet Governance?" Global Media and Communication 1, no. 3:359–75.

Melkote, Srinivas R., and H. Leslie Steeves. 2001. Communication for Development in the Third World. New Delhi: Sage.

Mittelman, James H. 2000. The Globalization Syndrome: Transformation and Resistance. Princeton, NJ: Princeton University Press.

Ng, Cecilia. 1997. "The Management of Technology and Women in Two Electronics Firms in Malaysia." Gender, Technology and Development 1, no. 2:177–203.

Omvedt, Gail, and Govind Kelkar. 1995. "Gender and Technology: Emerging Visions from Asia." Gender Studies Monograph 4. Bangkok, Thailand: Asian Institute of Technology.

Ottaway, Marina. 2001. "Corporatism Goes Global: International Organizations, NGO Networks and Transnational Business." Global Governance (September). www.ceip.org/files/publications/GlobalCorporatism.asp (accessed 12 October 2002).

Paine, Ellen. 2000. "The Road to the Global Compact: Corporate Power and the Battle over Global Public Policy at the United Nations." Global Policy Forum. http://globalpolicy.org/reform/papers/2000/road.htm (accessed 22 May 2005).

Robins, Kevin, and Frank Webster. 1989. The Technical Fix: Education, Computers and Industry. New York: St. Martin's.

Schiller, Herbert. 1996. *Information Inequality.* New York: Routledge.

Sreberny-Mohammadi, Annabelle. 1991. "The Global and the Local in International Communications." In *Mass Media and Society*, eds. James Curran and Michael Gurevitch, 118–38. London: Edward Arnold.

Staudt, Kathleen. 1997. "Gender Politics in Bureaucracy: Theoretical Issues in Comparative Perspective." In *Women, International Development, and Politics: The Bureaucratic Mire*, ed. Kathleen Staudt, 3–35. Philadelphia: Temple University Press.

Sussman, Gerald. 1998. "Electronics, Communications, and Labor: The Malaysia Connection." In *Global Productions: Labor in the Making of the Information Society*, eds. Gerald Sussman and John A. Lent, 11–144. Cresskill, NJ: Hampton Press.

Utsumi, Yoshio. 2005. "Message from Yoshio Utsumi, ITU Secretary-General and Secretary-General of the Summit." International Telecommunication Union. www.itu.int/wsis/messages/utsumi.html (accessed 20 January 2006).

Wajcman, Judy. 2002. "Addressing Technological Change: The Challenge to Social Theory." *Current Sociology* 50, no. 3:347–63.

Webster, Frank. 1994. "What Information Society?" *The Information Society* 10, no. 1:1–23.

Webster, Juliet. 1996. *Shaping Women's Work: Gender, Employment, and Information Technology.* New York: Longman.

———. 2000. "Today's Second Sex and Tomorrow's First? Women and Work in the European Information Society." In *The Information Society in Europe: Work and Life in the Age of Globalization*, eds. Ken Ducatel, Juliet Webster, and Weiner Herrman, 119–40. Lanham, MA: Rowman and Littlefield.

Wilkins, Karin Gwinn. 1999. "Development Discourse on Gender and Communication in Strategies for Social Change." *Journal of Communication* 49, no. 1:46–68.

Wilkins, Karin Gwinn, and Bella Mody. 2001. "Reshaping Development Communication: Development Communication and Communicating Development." *Communication Theory* 11, no. 4:385–96.

World Summit on the Information Society (WSIS). 2003. Civil Society Secretariat. www.geneva2003.org (accessed 20 February 2003).

CHAPTER SIXTEEN

Empire and Sweatshop Girlhoods: The Two Faces of the Global Culture Industry

Leslie Regan Shade and Nikki Porter

"This is not an attack against Mary-Kate and Ashley; it's an appeal," said Charlie Kernaghan, the director of the National Labor Committee. "We don't have to kid ourselves. They have power, enormous power."[1]

As part of the eighth annual Holiday Season of Conscience Candle Light March to End Childhood and Sweatshop Abuses, sponsored by the National Labor Committee (NLC) and the New York University (NYU) chapter of United Students Against Sweatshops, focus centered on the famous American entertainment-lifestyle product moguls Mary-Kate and Ashley Olsen, then new freshmen at NYU. The Olsen's privately held Dualstar Entertainment Group (DEG), whose 2002 revenues were estimated to be US$1 billion, was targeted by NYU students and the NLC because, they alleged, female Bangladeshi workers who made the Olsen clothing line for Wal-Mart were not paid maternity leave mandated by Bangladeshi law. While the NLC was able to get other garment companies to sign a no-sweatshop pledge, the Olsens were immune to various entreaties, including students attempting to contact Ashley Olsen "via notes in some of her classes" (Pilon 2004). Kernaghan calculated that a Bangladeshi woman would have to work 109 years to earn the equivalent amount of NYU tuition, exclusive of housing and a meal plan. "This is the great gap in the world today . . . [The Olsens] have that power, that visibility. There is so much good they could do for the world" (Pilon 2004).

While the Olsens vigorously denied receipt of the petition from the NLC, they quickly issued a press release right before the march, stating that all Dual-star vendors "are required to comply with the most rigorous health and safety standards in the retail industry" (Silverman 2004) and pledging that "to the best of our abilities, we will guarantee that any woman sewing our garments in Bangladesh will be afforded her legal maternity leave of at least three months with full pay" (Susman 2004). This news and their subsequent statement appeared in several online entertainment magazines, thus averting negative publicity for the young stars who, since turning eighteen six months before and assuming control of their entertainment-lifestyle empire, had become the subject of much media adulation.

This poignantly stark disjuncture between the lives and livelihoods of women workers in Bangladeshi—who earn between 8 and 18 cents an hour (or between US$189.28 and $436.80 a year)—and the Olsen twins, whose 2004 gross sales were $1.4 billion, with retail revenues at $21 million (Forbes 2004), and who earned the distinction of being ranked number eleven on *Forbes* magazine's 2007 list of the twenty richest women in entertainment,[2] with a net worth of $10 million, is the focus of this chapter.

It takes up Teresa Ebert's argument to embrace materialist feminist cultural critiques, understood as "politics as the practice aimed at 'equal' access for all to social, cultural, and economic resources and also as an end to the exploitative exercise of power . . . [the achievement] of economic equality through social struggle" (1992–93, 18), and the recognition of gendered divisions of labor in the "global reconfiguration of patriarchal capitalism" (42); and the later challenge from Toby Miller (2004), who urges cultural studies scholars to turn away from a preoccupation with consumption toward a consideration of labor, and how this new international division of labor "links productivity, exploitation and social control" (62). Thus, rather than look just at the consumption practices—the cultural formations of the Mary-Kate and Ashley empire, and the subjectivities engendered by their myriad products on young girls—Miller urges us to look at the life of these commodities and the various subjectivities complicit in the international cultural division of labor.

In the burgeoning girls studies movement in media and cultural studies, feminist analyses have not typically adapted a political-economic perspective in scrutinizing the creation of tween and teen girl content, although there have been some notable exceptions (Record 2001; Kearney 2006). This chapter thus applies a feminist political-economic analysis to the phenomenon of Mary-Kate and Ashley Olsen, arguably one of the most financially successful teen enterprises ever, whose television, film, and video ventures have expanded to include a range of products, including clothing, magazines, books, cosmetics, accessories, and home decorating items, some of which are sold exclusively at the megastore Wal-Mart. This analysis also aims to contribute to childhood studies, where recent scholarship has examined global youth media and consumption (Buckingham and Sefton-Green 2003; Langer 2004; Maira and Soep 2004; Cook 2005; Lemish 2007), and to international communication, which rarely interrogates global youth culture, with the exception of analyses of coproduction and glocalization (Grixti 2006; Moran 2006).

The chapter first describes the rise of the Olsen twins' stardom and maps out their media holdings, which are managed through their Dualstar Entertainment Group, created in 1993 to manage the Olsen brand and now rapidly expanding transnationally. It then shifts from the first-world fanciful fortunes of the Olsens to focus on the stark realities of the many women and child laborers in developing countries who produce the very material goods that make it possible for the Olsens to be feted as fashionista billionaires by fans, the business press, and high-powered fashion magazines.

The MK&A Empire

"If we buy something we think is too much, of course we have buyer's remorse," says Ashley (Tauber and Dagotino 2004, 112).

Mary-Kate and Ashley Olsen debuted as baby actors in the U.S. television sitcom *Full House* in 1986, starring as Michelle Tanner, youngest daughter of a San Francisco widower played by Bob Saget. The popular series, which ran from 1987 to 1995, is still in syndication. In 1993, Dualstar Entertainment Group was established by their then-manager Robert Thorne, and over the next six years the Olsens were the stars of books, videos, and music videos. In 2001, when the twins were fifteen, they launched a teen clothing line with Wal-Mart and were lauded by the *Hollywood Reporter* as "the most powerful young women in Hollywood." Entertainment magazines were abuzz in the spring of 2004, when Mary-Kate and Ashley turned eighteen and assumed control of Dualstar. That year *Fortune* magazine estimated the twins' wealth at $137 million each. Although the private company does not disclose revenues, *Forbes* magazine estimated the twins' 2004 gross sales at $1.4 billion, with their retail revenues at $21 million (Forbes 2004).

Since assuming control of Dualstar, the twins have taken a vested interest in their company, tracking "business in weekly telephone conference calls, examining product design shipped via e-mail, and in less-frequent face-to-face meetings with executives" (Hopkins 2005, 2B). The MK&A brand is available outside the U.S. in Canada, Australia, New Zealand, Mexico, the UK, France, Germany, Spain, Italy, and Japan. Mary-Kate described their future plans in a 2006 *Women's Wear Daily* interview as developing a high-end fashion brand by investing in a different company or bringing in an outside

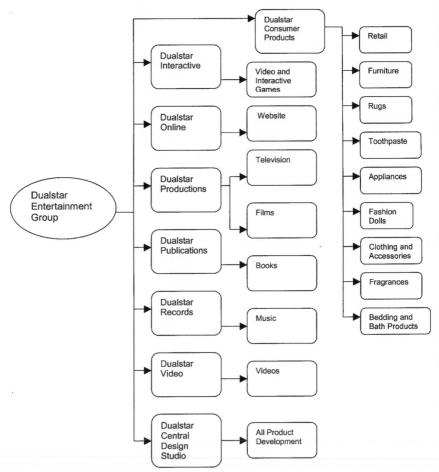

Figure 16.1.　Map of Ownings, Dualstar Entertainment Group
[Created by the authors]

designer; transforming their thirty-person enterprise, with offices in Culver City, New York, and London, into a boutique brand management firm supervising emerging labels and talent in both the fashion and entertainment world; generating ideas for a so-called incubator, a separate division formed in Dualstar to research and test new brands in fashion, home, and beauty; and taking a more active role in the film production division by producing and purchasing properties, meeting with directors, and making movies for brands managed by Dualstar (Heyman 2006).

A brief overview of their professional trajectory reveals their dizzying and indubitable success in creating teen-oriented cross-ownership media and synergistic entertainment and lifestyle products (see the chapter appendix below). As Mary-Kate boasted, "The difference between us and other celebrity brands is that we've been making movies, TV series, videos, CDs, fashion dolls, and books since we were infants. So there is something fun and age-appropriate for kids to have at every stage. We are able to grow creatively, do projects that are geared towards our peers and not have to worry about all the 'marketing' issues for the younger fan. The product is already there. It is really a unique situation" (Checking In 2004).

Alongside their miscellaneous forays into branded consumer products, the twins, as they left adolescence to young adulthood, have become the focus of intense media scrutiny, from their questionable fashion tastes to their alleged eating disorders. As they entered NYU, they were featured in the *New York Times* for their "ashcan" attire, a combination of funk, bohemian, and grandma all wrapped in one; they were seen "dashing around Greenwich Village wearing floppy hats, huge sunglasses, dust-catcher skirts and street-sweeping cable-knit cardigans . . . the twins are trendsetters for the latest hipster look. They are influencing the same generation of girls and young women who fell for them as wholesome child stars, buying their Mattel dolls, and who later, as tweens, spent $750 million a year on denims and pastel tops from the mary-kateandashley line at Wal-Mart." While at a quick glance it might appear that the "bobo" (bohemian bourgeois) style eschews ostentatious displays of wealth, an analysis of the actual accoutrements reveals high-end designer labels and vintage specialties. Said stylist Karen Berenson, "The Olsens are the real thing, fashion role models for a generation entering adulthood" (La Ferla 2005).

The Olsens' eclectic and very personal style is far removed from the wholesomeness of their brand products available at Wal-Mart. Their "bobo-ness," said to be the inspiration for designer John Galliano's fall 2005 collection, also provoked *Jane* magazine to call them "smaller, female versions of Andy Warhol." Their celebrity and wealth has allowed them to drop out of NYU and conduct internships with New York fashion designer Zac Posen and *Rolling Stone* and *Vanity Fair* photographer Annie Leibovitz, while being endlessly photographed and gossiped about on myriad fan websites. Their revolving wardrobe, boyfriends, charity events, parties, shopping expeditions, and Hollywood events are ruthlessly dissected and gushed over by fans. Not always appearing together, they have separately graced the pages of *Harper's Bazaar, Vogue, Nylon,* and *W.*

One of their latest forays is in promoting the Sprouse brothers, teen blond actors who star on a Disney Channel television show and are now creating computer wallpaper, buddy icons, iron-on transfers of their logo, video podcasts, DVDs, books, and a quarterly magazine (Bahney 2006).

In their sixteenth birthday *Hollywood Reporter* issue, where full-page ads from corporate liaisons congratulated the twins on their industry success (these included AOL Time Warner, the Beanstalk Group, Fox Family, Bear Stearns, Wal-Mart, K-Mart, Toys"R"Us, Warner Home Video, and Borders), an article on their merchandising arrangements with over 114 manufacturers and distributors was featured. According to the article, the twins design most of the various products in-house, ensuring "that every Olsen-related object on the market has passed muster in the quality-control department" (Spalding 2001). Two years later, the Olsens became poster girls for corporate greed, with the scandal over the sweatshop labor practices of the Bangladeshi women who manufacture their exclusive Wal-Mart clothing line.

Globalization Gone Awry: The Other Side of the Empire

In 2004 the National Labor Committee[3] issued a call for action in support of the rights of women Bangladeshi garment workers. According to the NLC, an estimated 90 percent of the more than 3,780 export garment factories denied women their legal right to a three-month maternity leave with full pay. Some companies pressured their women workers to quit, others made them quit and then come back as new employees, and only a few of the companies paid them benefits. Citing Disney, Kohl's, and Wal-Mart as the corporate culprits, the NLC urged them to sign the following pledge: "that any woman in Bangladesh sewing their garments will be guaranteed her legal right to maternity leave with benefits." While some of these companies professed to sign the pledge and uphold local labor laws, others, as investigated by the NLC and the Bangladesh Center for Workers Solidarity, continue to deny both women and child laborers their rights as workers and citizens.

As Suzanne Bergeron highlights in her overview of feminist political economic perspectives on globalization, focus has been attuned to "the conflictual interactions among multinational corporations, households, the nation-state, and women" (2001, 990), from studies in the 1980s on emergent international divisions of labor with heightened economic globalization and the resultant "feminization of labor" and the myth of women's "nimble fingers" (see McLaughlin in this volume) to later studies focusing on the politics of structural adjustment policies wrought by the Bretton Woods institutions. Challenging the gendered assumptions of the public-private divide (see Youngs in this volume) and addressing the tensions between the role of the nation-state and transnational governance in the labor market has been an ongoing struggle.

Chandra Talpade Mohanty has argued that studies of developing country women and international divisions of labor "must draw upon the histories of colonialism and race, race and capitalism, gender and patriarchy, and sexual and familial affiliations" (1997, 28). For Valentine Moghadam (1999) economic globalization is characterized by the creation of jobs for women in export-processing free-trade zones and the outsourcing of factory work to corporately owned factories. While such jobs do allow women to gain a level of economic and personal autonomy apart from traditional and patriarchal structures, these jobs are low-paid and precarious, thus ironically (or not) contributing to the feminization of poverty. This female proletarianization is especially acute in the textile and garment industries:

> The global economy is maintained by gendered labor, with definitions of skill, allocation of resources, occupational distribution and modes of remuneration shaped by asymmetrical gender relations and by gender ideologies defining the roles and rights of men and women and of the relative value of their labor. (379)

Assessing shifts in transnational labor flow, Patricia Fernández-Kelly (2007) outlines how globalization and trends toward economic integration have shifted from the relocation of low-skilled jobs to Mexico, the Caribbean, and Asia in the 1970s to the movement of professional jobs from the U.S. to India, as in the case of the computer industry. However, as she emphasizes, it is the low-skilled workers who have experienced a continual decline in their wages and quality of life.

For Mary Beth Mills (2005), the global iconography of the female third-world worker is one that is nimble-fingered and dexterous, patient, obedient, and respectful, and hardworking amidst the brutal boredom and fast-paced fastidiousness of the global assembly line. While it is generally assumed that these women are too compliant and thus resistant to labor organizing, her study of labor activism in Thailand reveals how important it is to consider the politics of place, wherein "structural constraints, and contested identities within women's labor struggles require close attention to participants' own gender and place-based politics" (140).

Dong-Sook Gills (2002), considering the feminization of labor in Asia, echoes Moghadam (1999) in her characterization of the attendant proletarianization of labor, with a key feature of the political economy workers drawn from rural household economies distinct from capitalist production. Aligned with low wages is the "flexibility" of the work—flexible in terms of its contingent, casualized, part-time, and nonunionized status (see also Wright 2006).

Apparently Corrupt:
Sweating in the Global Garment Industry

The history of the early garment industry and its association with women and immigrant succession labor in the U.S. and France has been copiously documented by Nancy Green (1996). In the late twentieth century, because of the relatively low cost of entry, the use of female labor, and neoliberal free-trade policies, the apparel industry was able to seamlessly move from urban centers such as Los Angeles and New York City to farther and more remote regions of the world, from Mexican *maquiladoras* to the Caribbean and Asia. Jane Collins (2003) and Andrew Ross (2004) both recount how, for many first-world citizens, the global garment industry in many ways characterizes negative aspects of economic globalization, with news reports and exposés on sweatshop corruption, child labor, and factory fires fueling renewed and heightened urgency for global justice. This is especially the case for postsecondary students, who have rallied for an end to sweatshop labor, including the manufacture of their collegiate gear by sweatshop-free companies (Featherstone and USAS 2002).

The ubiquity of apparel factories is also a product of the fashion industry, as designer duds are translated into cheaper knock-offs, and as the fashion season escalates into multiple miniseasons. Large retailers with vertical holdings now make their own private-label clothing lines, which are sent off for manufacturing at the cheapest locales, evading local unionized factories with more humane working conditions, including environmental standards. The gendering of labor accelerates faster production processes and propels more corporate profit, even as it leads to a contemporary proletarianization of women akin to the Industrial Revolution's exploitation of women and children. As Ross (2004) comments, "The worst manifestations of the global sweatshops are all the more tragic when adolescents in poor countries are toiling to meet the style demands of their age peers in the North who are fortunate enough to have disposable income" (25).

Ahmed (2004) traces the current garment factories in Bangladesh to post-1975, when a wave of liberalization, privatization, creation of export-processing zones, and the reduction of trade barriers occurred. After a short span of eight years, by 1991 Bangladesh emerged as the eighth largest garment exporter to the U.S., and many in Bangladesh hail the industry as the "liberator for women" (35). Middle-class (but cash poor) rural women were recruited to work in the new garment factories, with male owners promising their families and their fathers that the women would live in segregated and protected compounds. Thus was produced an uncomfortable paradox between what women garment workers in Bangladesh have gained (new employment opportunities necessary for family income) versus their lack of worker and financial autonomy and their resultant exploitation. By 2006, Bangladesh was the third largest exporter to the U.S., behind Mexico and China. Current production figures forecast that Bangladesh will surpass Mexico by March 2007. In 2005, 785 million garments were shipped from Bangladesh to the U.S, with a wholesale value of US$2.4 billion. One billion garments are scheduled to ship to the U.S. in 2006, amounting to "over three garments for every man, woman, and child in America," according to the NLC (2006), made by a labor force composed of 80 percent young women aged sixteen to twenty-five.

Four years after the NLC chastised and received pledges from corporations that they would guarantee Bangladeshi women their guaranteed maternity leave, the NLC issued a scathing report on child labor in a Harvest Rich plant in Bangladesh. They alleged that Wal-Mart, Hanes, Puma, and J. C. Penney were employing and abusing an estimated two hundred to three hundred children, aged eleven years of age or even younger. This report, issued after the NLC's infamous exposure of celebrity Kathy Lee Gifford's Wal-Mart clothing line made by Honduran child labor brought to public furor this human rights issue a decade ago, was even more condemnatory. Citing children's accounts of beatings, slaps, and harsh and long working hours, the NLC report urged U.S. companies to issue wage and educational stipends for the children, the hiring of their older siblings and parents, and a wage increase to at least thirty-six cents an hour in order that they might "live with a modicum of decency." This, despite Bangladeshi law prohibiting child workers under the age of fourteen, and their mandated eight-hour-day, six-day-week, and voluntary overtime labor laws. "We have protected the corporate label. Now it is time to protect the sixteen-year-old girl in Bangladesh who made the garment," the NLC urged (NLC 2006).

Liza Featherstone's book *Selling Women Short* (2004) is a fascinating and disturbing chronicle of *Dukes v. Wal-Mart*, a class-action suit launched in 2004 by women Wal-Mart workers that is currently winding its way through the U.S. courts. In telling the employees' stories, Featherstone discusses the broader societal impact of the retail giant, which is the largest private employer in the U.S.: how its success is derived by offering poor, raced, and working-class people (its primary consumer base) the lowest prices around, while hiring workers at minimum wage (many of whom need a second job to survive) and discriminating against women, particularly women of color.[4]

Dukes refers to Betty Dukes, a fifty-four-year-old African American Wal-Mart employee who became the lead plaintiff in the largest ever class-action suit in the U.S. *Dukes* represents 1.6 million women—past and present employees of Wal-Mart—who allege that Wal-Mart discriminates against women in pay, promotion, and job assignments, all in violation of Title VII of the 1964 Civil Rights Act. This act protects workers form discrimination on the basis of race, religion, national origin, and sex.

The National Organization of Women (NOW) named Wal-Mart one of its "merchants of shame" in its Women Friendly Worker Campaign. "Wal-Mart women workers deserve equality," the campaign material reads:

Wal-Mart pays its women employees an average of *$5,200 per year less* than it pays men. Women are *denied promotions* to higher-paying jobs. Men hold 85% of store manager positions and ⅔ of all management jobs, even though ⅔ of its "associates" are women. This is no way for the country's largest private employer to behave. Wal-Mart earned more than $9 billion in net profits—after taxes—in 2004.[5]

Wal-Mart is savvy in catering to the female consumer, whether through entreaties of "Always Low Prices!" or by creating in-house clothing lines for the tween or the plus-size woman. Says Featherstone on Wal-Mart's exclusive relationship with Mary-Kate and Ashley: "Tapping into the popularity of these bland teens, described by Wal-Mart CEO Lee Scott as 'fashion magnets,' demonstrates that Wal-Mart brilliantly understands not only overworked middle-aged women, but also their daughters who, after all, do plenty of shopping" (2004, 215). Recognizing that the plus-size market is the fastest-growing category, Wal-Mart carries teen brands, including Mary-Kate and Ashley, in their Girlswear Plus lines. But as Featherstone ruefully remarks, Wal-Mart is merely tapping into its largest consumer base—low-income women ("those living on incomes below 130 percent of the federal poverty line"), who, regardless of race or ethnicity, "are about 50 percent more likely to be obese than women of higher economic status" (217).

Role Models?

> If Mary-Kate and Ashley continue to stand up for other young women their same age who are sewing their garments all across the developing world, this could have a profound impact, highlighting the problem of sweatshop abuses, while working concretely to improve conditions and wages. (Charles Kernaghan, NLC 2004)

Is it naïve of Charles Kernaghan to suggest that the Olsens could be role models for socially responsible consumption and labor practices amidst the current North American glut of celebrity culture? Obsession over Mary-Kate's $1,700 wool wrap dress from designer Marc Jacobs, the twins' return to their natural honey-blond hair color after escapades with platinum blonde and dark brown, Ashley Olsen's dubious distinction of making it as number two on PETA's worst-dressed list for her fur-wearing ways, or speculations on the height of their shoes, have all been fodder for the tabloids in just the past few months.

Profitable tabloids specializing in celebrity gossip and gratuitous titillation are an unfortunate mainstay of our current media system. Whether the twins will jump on the latest vogue for celebrity philanthropic ventures and start advocating for the gender rights of their sisters—who can barely eek out a living wage sewing the MK&A line of latest fashion trends that are then sold by a megacorporation that is infamous for exploiting its women workers—remains a vague and unlikely possibility. There are some exceptions to such everyday exploitation—Eraydin and Erendil (1999) provide the example of Istanbul apparel workers, composed of second-generation rural female migrant workers who, because of positive bargaining and wage increases, see themselves as active agents in the labor market.

Yes, there are pioneering and brave organizations such as the NLC that expose injustices and promote the labor rights of women and children working in the export garment industry. Transnational resistance to global capitalist structures that reinvent, overlap, and reimagine feminist communities at the local, national, and global levels (Bergeron 2001) are also incredibly encouraging and vital. The Clean Clothes Campaign is one such example; their Made by Women campaign of 2005 highlights the activism, resilience, and liveliness of women working in northern and southern countries to ensure gender equality and social justice for all women.

But it is difficult for these stories to get reported in the mainstream media. The NLC has been somewhat successful in gaining mainstream media attention, but this media notoriety has come about because of their exposure of American celebrity complicity in using offshore sweatshops that exploit the children and women who manufacture their branded clothing lines. Mainstream media typically do not report the everyday economic realities of men and women struggling to survive in southern countries or the environmental and social challenges they face. Disasters—whether natural or man-made, such as factory fires—usually are covered, thus allowing Westerners a glimpse into the deplorable and inhumane working conditions of the child laborers that manufacture the clothing, toys, and other consumer goods that they voraciously consume. Meanwhile, we are bound to hear more about the fashion histrionics, the boyfriend breakups, and the newest licensed products of the MK&A empire. This is a different kind of power than that envisioned by Charles Kernaghan—a power that starkly reminds us how slanted economic globalization can be for the lives and livelihoods of many women.

Appendix: Mary-Kate and Ashley Timeline

1986
(June) Mary-Kate and Ashley Olsen are born on Friday the thirteenth.

1987, 1 year old
Full House, their first series, premieres. Each girl earns $24,000 per episode.

1990, 4 years old
MK and A each earn $25,000 per episode.

1992, 6 years old
Brother for Sale, the twins' first album, is released. It sells 325,000 copies. Their first TV movie, *To Grandmother's House We Go*, premieres and makes it onto Nielsen's Top 10.

1993, 7 years old

The Dualstar Entertainment Group is established. The twins release *Our First Video*, their first direct-to-video production. It tops Billboard video charts and sells 35 million copies. They sign a new deal with ABC for *Full House* and television movies worth $5 million each. The girls are worth $10 million.

1994, 8 years old

BMG signs MK and A for thirty-two album and video projects over the following three years. The deal is worth $5 million to $7 million.

1995, 9 years old

The twins' first feature film, *It Takes Two*, is released. The girls take is $1.6 million for acting; the movie makes $19 million at the box office and $75 million in home video sales. WarnerVision buys MK and A video distribution rights from BMG.

1996, 10 years old

WarnerVision is absorbed by Warner Home Video. The twins' books are introduced.

1997, 11 years old

Lightyear Entertainment (sister company of Warner Home Video) picks up the MK and A music line from BMG. The music videos sell over 500,000 copies. Book sales hit $25 million; and video and CD sales hit $80 million. The girls make $3 million from *Full House* syndication and over $6 million from video royalties.

1998, 12 years old

The girls are worth $17 million. They sign a seven-figure pay-or-play deal with ABC. Their second series, *Two of a Kind*, premieres. Their video, *Our Lips Are Sealed*, sells more copies than the video release of *Erin Brockovich* and the first season of *The Sopranos*.

1999, 13 years old

MK and A's first Christmas album is released.

2001, 15 years old

Teen clothing, bedding, and bath line is launched at Wal-Mart in the United States, bringing in an estimated $300 million for Wal-Mart. Home video soundtracks are released. *Mary-Kate and Ashley in Action* cartoon is broadcast on ABC's Saturday morning lineup. *Mary-Kate and Ashley Magazine* is launched with focus on "fashion, boys, and beauty." Publisher goes under after three issues and the magazine folds. *So Little Time* premieres. Mary-Kate earns a daytime Emmy nomination. *The Hollywood Reporter* produces a special issue on MK and A, naming them "the most powerful young women in Hollywood."

2002, 16 years old
The "mary-kateandashley" brand is launched in the UK at ASDA stores. The brand brings in an estimated $500 million to $600 million for Wal-Mart. Mary-Kate and Ashley Olsen's official online fan club is launched.

2003, 17 years old
The first global video fashion show is filmed at a Wal-Mart in Toronto, then broadcast simultaneously at Wal-Marts across Canada in March and at Wal-Marts across the United States in April. The girls' first set of fragrances is launched at Wal-Mart: "Mary-Kate and Ashley One" and "Mary-Kate and Ashley." It is estimated that the brand brings in over $1 billion for Wal-Mart, that the girls are each worth $80 million to $150 million, and that Dualstar is worth over $1 billion. GlaxoSmithKline introduces MK and A Aquafresh toothpaste in Bubble Cool flavor.

2004, 18 years old
A line of rugs is introduced. Close to twenty dolls have been created, seventeen albums are released, there are nearly thirty mostly direct-to-video titles, fourteen feature-length films have been made for television and direct-to-video, and there are one hundred book titles in print. MK and A become copresidents of Dualstar on their eighteenth birthday. The feature film *New York Minute* is released and receives lukewarm reviews. They host the season finale of *Saturday Night Live* and are slimed on Nickleodeon's Kid's Choice Awards. Their website, www.mary-kateandashley.com, is relaunched. MK and A get a star on the Hollywood Walk of Fame. Warner Home Video agrees to distribute Olsen titles for another ten years, earning them an advance "in the millions."

2005, 19 years old
Robert Thorne leaves Dualstar; the girls reportedly buy him out. Diane Reichenberger becomes the new CEO. A line of furniture is launched, available in twenty-five stores in Canada and fifty stores in the United States. A second set of fragrances is launched: "Mary-Kate and Ashley Coast to Coast L.A." and "Mary-Kate and Ashley Coast to Coast New York," sold at Kohl's, Claire's, CVS, and Walgreens in the United States. Apparel counts for approximately 80 percent of Dualstar's business. Dualstar Entertainment Group announces a deal with boy twins Cole and Dylan Sprouse for boy-twins-themed clothing, sporting goods, video games, CDs, and DVDs. There are plans to launch in Australia.

2006, 20 years old
Dualstar inks deal with Simon Spotlight, an imprint of Simon & Schuster Children's Publishing for the Sprouse brothers books. The first books in the series are expected in summer 2007. Dualstar launches a partnership with "teen expert and author" Jessica Weiner, who will write an advice column for

mary-kateandashley.com. Plans are made to widen distribution of beauty products beyond Wal-Mart through retailer Claire's. They are set to launch e-commerce on mary-kateandashley.com. Dualstar partners with Airborne Entertainment Inc. (a subsidiary of CYBIRD Co., Ltd.) to create branded mobile products for both mary-kateandashley and Sprouse Bros. (ring tones, wallpapers, ringback tones, and mobile games). Airborne will create the content. MK and A star in Badgley Mischka advertising campaign, the first time they represent a brand other than their own.

Sources: Andreoli 2004; Ault 2004; Bittar 2003; Dualstar press releases; E'Innocenzio 2002; Lefevre 2001; Marr 2004.

Notes

Acknowledgment. Thanks to the Social Sciences and Humanities Research Council of Canada for their support of this research.

1. Mary Pilon, "Labor Groups to Picket Olsens." *Washington Square News*, December 9, 2004. http://media.www.nyunews.com/media/storage/paper869/news/2004/12/09/UndefinedSection/Labor.Groups.To.Picket.Olsens-2388681.shtml (accessed 30 April 2007).

2. For the *Forbes* List of Top 20, see www.forbes.com/digitalentertainment/2007/01/17/richest-women-entertainmsnt-tech-media-ca_lg_richwomen07_0118womenstars_lander.html (accessed 26 January 2007).

3. The National Labor Committee was founded in 1980 by three U.S. labor presidents in order to organize and boost national labor organizations in light of then-president Ronald Reagan's wave of anti-unionism, and to lend solidarity to international labor movements, such as the assassination in Central America of union organizers and the rise of Mexican *maquiladoras*. See Ross 2004, p. 34, and the NLC at www.nlcnet.org.

4. The anti–Wal-Mart literature is voluminous; selected books and films include Bill Quinn, *How Wal-Mart Is Destroying America (and the World) and What You Can Do about It* (Berkeley: Ten-Speed Press, 2000); Charles Fishman, *The Wal-Mart Effect* (New York: Penguin, 2006); *Wal-Mart: The Face of Twenty-First-Century Capitalism*, ed. Nelson Lichtenstein (New York: The New Press, 2005); and Robert Greenwald's film *Wal-Mart: The High Cost of Low Price*, 2005.

5. See NOW's Wal-Mart Campaign at www.now.org/issues/wfw/wal-mart.html (accessed 2 February 2007).

References

Ahmed, Fauzia Erfan. 2004. "The Rise of the Bangladesh Garment Industry: Globalization, Women Workers, and Voice." *NWSA Journal* 16, no. 2:34–45.

Andreoli, Teresa. 2004. "Mary-Kate & Ashley: How the Brand Found Stardom at Wal-Mart." *Furniture Today*, June.

Ault, Susanne. 2004. "Warners Extends Olsen Pact." *Video Business* 24, no. 40, October 4.

Bahney, Anna. 2006. "Boys Just Want to Be . . . Olsens." *Sunday New York Times*, April 30.

Bergeron, Suzanne. 2001. "Political Economy Discourses of Globalization and Feminist Politics." *Signs: Journal of Women in Culture and Society* 26, no. 4:983–1006.

Bittar, Christine. 2003. "GSK Gets Aquafresh with Mary Kate, Ashley." *Brandweek* 44, no. 18, May 5.

Buckingham, David and Julian Sefton-Green. 2003. "Gotta Catch'em All: Structure, Agency and Pedagogy in Children's Media Culture." *Media, Culture & Society* 25, no. 3:379–99.

"Checking In with Mary-Kate and Ashley." 2004. *Children's Business* 19, no. 4:15.

Clean Clothes Campaign. 2005. *Made By Women: Gender, the Global Garment Industry and the Movement for Women Worker's Rights*, eds. Nina Ascoly and Chantal Finney. Amsterdam: Clean Clothes Campaign International Secretariat. www.cleanclothes.org/pub.htm (accessed 1 February 2007).

Collins, Jane L. 2003. *Threads: Gender, Labor and Power in the Global Apparel Industry*. Chicago: University of Chicago Press.

Cook, Daniel Thomas. 2005. "The Dichotomous Child In and Of Commercial Culture." *Childhood: A Global Journal of Child Research* 12, no. 2:155–59.

Corliss, Richard. 2004. "Olsens in Bid to Buy Disney." *Time*, May 17.

Ebert, Teresa L. 1993. "Ludic Feminism, the Body, Performance, and Labor: Bringing 'Materialism' Back into Feminist Cultural Studies." *Cultural Critique* no. 23:5–50.

E'Innocenzio, Anne. 2002. "Olsen Twins Extend Brand to Teen Demo." *Marketing News* 36, no. 14, July 8.

Eraydin, Ayda, and Asuman Erendil. 1999. "The Role of Female Labor in Industrial Restructuring: New Production Processes and Labor Market Relations in the Istanbul Clothing Industry." *Gender, Place and Culture* 6, no. 3:259–72.

Featherstone, Liza. 2004. *Selling Women Short: The Landmark Battle for Worker's Rights at Wal-Mart*. New York: Basic Books.

Featherstone, Liza, and United Students Against Sweatshops (USAS). 2002. *Students Against Sweatshops*. London: Verso.

Fernández-Kelly, Patricia. 2007. "The Global Assembly Line in the New Millennium: A Review Essay." *Signs: Journal of Women in Culture and Society* 32, no. 2:509–21.

Forbes Magazine. 2004. "The Celebrity 100." www.forbes.com/2004/06/16/celebs04land.html (accessed 30 April 2007).

Gills, Dong-Sook S. 2002. "Globalization of Production and Women in Asia." *Annals of the American Academy of Political and Social Science* 581:106–20.

Green, Nancy L. 1996. "Women and Immigrants in the Sweatshop: Categories of Labor Segmentation Revisited." *Comparative Studies in Society and History* 38, no. 3:311–433.

Grixti, Joe. 2006. "Symbiotic Transformations: Youth, Global Media and Indigenous Culture in Malta." *Media, Culture & Society* 28, no. 1:105–22.

Heyman, Marshall. 2006. "Profile: Mary-Kate Olsen." *W Magazine*, January: 136–37.

Hopkins, Jim. 2005. "Billion-dollar Teens: Celebrity Pair Takes Business Seriously." *USA Today*, May 6.

Kearney, Mary Celeste. 2006. *Girls Make Media*. New York: Routledge.

La Ferla, Ruth. 2005. "Mary-Kate: Fashion Star." *Sunday New York Times*, March 6. www.nytimes.com/2005/03/06/fashion/06olsen.html?ex=1267765200&en=aac4f88e8a8a2fa8&ei=5090&partner=rssuserland (accessed 26 January 2007).

Langer, Beryl. 2004. "The Business of Branded Enchantment." *Journal of Consumer Culture* 4, no.2:251–77.

Lefevre, Lori. 2001. "The New Kids." *Mediaweek* 11, January 15.

Lemish, Dafna. 2007. *Children and Television: A Global Perspective*. London: Blackwell.

Maira, Sunaina, and Elisabeth Soep, eds. 2004. *Youthscapes: The Popular, the National, the Global*. Philadelphia: University of Pennsylvania Press.

Marr, Merissa. 2004. "Hollywood Report: Double Jeopardy?: Olsen Sisters Act Their Age in Appeal for New Fans." *Wall Street Journal*, April 9.

Miller, Toby. 2004. "A View from a Fossil: The New Economy, Creativity, and Consumption—Two or Three Things I Don't Believe In." *International Journal of Cultural Studies* 7, no.1:55–65.

Mills, Mary Beth. 2005. "From Nimble Fingers to Raised Fists: Activism in Globalizing Thailand." *Signs: Journal of Women in Culture and Society* 31, no. 1:117–44.

Moghadam, Valentine M. 1999. "Gender and Globalization: Female Labor and Women's Mobilization." *Journal of World-Systems Research* V, no. 2:367–88.

Mohanty, Chandra Talpade. 1997. "Women Workers and Capitalist Scripts: Ideologies of Domination, Common Interests, and the Politics of Solidarity." In *Feminist Genealogies, Cultural Legacies, Democratic Futures*, eds. M. Jacqui Alexander and Chandra Talpade Mohanty, 3–29. London: Routledge.

Moran, Kristin C. 2006. "The Global Expansion of Children's Television: A Case Study of the Adaptation of Sesame Street in Spain." *Learning, Media & Technology* 31, no. 3:287–300.

National Labor Committee (NLC). 2004. "Under Pressure, Celebrities Mary-Kate and Ashley Olsen Do The Right Thing." NLC Human & Worker Rights Update, December 15. http://mailbox.gsu.edu/pipermail/tedlog/2004-December.txt (accessed 22 January 2007).

———. 2006. "Child Labor Is Back: Children Are Again Sewing Clothing for Major U.S. Companies." www.nlcnet.org/article.php?id=147 (accessed 1 February 2007).

Pilon, Mary. 2004. "Labor Groups to Picket Olsens." *Washington Square News*, December 9. http://media.www.nyunews.com/media/storage/paper869/news/2004/12/09/UndefinedSection/Labor.Groups.To.Picket.Olsens-2388681.shtml (accessed 30 April 2007).

Record, Angela. 2001. "Born to Shop." In *Sex and Money: Feminism and Political Economy in the Media*, eds. Eileen R. Meehan and Ellen Riordan, xx. Minneapolis: University of Minnesota Press.

Ross, Andrew. 2004. "The Making of the Second Anti-Sweatshop Movement." In *Low Pay, High Profile: The Global Push for Fair Labor*, 15–55. New York: The New Press.

Silverman, Stephen M. 2004. "Mary-Kate, Ashley, Petition to Stop Abuses." *People Online*. December 10. www.people.com/people/article/0,,956032,00.html (accessed 30 April 2007).

Spalding, Rachel Fischer. 2001. "Quality Control." *The Hollywood Reporter*, October 12–14.

Susman, Gary. 2004. "Rags to Riches." *Entertainment Weekly Online*, December 10. www.ew.com/ew/article/0,,956075,00.html (accessed 22 January 2007).

Tauber, Michelle, and Mark Dagotino. 2004. "Two Cool." *People*, May 3.

Wright, Melissa W. 2006. *Disposable Women and Other Myths of Global Capitalism*. New York: Routledge.

PART FIVE

GLOCALIZING MEDIA AND TECHNOLOGIES

CHAPTER SEVENTEEN

Feminist Print Cultures in the Digital Era

Simone Murray

During the last decades of the twentieth century, book publishing increasingly became subsumed by the global media industries. Many formerly independent publishers were bought by multinational conglomerates with interests in an array of communications media. Once well-known publishing houses were merged with conglomerates' existing publishing interests, their names sometimes retained as specific imprints within the conglomerate, or their lists simply stripped of profitable titles and the original imprint name discarded (Miller 1997; Schiffrin 2001). In parallel with such globalized acquisition and merger activity, the firmly international character of the book publishing industry was reinforced by the rise of the long-established Frankfurt Book Fair to the status of unrivalled annual marketplace for the buying, selling, and licensing of book rights. Such supranational production arrangements required comparable growth in international policy mechanisms for policing intellectual property in the book. Hence the late twentieth century witnessed marked shifts from national to bilateral or multilateral copyright agreements under the auspices of free-trade negotiations, or the World Intellectual Property Organization (WIPO), or both. As standard book contracts came increasingly to apportion world rights, translation rights, and an extensive range of subsidiary rights, it was clear that if book publishing could ever have been considered a nationally focused industry, those days were resoundingly over.

Such longer-term trends toward internationalization of the book industry were massively accelerated by the globalizing impact of digital technologies from the 1980s onward, particularly with mainstream Western adoption of the Internet from the mid-1990s. Suddenly publishers began to construct Web pages designed as publicity and marketing portals for global readerships, and on-line book retailers such as Amazon.com overturned the idea of a bookstore servicing a particular geographic or metropolitan locale. As the phenomenon of digital piracy confronted all media industries from the last decade of the twentieth century, it was apparent that book publishers shared common interests—and frequently common corporate owners—with the music, screen, and newspaper industries, and that the battle to protect copyright in cyberspace required medium-neutral and globally enforceable legislative regimes.

Against the background of these industry-wide changes, the feminist book publishing sector faced its own set of challenges, some reflections of macro-level changes and some specific to the particular feminist publishing project. Women-run print enterprises had evinced a strongly internationalist orientation since their emergence in the early 1970s: presses frequently entered into rights agreements, republishing each other's titles in different territories; the International Feminist Book Fairs of the 1980s and 1990s were important trade shows as much as cultural and political events;[1] and presses such as The Women's Press in the UK based their imprint identity upon translations and English-language titles from Commonwealth authors (Murray 2004). The issue this chapter examines is how the digital era has impacted upon the feminist book sector in particular. The rise of digital information and communication technologies (ICTs) has been widely recognized as reconfiguring the twenty-first-century book industry (Birkerts 1994; Nunberg 1996; Epstein 2002; Basbanes 2004). Has its effect been similarly transformative for the feminist press sector, or do the particular dynamics of feminist print culture generate more complex and ambiguous patterns?

Feminism and the "Death of the Book" Debate

In comparatively rare instances when the research trajectories of gender studies, print cultures, and digital technologies have intersected, feminist commentary on the relationship between print and the Internet has tended to follow one of three interpretative modes. The first generally ignores the successes of the women-in-print movement in a wave of euphoria at the liberatory potential of interactive multimedia. These technologies are posited as potentially emancipatory tools yet to be fully colonized by patriarchal power structures, unlike the more familiar medium of print, which is understood as complicit in the "dominant masculinist Western" paradigm of linearity, uniformity, univocality, and

reader disenfranchisement (Josie Arnold 1999, 264). A second, better historically informed stream acknowledges the successes of the women-in-print movement as a significant challenge to the gatekeeping power of the culture industries, but explicitly rejects further feminist investment in book cultures as
self-defeating nostalgia for a superseded technology. As Dale Spender's *Nattering on the Net* (1995), the archetypal enunciation of this renunciatory position,
puts it, "On every index, the book is making way for the new medium" (65). "If
the present generation of women cannot hand on this knowledge that they
have created, then the entire tradition is at risk—and it could be lost. This is
the pattern of the past; it should not be the prediction for the next century"
(xxiv). A third, less explicitly renunciatory, modulation of Spender's position
acknowledges feminist book industries as culturally significant but as prelude to
the newer, and by implication more significant, feminist embrace of digital
technology. Leslie Regan Shade's discussion of gender and the Internet nods re-
spectfully to feminist book cultures, but in elegiac mode: "In the mid-1970s,
North America was home to a plethora of independent women's presses and independent women's bookstores; by the 1980s, these numbers had dwindled, and
by the end of the 1990s only a handful of feminist presses remained" (2002, 34).

Despite their gradations of enthusiasm for digital media, all three approaches
are implicitly wedded to a conception of the book and digital culture as locked
in opposition; the Internet is perceived by all three approaches as eclipsing print
culture, the key differential being the rate of eclipse. In adopting such a binary,
historicist paradigm, feminist critics overlook a fruitful body of medium theory
arguing for the mutually constitutive and complementary coexistence of media
formats, which originates in the work of Marshall McLuhan (McLuhan 2001;
Marvin 1998; Holmes 2005). In particular, binary conceptions permit no means
to understand how, in this era of digital incunabula, the book and the Internet
may be engaged in a complex process of mutual "remediation"—each attempting to repurpose the characteristics of the other to win medium-loyalty of users
and to secure a place in an ecology of competing media (Bolter and Grusin
1999). Feminist cultural sociologist Elizabeth Long, for example, perceives "a
burgeoning world of literature online," in which "modern channels of communication have enabled the book to assume a newly powerful presence for some
readers" (2003, 216, 218). Similarly, Susan Hawthorne and Renate Klein's *CyberFeminism* (1999) not only exemplifies how the Internet constitutes a new
niche topic for book publishers, but moreover it attempts to reproduce the hy-
pertextual links of a Web page through use of a marginal eye of Horus icon,
cross-referencing the reader to related topics elsewhere in the anthology (vii).
It is not simply that newer media cannibalize older media forms but, more surprisingly, traditional media formats retaliate by themselves remediating the
unique interactive functions of new media. One contributor to Hawthorne and

Klein's volume may dismiss books as "reinforc[ing] the dominance of patriarchal society," but this feminist press volume in its very materiality indicates that feminism, the book, and the Internet enjoy a more subtly interdependent and mutually constitutive relationship than she allows (Josie Arnold 1999, 270).

The present discussion takes up the idea of remediation as emblematic of a feminist book culture both enervated and energized by the rise of digital technologies. The Internet appears to have had a bifurcating effect on the feminist culture of women-run publishing houses, magazines, bookshops, book clubs, and reading groups established during the 1970s and coming to mainstream prominence during the 1980s. For midsize feminist presses, the advent of the Internet coincided with successful mainstreaming of women writers and female editors within literary and academic culture, such that feminist operations lost their specifically oppositional raison d'être and became effectively incorporated into publishing conglomerates, mainstream book distribution, and chain bookstores. When it became possible to purchase such formerly underground publications as lesbian erotica from Amazon.com—published under a mainstream colophon no less—it had become clear that the staunchly separatist self-conceptions of the early 1970s women-in-print movement had been thoroughly superseded (Moberg 1974; Arnold 1976). Yet conversely, the Internet had a catalyzing effect on smaller-scale and fringe feminist book operations, as it dissolved long-standing problems such as barriers to market entry and costs associated with distribution and publicity infrastructure. Simultaneously it expanded niche markets from metropolitan or predominantly national scale to global special-interest audiences. Media Report to Women encapsulated this bifurcating and complicating impact of the Internet on an already complex feminist publishing sector in its observation that the news for feminist publications after the millennium is "both happy and sad": "As some publications rooted in the modern feminist era produce their final issues, new ones are appearing, often on the Internet, where their potential reach is far beyond what could have been envisioned by 1970s-era women limited to mimeograph machines, mailing labels and stamps you had to lick" (Media 2003a, 6). Changes in digital technology, shifts in political climate, and concentration of media industries have reformulated feminist book cultures beyond recognition from the seemingly halcyon days of the ubiquitous Virago Modern Classics list in the mid-1980s. But the relationship between these media formats has become too intertwined, mutually dependent, and cross-pollinating to be adequately encapsulated by the metaphor of eclipse and hence warrants more sustained empirical investigation.

Production

The widespread sense that feminist book culture has changed beyond recognition is due to two simultaneous forces that, taken together, atomized the industry as formerly known. These forces can be best conceptualized as a matrix model, with the horizontal axis representing the overriding technological change of the late twentieth century—the remediating tension between the book and the Internet. Transversely, represented by the vertical axis, are contemporaneous industry, political, and cultural changes, which saw elements of feminism incorporated into mainstream culture and the academy and certain strands of feminist thought appropriated as profitable niche markets by publishing multinationals. The complexity of contemporary feminist book cultures arises from the unpredictable interplay between these two axes. The forces of technological remediation on one hand, and sectoral polarization on the other, played out differently across national book markets, let alone across international Anglophone markets or the global book industry in all its diversity. To give some indication of the breadth of change confronting feminist print producers, this discussion selects four case studies, broadly representative of each of the quarters formed by this matrix model: book publishing within conglomerates, conglomerates with an Internet orientation, independent book-focused producers, and online independent publishers.

It is safe to begin with the observation that all involved in feminist print production—as in the publishing industries generally—now acknowledge the crucial importance of having a presence on the World Wide Web; as Spinifex Press cofounders Hawthorne and Klein recall their early-1990s awakening to the possibilities of digital media, "We were soon convinced that Spinifex Press needed to get a Home Page operating, and to do so quickly" (1999, 12).[2] Chiefly this online presence is attributable to the highly cost-effective marketing potential of the Web for publicizing new releases, backlist titles, author information, and forthcoming book-related events. Martha Leslie Allen, of the Washington-based Women's Institute for Freedom of the Press, encapsulates this power to grow potential readership exponentially for minimal outlay: "Inexpensively, we're able to communicate on a global level" (Media 2003a, 6). Aimed additionally at fellow industry professionals, publishers' websites are also capable of reducing administrative time spent on processing routine and labor-intensive inquiries regarding rights, permissions, employment, internships, or submissions policy. But it is in the domain of electronic commerce that feminist publishers have exploited most fully the interactive potential of the Internet, with online ordering eradicating the problem of securing display of small-press titles in mainstream book retailers and eliminating the retailers' markup to boot. Any market research or customer-loyalty benefits that may accrue from publisher home pages simply constitute additional benefits. The fact that feminist publishers, whether conglomerate-owned or fiercely independent, have universally embraced the Web makes its advantages appear unalloyed. If there is a drawback, it is probably more for feminist periodical publishers than for book producers, as the shift from hard copy to digital format can heighten concerns about archiving and preserving the feminist print record. Well acquainted with feminism's periodic reexcavations of its own obscured past, Allen cautions, "The historical record will not be documented as well for the online magazines, and as an historian, I find that very unfortunate" (Media 2003a, 6).

The multinational publishers with the greatest market presence in the field of feminism are academic publishers Sage and Routledge, whose lists almost define the lineaments of contemporary feminist thought within many subfields of women's studies. To maintain this market dominance, Sage and Routledge's use of the Internet is conspicuously book- and publisher-centric, with their Web pages geared almost solely to more commercial Web applications, such as catalogue searching, marketing, and sales.[3] Routledge previously hosted a more researcher-focused gender studies forum, with information not only about house titles but also including lists of women's studies courses and useful library resources, but this appears to have been scrapped and the previously distinct gender studies list dissolved into the lists of affiliated humanities subdisciplines.[4]

Yet the success of multinational academic publishers in cultivating feminism as a lucrative niche market has never been without its critics from within second-wave feminism (Murray 2004, 97–125). Most recently, third-wave feminist authors have revolted against the increasing theorization and academicization of women's studies during the 1990s by choosing to publish instead with mainstream trade presses, characterizing mainstream academic feminist publishing as a deadening gatekeeper in its power to deem "only certain kinds of voices, narratives, and consumer goods fashionable and profitable enough to be marketed and sold" (Piano 2002). Third-wave feminists appear also to have diagnosed a lingering second-wave ambivalence toward popular culture, in spite of publishers such as Routledge profiting hugely from the institutionalization of media and cultural studies curricula since the 1980s:

> Third-wavers are concerned with publishing in popular formats and venues, so as to be a part of the culture they critique; they are not interested in being confined to academia, nor do they feel academic feminism gives them the freedom to theorise in new ways. For this reason, third-wave writings have been published by popular presses, and use witty titles and catchy graphics whenever possible to draw in the average reader. (Gilley and Zabel 2005, 191)

The concept of authors actively deciding *against* mainstream feminist publishers as not mainstream enough is intriguing, in that it directly contradicts the more familiar feminist critique of publishing multinationals as opportunistically poaching feminist "stars" while having failed to support the discipline that nurtured them (Murray 2004, 120–25, 179). The third-wave critique suggests instead a younger generation of authors perceiving themselves as active agents rather than corporate dupes—women who believe feminism's entrenchment within the academy has been won at the high price of theoretical obfuscation and mass exclusion.

A conglomerate-owned feminist publisher that has taken a more reader-centric approach to its website is Virago Press, the once emblematic UK feminist press, which was bought by Time Warner Books in late 1995 (Murray 2004, 29).[5] Virago's extensive Web presence includes interactive applications such as the Virago Forum, featuring book groups, author discussion, and vociferous debate, particularly about the BBC adaptations of Virago author Sarah Waters's novels *Tipping the Velvet* (1998) and *Fingersmith* (2002).[6] Virago innovatively explores the potential of the Internet for feminist publishers in offering a print-on-demand facility for eighteen out-of-print Virago Modern Classics titles: "You may find yourself paying something more like a hardback price, but this new approach keeps our books in print longer."[7] Regarded as in many ways an heir to Virago and its pioneering female canon-building of the late-1970s, London-based independent publisher Persephone Books similarly uses the Web to remediate, reinforce, and multiformat book culture (Ducas 1999). Persephone's standard grey-jacketed reprints of predominantly interwar women's fiction appear at first glance to fetishize the book format beyond taint of competing technologies, with their choice of vintage fabric prints for endpapers and tastefully understated bindings. But Persephone's artfully constructed website is in fact integral to the firm's celebration of a certain kind of middle-class female bookishness, with online ordering, readers' fora, advertising for in-store events, and extensive book-club materials (Hartley 2001, 8).[8] This is the Internet consciously remediated to affirm biblio-superiority.

Representing the fourth quarter of the matrix model are a number of staunchly independent fringe publishers who conceive of the Internet as integral to their feminist publishing project. For some, embrace of digital interactivity and multimedia serves as a manifestation of poststructuralist feminist thought, such as the online feminist poetics journal *HOW2*, which celebrates the Internet as enabling the kind of open, dialogic texts that testify to their plurality and polysemy in their very format (Kloo and McMillan 2002, 194).[9] The bilingual journal *Lola Press*, by contrast, tempers its theoretical justifications for an online presence with pragmatic utility; as a joint English–Spanish journal edited by women in three continents and producing two hard-copy and one online issue per annum, the communications infrastructure of the Internet makes joint production of the journal possible, as well as building a sense of producer/consumer community: "Send us your comments, suggestions and exploit the advantages of e-mail-correspondence [sic] with other readers, editors and authors."[10] For academic women's studies journals based solely in developing countries, dual print and digital publication serves strategic purposes. As the website of the journal *Feminist Africa* states, producing hard-copy issues ensures access for "those based at African institutions," while the website is "a key tool for knowledge-sharing and communication."[11] But for developing-world feminist publishers, Internet publication is always a double-edged sword, reducing barriers to entry and creating valuable economies of scale, but excluding the majority of women their development-informed work most seeks to reach. Tahera Aftab, editor of *Pakistan Journal of Women's Studies: Alami-Niswan*, records her delight at hearing from a network of other feminist journals internationally, particularly because "regular email connections are not a routine affair in Karachi" (2002, 153). This ambivalence suggests that one impact of the Internet on feminist publishing has been a further polarization—not just between fringe independents and conglomerate imprints within the Western world, but also between an educated and ICT-literate elite of feminist activists in the developing world and potential mass indigenous audiences for their work.

Distribution and Retailing

In the sphere of book production, technological rivalry proved the dominant force for change as the book and Internet sought to remediate each other in their own image. Progressing through the book industry cycle to consider distribution and retailing, it becomes apparent that, although digital media have had considerable impact, the dominant pressure has been bifurcation of the industry, with the extinction of many formerly women-run operations by mainstream retailers. The network of feminist bookshops that sprang up to supply the demand for women-authored books and periodicals during the second-wave's key years of the early 1970s had, by 2005, been roughly halved in number.[12] A more symbolic loss to the sector occurred in 2000, when *Feminist Bookstore News*, long the bible of the trade and a general resource for the cognate areas of women's writing and feminist cultural politics, ceased print publication (Douglas 2000b; Media 2003b; Onosaka 2006). Announcing the closure, founding editor Carol Seajay stated that the periodical was shifting to an online network instead and spoke of a "generational shift" under way—casting the move as emblematic of changes affecting feminist book distribution and retailing as a whole (Kawaguchi 2000, 26).[13]

The decimation of the feminist bookshop sector occurred due to a pincer movement for market control effected by chain superstores, from one direction, and online book retailers from the other. Big-box stores (as they are disparagingly termed by feminist and independent book retailers) such as Borders and Barnes & Noble expanded massively during the 1980s and 1990s, first in North American markets and subsequently throughout Anglophone countries (Felesky 2004, 21; Epstein 2002). Aggregating economies of scale through huge infrastructure and capital resources, these book retailers appropriated markets of independent bookstores by offering vastly larger stockholdings, by sometimes predatory outlet siting in established independent bookstore hubs, and by wielding their market power to secure increased discounts from publishers (Schiffrin 2001; Klein and Hawthorne 2006). More subtly, chain retailers astutely recast book-buying as a leisure activity and provided attractive, well-lit, clean, and amenity-filled outlets that highlighted by contrast the shabbiness and inhibiting proprietorialism of many an independent bookstore (Wirtén 2004, 82; Finkelstein and McCleery 2005, 129; L. Miller 2006). Given the tightly interdependent feminist literary ecosystem, the knock-on effects of chain retailers' expansion were felt by feminist publishers as well. The retailer discounts, returns policies, and often protracted accounting periods characterizing the chain stores' operations exacerbated the financial pressures faced by undercapitalized and understaffed feminist presses (Douglas 2000b). The irony was that feminists, who had spent years lobbying for display of their titles in mainstream retailers, had now conclusively demonstrated a market for feminist books; the problem was that such volumes could now be more cost-effectively ordered in bulk from mainstream publishers.

Feminist responses to the book industry transformation instigated by chain and online retailers such as Amazon fall into three discernible strands. At one extreme lies a defensive insistence on consumer loyalty to feminist enterprises and accusations of political bad faith: "All too many feminists have bought discount books at chain bookstores or preferred the convenience of shopping online at Amazon.com, not admitting to themselves that their actions had an impact on feminist bookstores" (Douglas 2000b).[14] More politically innovative have been bricks-and-mortar feminist bookshops such as Britain's well-known Silver Moon which, facing rent hikes on its central London premises in 2001, reestablished itself across the road as a self-branded franchise within long-established independent bookstore Foyles (Murray 2004, 135). Silver Moon's brand recognition as "officially Europe's largest women's interest bookshop" enabled it to set up an extensive online book retailing division as well as to offer a selection of twelve print-on-demand books by cult lesbian author Radclyffe— a revealing demonstration of how digital technologies are further blurring inherited book industry production/distribution demarcations.[15]

Internet retailers and chain booksellers strive in their online reviews features and in-store promotions to replicate the independent bookshop's sense of community engagement (Long 2003, 192-98). But as mass-market retailers' raison d'être remains unswervingly one of profit maximization, feminists have been able to gain some leverage around the resonant issue of local community, as well as establishing feminist book-culture hub-sites styled as "the ultimate resource for readers who miss browsing in a good community bookstore" (Hogan 2003;

Liddle 2005).[16] Reimagining the political and networking function of a feminist bookshop for cyberspace, sites such as Mev Miller's Women in Print offer details on new titles; author profiles; information about women's presses, periodicals, and other media; as well as a bibliography of research into the history of the women-in-print movement.[17] Such hub-sites may direct browsers' spending back to real-world feminist enterprises, but they do not themselves offer e-commerce facilities. Tellingly, an online-only feminist book retailer does not appear to exist. This fact serves to underline how near-complete the mainstream absorption of feminist book retailing has been: with their market niche successfully coopted by mainstream retailers and without economies of scale in their bricks-and-mortar operations, feminist bookstores were so culturally successful as to engineer their own commercial atomization. "Are we," questions Catherine Sameh, owner of Portland's In Other Words bookstore, "victims of our own success?" (Kawaguchi 2000, 25).

Consumption

Book historians have frequently remarked upon the difficulties of recovering past reading practices because of the intensely private and interiorized nature of reading, a problem that becomes more acute for feminist scholars given women's long relegation to the lesser-documented private sphere (Manguel 1997; Cavallo and Chartier 1999; Rose 2001). Second-wave feminism challenged the idea of reading as autonomous mental communion with a text by means of the collectivism of the consciousness-raising group, which often incorporated mimeographed feminist articles or position papers as catalysts for discussion (Echols 1989). But the seemingly unstructured nature of such group dynamics and the prioritizing of free-associative talk mean records or minutes of such meetings are a veritable contradiction in terms. The Internet and the book's current phase of mutual remediation thus provides rare documentary evidence of the structures enabling feminist reading, as well as of the ways in which women's reading—long coded by feminists as potentially oppositional—has become structured into the book industries themselves (Radway 1984). As highlighted by the Virago and Persephone Web pages discussed earlier, in the digital era consumption is no longer confined to the final phase of the book product-cycle but is factored into *all* phases, collapsing long-standing industry distinctions between publishers, retailers, and consumers.

Feminist book consumption is most in evidence on the Internet in the plethora of reading groups (in UK parlance) or book clubs (in North American terminology). Popular culture overwhelmingly codes the reading group as female, and participants in both embodied and online book groups are predominantly women (Hartley 2001, 114, 137; Flax 2002; Sedo 2003, 71–73). For feminist readers, the phenomenon of the online book group has clear attractions: the ability to congregate individuals with an interest in highly niche topics such as academic feminist theory or the work of specific authors; transcendence of geographic (if not linguistic) boundaries; the convenience of asynchronous communication via e-mail Listservs or message boards; and the possibility of archiving group discussions for later reference. The disembodiment characterizing most cyber-communication leads equally to potential problems of impersonation, inactive lurkers, and provocative flaming, which may be why some online book groups use the Internet as a complement for in-person discussions in a dual embodied–disembodied format. The remediating tensions underpinning the online book group can extend equally to other media platforms; Oprah's Book Club harnesses consumer loyalty to multiple media formats—book, television, the Internet, magazine—into an unstable but broadly cross-promoting synergy (Farr 2005).

Book clubs are a burgeoning subject for academic research, but current critics' focus on members' interpersonal dynamics tends to elide the issue of how the book club might be considered within the context of a *materialist* feminist print culture (Hartley 2001; Long 2003; Sedo 2003). Examining this issue highlights how the dual forces of remediation and polarization have so atomized earlier conceptualizations of "feminist book culture" that the idea is in need of complete rethinking. Considered from the perspective of authors, the book club would appear to celebrate the mainstreaming of women's writing into broader popular culture, with Canadian Margaret Atwood (published in the UK by Virago), and Americans Alice Walker (formerly published in the UK by The Women's Press) and Toni Morrison (long a favorite of feminist literary critics) staples of book club lists.[18] Mary Greenshields' online reading group diary quotes novelist Elizabeth Noble's observation that "you're not a proper reading group until you've read a Margaret Atwood," suggesting that the percolation of feminist authors through book group culture is so pervasive as to be truistic, and is now appropriated for self-ironic badging by groups themselves.[19] From the perspective of the book club participants, the sense of community, empathetic support, and intellectual challenge characterizing book discussion would appear to harmonize with second-wave strategies for women's empowerment (Long 2003, 209; Sedo 2003, 85). Yet if Oprah's Book Club can be taken as emblematic of broader trends within the admittedly heterogenous field of book clubs, feminists should be chary of valorizing any celebration of emotional identification that remains devoid of critical analysis. So too should they be justly wary of the Oprah's Book Club program's relentless emphasis on individual self-actualization divorced from politico-economic context (Farr 2005, 27).

A related question for feminist print culture is whether book clubs are bottom-up, women-run, organic entities co-opted by media industries, or whether they are themselves the creation of commercial structures. This vexed issue goes to the heart of feminism's deep-seated ambivalence about reading—does it constitute an act of political resistance or is it mere self-indulgent, privatized, capitalist consumption (Murray 2004)? As with feminist print production, book consumption evidences the bifurcating impact of conglomerate media on feminist practices. At one end of the spectrum, mainstream culture's willing cooptation of certain aspects of second-wave feminism has strengthened feminist readers' oppositional resolve to distance themselves from and critique its products, such as the New York City–based Feminist Book Club, which meets at independent bookstore Bluestockings, and (the bookstore's Web page announces) discusses texts such as Ariel Levy's *Female Chauvinist Pigs* (2005). Firmly prioritizing community over revenue, the store's events page promises, "You will not be turned away from an event at Bluestockings for lack of $."[20]

Conversely, the website for the women-only Orange Prize for Fiction contains much evidence that the agenda for feminist writing and reading is now set by corporate sponsorship and book retailing interests: the site carries book club discussion notes and diaries of UK book groups engaged in reading the Orange Prize shortlist, and it encourages reading groups to register their details online.[21] Penguin, a publisher of Orange Prize short-listed titles, cosponsors an annual Readers' Group Prize for UK residents.[22] Most literary fiction imprints publish free book group discussion guides and offer Web facilities to maximize book-club selections, while large book retailers have understood book-club hosting as enhancing the consciously bibliophilic atmosphere they cultivate in their outlets (York 2000, 100; Long 2003, 192–98). Critics such as Long and DeNel Rehberg Sedo have urged understanding of book clubs as mediating sites between the power of the book and other media platforms, accepting that "mass media institutions have had some influence" but asking, "How much? And how? These questions remain unanswered" (Sedo 2003, 86; Long 2003, 190). While endorsing their remarks, I would add that it is important to contextualize such a specifically gendered social phenomenon as book groups against an additional history of feminist print cultures. Researchers need to examine the complex ways in which book consumption appears to endorse female—even feminist—cultural centrality, while corralling that presence into predominantly commoditized forms. Equally researchers need to consider the ways in which the rise of the Internet appears to reinforce, as well as provide alternatives, to that structuring dynamic.

Conclusion

With the atomizing forces now transforming feminist print cultures, it is tempting retrospectively to idealize the women-in-print movement of the 1970s and

1980s as unified in politics and practice. This unity is—and always was—specious. From its second-wave origins, the women-in-print movement was racked by internal debates over appropriate structures, sexual identity, politics of race, and degrees of involvement with corporate interests (Murray 2004).

Nevertheless, while the definition of *feminist* may have been fiercely contested during this period, the concept of the book was largely unproblematic. Since the latest round of the "death of the book" debate began in the early-1990s, feminist print culture practitioners have attempted to keep pace with technological change in the sector. Among third-wave feminists in particular, the sense of digital technology as building productively upon, but not eclipsing, a feminist print culture inheritance is strong.

Yet the book's rival technologies have themselves been largely superseded (CD-ROMs), have stalled in the face of consumer indifference (e-books), or rely upon as yet unproven business models (print-on-demand). Hence, feminist print producers and distributors have been astute in not abandoning the resiliently popular book format. In the twenty-first-century media economy of multiple co-existing and avidly remediating communications platforms, the key value of books may inhere in their intellectual property (IP) rights—the potential to re-format book content across multiple digital platforms to create cross-media phenomena. Engineering such multiplatform "content streaming" requires extensive holdings in various media sectors, an asset-sheet no feminist print enterprise can hope to boast (Murray 2003, 2005). As a result, feminist print producers are faced with the choice of either trusting to globalized media multinationals to produce feminist-informed content (unlikely at best) or acting as brokers, selectively trading subsidiary book rights with other media interests, and relying upon the success of film, television, or even game adaptations to cross-promote the originating book (Wirtén 2004, 81–96). The fact that so-called subsidiary rights are increasingly valuable in book industry transactions underlines feminist publishers' need to prioritize securing their IP interests, particularly in backlist titles. For companies contracting new titles, the quality of the writing must—as ever—be the primary consideration, but commissioning editors now need additionally to factor in any prospective title's cross-platform potential.

Such considerations may confirm suspicions that, for all that has changed in the women-in-print movement over the past thirty-five years, more has remained the same. The mainstream emergence of the Internet in the mid-1990s promised to democratize media production by reducing barriers to entry, yet the logic of content multipurposing made possible by digital technology can only be optimally exploited by conglomerates with access to an array of media platforms. There is some truth to such pessimistic reflections. But the Internet's impact on the book industries has, in other ways, delivered upon its promise of more egalitarian media. The distinct production/distribution/retail/consumption demarcations that arose from the structure of the book trade during the industrial era have been radically undermined by digital media, so that now a publisher such as Persephone Books may produce titles, publish reviews in its own journal, operate a retail outlet, sell directly to customers online, and host reading groups to boot. Feminist publishers have always enjoyed strong brand loyalty among book readers (Murray 2004). The digital era's brand-centric logic may now require feminist publishers to concentrate on establishing more direct relations with those readers. Again, a matrix model may be appropriate to conceptualize the challenge: just as the digital rights regime of globalized, multiformat media may appear to work against feminist publishers, collapsing sectoral distinctions within the book trade create room for new maneuvers.

Appendix: Selected Feminist Publishers

Feminist Africa (South Africa): www.feministafrica.org

How2 (US/Australia): www.how2journal.com/

Lola Press (Uruguay/South Africa/Germany): www.lolapress.org/index.htm

Persephone Books (UK): www.persephonebooks.co.uk/index.htm

Spinifex Press (Australia): www.spinifexpress.com.au

The Feminist Press at the City University of New York (US): www.feministpress .org

The Scholar and Feminist Online (US): www.barnard.edu/sfonline

Virago Press (UK): www.virago.co.uk/

Sumach Press (Canada): www.sumachpress.com/

Notes

1. The first International Feminist Book Fair was held in London in 1984, and the sixth and final fair took place in Melbourne in 1994 (Murray 2004, 56). Director Catherine Marciniak's documentary film *Life on the Rim* (1995) gives some sense of the scale of these book fairs, with the indigenous- and Asia-Pacific-focused Melbourne Book Fair hosting over two hundred women writers and prominent displays by international feminist publishers. See also Klein and Hawthorne, 2006, p. 28.

2. Spinifex Press announced in February 2006 that, after fifteen years in operation, it would cease publishing new titles and would instead continue to promote and sell its 170 backlist titles. Hawthorne and Klein attribute the demise of Australia's only remaining feminist book publisher predominantly to "lack of interest from media and all but the best bookshops" (2006, 28).

3. www.sagepub.com/

4. www.routledge.co.uk/

5. The Time Warner Book Group was itself bought by French-based multinational Hachette Livre in February 2006, with the announcement that "the Time Warner name will disappear . . . given the association both parts of that name have with other businesses, though that could take up to five years" (*Publishing News* 2006).

6. www.virago.co.uk/virago/forum/default.asp?

7. www.virago.co.uk/virago/virago/oop.asp?

8. www.persephonebooks.co.uk/index.htm

9. www.how2journal.com/

10. www.lolapress.org/index/about_us.htm

11. www.feministafrica.org/2level.html

12. *Media Report to Women* provides statistics for U.S. and Canadian markets, recording about 120 feminist bookstores in the mid-1990s, falling to 74 by 2001 (2003b, 7). Ann Weber cites more recent and alarming figures for the same markets, showing a decline to 56 feminist bookstores still trading (2005, 1). Kristen A. Hogan's doctoral research statistics for North America indicate rapid decline: 70 stores in 1998, reduced to less than 40 by 2000 (Hogan 2003). Personal correspondence with Hogan indicates that further stores have closed since her article's 2003 publication. Reliable statistics for other regional markets are not available but are likely to demonstrate a similar downward trend.

13. www.litwomen.org/WIP/stores.html

14. This representative article in the long-running second-wave publication *Off Our Backs* closes with the promise of a regular listing of feminist bookstores noting "which ones take online orders," but the gesture is largely tokenistic and fails to overturn the article's subtextual positing of digital technologies as inherently threatening to the broader feminist project. See also Norman 2001.

15. www.foyles.co.uk/foyles/sm/default.asp

16. www.litwomen.org/WIP/

17. www.litwomen.org/WIP/. There is clear overlap here with more academically focused hub-sites such as the University of Wisconsin's Women's Studies Librarian's website, which act as portals for information about feminist literary cultures in specifically materialist— as well as more broadly textual—guises; www.library.wisc.edu/libraries/WomensStudies/.

18. Alice Walker was published in the UK by The Women's Press until 2004, when Phoenix Press (an imprint of Orion Publishing Group) picked up the UK rights to all of Walker's titles upon the demise of The Women's Press.

19. www.orangeprize.co.uk/readers/diaries/goma_2.html

20. www.bluestockings.com/events.html

21. www.orangeprize.co.uk/projects/reading_gr.php4

22. http://readers.penguin.co.uk/nf/shared/WebDisplay/0,,75447_1_2,00.html

References

Aftab, Tahera. 2002. "Lobbying for Transnational Feminism: Feminist Conversations Make Connections." *NWSA Journal* 14, no. 2:153–56.

Arnold, Josie. 1999. "Feminist Poetics and Cybercolonisation." In *CyberFeminism: Connectivity, Critique and Creativity*, eds. Susan Hawthorne and Renate Klein, 250–77. Melbourne: Spinifex.

Arnold, June. 1976. "Feminist Presses & Feminist Politics." *Quest: A Feminist Quarterly* 3, no.1:18–26.

Basbanes, Nicholas A. 2004. *A Splendor of Letters: The Permanence of Books in an Impermanent World*. New York: Harper Perennial.

Birkerts, Sven. 1994. *The Gutenberg Elegies: The Fate of Reading in an Electronic Age.* Boston: Faber and Faber.

Bolter, Jay David, and Richard Grusin. 1999. *Remediation: Understanding New Media.* Cambridge, MA: MIT Press.

Cavallo, Guglielmo, and Roger Chartier, eds. 1999. *A History of Reading in the West.* [1995] Trans. Lydia G. Cochrane. Amherst: University of Massachusetts Press.

Douglas, Carol Anne. 2000a. "NWSA Meeting Features Lesbian Institute." *Off Our Backs* August/September:1.

———. "Support Feminist Bookstores!" 2000b. *Off Our Backs* December:1.

Ducas, Jane. 1999. "Banking on Nostalgia." *Financial Times* [UK] 20 March.

Echols, Alice. 1989. *Daring to Be Bad: Radical Feminism in America, 1967-1975.* Minneapolis: University of Minnesota Press.

Epstein, Jason. 2002. *Book Business: Publishing Past, Present and Future.* New York: Norton.

Farr, Cecilia Konchar. 2005. *Reading Oprah: How Oprah's Book Club Changed the Way America Reads.* Albany: State University of New York Press.

Felesky, Leigh. 2004. "Feminist Ink: Politics and Publishing in a Big Box World." *Herizons* 17, no.4:21–23, 45–46.

Finkelstein, David, and Alistair McCleery. 2005. *An Introduction to Book History.* New York: Routledge.

Flax, Peter. 2002. "Confessions of a Book Club Outcast." *Salon.com.* 26 March. www.salon.com/books/feature/2002/03/26/book_club (accessed 3 November 2005).

Gilley, Jennifer, and Diane Zabel. 2005. "Writings of the Third Wave: Young Feminists in Conversation." *Reference & User Services Quarterly* 44, no. 3:187–98.

Hartley, Jenny. 2001. *Reading Groups.* Oxford: Oxford University Press.

Hawthorne, Susan, and Renate Klein, eds. 1999. *CyberFeminism: Connectivity, Critique and Creativity.* Melbourne: Spinifex.

———. 2006. "Spinifex Press to Cease Publishing New Books." Press release. February. www.spinifexpress.com.au/ (accessed 12 September 2006).

Hogan, Kristen A. 2003. "Defining Our Own Context: The Past and Future of Feminist Bookstores." *thirdspace: the journal for emerging feminist scholars* 2, no. 2. www.thirdspace.ca/articles/hogan.htm (accessed 11 September 2006).

Holmes, David. 2005. *Communication Theory: Media, Technology, Society.* London: Sage.

Kawaguchi, Karen. 2000. "Feminist Feast and Famine." *Publishers Weekly,* July 24.

Klein, Renate, and Susan Hawthorne. 2006. "Women's Work at an End.' *The Australian,* Higher Education supplement, March 22, 2006: 28.

Kloo, Julie O'Neill, and Laurie McMillan. 2002. "Choose Your Own Critical Adventure in (Cyber)Space: HOW2 and the Impact of the Online Medium." *Women's Studies Quarterly* 30, no. 3/4:193–208.

Liddle, Kathleen. 2005. "More than a Bookstore: The Continuing Relevance of Feminist Bookstores for the Lesbian Community." *Journal of Lesbian Studies* 9:147–61.

Long, Elizabeth. 2003. *Book Clubs: Women and the Uses of Reading in Everyday Life.* Chicago: University of Illinois Press.

Manguel, Alberto. 1997. *A History of Reading.* London: Flamingo.

Marciniak, Catherine. 1995. *Life on the Rim.* Conversations with Women Writers series. Flaming Star Films/Open Channel.

Marvin, Carolyn. 1998. *When Old Technologies Were New: Thinking About Electronic Communication in the Late Nineteenth Century.* New York: Oxford University Press.

McLaughlin, Lisa. 1998. "Beyond 'Separate Spheres': Feminism and the Cultural Studies/Political Economy Divide." *Journal of Communication Inquiry* 23, no. 4:327–54.

McLuhan, Marshall. 2001. *Understanding Media: The Extensions of Man* [1964]. London: Routledge.

Media Report to Women. 2003a. "Retirement Hits Veteran Feminist Publications as New Titles Surface." 1 January: 6.

———. 2003b. "The 'Women-in-Print' Movement and its Status Today." 1 April: 5–10.

Miller, Laura J. 2006. *Reluctant Capitalists: Bookselling and the Culture of Consumption.* Chicago: University of Chicago Press.

Miller, Mark Crispin. 1997. "The Crushing Power of Big Publishing." *Nation*, March 17.

Moberg, Verne. 1974. "The New World of Feminist Publishing." *Booklegger* 1, July–August.

Murray, Simone. 2003. "Media Convergence's Third Wave: Content Streaming." *Convergence: The Journal of Research into New Media Technologies* 9, no. 1:8–18.

———. 2004. *Mixed Media: Feminist Presses and Publishing Politics.* London: Pluto Press.

———. 2005. "Brand Loyalties: Rethinking Content within Global Corporate Media." *Media, Culture & Society* 27, no. 3:415–35.

Norman, Rose. 2001. "Support Your Feminist Bookseller: She Supports You!" *NWSAction: National Women's Studies Association* 13, no.1:30–32.

Nunberg, Geoffrey, ed. 1996. *The Future of the Book.* Berkeley: University of California Press.

Onosaka, Junko. 2006. *Feminist Revolution in Literacy: Women's Bookstores in the United States.* New York: Routledge.

Piano, Doreen. 2002. "Congregating Women: Reading 3rd Wave Feminist Practices in Subcultural Production." *Rhizomes* 4. www.rhizomes.net/issue4/piano.html (accessed 2 September 2005).

Publishing News. 2006. "Surprise and Delight as Hachette Livre Buys TWBG." February 7. www.publishingnews.co.uk/pn/forum_pn/topic.asp?TOPIC_ID=886 (accessed 11 September 2006).

Radway, Janice A. 1984. *Reading the Romance: Women, Patriarchy, and Popular Literature.* Chapel Hill: University of North Carolina Press.

Rose, Jonathan. 2001. *The Intellectual Life of the British Working Classes.* New Haven: Yale University Press.

Schiffrin, André. 2001. *The Business of Books: How International Conglomerates Took Over Publishing and Changed the Way We Read.* London: Verso.

Sedo, DeNel Rehberg. 2003. "Readers in Reading Groups: An Online Survey of Face-to-Face and Virtual Book Clubs." *Convergence: The Journal of Research into New Media Technologies* 9, no.1: 66–90.

Shade, Leslie Regan. 2002. *Gender and Community in the Social Construction of the Internet.* New York: Peter Lang.

Spender, Dale. 1995. *Nattering on the Net: Women, Power and Cyberspace.* Melbourne: Spinifex.

Weber, Ann. 2005. "Feminist Bookstore Focuses on People." *Toledo [OH] Blade*, 26 June 2005.

Wirtén, Eva Hemmungs. 2004. *No Trespassing: Authorship, Intellectual Property Rights, and the Boundaries of Globalization.* Toronto: University of Toronto Press.

York, Lorraine. 2000. "'He Should Do Well on the American Talk Shows': Celebrity, Publishing, and the Future of Canadian Literature." *Essays on Canadian Writing* 71:96–105.

CHAPTER EIGHTEEN

Communication and Women in Eastern Europe: Challenges in Reshaping the Democratic Sphere

Valentina Marinescu

Seventeen years after the fall of communism in Eastern Europe, the relation between communication and women is still vexed. Studies made during this period were obviously segmented and mainly centered on communication or women but not their interrelationship. The reason is twofold: On the one hand, communication researchers (both from Western and Eastern countries) were exclusively interested in analyzing and understanding the direction of mass media systems as functional totalities (Lánczi and O'Neil 1997). As a result, the study of East European (EE) media during that period was characterized by historical and macroperspectives and, as a consequence, was less interested in understanding the relations media had with other social dimensions of those societies, such as gender, age, or ethnic group (Kideckel 1993) On the other hand, "gender-sensitive" social analysis had to take into account and face the pressure of gender perspectives from scientific researchers and public opinion in those countries. A strange mix of socialist-biased ideas and a liberal thesis underpinned the social research devoted to gender in those countries, a situation that was well synthesized by Gal and Klingman (2000):

> The acclaimed "women's emancipation" during the communist period exhibited a particular paternalism that was in concert with liberal thought in seeing production (public) as the main site of historical and revolutionary change.

This chapter fleshes out common points between the two poles of the relationship between gender/women and communication in the case of EE countries. It answers the following questions: What have been the characteristics of the EE mass media and of the women's movement from those countries in the last seventeen years? How were the relations between media ownership and gender representations for the EE countries structured? What is the place and weight of women's communicative actions in shaping the democratic sphere in those countries?

Televised Revolutions and Secluded Issues: Mass Media and the Women's Movement in Eastern Europe

Mass media in the former communist countries are characterized both by the absence of a general, panoramic, encyclopedic image and by the presence of a typological map drawing of the status quo, a map made possible by vast references (De Bruyker 1994; Splichal 1995, 2001; Paletz, Jakubowicz, and Novlosel 1995; Cluzel 2006; Giorgi and Schlesinger 1995; Sparks and Reading 1998; Feigelson and Pelissier 1998; Aumente et al. 1999; Gross and Walker 2002). The main hypothesis, which the analyses in the field are based upon, is that mass media transformations in all these countries are not chaotic and that there is a general scheme (still partially known) that generates this transition process. The main idea underlying those explanations is that of the unity of the transition process from the communist press to a democratic one, which had led to a common route for EE mass media changes in those varied countries characterized by

1. eliminating the control system by the abolition of the states' and parties' monopolies on the press, paper production, and the means of production in the press, including distribution, the national news agency, and press censorship; and, finally, abolishing public investments (except in the radio and television public service);
2. the setup of a proper legal framework, endorsed by constitutional guarantees and special laws, for freedom of expression and free access to information, which is expected to consider press operations, intellectual property, mass media campaigns, telecommunications, and antitrust law;
3. the promotion of a democratic political life through a set of norms referring to the limitation of political forces' intervention in the press, by councils that may ensure the implementation of these provisions and laws, by the presence of a just system that guarantees access to mass

media for the representatives of civil society and by supporting mass media decentralization;

4. the journalists' professionalization, by the use of laws and norms intended to ensure their professional autonomy, creation of ethics codes and modalities of implementing them and emphasis on the responsibility involved in this profession, creation of systems of observing and monitoring the press by representatives of civil society, the development of journalistic education, and ongoing professional training and development. (Jakubowicz 1996)

This list of the conditions necessary for transforming a press dominated by the interests of a political control system into a press sensitive to the priorities of a democratic system is obviously a normative one, discretely utopian and openly based on an ideal image of the Western press. In fact, mass media in these EE countries did not create a new theoretical model in communication studies or a new type of press on a real, pragmatic level. They rather represented a mixture of the already known theoretical models (the well-known typology of mass media systems developed by Siebert, Peterson, and Schramm [McQuail 1987]), combined in variable proportions according to the historical, geographical, and cultural differences of each country in this European region (Gross and Walker 2002). The main shortcoming of this eclectic theoretical framework is its pure functionalist character, the lack of sensitivity to secluded or hidden issues, such as gender, ethnicity, and national and transnational identity (King and Cushman 1992; Stoiciu 1995; Coman 1996). But what were the main characteristics of the gender relations in Eastern European countries during the same period?

The postcommunist transition involves mainly a transformation of gender relations in both public and private life. The structure of gender relations in EE communist societies was especially configured by political pressures focused mainly on enhancing the equal participation of women and men in the labor market, implementing the principles of equality, and integrating women into social and political life. Due to the changing of the political regime in 1989 and—on an economic level—the replacement of state property with private property, many of these pressures disappeared and were replaced by other mechanisms of structuring gender relations similar to the pan-European ones, which were made explicitly clear by the community *acquis* or by the reappearance of some important precommunist actors in the forefront of political life (for instance the Catholic Church in Poland or nationalist movements in Romania).

At a general level of analysis (Corrin 1992; Einhorn 1993; Funk and Muller 1993; Verdery 1994, 1996; Nicolaescu 1996; Renne 1997; Gal and Klingman

2000; Weber and Watson 2000; Haney 2002; Cosma, Magyar-Vincze, and Pecican 2002; Matland and Montgomery 2003; Johnson and Robinson 2004), the main characteristics of gender and feminist movements in Eastern Europe are women's obvious recoil from the public sphere to the private sphere, a phenomenon that constantly increased during the last seventeen years. Among the causes that contributed to this phenomenon was, for one, that communism did not have a feminist agenda but rather a homogenizing and equalitarian one. The fall of the equalitarian/egalitarian ideology also affected the politics of gender equalitarism/equality/equity. The communist state did not lead to a balanced redistribution of gender relations, but it created its own patriarchate/patriarchy. It did not change the relations between men and women, but it diminished the differences between them. As a result, the postcommunist inheritance included (a) a traditional patriarchate/patriarch in the family sphere; (b) a gender equalitarism/equalitarianism in the official ideology and mass media; and (c) a state patriarchate/patriarch in the state-citizen relation. Further, in most EE countries the "rescue" from communism meant the return to traditional institutions: the Church, the precommunist tradition, and parties and intellectuals belonging to the conservative right wing. This resulted in a strengthening of the antifeminist reaction (Poland is the extreme case where, under the influence of the Catholic Church, abortion was forbidden until after the fall of the communist regime).

Moreover, the communist indoctrination led to an explicit and massive rejection of all kinds of ideologies, especially those that had not been present in the precommunist period—as was the case for feminist ideology. At the same time, a widespread acceptance and popular adhesion to the populist and nationalist ideologies—both less compatible with feminism—exploded in the EE countries in the last decade.

In addition, the feminist movement developed in these countries mainly in the academic field and in nongovernmental organizations. EE feminism is not politically colored and is not a mass movement. According to Gal and Klingman (2000, 2003) women from this region do not understand their interests and conditions, so their mobilization into the feminist movement is especially difficult.

Finally, the most significant modernization of the social, economic, and political relations in EE takes place under the influence and intervention of international organizations, such as the European Union and United Nations, especially as constituted in the inclusion of these countries into the European Union. Because all these new norms are not the result of women's internal movement, a phenomenon of adjusting them to the local conditions has emerged, the shape of which is the perpetuation of the woman's de facto subordination in the social, political, and communicative spheres.

Nongendered Media
Ownership in Eastern European Countries

From a general theoretical view, the main difficulty one finds in studying the relationship between mass media and women in these countries is the absence of a specific EE feminist theory. Such a theory should be simultaneously inspired from and adequate to the transition realities specific to this region and not imported from general Western feminist ideas and concepts. Feminist analyses of communication in EE are mainly punctual—focused on a present state in a certain country from the region (and often published in the national language, thus limiting their international availability), or fragmentary—encompassing two or more countries from this region in a larger pan-European, transcontinental project. Therefore it is quite difficult to have a complete image from a gender-biased perspective: type of property on media, type of content disseminated by the national media, the public/audience structure of mass communication channels.

The relationship between globalization, gender issues, and the economic transition of media is the first challenge. For EE countries the changes in the type of media ownership (from the state to private property) led to changes in the nature of public space from that region. In general, referring to the last seventeen years, EE analysts (Watson 1997b) stressed the fact that, during the communist period, gender (or other social characteristics) had no relevant public role because everyone was deprived of political rights in this state-dominated "curved" political space. From here we assumed that a greater degree of gendered ownership in the media field could lead to an increase of women's public (social and political) participation. Is the present economic status of media enterprises gender sensitive, and if so, to what degree?

The answer to this question offered in the report "South East European Network for Professionalisation of the Media" (Capital 2004) is not positive. The report revealed that the available data only accentuates a powerful entrance of foreign capital into the local media market in this region and the nongendered character of ownership. In short, the entrance of external capital in Eastern European media improved during the last seventeen years. The main pan-European (or transnational) media groups that dominate the EE media market include Axel Springer Verlag, Bertelsmann, SBS Broadcasting, Ringier, WAZ, Sanoma, Grafobal, Petit Press, Westdedeutsche Allgemeine Zeitung, and Verlagsgruppe Passau. The degree of penetration for transnational media corporations varies from one country to another, and one therefore cannot speak about a general pattern that applies to the entire region. Thus the Slovakian press is concentrated in a few major groups: Markiza, Grafobal, Petit Press, Ringier, and the public stations. Markiza (owned by, among others, CME, an American company which is also a shareholder at Pro TV) was founded by Pavol Rusko, presently minister of the economy, who last year sold his shares to a friend (who, in the meantime, has become his counselor at the ministry). The television station attracts 80 percent of the publicity marketing/advertising revenue and dominates the market share.

Ivan Motrik holds the second Slovakian media group, Grafobal, which includes, among others, TV Joj, the largest network of distribution and the largest advertising agency. News Channel TA3 is the property of an investment group, J&T, which has the reputation of being aggressive and almost unlawful in its pursuit of more opportunities. Apart from the public stations, the largest private radio station, Express, is owned by a number of financial institutions.

At the same time, in the Czech Republic, media companies are almost entirely private, except for the public radio and television and the CTK news agency, controlled by the Parliament. The newspaper with the highest circulation (Blesk) is owned by the Ringier group. The main station, Nova TV, is owned by the PPF group of investments, which also has other media holdings. Another group, Vltava-Labe-Press, controls almost all the regional and local press and is owned by German Verlagsgruppe Passau. In general there are no genuine concerns about media concentration in this country, and the number of radio stations and titles in the written press guarantees a favorable climate for media pluralism. The main trait of the Czech media system is that media industries have not encountered powerful attempts of manipulation from politicians.

Mass media in Hungary are dominated by foreign companies: Axel Springer Verlag, Bertelsmann, SBS Broadcasting, Ringier, WAZ, Sanoma. The largest distribution network is controlled by the French group Hachette. The first two commercial television stations/networks belong to SBS (involved in Prima TV) and Bertelsmann. The largest publications (Metro, Blikk, Nepszabadsag) are owned by Metro International, Ringier, and, in Nepszabadsag's case, by a shareholder of Ringier, Bertelsmann, and the Free Press Foundation. However, there is no sign that the press with foreign shareholders wants to interfere with the political world.

The magnate Rupert Murdoch controls the first Bulgarian national TV station, BTV. The first titles in the press are the property of Westdedeutsche Allgemeine Zeitung German group (WAZ is also involved in Romania by the ownership on Romania Libera and National newspapers). There is an interesting relationship among media, political life, and large businesses. In the view of many analysts of the Bulgarian media, mass media is considered a weapon used in public relations. Following the Italian model, many media owners also have businesses in other domains, a fact that is considered to be a potential threat to media independence.

Three main tendencies are present in the biggest media market in Central Europe—Poland. Powerful foreign groups, especially from Germany, such as Axel Springer, are concentrated in some stable domains (in this case, the written press). Local corporations, such as Agora or Holding FM, also own important titles both in newspapers (as with the Wiborcza newspaper) and in radio or TV. Only in a small number of cases does it happen that firms from other domains than media invest in this sector. The most famous example is Polsat Capital Group, which owns the main private TV channel, Polsat. There are some media channels, mostly TV stations with a clear "gender-assumed identity," among which is Senso TV station in Romania (owned by Anca Vlad, a manager in the pharmaceutical industry) or Irisz TV, a women-owned station in Hungary, which is the shared property of TV2 Hungary (the state television station) and of Digital Media Centre (in Holland) (Broadband TV News 2005). But these cases seem to be exceptions in a media landscape dominated by transnational, male-dominated corporations.

Representation of Women in Eastern European Media

Analyses of the nexus of women in communication are centered on some key dimensions: women as social actors in the journalism profession, the gender image conveyed by media, and content for women as it is built up within gender-oriented messages.

Research by MediaWatch Canada (1995) emphasized the presence of a split between women as news authors and as news objects. Thus, if in 1995, 37 percent of all the journalists were women (more on radio and TV than in print), only 15 percent of the people interviewed during the reportages broadcast by EE media were women. In the same year, the percentage of EE women journalists was subcategorized as follows: 18 percent in local news, 42 percent in national news, and 41 percent in international news; the women interviewed made up 16 percent of local stories, 24 percent of national stories, and 30 percent of international stories. The thematic focus of the news programs was also different: Art, entertainment, and social issues were covered by women journalists, while the economy, sports, war, and terrorism were constantly presented by men journalists.

Ten years later, in a study for the World Association for Christian Communication, the Global Media Monitoring Project (WACC 2005) pointed out an interesting segmentation of the journalist profession in Eastern Europe. Thus, if women journalists dominated the occupational category of media presenter (with an average of 72 percent to men's 28 percent), they were underrepresented in the case of reporter-journalists (an occupational category clearly dominated by men: 60 percent versus 42 percent women reporters).

Table 18.1. News Subjects in Mass Media in East Europe

	Television		Radio		Newspapers	
	Women (%)	Men (%)	Women (%)	Men (%)	Women (%)	Men (%)
Hungary	15	85	5	95	12	88
Romania	28	72	10	90	18	82

Source: Global Media Monitoring Project, 2006. Annexe D, 2, News Subjects in Television, Radio, Newspapers, GMMP 2005, 121.

As news subjects, women were more visible in the programs of local TV stations, while in newspapers and on the radio they were less present in 2005.

The same study emphasizes, again and at a significant temporal distance, the maintenance and consolidation of the split between women as authors in the media and women as subjects of the media message: 22 percent of the news subjects were women compared to 62 percent that were women journalists. The gender difference is found again in the fields in which the news subjects are presented: The highest number of interviewed women were in sports and celebrity areas (15 percent), while men dominated the sphere of political debates (92 percent) (GMMP 2006).

An important aspect stressed by the study concerns the ways in which women are represented as stereotypes and whether the gender equality principle exists inside media coverage of an issue. Here we have one of the characteristics of the paradox of objectivity practiced in EE journalism: If most of the analyzed news presents journalistic neutrality (meaning that these messages did not convey or/and did not consolidate a series of gender stereotypes), the analysis of the message pointed out that the great majority (97 percent) tended to strengthen gender inequality. In my opinion, these facts result from the influence exercised by the general image of women that EE media convey, directly or indirectly. What kind of woman, then, is promoted by the EE media messages? Is it a unique model or a plurality of models?

Before approaching the issue of media images specific to the seventeen years of postcommunist transition, we need to consider some characteristics of the gender self-perceptions (feminine vs. masculine) specific to the journalists' activity in some of the countries from that region. Research from 2004 in the Romanian printed press (Munteanu 2004) showed that 76 percent of women journalists included in a national sample declared that they had never felt discriminated against in relationship to their male colleagues, while 21 percent stated that they had been discriminated against at least once (3 percent asserted that the discrimination had been positive and 13 percent said that the discrimination had been negative). The main situation in which the women journalists stated discriminatory practices was in the provision of press coverage of certain topics by the editorial staff according to the gender of the journalist—the reason invoked in this case being that men are more suitable for the "high-risk" areas. For the same set of data, the question of whether there were perceived differences between journalism practiced by men and by women, the answers of the majority of Romanian women journalists (70 percent) were included under the answer: "This was a variable situation and, as such, it varies from an individual to another"; 20 percent of the journalists claimed that there was no difference in this respect.

Although limited to the experience of a unique country (Romania), this research indicates the presence of a dual mentality in the case of women journalists: On the one hand they adhere to the traditionalist, protective perception of the journalistic profession (the interviewed women journalists did not indicate any gender discrimination in the practice of journalism) and, on the other, they have a modern attitude toward the presence of an imposed boundary in practicing their profession.

A phenomenon signaled by sociological research dedicated to Eastern Europe (Daskalova 2000) is the invasion of neotraditional models of women, an incursion precipitated by the fall of all types of ideological censorship in EE media. For the excommunist countries, the importance of female images belongs to the category of those rejected by Western feminists. Nowadays in Eastern Europe more mythic images of women coexist. One is the sexual beauty cult (promoted in magazines intended for male audiences, such as *Playboy* and *FHM*); another is the traditional image of woman as mother. According to Johnson and Robinson (2004), "These two apparently incompatible ideologies are made to last together by the fact that, no matter if they are treated as angels or whores, women are not simply regarded as people who have the same impulses and aptitudes as men."

From this point of view, Eastern Europe can be considered a territory of massive gender identity renegotiations. Thus a study by Svetlana Taraban (Johnson and Robinson 2004) focuses on images and myths of EE brides on the Internet. The results of Taraban's analysis indicate that in this type of communication EE women's images combine femininity with maternity, including constructions of fantasies about "real love" and "the perfect wife," while pictures showed images of sexy and available women. Under such circumstances, it is worth noticing that the bulk of academic approaches to women in communication in Eastern Europe are centered on the decoding and presentation of women's mythic images in the media from postcommunist countries.

I identified five central axes where social research centered on gender issues in these countries. From a quantitative point of view, written and broadcast media in this region indicates the presence of three main categories of images of the feminine gender.

One is woman presented as victim. Data synthesized in the Global Media Monitoring Project (2005) indicate the maximization of this gender stereotype; 36 percent of the subjects in news media are women (compared to 22 percent men).

Second is the expert woman (analyst or specialist). In this case data from the same report also indicate an underrepresentation of women in the EE news flow. In 2006 women were presented as experts in the news in 7 percent of instances and as spokespeople in 22 percent of stories in the programs of the EE mass media.

Finally is the "ordinary" woman, a category that represented, according to the same statistical source, 36 percent of the total subjects presented in the news in the EE media.

Separate from those primary data (and implicitly beyond the impact of the negative image conveyed by them) one can notice a persistency of these mythic images at the level of the discursive construction of the EE feminine gender. Thus, research from 1995 in Romania on the content of the feminine press indicated the perpetuation of the woman-victim image—12 percent of the subjects in the analyzed news were women victims of male abuse (rape, violence). A second stereotype is that of women as a sexual objects for mass consumption, "for men's eyes" (Rovenţa Frumuşani 2002). In this respect, referring to the dominant stereotypes in Eastern Europe, Gail Klingman (1996) quoted a news report from the 26th of August 1995 edition of *Nepzsabadsag* newspaper regarding the percentage of the pornographic movie market owned by Hungary:

> Pornography raises questions about the representation of women as sex objects and complicates women's struggles in defining their identities in a changed world. The price for controlling the marketization of such images is assumed to be censorship, which is highly problematic for the reconstruction of a public sphere that was formerly held captive to state censorship. (xx)

If Western mass media include nonconventional feminine roles both in news and in televised fiction (woman sheriff, policewoman, black woman prosecutor, etc.), in postcommunist countries, at present, after a long period of top-down emancipation (women tractor drivers, police inspectors, heroines of socialist labor, etc.), one witnesses the rebirth of women as sexual objects, heroines of fancy parties, fashion shows, and beauty contests, as seen for example in the explosion of sexist advertising and commercial media content, both beneficiaries of the feminine body instrumentalization (Rovenţa Frumuşani 2002).

Another important trend in the development of women in communication in EE countries is the focus of recent studies on the image of women politicians. This partially new image is sometimes considered part of the media's attempts to adapt, alongside with the rest of Eastern societies, to the requirements of the European common acquis. The study, Gender and Media in Czech Republic (Maříková and Kolářová 2005), describes the stereotypes associated with the political image of the woman politician in the Czech Republic: In political debates the women were generally associated with social issues (health, education, society, culture). In Hungary, a study made within the same trans-European, comparative project, centered on the media image of EE women politicians (Jenei 2005) pointed out the gender differences: When invited to an interview or talk show, male and female politicians must answer to different questions. For instance, a man is seldom asked if he is able to deal with the family obligations in parallel to his public activities. In political life, women are usually presented as agreeable persons on a discursive level; they are rarely confronted with uncomfortable questions from journalists during a televised debate. Thus an image of vulnerable and weak women is transmitted. Women politicians are rarely invited to participate in conflicting political debates, while male politicians are routinely asked to do so.

Given the presence of such a great difference between the ways of initiating and maintaining the dialogue and of representing the two genders in EE mass media, one could consider that the state of affairs fits the characterization of the gendered political status quo in the media. It is obvious that, in the case of the formerly communist countries, mass media stereotypes in presenting women leads directly to their low participation in political life, as some feminist theory has stressed, referring to Western democracies (Sreberny and Van Zoonen 2000).

Where from Here? Some Concluding Remarks

Women's campaign for gender equality in Eastern Europe has clearly been affected by the legacy of communism during the last seventeen years. Following the transition from communism to liberal (Western) democratic societies, a feminist movement was seen as unnecessary because the demagogic communist agenda damaged awareness of women's rights by emphasizing women's (supposed) emancipation as an integral part of a communist society. In other words, EE women have yet to conquer the political domain: "the arduous task of campaigning against the general political conservatism that sustains the misapprehension of gender equality and undermines the social significance of women's emancipation" (Eberhardt 2004).

There exist two competing perspectives: one that strengthens the social position of women on the basis of traditional gender roles, and another that seeks a more radical notion of gender equality by challenging such gender classifications. It is becoming increasingly clear that a framework for the promotion of women's rights must combine both approaches:

> The strategies reinforcing a familiar conception of gender identity could be effective in mobilizing women and women's groups, while the strategies questioning the essential difference between the sexes could be helpful in initiating major changes of social and personal relations." (Eberhardt 2004)

But what are the communicative means women should deploy in order to gain public and political visibility along with socioeconomic empowerment? One solution is advancing women's rights within and through the media. This relates to the efforts made by women's NGOs from the region on the following axes: the creation of alternative women's media, the reshaping of collaboration with existing media watch groups, media-related advocacies within and with governments and nongovernment organizations, and the integration of gender perspectives in media codes of conduct (Peters 2002).

Moreover, women's innovative use of new communication technologies (especially the Internet) in EE countries is very important (see also Huws in this volume). EE women realize that the only way to earn citizenship rights is to participate in an open dialogue that critiques their political silencing and their loss of rights. Among the examples of such a proactive feminine discourse, an analysis made by Lengel (1998) indicates the existence of women's networks of communication and action. This is the case with the projects Balkan Neighbors (Bulgaria), Magyar Nok Elektronikus Lapaj (Ungaria), Prague's Gender Studies Center (Czechoslovakia), and the Gender Project for Bulgaria. As an alternative to more traditional, gender-blind mass media, the Internet and women's network of communication made possible through ICTs are hoped to "foster both gender equity and, more broadly, the future growth of participatory democracy. Through increases in access and opportunity, women can communicate as active, vital dialogic agents" (Lengel 1998).

It becomes obvious that one of the exits of this "antifeminism without women" (Watson 1997a) that characterizes contemporary Eastern Europe is that citizens need to be aware of women's economic, social, and political roles through the means of mass media. In this case, the role of initiator and active agent has to be attributed not to some impersonal, gender-blind organization (such as in a newsroom or a radio or television station), but directly to the women, formally or informally organized. This also implies an increase of EE women in new and challenging professional and social roles: more women as owners of newspapers and TV stations, a higher percentage of women in journalism professions and in the advertising industry, and a greater number of women NGOs promoting gender-sensitive coverage in those societies.

References

Aumente, Jerome, et al. 1999. "Lessons Learned and Predictions for the Future." In *Eastern European Journalism: Before, During and After Communism*, eds. Jerome Aumente, Peter Gross, Ray Hiebert, Owen, Johnson, and Dean Mills. Cresskill, NJ: Hampton Press.

Brikše, Inta. 2005. "Comparative Analysis Report on Media." www.medijuprojekts.lv/?object_id=423 (accessed 1 October 2006).

Broadband TV News. 2005. Central and East Europe, 11 March. www.central.broadbandtvnews.com (accessed 22 February 2007).

Capital. 2004. "Esticii au fost cuceriti de presa occidentala." 10 June. Bucharest, Romania.

Cluzel, Jean. 2006. *Regards sur l'audiovisuel en Europe Centrale et Orientale*. Paris: Librairie générale de droit et de jurisprudence.

Coman, Mihai. 1996. "De la télévision d'état a la télévision privée. Le décline de la télévision publique en Roumanie." In *Société et médiatisation—Actes du troisième colloque roumain—français*, Bucharest, Romania.

Corrin, Chris. 1992. *"Superwomen" and the Double Burden: Women's Experience of Change in Central and Eastern Europe and the Former Soviet Union*. Toronto: Second Story Press.

Cosma, Gisela, Eniko Magyar-Vincze, and Ovidiu Pecican, eds. 2002. *Prezenţe feminine. Studii despre femei ăn România*. Cluj: Ed. Desire.

Daskalova, Krassimira. 2000. "Women's Problems, Women's Discourse in Bulgaria." In *Reproducing Gender: Politics, Press and Everyday Life after Socialism*, eds. Susan Gal and Gail Klingman, 337–69. Princeton, NJ: Princeton University Press.

De Bruyker, Chris. 1994. "Le marché des médias en Europe Centrale et Orientale." Paris: DATAR.

Eberhardt, Eva. 2004. Mapping Women's Campaign for Change: Hungary. Unpublished report.

Einhorn, Barbara. 1993. *Cinderella Goes to Market: Citizenship, Gender and Women's Movements in East Central Europe*. London: Verso.

Feigelson, Kristian, and Nicholas Pelissier. 1998. *Télé-révolutions Culturelles: Chine, Europe Centrale, Russie*. Paris: L'Harmattan.

Frunza, Miheala, and Theodora-Eliza Vacarescu, eds. 2005. *Gender and The (Post) "East"/"West" Divide*. Cluj: Limes.

Funk, Nanette, and Magda Muller, eds. 1993. *Gender Politics and Post Communism*. New York: Routledge.

Gal, Susan, and Gail Klingman, eds. 2000. *Reproducing Gender: Politics, Press and Everyday Life after Socialism*. Princeton, NJ: Princeton University Press.

———. 2003. *The Politics of Gender After Socialism*. Princeton, NJ: Princeton University Press.

Gallagher, Margaret. 2002. "Women, Media and Democratic Society: In Pursuit Of Rights and Freedoms." Un.org/womenwatch/daw/egm/media2002/reports/BPIGallagher.PDF (accessed 1 October 2006).

Giorgi, Liana, and Philip Schlesinger. 1995. *The Post-Socialist Media: What Power the West?* Aldershot, UK: Avebury-Ashgate.

Gross, Peter, and Carol Walker. 2002. *Entangled Evolutions: Media and Democratization in East Europe*. Washington, D.C.: Woodrow Wilson Center Press.

Haney, Lynne. 2002. *Investigating the Needy: Gender and the Politics of Welfare in Hungary*. Berkeley: University of California Press.

Jakubowicz, Karol. 1996. "L'évolution vers des médias démocratiques et libres en Europe Centrale: combien faudra-t-il de temps pour y parvenir?" *L'autre Europe*, éd. L'Age d'Homme, no. 32–33, Lausanne.

Jenei, Rita. 2005. "Portrayal of Female and Male Politicians in Media: Hungary." www.medijuprojekts.lv/?object_id=439 (accessed 1 October 2006).

Johnson, Janet Elise, and Jean C. Robinson, eds. 2004. Living with Gender in Post-Communist Central and Eastern Europe. Unpublished ms.

Kideckel, David A. 1993. The Solitude of Collectivism: Romanian Villages to the Revolution and Beyond. Ithaca: Cornell University Press.

King, Sarah Sanderson, and Donald P. Cushman, eds. 1992. Political Communication: Engineering Visions of Order in the Socialist World. Albany: State University of New York Press.

Klingman, Gail. 1996. "Women and Negotiation of Identity in Post-Communist Eastern Europe." In Identities in Transition: Eastern Europe and Russia after the Collapse of Communism, ed. Gail Kligman, 68–91. University of California Press/International and Area Studies Digital Collection, edited volume 93. http://repositories.cdlib.org/uciapubs/research/93/6 (accessed 9 February 2006).

Lánczi, Andras, and Patrick O'Neil. 1997. "Pluralisation and Politics of Media Change in Hungary." In Post-Communism and Media in Eastern Europe, ed. Patrick H. O'Neil, 82–101. London: Frank Cass.

Lengel, Laura. 1998. "New Voices, New Media Technologies: Opportunity and Access to the Internet in East Central Europe." Convergence: Journal of Research into New Media Technologies 4, no. 2 (June): 38–55.

Maříková, Hana, and Marta Kolářová. 2005. "Gender and Media in Czech Republic." www.medijuprojekts.lv/?object_id=439 (accessed 1 October 2006).

Marin, Noemi, and Laura Lengel. 2002. "Impact of Media on Conflict Resolution and Education in the New Europe." lass.calumet.purdue.edu/cca/gmj/fa02/gmj-fa02-marin-lengel.htm (accessed 1 October 2006).

Matland, Richard E., and Kathleen A. Montgomery, eds. 2003. Women's Access to Political Power in Post-Communist Europe. Oxford: Oxford University Press.

McQuail, Denis. 1987. Mass Communication Theory. London: Sage.

MediaWatch Canada. 1995. Global Media Monitoring Project. In Femei, Cuvinte şi Imagini, eds. A. Bradeanu, O. Dragomir, D. Roventa-Frumusani, and R. Surugiu. Iaşi: Ed. Polirom.

Munteanu, Cristina. 2004. "Jurnalistele din Romania—un profil socio-profesional." Jurnalism şi Comunicare, no. 4/2004: 22–31.

Nicolaescu, Madalina, ed. 1996. Cine suntem noi? Bucureşti: Ed. Anima.

Paletz, David, Karol Jakubowicz, and Pavao Novlosel, eds. 1995. Glasnost and After: Media Change in Central and Eastern Europe. Cresskill NJ: Hampton Press.

Peters, Bettina. 2002. Equality and Quality: Setting Standards for Women in Journalism. Brussels: IFJ. www.ifj.org/pdfs/ws.pdf (accessed 9 February 2007).

Ramet, Sabrina P. 2005. "Sliding Backwards: The Fate of Women in Post-1989 East-Central Europe." www.kakanien.ac.at/beitr/fallstudie/SRamet1.pdf (accessed 1 October 2006).

Renne, Tanya, ed. 1997. Ana's Land: Sisterhood in Eastern Europe. Boulder, CO: Westview Press.

Roman, Denise. 2001. "Gendering Eastern Europe: Pre-Feminism, Prejudice, and East-West Dialogues in Post-Communist Romania." Women's Studies International Forum, no. 24:53–66.

Roventa Frumuşani, Daniela. 2002. "Identitatea feminină şi discursul mediatic în România postcomunistă." In Femei, Cuvinte şi Imagini, eds. A. Bradeanu, O. Dragomir, D. Roventa-Frumusani, and R. Surugiu. Iaşi: Ed. Polirom.

Sparks, Colin, and Anna Reading. 1998. Communism, Capitalism and the Mass Media. London: Sage.

Splichal, Slavko. 1995. Media Beyond Socialism. Boulder, CO: Westview Press.

———. 2001. "Imitative Revolutions: Changes in the Media and Journalism in East-Central Europe." Javnost (The Public) 8, no. 4:31–58.

Sreberny, Annabelle, and Liesbet Van Zoonen, eds. 2000. Gender, Politics and Communication. Cresskill, NJ: Hampton Press.

Stoiciu, Gina. 1995. "Le post-communisme en déroute mythologique." *The Global Network*, no. 2:2.

Verdery, Katherine. 1994. "From Parent-State to Family Patriarchs: Gender and Nation in Contemporary Eastern Europe." *East European Politics and Societies*, no. 8:225–55.

———. 1996. *What Is Socialism and What Comes Next*. Princeton, NJ: Princeton University Press.

Watson, Peggy. 1997a. "(Anti)feminism after Communism." In *Femei, Cuvinte și Imagini*, eds. A. Bradeanu, O. Dragomir, D. Roventa-Frumusani, and R. Surugiu. Iași: Ed. Polirom.

———. 1997b. "Civil Society and the Politics of Difference in Eastern Europe." In *Transitions, Environments, Translations: Feminisms in International Politics*, eds. J. W. Scott, C. Kaplan, and D. Keates, 21–29. New York: Routledge.

Weber, Renate, and Nicole Watson, eds. 2000. *Women 2000. An Investigation into the Status of Women's Rights in Central and South-Eastern Europe and the New Independent States*. Vienna: International Helsinki Federation for Human Rights.

World Association for Christian Communication (WACC). 2005. Global Media Monitoring Project. www.wacc.org.uk/wacc/content/pdf/488 (accessed 1 October 2006).

CHAPTER NINETEEN

GodZone? NZ's Classification of Explicit Material in an Era of Global Fundamentalism

Mary Griffiths

There are signs that vocal attacks on the gains that New Zealand (NZ) state feminism has made in many areas are coming from a small but mobilized religious and moral right, encouraged by the apparent successes that similar groups have had elsewhere, particularly in the U.S. This can be seen as a reaction to the country's pragmatism in social policy making in a global age. NZ has a reputation for finding bicultural answers to the colonial past in the Treaty of Waitangi's continued influence on most legislation, and for state feminism in progressive social policies, such as those provided in more recent Labour government legislation (the 2005 Civil Unions Bill and the adoption of Human Rights). In the policy area of the classification of sexually explicit or violent material, significant public challenges from the right are occurring, launched both legitimately through legal requests for the review of classification decisions and also, unacceptably in a democracy, through campaigns of personal attacks on the chief officer and deputy of the state body with the remit to act: the Office of Film and Literature Classification (OFLC) or, as Kiwis know it—the chief censor's office. The change is not simply the result of a reenergized backlash (against a liberalizing government) spearheaded by a newly led political right, but it appears to be a local convergence of traditionally conservative individuals and groups in a new discursive formation based on moral thinking, set on influencing NZ nation-building, and the formation of citizens. Attempts have been made to turn debates on NZ's censorship practices to normative, Christian "family first" considerations. Kiwis stand to be divided, through this rhetorical trope, into "good" people and "others." Diane Richardson has argued that "the discourses of citizenship have produced a particular version of the responsible/good citizen focussed on the values and norms associated with the heterosexual, nuclear family" (2000, 269).

This certainly seems true of NZ.

This chapter presents the argument that, in NZ, fundamentalist conflict over classification is the locus for deep divisions over the future shape of "Godzone," the term used to embody patriotic settler love of a land of opportunity, a belief in its can-do people, and (only half-ironically) a new confidence in the country's globalized economy, its capacity, and its "fairness." This case study focuses on the work of the OFLC and the fundamentalist challenges to its decisions, within a context of wider social change and global content flows in NZ, its geographical isolation, and its postcolonial history.

Biculturalism and State Feminism

We are tuakana or teina[1] to other women, with sets of obligations according to these culturally defined relationships . . . Mana Wahine[2] for me is not elevating the status of women above men. It is about that complementary, co-operative, respectful relationship between all our peoples, that honours them. (Tariana Turia, Maori Party)

NZ's 4 million people live four to six hours' flying time from their trading neighbor, Australia, yet a close, dependent, and symbiotic relationship exists on many levels. Postcolonial nation-making, in such relative isolation, is a central concern of both countries, although NZ has to negotiate a distinctively different indigenous history. The 1840 Treaty of Waitangi (thirteen Maori women signed) governs contemporary bicultural legislation and relationships. NZ has sensitive global trade dependencies for the sale of its primary produce, and memories of the social impact of past harsh market reforms have made it cautious about taking any extreme measures. Traditional roles in Maoridom, allied to feminism's state successes, mean that NZ female education and employment participation rates are relatively high: Tertiary education between the ages of eighteen and twenty-four is 44.1 percent non-Maori, and 34.5 percent Maori—both percentages higher than those for men.[3] Sixty percent of women were in paid employment, compared to 74 percent of men (according to the 2001 census). Maori women are 14 percent of the female population, and they once participated more fully in employment, but the market ideologies of the 1980s badly affected Maori women's workforce participation, directly leading to the current economic disadvantage for Maori families. This might partly explain why aspirational Maori are so often found supporting Pentecostal churches, like Destiny Church, which militates against the liberal tenets of a global consumer society yet promises the rewards on earth of "a good life."

Women occupy significant positions in New Zealand. Helen Clark's Labour governments rely on minority parties like the Greens, whose senior women are committed to social change (Jeanette Fitzsimmons, Sue Bradford, Sue Kedgeley, and Metiria Turei).[4] Media frequently note that the powerful, most highly paid CEO is Telecom's Theresa Gattung. Locally, routine media coverage of the powerful Maori women who intervene in NZ society include the highly respected Maori Queen, Te Arikinui Dame Te Atairangikaahu, who up to her death in 2006 had a North Island ceremonial role, and Maori MPs like Waikato's Nania Mahuta (Labour) and the coleader of the breakaway Maori Party, Tariana Turia. Both have high profiles in Parliament and are determined to fight for social justice to improve health, education, and employment opportunities for Maori. When Turia launched Mana Wahine, she defined the term within a Maori worldview of interdependent and enduring relationships of family, tribe, and nation. The excerpt from her speech quoted above is typical of the discourses of Maoridom, but it has relevance for powerful, prevalent bicultural attitudes in NZ, especially in the conservative heartland. Multi-issue feminist anarchist groups exist (involved most recently in street and Internet activism in the breaking of suppression orders over evidence in a notorious and nationally significant rape case),[5] but NZ women activists are mainly engaged in other kinds of civic participation, since earlier groups like Women Against Pornography dealt with the issues raised by changing social mores (see Watson and Shuker 1998 for a history of NZ censorship).

Rape crisis centers, peace activism, and working for equal employment conditions and equal representation are the feminist issues to the fore. Policy input is made through the largest umbrella women's organization, the nonpartisan, 200,000-member National Council of Women of New Zealand (NCWNZ), set up in 1896 by Kate Sheppard, a leader in female suffrage. Ten specialist committees, drawn from forty groups, study issues affecting women and children and help select committees draft relevant legislation. Their advice was sought on the Films Video and Publications Classification Amendment Bill (see S04.21 2004) and on the Crimes (Intimate Covert Filming) Bill (see S05.32 2005). This is powerful activism, but its targeted feminist civic commitment to social justice for women and children rarely makes headlines in the popular press.

Despite these achievements, its size, isolation, ethnic composition, and history make New Zealand a conservative society, demonstrably anxious to find considered, workable twenty-first-century identities that avoid social conflict. Attorney-General Margaret Wilson, in addressing the first sitting of the Supreme Court in mid-2004, mentioned how long it had taken NZ (almost the last Commonwealth country) to act upon the desire to leave the Privy Council's Appeals connection. She said: "NZ can never be accused of rushing into things."[6]

Thus, eccentrically, divisive conflicts over private freedoms have been fought out in public, not by women (with the exception of the prime minister), but by high-profile NZ men located in government or in religious organizations like the Society for the Protection of Community Standards (SPCS), a minority activist group, and Destiny Church, whose outspoken Bishop Brian Tamaki mobilizes moralistic media events in response to all liberal legislation. Both groups have become more active in their criticism of all liberalization of gender legislation, creating connections and a climate of moral panic over both gay rights and censorship decisions. The SPCS, an organization with about 1,500 members, uses the technique of guilt by association by focusing on the sexual preferences of highly placed appointees in the Classification Office, at the same time as hitting out at other kinds of liberal legislation before the New Zealand Parliament. They have opponents in the activist groups Libertarianz and GayNZ.

Tamaki has no scruples about overtly linking all incidents, legislation, or people associated with liberal legislation—which signifies, from their perspective, the "moral decay" of a government "gone evil, antifamily and anti-Christian," as expressed in a downloadable DVD, "Exposé, A Nation Under Siege," released prior to the 2005 national election. Rated M (recommended for mature audiences sixteen and over) by the OFLC to media inquiries about its homophobic content, it is similar to "Living Word" video materials produced by American Christians.[7] Tamaki states unequivocally that the "nation was under siege" from a national "homosexual agenda." Among those named responsible are politicians Helen Clarke, Don Brash, Peter Dunne, and Steve Maharey, as well as the "world's first transgender MP," Georgina Beyer, and finally Bill Hastings, the chief censor. Destiny Church is the fastest growing church and it mobilized the March 5, 2005 Enough is Enough march of black-tee-shirted conservatives, who had a row of targets in their sights: the Civil Unions Bill, homosexuality, prostitution law reform, liberal classification policy, and draft hate speech legislation. The discourses of nationhood used included speeches and media interviews and the idea of protecting the legacy of a family-oriented nation of god-fearing Kiwis, concerned about their children's future and the creeping relativism in moral values. What is really at stake is not whether a foreign import receives a too lenient classification but what kind of nation NZ is becoming.

Yet the idea that a certain group of powerful individuals or the secular state is responsible for such an agenda is patently false. The unicameral Parliament, with its emphasis on the work of select committees in drafting legislation, and a national system of voting that guarantees multiparty membership of those committees, means that "governance by consensus" in manageable small groups has more of a chance of resulting in what is seen as commonsense, compromise, social legislation. In recognition of statistics on the actual constitution of diverse groups who identify as families, the whole concept of the family was recently liberalized by the passing of the Civil Unions Bill (in December 2004). Simultaneously, an amendment to the 1993 Films, Videos and Publications Classification Act (FVPC) (which deals in part with the discretionary powers of the chief censor and the contextualizing of images of naked children) was being read in Parliament. These two pieces of legislation pleased liberal thinkers but also crystallized conservative fears. Antiliberal claims were made using derogatory vocabulary. The frequent epithet "nanny state," Janiewski and Morris argue, is the sign of confusion about social liberalism and market liberalism with their apparently similar, but actually opposing, emphasis on the individual's rights (2005, 119). The biblical myths do service in new "rights" narratives of New Zealand, which Janiewski and Morris see as part of a long history of national conflict over gender and sexuality shaped both by secularity and by religious tradition:

> We usually think of ourselves as living in a predominantly secular society, despite the evidence of our Christian heritage . . . There are some New Zealanders, however, who want to return to traditional values as they chant "enough is enough," repeat the familiar biblical phrases and warn about the power of the "sisterhood." (120–21)

In practice, how is the freedom to view what one chooses balanced with the need to limit social harm? Greater liberalization and policy input in NZ were facilitated by the New Zealand Bill of Rights Act (1990),[8] although the Human Rights Commission's Submission to the Administrative Committee into the Enquiry into Hate Speech (2005) for example, noted that "the failure to wholeheartedly accept difference and diversity" still militated against certain groups having full human rights, including people who are "non-Pakeha[9] New Zealanders, women, and gay, lesbian, transgender and intersex people" (2). The improvements recommended were "greater participation in decision making; the empowerment of individuals and groups to use rights as leverage for action and to legitimate their voice in decision making; and the linking of decision making at every level to the agreed human rights norms." The Submission did not endorse the civil libertarian, or absolutist, position, despite its democratic usefulness in "ensuring a marketplace of ideas" (3).

The next section focuses on NZ classification policy and routines as they attempt to balance rights. The trigger for controversy is still explicit material (for example, the banning of the video games *Manhunt* and *Postal 2* and the classification of films as different as *Baise-Moi*, *9 Songs*, *Irreversible*, and *The Passion of the Christ*) but other debates (about gay rights or liberal reforms) also have converged. Traditional perspectives on censorship usually include the focused, strategic regulation of content as an informative exercise for citizens—as classification,[10] or the perspective that any limit imposed on an adult's freedom to view as the censorious act of spoilers or "nanny statists." Recent NZ debates cannot be so neatly précised.

Explicit Material

The country's "precautionary risk management"[11] of content regulation results in a three-tiered approach to film censorship, operated with a light touch in an effort to inform and find "workable limitations on freedom" in and for all citizens. It results in relatively sophisticated arrangements for managing the "risks" to a local population from (often) foreign materials. A democratized, transparent monitoring system for film and video content exists, with limited state discretionary powers, where individual citizens and groups can have their say, and where a number of checks and balances operate. Classification rather than censorship prevails. NZ produces more liberal judgments than its Australian counterpart—with the exception of the ACT (Australian Capital Territory). Unlike the British system, where devolved responsibility to cities and boroughs results in their reliance for classification of publications on the British Board of Film Censorship (BBFC), in NZ the agency operates on a national level as most content (except Internet material) enters the country through customs.

NZ is on the ring-fenced end of a global chain of media exchanges and flows, despite Peter Jackson's determinedly nationalist work, which produced the *Lord of the Rings* phenomenon, and glocalized NZ film production. A number of agencies, under the oversight of the Ministry of Justice and the Department of Internal Affairs, are involved in ensuring compliance with the defining 1993 FVPC Act, which received significant amendments in 2005: the New Zealand Customs; the Censorship Compliance Unit of the Department of Internal Affairs (DIA); the Crown entity, the OFLC, headed by the chief censor and his staff, of whom nearly half are censors; and a Film and Literature Board of Review (FLBR). The OFLC independently classifies all films, videos, DVDs, and computer games. FLBR's president is empowered to issue an interim restriction order on any publication, pending independent review. Public servants able to ensure a review include the chief officers of Internal Affairs, Customs, and the police. Other citizens and groups, apart from direct parties to a review (those with rights to the publication referred), have to request permission from the Secretary of Internal Affairs for a review. This is one area of discretionary power.

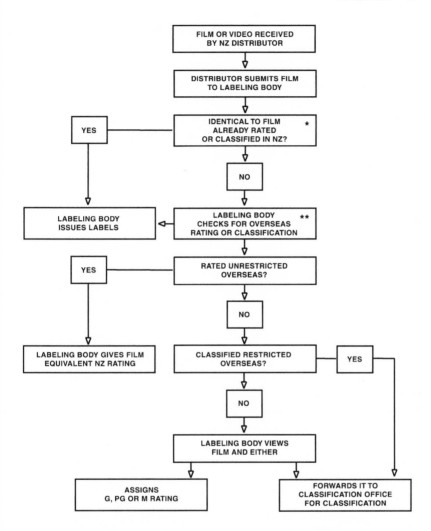

Figure 19.1.   Regulatory Processes
Source: Adapted from www.censorship.govt.nz

Membership of the Review Board is appointed by the Governor-General (the role still a colonial remnant) with advice from the Ministry of Justice and, notably, from Women's Affairs. The chief censor is a political appointment. The incumbent, Bill Hastings, is gay and has chosen a high public profile, a fact that empowers opposing claims made by an outspoken activist minority that the censor is not impartial, and that the office does not serve the interests of the whole of the NZ population, but his profile also allows the censor to speak out personally and passionately about the power of representational practices to wound minority groups.

The first step, after DIA's scoping of imports, is taken by the industry-based Labelling Body, which is obliged to cross-rate publications using any prior G (general), PG (parental guidance recommended for younger viewers), or M (mature, over sixteen) classifications from the Australian OFLC or the British Board of Film Censorship. The Labelling Body submits a film to the Classification Office if it has been restricted or refused permission in Australia or the UK, or if there is uncertainty about its rating, or if it is seen to be likely to be restricted or objectionable.

The flowchart (see figure 19.1) shows that by the time a publication reaches the censor, it will have passed through a number of checks and been subject to a series of informed, "expert" discussions. Restrictions on publications are governed by the terms "objectionable" and "likely to be injurious to the public good"—for example, the promotion or support of sexual exploitation of children, sexual coercion, torture or extreme violence, and so on. The manner and likely contexts of viewing and potential representational outcomes are taken into account in consideration of each publication, as well as the way publications deal with "degrading, dehumanising or demeaning conduct" and "representations of a particular class of person as inherently inferior by reason of a *prohibited ground of discrimination*" (emphasis in OFLC website). NZ's OFLC makes an important distinction between "representation" and "promotion" of activities. At the Review Board, a publication goes through the classification process again, after submissions from all interested parties are heard, and a decision is made without regard to ones made previously.

There are a few differences between NZ and Australian regimes (OFLC 2005). NZ's chief censor is empowered to examine any publication, whatever prior classification it has been given in Australia, and also serves on the Australian body. Since 1916, a trans-Tasman traffic in ideas about regulation and a history of shared development has taken place. Previous Chief Censor Kathryn Paterson served in similar roles in both countries. This exchange of "expert" state knowledge, and officials responsible for classification, moves the debate into the field of international policy compliance to rights-based legislation, and out of the "moral" arena or more subjective—and hard to defend— culturally formed "taste and decency" grounds. This is exactly what has drawn criticism from the right, although working examples of human rights defense are much needed in the geopolitical region.

To combat the notion that selected and self-selected individuals are policing a nation's viewing according to subjectively formed "taste," OFLC communicates a high level of online and hard-copy information about the classification process and its other work. The website is excellent from a citizen-usability perspective; it includes a brief history of censorship, links to movie sites and other codes (British, Australian, Canadian, French, Finnish, Swiss, Hong Kong), provides updates on legislation and rulings, and answers FAQs. The New Zealand Censorship Database (2005) is searchable, with password log-in quickly granted to adults on application, a security measure protecting minors and those who may be offended by the titles of "adult" publications. All the historical data is available, and online information has resulted in a 52 percent drop in user inquiries, as users, many of whom may be buying material online globally, search the classifications themselves. (OFLC 2005, 7).

"Push" communication strategies aside, OFLC seeks feedback from diverse sections of the community, as part of its outreach educational and research programs. An annual Censor for a Day high school activity is run, with students involved in "real-life" classification procedures. Student censors were also research subjects for a study of informed use of video game labeling. OFLC sends its officials to address the public (Wilson 2005) and researches user practices—contacting Hawkes Bay participants for a survey of "users of sexually explicit material" through sex stores and video outlets, and asking a self-selected sample to comment on their uses of the material (OFLC 2005, 45–46). From a Foucauldian perspective, the "conduct of conduct" in classification is an interactive process, involving the OFLC and the citizens it protects. Bill Hastings used his 2005 Annual Report summary to refer to the work of Andrea Dworkin and Catherine MacKinnon, whose ideas, he wrote, "informed debate at the time the Films, Videos and Publications Classification Act was being drafted, and found their way into the provisions that concern degrading, dehumanising and demeaning sexual conduct" (17). This historicizes the contribution of, and pays tribute to, early feminist pioneers.

In combination, these agencies, and the processes they represent, are designed to be pragmatic. They aim to restrict according to a consensual notion of "human rights" and "public good" not, as in the UK, by "taste and decency"; and they may restrict not only according to age, but to purpose (such as film festivals and media studies courses), or class or persons (such as psychologists). They provide the targeted checks and balances to protect the relatively small, isolated set of different publics from inadvertent viewing of "objectionable" material—a term that is, of course, open to testing and challenge by those publics and by individual citizens. The OFLC is active: In 2004, it classified 534 videos, 464 DVDs, and sixty-two films. It banned 149 computer files, twenty-six photographs, eighteen magazines, forty videos/DVDs/VCDs, five letters, two video slicks, and one video game (Wilson 2005).

Activists and Censors

NZ's acceptance of the OFLC "expert" approach to managing a small but important area of human rights was increasingly tested by activists beginning in 2001. SPCS members were prominent:

> The SPCS are rather a queer outfit, to be honest. Founded in 1970 by Patricia Bartlett, an ex-nun, they cut their teeth opposing the release of various written works. They currently seem to operate as a general Christian pressure group: opposing the Civil Union Bill and abortion, but with a particular focus on censorship or, as they see it, the lack of it . . . The hardest question to ask is: do the SPCS actually have a point?' (Crawford 2004)

The last three of the organization's six objectives, as published on the official website, deal explicitly with objectionable publications and activism and summarize their self-appointed watchdog brief on the "harmful nature and consequences of sexual promiscuity, obscenity, pornography and violence" on "the public good." The SPCS began to use the legal processes not only to "focus attention" but, from its perspective, to "uphold and press for the proper enforcement of applicable law" over the content of published material. The battle was conducted by press release—submissions to the Review Board; and mainstream, blog, and website commentary. Had they overstepped their watchdog brief and become de facto moral censors, as Crawford argues? Or were they simply, as OFLC officials believe, exercising their legal rights?

The public focus on review requests tends to broaden to a general scrutiny of the processes of the OFLC. The New Zealand story of the classification of the French film *Baise-Moi* began in 2001, for example, and continues with parliamentary questions being asked (by Peter Brown, a long-time critic) in December 2005. Brown wanted to know how the film originally came into the chief censor's hands,[12] how much the final cost of classification, review, and appeals cost the public,[13] and whether the Minister of Internal Affairs trusted the censor and his staff. The government's reply to the last question was, "Yes, because they are hard-working people trusted to serve the community in a difficult area."[14]

SPCS campaigns have become more targeted over the years. It objected to the film festival screenings of foreign films such as *Y Tu Mamá Támbien* and *The Piano Teacher*, following earlier objections to *Visitor Q*. With *Baise-Moi's* descriptor of frequent disturbing depictions of violence and "repeated explicit sexual content and violence," the chief censor's direction to restrict the viewing of the VHS to R18, and to a purpose (tertiary media study) and a set of audiences (film festivals), it was guaranteed to be challenged. The conflict continued with the 2002 Board of Review decision to reduce the restrictions to R18, finding against the SPCS. In the case of the film, in 2003 the Review Board kept the over-eighteen restriction but allowed it to be seen in cinemas and in tertiary media studies courses. In 2005 the Court of Appeals kept the over-eighteen restriction, but allowed theatrical exhibition and tertiary study. The final classification of *Baise-Moi* was a long, drawn-out procedure in which the SPCS honed its use of legal review and injunction application processes, persisting, despite failures, to secure higher ratings for or the banning of films. It gave rise to some interesting alliances between global libertarians and those who trusted the local classification system even for foreign products against those who wanted to return to an older, more "moral," ideal of NZ.

A letter to "friends of the festival" published on the Film Festival website on November 27, 2002,[15] by Bill Gosden, the director of the New Zealand Film Festival Trust, showed the anger caused in liberal and libertarian circles by the early successes of the SPCS. SPCS's power to impact on others' viewing freedoms—especially on the informed audiences at independent film festivals— is described by Gosden as "vexatious in the extreme" and, given the strategic withdrawal of appeals by David Lane, the SPCS spokesperson, the anger at the cost to the public of a small organization holding others to ransom placed the liberal film festival boss in a self-confessed and unaccustomed alliance with the experts at the OFLC: Gosden called for "common-sense" and for compliance to existing state processes. This appeal cut to what he saw as a significant issue: that a small and "highly committed organisation" had "made a mockery of the elaborate and expensive processes" of classification. "Who would have thought the director of a Film Festival would be staking such a claim for the credibility of the Classification Office?" his letter ends. Indeed!

Michael Winterbottom's 9 *Songs*, which attracted an R18 rating from the BBFC, caused the most media inquiries and complaints to the OFLC, over the 2004–2005 period (OFLC 2005, 43). As is usual with a sexually explicit or violent foreign film, community awareness of overseas classification disputes had preceded its NZ arrival. The film trailer labeled "contains drug use and sex scenes" was classified objectionable and restricted to persons over the age of sixteen; the DVD was classified as restricted to persons over the age of eighteen by the Labelling Body (25 February 2005) and, after review, no excisions were recommended by the Board of Review (27 July 2005). Again the SPCS had been a committed "interested party," in the Review Board process.

Gaspar Noe's *Irreversible*, the OFLC reports, attracted the "second largest number of complaints" and had been classified and reclassified "at the request of its Australian distributor," (2005, 43) (no doubt as a precautionary measure) because of the nine-minute rape sequence. Predictably the SPCS applied for a review in 2003, after the OFLC R18 classification and the viewing restriction to tertiary institutions or film festivals. OFLC consultations had included the

Wellington Rape Crisis Centre, a clinical psychologist, a film reviewer, and a twenty-six-member focus group (Wilson 2005). The SPCS, nevertheless, opposed what it saw as the chief censor's personal investment in liberal classification, convincing another activist group, the Viewers of Television Excellence (VOTE)—who also sought to overturn the classification decision—that late-night television screenings were probable.[16] Its 11 November press release states that Hastings had "aided and abetted the dissemination of this sick R18 film throughout Rialto Cinemas in New Zealand" (SPCS 2005).

On the other hand, the violent American film *The Passion of the Christ* elicited a different fundamentalist response because, although there was abundant visual evidence for imposing a viewing restriction given the lengthy representations of violence and torture, it was a film supported by NZ Christians. Its first OFLC rating was restricted to age sixteen and over. The significant difference between the fights over the earlier films described and Mel Gibson's film was that those who now saw themselves as primary stakeholders were in opposition to the age restriction classification, not because they wanted to further restrict viewing but because they wanted it liberalized so that schoolchildren could see the uncut film. Eventually the age restriction was lowered to R15.[17]

GayNZ keeps a careful watch on the activities and press releases of the SPCS, because of that organization's outspoken antagonism to the censor. In 2003 they profiled the censor in an interview about his work and beliefs, on a regular GayNZ website feature, Our People. Hastings, who said he "became a censor by accident," reveals himself as deeply committed to helping people understand "the power of words to damage and to heal." In this he takes a more public stance than his deputy, who nevertheless draws personalized (and risible) attacks from the SPCS as an "experienced lesbian." Hastings says: "I don't think I can change the whole world . . . I see the Classification Office as a sort of environmental regulation agency." He continues: "Being out allows me to show anyone who wants to see that being openly gay will not stop you from being the chief executive of a crown entity, being the Chief Censor." (GayNZ 2003) Hastings's beliefs are those of a rights-driven liberal.

In fact SPCS fears are unfounded: The record shows that only one classification review has resulted in a higher rating from the original one given by the OFLC (Wilson 2005). These limits on freedom are acceptable to the majority of citizens. Management of competing rights informs OFLC policy and its practices as an active provider of information and public education. The passionate commitment of the OFLC to educate and inform arises from the chief censor's leadership, and from his membership in one of New Zealand's minority groups. As feminists have traditionally argued, personal experience shapes one's politics, and one's choice of, in this case, state activism.

Conclusion

NZ's regulation of explicit content shows a deliberative, reflexive light touch, despite its negative reception by a small but committed number of activist individuals and groups. The SPCS represents a minority rights perspective on representations of sexual violence. Christian groups, which support few or no restrictions on young children watching depictions of brutality in the name of religious observance, represent a more powerful but still minority lobby. Janiewski and Morris may have mistaken noise for numbers. Nevertheless NZ's fundamentalist mobilizations show that vigilance has to be maintained in the area of hard-won rights.

Of the SPCS failures to change classifications or to have content censored, and the accusations of frivolous conduct they have drawn, it can be argued that they are meeting their group's democratic objectives in keeping the classification of content a live issue in public debate and, in doing so, they are exercising their rights as NZ citizens to put opposing views using existing laws. What is less acceptable is the personalizing focus on the private life of state officials and the use of knowledge about their sexual preferences to restage arguments about the perceived links between classification regimes and homosexuality, or homosexuality and pedophilia, or liberal thought and "moral decline."

In a democracy, the management of competing rights is a difficult terrain. The philosophical arguments about representation and promotion, which are the crucial points distinguishing the OFLC from the SPCS, are ones dominated by beliefs about the effects of media as well as attitudes to democratic rationalities. The discourse of expert knowledge in the OFLC and about the OFLC may in fact be responsible for generating the homophobic tropes and personalizing language used by OFLC's opponents. By drawing the argument about particular films back to individual sexual preferences of those charged to regulate by the state, the SPCS remarks attempt to mobilize a panic about declines in national moral health; thus ironically, in a double move, they can damage the civic respect for difference, without which no democracy can stay healthy for long.

The biggest challenge facing the NZ Crown entity and its opponents is the digital environment, which will mean more classifications and possibly evoke more trenchant reactions. The digital future presents a deterritorialized world, in which representation and promotion will be treated differently. Fragmented audiences will emerge who are not tied to a safe, ring-fenced national space of viewing but can download and view any material, anywhere, anytime. Education, information, and consensus, the approaches taken in NZ policy and practice, seem to be the way to go to promote a rights-based, responsible, civic arena in an age of global fundamentalism.

Notes

1. *Tuakana* (support person); *teina* (learner).

2. *Wahine* (women). *Mana* is more difficult to translate and refers to power and earned respect, spiritual and worldly.

3. The Social Report, 2005. www.socialreport.msd.govt.nz/knowledge-skills/participation-tertiary-education.html.

4. www.greens.org/nz.

5. Louise Nicholas accused three senior police officers of brutally raping her eighteen years earlier in Rotorua. They were acquitted, but feminist anarchists have since late March 2006 begun a high-profile leaflet and e-mail campaign, "We believe Louise Nicholas," (see Watt 2006). Meanwhile, the Department of Internal Affairs has appointed a commissioner, Dame Margaret Bazley, as the sole investigator into its Enquiry into Police Conduct.

6. Her speech can be found at www.beehive.govt.nz/Portfolio.aspx?PortfolioID=37?tid=2.

7. "AIDS: What You Haven't Been Told" and "Gay Rights /Special Rights: Inside the Homosexual Agenda" were both banned and then released in the mid-1990s because the censorship law could not restrict an opinion, only the representation of an activity.

8. The 1993 amendment extended the grounds on which employment discrimination could be considered illegal to include sexual orientation. The same year, the FVPCA was passed which, in the view of the 2005 "Focusing on Women" report, is "seen as a positive step towards recognising that violence and sexual violence against women and children is not acceptable." www.mwa.govt.nz/women-in-nz/timeline/1990.html.

9. *Pakeha* refers to New Zealanders of British descent. Non-Pakeha thus includes Maori, Pacific Islanders, and other more recent immigrant groups of different ethnicities.

10. OFLC 2005.

11. Violent content on television is regulated by the Broadcasting Standards Authority's (BSA) Precautionary Risk Management Model based on research into number and contexts of violent incidents represented. Yet as GayNZ writers frequently point out, the SPCS blurs the jurisdictions when attacking the chief censor.

12. It came "informally."

13. The whole process was calculated to cost $NZ72,000.

14. Parliamentary Question 10742 for December 1, 2005. Questions for Written Answer: 17 November–14 December 2005. http://publications.clerk.parliament.govt.nz.clients.intergen.net.nz/QuestionsForWrittenAnswer.aspx?Mode=Lodged&Days=0&Sets=20.

15. www.nzff.telecom.co.nz/grids/b-grid-text.asp?=185&area=5.

16. SPCS 2004.

17. A U.S. Christian site pointed, on the other hand, to the "vileness" of the film and a female star, shared with Noe'e *Irreversible*, while reporting the NZ SPCS media releases on the latter. www.wayoflife.org/fbns/melgibson-thepassionofthechrist/moral-vileness.html.

References

Baise-moi. 2000. Film. Director Virginie Despentes.

Beck's Incredible Film Festival Feedback. www.becksincrediblefilmfest.co.nz/feedback.html (accessed 12 December 2005).

British Board of Film Classification (BBFC). www.bbfc.co.uk (accessed 1 July 2005).

Crawford, Matt. 2004. "Protecting Society from Art." http://critic.co.nz/showfeature.php?id=486. 2 August. (accessed 3 December 2005).

Gay Lesbian NZ. www.gaynz.com.

GayNZ 2003. "At a Glance: Bill Hastings." *Our People*. 1 August. www.gaynz.com/aarticlestemplates/ At-A-Glance.asp?articleid=443&zoneid=15 (accessed 12 December 2005).

Index on Censorship. www.indexonline.org.

Irreversible. 2002. Film. Director Gaspar Noe.

Janiewski, Dolores, and Paul Morris. 2005. *New Rights New Zealand: Myths, Moralities and Markets*. Auckland, NZ: Auckland University.

King, B., et al. *Television Violence in New Zealand: A Study of Programming and Policy in the International Context*. Lesbian and Gay Archives of New Zealand. www.laganz.org.nz/resources/ keyevents.html.

Liberarianz. www.libertarianz.org.nz.

National Council of Women. www.ncwnz.co.nz.

New Zealand Censorship Database. www.censorship.govt.nz/ofcdd/Summaryresults.asp.

New Zealand Film Festivals. www.nzff.telecom.co.nz.

Nightline. 2005. "Chief Censor Urges Review." TV3. November 9. www.tv3.co.nz/News/tabid/67/ articleID/725/Default.aspx. (accessed 12 November 2005).

NZ Customs Service. "Consolidated List of Decisions of the Indecent Publications Tribunal Video Recordings Authority, and the Office of Film and Literature Classification." www.customs.govt.nz/ library/Technical+Publications/Consolidated+List+of+Film+and+Literature+Classifications.htm.

NZ Government. 2005. *Films, Videos, and Publications Classification Amendment Act*. (accessed 21 February 2005).

"Offensive Brown." 2003. Libertarianz. www.libertarianz.org.nz/?libzpr=184. October 16. (accessed 12 December 2004).

Office of Film and Literature Classification (OFLC). www.censorship.govt.nz.

Office of Film and Literature Classification (OFLC) 2005. Annual Report. www.censorship.govt .nz/pdfword/Annual%20Report%202004-5.pdf (accessed 30 November 2005).

Refused Classification, Film Censorship in Australia. www.refused-classification.com.

"Response to Chief Censor Bill Hastings." 2004. *Scoop Independent News*. April 7. www.scoop.co .nz/stories/CU0404/S00031.htm (accessed 30 July 2005).

Richardson, D. 2000. "Claiming Citizenship? Sexuality, Citizenship and Lesbian/Feminist Theory." *Sexualities* 3, no. 2: 255–72.

Society for the Promotion of Community Standards (SPCS). www.spcs.org.nz.

Society for the Promotion of Community Standards (SPCS). 2004. "Irreversible Homophobia and 'Hate Speech.'" November 4. www.scoop.co.nz/stories/CU0411/S00037.htm (accessed 1 December 2005).

Society for the Promotion of Community Standards (SPCS) 2005. "Chief Censor's Office Identifies Film Complaints." Press Release. www.scoop.co.nz/stories/print.html?path=PO0511/ S00106.htm (accessed 15 November 2005).

Submission to the Government Administrative Committee into the Enquiry into Hate Speech. 2005. Human Rights Commission. www//hrc.co.nz/hrc/cms/files/documents/ (accessed 15 November 2005).

Submission to the Government Administration Select Committee of the Films, Videos and Publications Classification Amendment Bill. 2004. S04.21. National Council of Women. May 10.

Submission to the Government Administration Select Committee on the Crimes (Intimate Covert Filming) Bill. 2005. S05.32. National Council of Women. June 13.

Tamaki, Brian. 2004. DVD. "New Zealand: A Nation Under Siege–A Social Disaster Has Hit Our Nation." www.streamingfaith.com/viewer/viewerframes_parent.asp?action=odclist&b=ie&p=win& WMP=1&WMPv=7&RPIE=1&sp=&networked=3000320&gid=0&mt=552&tid=4000015.

"Towards Precautionary Risk Management of TV Violence." 2004. Report to the Minister of Broadcasting of the Working Group: TV Violence Project. Ministry of Culture and Heritage. April.

Watt, Emily. 2006. " 'Nice Middle Class Girls' with a Message to Deliver." *Sunday Star Times*. April 9.

Watch on Censorship. www.watchoncensorship.asn.au/guide.html.

Watson, Chris, and Roy Shuker. 1998. *In the Public Good: Censorship in New Zealand*. Palmerston North: Dunmore.

Wilson, David. 2005. "Film Classification in New Zealand." Lecture presented at University of Waikato, May 5.

CHAPTER TWENTY

Grounding Gender Evaluation Methodology (GEM) for Telecentres: The Experiences of Ecuador and the Philippines

Claire Buré

Within international development discourse, there is considerable debate over how the introduction, appropriation, and use of information and communication technologies (ICTs) through telecentres affect social change. Telecentres are public spaces offering a combination of ICT resources for community development purposes, in an effort to provide access to the global information and knowledge society, particularly for those who would not otherwise be able to make use of ICT services. To ascertain and enhance their effectiveness in meeting community needs, it is imperative to accurately assess how telecentres influence change in the communities where they are based. More specifically, the role of telecentres in providing ICT resources needs to be identified with respect to gender, since more men than women tend to have access to ICT resources and control them for their own benefits, and as a result, "women and girls are poorly placed to benefit from the knowledge economy" (Huyer 2003).

The need for an evaluation tool with a gender perspective resulted in the creation of the gender evaluation methodology (GEM) (Ramilo and Cinco 2005). GEM provides a framework to plan and evaluate ICT initiatives with a gender perspective, and it has been used with various ICTs for development initiatives, including telecentres. This comparative study presents the experiences of GEM use within four tester telecentres: two in Ecuador, and two in the Philippines. Feedback was gathered about experiences with the GEM evaluation process with telecentres, from which recommendations can be drawn to render the GEM methodology more effective for use specifically within telecentre contexts.

Although ICT use in development projects is not new, the potential is now prominently recognized as an important enabler in achieving long-standing development goals such as poverty alleviation (UNDP 2001). However, in many instances the actual effects of ICT implementation are "far from clear" (Gómez, Hunt, and Lamoureux 1999). Other studies describe how the use of ICTs has had no effect, or even harmful effects, on people's lives in developing countries (Mansell and Wehn 1998). Given the widespread implementation of ICT for development initiatives in many developing countries, research needs to focus not only on the *how* and *why* with respect to these projects and outcomes, but also—and perhaps more important—on the contextual factors that lead to successful (or unsuccessful) ICT initiatives (Ofir and Kriel 2004). This will allow for greater understanding of how technologies can be used to help build human capacity and the enabling environments that may allow this to occur more effectively.

The importance of telecentres is couched in their value as "an important component in universal access, and especially in harnessing ICTs for development" (Parkinson 2005). Telecentres, it is generally agreed, are public places offering shared access to a range of telecommunication and information services for specific social, educational, economic, and personal development purposes (Gómez, Hunt, and Lamoureux 1999). *Shared access* is a key concept in the definition of a telecentre, since it comprises a place where people gather to communicate and gain ICT awareness and ICT capability—meaning the required skills, knowledge, and confidence involved in using ICTs (Faulkner and Kleif 2003). Telecentres typically offer a variety of services and ICTs, which can include "photocopying, computer typesetting, faxing, internet (although many are beset by connectivity problems), phone and computer training, plus other value-added services that vary from site to site" (Parkinson 2005).

Although not all telecentres are successful (Benjamin and Dahms 1999), they are nevertheless part of a growing worldwide telecentre movement (Parkinson 2005). New telecentres are cropping up, even in a relative absence of funding, often adopting an entrepreneurial social enterprise approach (Ceballos and Buré 2006). As a result of years of collective research on telecentres, telecentre.org is a unique project based at the International Development Research Centre (IDRC) attempting to rethink the telecentre movement as a collaborative effort between cooperation agencies, private organizations, researchers, and key actors in the field. Telecentretelecentre.org focuses on building and supporting telecentre networks to help strengthen individual telecentres, allowing communities to share new and existing resources, improve skills, and facilitate innovative services.

Clearly defining telecentre goals and objectives is essential, particularly because multiple stakeholders may have different goals in mind (Benjamin and Dahms 1999). Additionally, it needs to be recognized that many changes brought about by ICT for development initiatives are long-term and often indirect, something that evaluation frameworks need to take into account. Above all, telecentre evaluation should be treated as a participatory learning process (Hudson 1999) and should be "useful, financially responsible, build local capacity and enable shared learning" (Reilly and Gómez 2001). Relatively little research exists on telecentre evaluation; one of the most significant contributions is a collection of research by Gómez and Hunt (1999). The Gender Evaluation Methodology presents an effective framework that upholds many of the positions in this research.

Gender should be understood as a multidimensional variable, cutting across other variables such as age, race, ethnicity, class, and geographical location. It is also important to challenge binary and essentialist understandings of gender, since not all men and women are necessarily the same (Faulkner 2004). Gender-ICT interplay is therefore a vital concern if women and girls are to be able to benefit from inclusion in the information and knowledge society (Hafkin 2002). That is, "Gender analysis of ICTs suggests that the existence of ICTs in public spaces does not entail access for all . . . since on average, women have less income, education, time mobility and face religious or cultural constraints that restrict their access to and use of technology" (Odame 2005). Engendering ICT policy and evaluation frameworks is therefore necessary because "ICT diffusion alone is not sufficient to close the gap altogether." Gender inclusion strategies need to be effectively tailored since they may be gendered themselves (Faulkner 2004).

Existing research on gender and telecentres is very limited (Holmes 1999; Johnson 2003; Jorge 2000). Yet as Jorge argues, "It is crucial to invest in gender analysis and training to ensure that telecentres can appropriately respond and address women's needs and demands, and consequently guarantee that women use and benefit from telecentre services, and consequently, more efficiently contribute to the economic development of their communities." Since universal service policies tend to exemplify gender-neutrality, "women's social and economic conditions are neglected." The gender evaluation methodology therefore plays a crucial role in understanding gendered spaces within telecentres and addresses the need for gender analysis to be an integral part of telecentre evaluations "rather than an 'add-on' task" (Jorge 2000).

Moreover, gender inclusion strategies into the information and knowledge society need to be more plural and dynamic to include various masculinities and femininities that exist, since "one size does not fit all" (Faulkner and Kleif

2003). Existing research shows that women-only ICT inclusion strategies are not always more effective than more plural strategies that include both men and women, a concept that holds significant implications for the findings presented here (Faulkner 2004).

What Is the Gender Evaluation Methodology?

GEM is a tool to integrate a gender perspective into evaluations of ICT initiatives for development and social change. It is designed to help ICT practitioners discover how technologies affect and interact with gender equality (particularly women's lives) at the individual and broader social levels. That is, GEM gives input into whether ICTs are having positive (or negative) outcomes in women's lives and gender relations (Ramilo and Cinco 2005).

The methodology includes a guide for conducting evaluations, and it provides a framework for evaluation processes, suggesting various approaches for incorporating a gender analysis in evaluation and project planning. GEM is an evolving guide that encourages user feedback and is based on the understanding that learning is fluid and interactive. Processes both of self-change (at the individual, organizational, and community levels) and social change (social, economic, political, and technological) are measured. Recognition of these changes in relation to ICTs allows for the measurement of how ICT use influences changing gender roles and stereotypes. GEM endorses a participatory, learning-by-doing approach, which leads to action and change. It also encourages critical reflection, sensitivity to context, and stakeholder bias, and it considers both quantitative and qualitative indicators (Ramilo and Cinco 2005).

GEM was developed by the Association for Progressive Communications Women's Networking Support Programme (APCWNSP), based on twenty-seven tester projects across nineteen countries (APCWNSP 2004). These projects included a broad range of ICT initiatives and practitioners, four of which involved telecentres. GEM has been used with various ICTs for development initiatives around the world, ranging from e-governance, education, and training programs to community-building initiatives, and it continues to be developed as it is applied as an evaluation tool. The implementation process involves workshops to provide training on gender awareness and the use of the GEM tool itself, so that participants can apply the methodology to their own ICT initiatives (acting as implementing agencies in this way), with help from the GEM team. Further, a GEM practitioners' network has been created, which aims to bring together GEM practitioners (online and in person) to share knowledge and resources on gender and ICT evaluation issues, as well as to develop new and useful resources. This includes development of the GEM tool itself by following up on various GEM projects after two years of field testing (APCWNSP 2004).

Methodology

This comparative study investigated how the gender evaluation methodology was used in four telecentres (out of the total of eight GEM tester telecentres) in Ecuador and the Philippines. Telecentre evaluations were carried out two to three years before this study was conducted, each evaluation process lasting approximately one year. For this study, interviews were conducted with twenty-six people, including sixteen women and ten men, representing a range of experiences with the GEM implementation process.[1] Additionally, two workshops were conducted with community members, in order to engage with local communities about gender issues and gain a better understanding of local context, including family roles and gender relations. The first workshop was held in El Chaco, Ecuador, with thirty-four participants; the second was held in Malingao, the Philippines, with twenty participants; each included both men and women.

Face-to-face interviews were conducted, either individually or in focus groups of no more than four people. Almost all interviews were audio recorded, with the permission of respondents, and all personal information was kept anonymous and confidential. The study was qualitative in nature; each interview was informal, semistructured, and reflexive. They featured open-ended questions based on three sets of interview guides geared toward GEM experts, telecentre leaders, and community members. Data collected was coded and analyzed to ensure consistency. The research is based on the understanding that gender and technologies are coconstructed, implying that strategies to involve more women in telecentres change both ICT and gender (Faulkner 2004). Although it is difficult to generalize qualitative findings from a small number of respondents, those who responded represented a variety of experiences with GEM, gender issues, and telecentres.[2] Further research is needed to draw deeper conclusions from the study's findings.

Evaluating Ecuadorian Telecentres: Project Background

In Ecuador, Fundación ChasquiNet was chosen to be the GEM implementing agency in both Colinas del Norte and El Chaco. Fundación ChasquiNet is a nonprofit organization based in Quito that helps strengthen individuals, communities, and organizations through the use of ICTs for development in education, improvement of life conditions, and strengthening of local culture. Both telecentres were fairly sustainable at the time of the study, despite a lack of Internet access.

Colinas del Norte is a neighborhood built on reclaimed land on the outskirts of Quito. Its telecentre is based at a community development organization that runs a number of programs in sectors including health, education, and environment.

A goal of one of their projects was to improve communication mechanisms within the community, for which a small group of male youth was identified, leading them to voluntarily run a telecentre initiative within local schools and to create a local newspaper based at the telecentre. Due to strong local cultural prejudices against women who work outside the home, very few young women became involved in the project. However, a number of young beauty contest winners self-organized as a group and became involved, claiming: "We don't want to be only pretty faces" (Galarza 1999).

It was within the planning and evaluation of this newspaper project that GEM was applied. Briefly, aims were twofold: first, to evaluate and integrate a gender perspective into the community newspaper material and the communications team; and second, to produce a manual to integrate a gender perspective into the telecentre's work. The project was successful in achieving both aims: it increased numbers of women in the communications team, it incorporated more gender sensitivity into newspaper content, and it increased gender equity in ICT project participation and decision making. Aims were achieved primarily through nine training workshops on a variety of issues, ranging from personal development to marketing training. Most important, a "GEM for Telecentres" manual was developed: a simplified, more holistic version of GEM adapted for the Ecuadorian telecentre context and which is still in circulation (Tipán Barrera 2002).

GEM was also applied in the telecentre of El Chaco, a rural village located about four hours from Quito. There GEM was used not in the planning or evaluation of a specific project, but rather for promoting gender equality among telecentre management and users. A series of training workshops focused on gender sensitization and personal development, to encourage higher levels of women's involvement with the telecentre and to increase gender sensitization in the community. Workshops were planned using the "GEM for Telecentres" manual, which helped raise local awareness and sensitivity about gender issues. Interestingly, even the telecentre manual was significantly adapted for the workshops in El Chaco, highlighting that adaptation to local contexts is crucial for effective gender planning and evaluation implementation. Efforts to bring more women to the telecentre (and to improve the quality of their participation) proved successful, particularly as a result of volunteers' social capital.

Evaluating Filipino Telecentres: Project Background

In the Philippines, GEM was used in two telecentres (known as multipurpose community telecentres) in remote neighboring communities in Mindanao: Malingao and Taguitic. These two small communities are similar in many ways;

variation can be attributed to differences in land tenure and community leadership. The GEM implementing agency was a nongovernmental organization called eDI (e-Development Initiatives), which promotes the use of ICTs in rural areas by training and empowering communities. eDI first became involved with the telecentres about three years after they had been created, to help with local "community preparation," since neither community recognized the value of the telecentres. As a result, six members of eDI relocated to the rural communities for over a year, and partially due to their presence, the two telecentres were chosen to be GEM testers.

Both Malingao and Taguitic are rural, leader-oriented communities, with local economies based on agriculture. Migration from rural communities in search of a "better life" is common, and a high level of community mobilization was apparent. When eDI first arrived in Malingao and Taguitic, it took much time for them to build rapport with the community and create telecentre leaders, particularly in Taguitic. Both telecentres had lost Internet access, and the ICT services available were becoming obsolete, leading to significant sustainability problems in both communities. Many telecentre volunteers made use of newly gained ICT skills for their own advantage, consequently leaving their communities for better-paying jobs elsewhere. The resulting lack of volunteers also proved to be a factor in the telecentres' unsustainability.

GEM was applied with similar aims in both telecentres: to investigate levels of community access to the telecentre and of gender sensitivity and usefulness of the information services in addressing community needs. In contrast to the Ecuadorian experience, which used GEM primarily as a project planning tool, GEM was used as an evaluation tool in the Philippines. The evaluations focused on telecentre use, telecentre information needs, and changes in users' confidence levels and social needs with respect to gender. Stories were gathered from community members and telecentre leaders through individual interviews, focus group discussions, and personal journals kept by each telecentre volunteer. Evaluation findings were analyzed at a major workshop, which was attended by APC, members of the community, the GEM implementing agency, and the telecentre implementation and monitoring agencies.

In general, those involved with the telecentre experienced an increase in self-esteem and self-confidence. However, as eDI explained, this may also be attributed to the ongoing presence and work of the implementing agency with community members. It was also recognized that the information accessible at the telecentres should be more closely related to community needs—in this case, to people's livelihoods—such as agricultural information on the crab hatchery. Experiences revealed the need for more telecentre volunteers and more community participation (in order to also improve financial sustainability).

GEM Use with Telecentres:
Commonalities among Local Adaptations

From this investigation of how GEM was used in each of the four telecentre projects, a number of commonalities were found in how the methodology was adapted to local contexts. In all four communities, GEM was implemented to fit within the local community culture, including goals and priorities (particularly in a way that made sense for the implementing agency), largely a result of the flexibility of the tool. When implemented with telecentres specifically, the GEM planning and evaluation methodology was rendered less conceptual and more concrete in how it was used. The creation and adaptation of the "GEM for Telecentres" manual is an example: the manual simplified language surrounding gender issues, and methodologically the manual simplified the GEM process by providing participatory exercises and facilitation techniques for workshop facilitators, as well as suggested indicators for telecentre evaluations (Tipán Barrera 2002). Additionally the basic FODA analysis tool (strengths, weaknesses, opportunities, and threats) was used for self-evaluation in Colinas del Norte. The simplification of concepts and methods for using GEM therefore seemed inherent to implementation, although this shift was not without its difficulties. For example, the implementing agency in the Philippines found it difficult to decide when would be the most appropriate time to involve men in the GEM process. For them, "there was no question about including men—but when to include them [in the evaluation process] was the question." One should therefore be sensitive about the timing of men's inclusion, since this likely differs with each context where GEM is applied.

Across all four cases, GEM was applied in a way that was highly inclusive of all community members, using community and telecentre leaders as examples for the rest of the community.[3] The GEM evaluation process in the Colinas del Norte newspaper project therefore focused on working with young men and women who already aspired to be community leaders. Similarly, eDI focused on building and working with community leaders regardless of gender:

It's really a case-to-case basis, how open [participants] are and how ready they are . . . for gender concepts. And the usual strategy is to start with people who are more open, and more respectful, and you build models for other people.[4]

Workshops conducted in each case were therefore not only about gender sensitization but also about personal development and skills training, designed to increase leadership skills. Further, in the Philippines, extra workshops were conducted before the official GEM training and evaluation workshop to more gradually introduce the concept of gender to the community, thereby adapting and relating to the community's understanding of gender issues. It is clear that in-clusion processes are not simple, underscoring the need for more research in this area to design effective gender inclusion strategies.

Evaluations were conducted within the available scope for human resources, time, and funding—limiting factors in each community. For eDI, funding short-ages restricted the time they could continue working in Taguitic and Malingao. With more time and funding, they claimed, they could have learned more, planned more strategically, and readjusted the intervention process. Instead, they were only able to gain a candid shot of the evaluation results, which they believed lowered the long-term sustainability of the evaluation process. Time commitment is also directly related to the process of building community lead-ers: In order for evaluation results to lead to significant changes, continued community participation is essential. Interestingly, in the Philippines this prompted a focus on more elderly people in the community to become leaders, because younger individuals were more likely to migrate from communities once they were empowered.

Outcomes of GEM Use in Telecentres

To make GEM for telecentres more effective, the outcomes of GEM use in each of these pilot cases must be investigated. First and foremost on the list of con-clusions is that changes occurred because GEM was used primarily as a reference tool, particularly for developing indicators through community participation. Generally use of GEM in telecentres helped effect small-scale changes in each community, which often resulted from rising confidence levels among GEM participants. This made a difference for individuals (particularly for women) and for family and community relations, and it helped introduce a new per-spective toward the potential benefits (and drawbacks) of ICTs in the local community through the telecentre.

Many participants who were involved in the GEM process experienced higher levels of confidence and self-esteem, often a result of their participation in personal development and gender sensitization workshops and ICT skills training. A number of participants described how their own lives consequently changed: Women in each community were inspired to pursue higher education, although the reasons behind these decisions were various. Others who gained ICT capacity used their new skills and confidence to pursue employment else-where, with the result that few or no telecentre leaders remained behind, in ef-fect lowering the numbers of telecentre users.

Additionally GEM training led to changes in family relationships, through personal or individual empowerment. In the Philippines, one finding revealed a general trend for men to be more likely to help their wives with household chores after training, and for women to be given more decision-making power within the family (particularly in Malingao, where gender roles were less rigid). These changes tended to result in more open communication flows between individuals, which led to higher levels of mutual understanding, according to individuals' reports. However, empowerment can be problematic between peers, who experience conflict and competition as they become local leaders. This occurred between the young individuals who were involved in the newspaper project in Colinas del Norte, as well as between volunteers and nonvolunteers in the Filipino telecentres in this study.

With respect to telecentres, the implementation of GEM brought about a greater awareness of the services that the telecentre could offer for the communities where evaluations took place. Participants in the evaluation process seemed more organized and more passionate about using and encouraging others to use the telecentre. Changes measured were short-term, however, because many of the volunteers moved away (leaving few behind to pass on ICT skills and encourage new users), and the telecentres themselves were experiencing low levels of sustainability. Although these changes were highlighted at the end of the evaluation, it is not clear to what extent they were sustained (or measured) afterward.

Recommendations for GEM Use with Telecentres

While the flexibility of GEM lends itself to its effectiveness and success across a broad range of ICT initiatives, similar trends were found in how GEM was adapted and used in four different community telecentre contexts for both project planning and evaluation purposes. A number of recommendations for future use of the GEM methodology specifically within telecentre contexts can therefore be drawn, namely

1. Conduct a feasibility scan for GEM project planning or evaluation in the community to determine available resource capacity, as well as local needs, priorities, and readiness, as preconditions for the GEM process to take place.
2. Steer the GEM methodology to become a more concrete tool through a user-friendly set of methods and strategies that are directly related to telecentre issues.
3. Ensure that GEM for telecentres is locally grounded, in that it is answerable to the needs and priorities of the individual community and telecentre.
4. Encourage participation and inclusion at all levels of the GEM planning and evaluation process to ensure a plural and dynamic gender inclusion perspective.

Each of these recommendations will be discussed in turn, with examples from the cases studied, and supported by a collection of existing research on telecentre evaluation that sets out ten "guiding principles for telecentre evaluation" (Reilly and Gómez 2001).

First, it is suggested that the feasibility of GEM implementation with the telecentre in question be assessed before implementation takes place. A feasibility scan could be applied as part of the GEM framework itself—as a tool for communities to assess their readiness for a telecentre evaluation or planning project with a gender perspective. To evaluate a telecentre's activities and usage requires a lot of people, time, and money, so it is likely that GEM use in a community would be more useful if implemented in telecentres that have achieved a relatively high level of sustainability and can provide the resources necessary to conduct the evaluation. Otherwise the results of the evaluation are rendered somewhat irrelevant, as knowledge gained becomes retained in small, disconnected pockets in the community. As eDI claimed,

If we had the choice, probably we would not have chosen Taguitic [to implement GEM] for example. Because it had too many problems . . . For us, we would have wanted to look at the social context first and see what was viable to implement: the criteria of putting the project at the same time . . . You should have some criteria [first], and probably [identify] what's the appropriate area for the project implementation process . . . Like I said, trust-building took us a very big time.[5]

Although complex community problems seem like a good reason to evaluate a telecentre initiative, the point here is that there should be a congruency between the resources needed and those available to conduct the evaluation. Inconsistency between these two factors may lead to an ineffective evaluation process. Nevertheless, more research is required on the basic needs and conditions necessary for a successful telecentre evaluation to take place.

Second, GEM might be more effective when used with telecentres if the tool were more concrete: "Something that we can easily apply, something operational. Not just a concept."[6] While it continues to evolve, it would be useful if the tool had a clearer set of strategies or methods to use "that you can just modify . . . meaning that it can work to the situation of what kind of communities, where."[7] Although overmodification should be avoided, it would be useful to produce a methodology more adaptable for particular telecentre contexts (such as for government-implemented telecentres versus community telecentres). This might streamline needed modifications when implementing GEM, thereby simplifying its application. Even after training, the implementing agency in the Philippines described: "We really still grappled with [GEM] after that [training] presentation, at least from our point of view, on how to implement it . . . And we didn't really know what would be the output." In part, this confusion resulted from the broadness of GEM, which also allowed for its flexibility. However, it is clear that further clarification would render the tool easier to use. Implementing agencies suggested that a GEM for telecentres could involve the creation of an indicator menu: a list that addresses common telecentre issues and needs. Although a discussion about developing indicators versus providing them is cumbersome for this chapter, it would nevertheless be useful to offer a number of evaluation indicators related to typical telecentre needs and priorities as examples.

Third, application of GEM for telecentres needs to be locally grounded and oriented to the needs of the telecentre and community. Generally the evaluations conducted in the cases studied were geared toward the aims of the implementing agency for the community, with some level of input from the community members and telecentre leaders. For example, in the Philippines the implementing agency began to collect stories from participants, who in turn decided that it would be more accurate for them to tell their own stories. Reilly and Gómez describe how telecentre evaluations need to be "incorporated into the project design and reflect project objectives" and focus "on clear questions that are important to stakeholders" (2001, 2). This is difficult, given that stakeholders will have different goals in mind for the evaluation outcomes. More study is needed to determine which methodologies are best suited to reflect project objectives for different telecentre contexts.

It also needs to be clarified whether GEM will be used as a planning or evaluation tool, something which the feasibility scan could identify in advance. For communities with wide-ranging socioeconomic problems, it is likely that evaluation is more useful for project planning through the telecentre, because it provides an opportunity for capacity building within the community development project. In Malingao, a number of individuals did not attend the gender sensitization workshops because they did not see what was in it for them—community concerns were instead focused on the more basic need of putting food on the table that day. However, since one of the biggest community priorities was to learn how to produce and sell virgin coconut oil, it is likely that the evaluation would have been more locally successful if GEM had incorporated this need, such as through training workshops held at the telecentre.

Last, participation in the evaluation process implies that all relevant stakeholders are involved at each stage of the process. The need for participation at all levels of GEM implementation with telecentres—particularly when choosing projects—was described by an individual at the GEM implementing agency in the Philippines who felt isolated from the planning process:

> Well I myself wasn't really oriented in what GEM was, they just said: "Oh, there's something that we'll be doing for women." So we were just waiting, and suddenly

they said, "Okay, this is what we're going to do." We were not really even part of the planning at the same time. So we just improvised along the way and what we can do to fit the community in at the same time.[8]

Similarly, involvement of community members is a key component of the evaluation process, because local understandings of gender need to be acknowledged and understood for the evaluation to be effective. For example, in Ecuador, it was difficult to apply GEM in a participatory manner within community telecentres, because gender issues and gender equality were issues not necessarily understood (and therefore not even relevant to everyone). It is likely that this lack of understanding of gender issues is linked to resistance toward gender issues, contributing to a perception that gender holds little or no importance for a community ICT project. Patton (1997, 183–84) describes utilization-focused evaluation (upon which GEM is theoretically based): "The processes of participation and collaboration have an impact on participants and collaborators quite beyond whatever findings or reports they may produce by working together." Although participation is a key principle of GEM, perhaps actual participation processes are more difficult to achieve in reality at all levels of GEM implementation with telecentres—an issue that therefore deserves more study.

Conclusion

In order to better identify the outcomes and potential benefits of telecentres for the communities they are intended to serve, and to further enhance their effectiveness within those communities, there needs to be a stronger effort to create and support solid telecentre evaluation frameworks. An important part of these frameworks should be dedicated to promoting gender equality and sensitization, as an embedded tool for learning within a larger evaluation framework. This is how the gender evaluation methodology was adapted for use within four telecentre contexts, in Ecuador and the Philippines, partly as a result of the flexibility of GEM for ICT initiatives in general. Given that it was adapted in similar ways according to similar factors (such as available time span and telecentre objectives), to fit within the culture and context of the community, a number of recommendations for further use of GEM with telecentres have been distilled.

It must be ensured that GEM effectively meets community and telecentre needs, for which a feasibility assessment would be useful. In so doing, consideration should be given to available time and economic and human resources, as well as community and telecentre needs and priorities, to ensure an effective evaluation. GEM for telecentres should provide a concrete and user-friendly framework that relates to common telecentre issues and concerns, thereby reducing the amount of modification that needs to be done. GEM for telecentres should be locally grounded through strong orientation to community and telecentre needs and priorities, and it should be fully participatory. Inclusion strategies should be plural and dynamic, in order to enhance gender equity throughout the process. Given these recommendations, the GEM tool can be more useful when extended to new community telecentre contexts. Only through this progressive learning process can a deeper understanding of gender relations and telecentre use be understood, where the ongoing use of GEM with telecentres and the sharing of experiences about this use provides us with this opportunity.

Notes

1. Respondents included GEM experts, GEM implementing agency members, telecentre implementing agency members, telecentre monitoring agency members, GEM training participants, telecentre leaders, community leaders, and community members.

2. It was difficult to distinguish clearly whether changes in the community were brought about by community use of the telecentre, the GEM process, or other external factors. Social development outcomes are often due to a combination of factors, including how dedicated the implementing agency is to community development.

3. It is important to note that findings on inclusivity in GEM application are consistent with the GEM analytical approach.

4. Interview, Philippines, April 2006.

5. Interview, Philippines, April 2006.

6. Interview, Ecuador, March 2006.

7. Interview, Philippines, April 2006.

8. Interview, Philippines, April 2006.

References

Association for Progressive Communications Women's Networking Support Programme. 2004. Extending the APC-WNSP Gender and ICT Evaluation Methodology: Final Technical Report. Unpublished document.

APCWNSP. 2006. "Gender Evaluation Methodology II: Building Gender and Evaluation Practice within the ICT for Development Community." Ottawa: International Development Research Centre. www.idrc.ca/en/ev-94819-201_103586-1-IDRC_ADM_INFO.html (accessed 20 August 2007).

Benjamin, Peter, and Mona Dahms. 1999. "Socialise the Modem of Production: The Role of Telecentres in Development." In *Telecentre Evaluation: A Global Perspective*, ed. Ricardo Gómez and Patrik Hunt, 49–67. Ottawa: International Development Research Centre.

Ceballos, Florencio and Claire Buré. 2006. "A Rejuvenated Pulse for the Telecentre Movement." *Public Service Review: International Development Incorporating Emerging Markets* 11: 129–30.

Faulkner, Wendy. 2004. "Strategies of Inclusion: Gender and the Information Society: Final Report." Strategies of Inclusion: Gender and the Information Society. www.sigis-ist.org.

Faulkner, Wendy, and Tine Kleif. 2003. "One Size Does Not Fit All! Digital In/Exclusion in a Rural Community." *Strategies of Inclusion: Gender and the Information Society*. www.sigis-ist.org.

Galarza, Marcelo. 1999. "Together for Our Future: Gender Sensitive Communication for Community Initiatives." Gem Practitioner's Network: Evaluator Reports. www.apcwomen.org/gem/practitioners/reports.shtml?x=63582.

Gómez, Ricardo, and Patrik Hunt. 1999. "Telecentre Evaluation—A Global Perspective." Report of an International Meeting on Telecentre Evaluation. Ottawa: International Development Research Centre. www.idrc.ca/uploads/user-S/10244248430Farhills.pdf.

Gómez, Ricardo, Patrik Hunt, and Emmanuelle Lamoureux. 1999. "Telecentre Evaluation and Research: A Global Perspective." In *Telecentre Evaluation: A Global Perspective*, ed. Ricardo Gómez and Patrik Hunt, 15–29. Ottawa: International Development Research Centre.

Hafkin, Nancy. 2002. "Gender Issues in ICT Policy in Developing Countries: An Overview." Paper prepared for the Expert Group Meeting on Information and Communication Technologies and Their Impact On and Use as an Instrument for the Advancement and Empowerment of Women.

Holmes, Rebecca. 1999. "Gender Analysis of Telecentre Evaluation Methodology." In *Telecentre Evaluation: A Global Perspective*, ed. Ricardo Gómez and Patrik Hunt, 139–48. Ottawa: International Development Research Centre.

Hudson, Heather. 1999. "Designing Research for Telecentre Evaluation." In *Telecentre Evaluation: A Global Perspective*, ed. Ricardo Gómez and Patrick Hunt, 15–29. Ottawa: International Development Research Centre.

Huyer, Sophia. 2003. "Gender, ICT, and Education." www.wigsat.org/engenderedICT.pdf.

Johnson, Kelby. 2003. "Telecentres and the Gender Dimension: An Examination of How Engendered Telecentres Are Diffused in Africa." Thesis, Georgetown Univ. www.schoolnetafrica.net/fileadmin/resources/KelbyJohnson.pdf.

Jorge, Sonia N. 2000. "Gender Perspectives on Telecentres." Paper prepared for ITU Telecom Americas 2000 Telecom Development Symposium.

Mansell, Robin, and Uta Wehn, eds. 1998. *Knowledge Societies: Information Technology for Sustainable Development*. New York: Oxford Univ. Press.

Odame, H. H. 2005. "Gender and ICTs for Development: Setting the Context." In *Gender and ICTs for Development: A Global Sourcebook*, 13–24. Amsterdam: KIT (Royal Tropical Institute).

Ofir, Z., and L. Kriel. 2004. *Evaluating Policy Influence of ICTs for Rural Areas: The MSSRF Information Villages Research Project*. Johannesburg: Evaluation Networks.

Parkinson, Sarah. 2005. *Telecentres, Access and Development: Experience and Lessons From Uganda and South Africa*. Ottawa: International Development Research Centre.

Patton, Michael Quinn. 1997. *Utilization-Focused Evaluation: The New Century Text*, 3rd ed. Thousand Oaks, CA: Sage Publications.

Ramilo, Chat Garcia, and Cheekay Cinco. 2005. *Gender Evaluation Methodology for Internet and ICTs: A Learning Tool for Change and Empowerment*. Melville, South Africa: APC.

Reilly, Katherine, and Ricardo Gómez. 2001. "Comparing Approaches: Telecentre Evaluation Experiences in Asia and Latin America." *Electronic Journal on Information Systems in Developing Countries* 4:3 (2001): 1–17.

Tipán Barrera, Giovanni. 2002. "Validando GEM en los telecentros: Una apuesta equitativa de las TIC's." www.tele-centros.org/index.php?module=articles&func=display&catid=799&aid=734.

United Nations Development Programme. 2001. "Information Communications Technology for Development: Synthesis of Lessons Learned." UNDP Evaluation Office, paper no. 5. www.undp.org/eo/documents/essentials_5.PDF.

Index

About the Contributors

Salam Al-Mahadin, PhD, is associate professor in the English Department at the University of Petra in Jordan. Her research interests include identity politics, power relations in tourism, media discourse, critical theory, and women's issues in both Jordan and the Arab world. She has published extensively in both English and Arabic in journals and books, in addition to translating two novels into English. She is the coauthor of a trilingual dictionary of tourism and hospitality terms. She can be reached at smahadin@go.com.jo.

Alison Beale, PhD, is a professor in the School of Communication at Simon Fraser University, Vancouver, BC, Canada. She has also taught in the Department of Communication at the Université du Québec à Montréal. She obtained a PhD in communication from McGill University, Montreal, in 1989. Her principal research and teaching areas have been film and video, communication history and historiography, and cultural policy. She has been a visiting scholar at the University of Western Sydney and the Canadian Studies Fellow at Macquarie University, Sydney, where she worked on a comparative study of Australian and Canadian cultural policies from a critical feminist perspective. She has also been a visiting researcher at Edinburgh University and was a Rockefeller Foundation Fellow in the Privatization of Culture Project at New York University. She is currently working on a monograph on globalization and cultural policy and is editing a special issue of *Feminist Media Studies* on feminist approaches to critical cultural policy. She is a member of several research networks in cultural policy and the national advisory group of the recently created Centre of Expertise on Culture and Communities at Simon Fraser University.

Claire Buré is a researcher with telecentre.org at the International Development Research Centre (IDRC) in Ottawa, Canada, where she is currently conducting a study about the synergies between community radio and telecentre initiatives. Her key research interests concentrate on the appropriation and use of ICTs for community development, and the outcomes of this use. Prior to joining IDRC, she was based at the Research Centre for Social Sciences in the UK, where she worked with a research project on strategies for inclusion with respect to gender issues. Her publications include a study about how homeless people use mobile phones and the Internet in Scotland, and more recently she coauthored an article about the global telecentre movement. She holds a master's degree in Science and Technology Studies from the University of Edinburgh, UK.

Barbara Crow, PhD, is an associate professor and the incoming director of the graduate program in Communication and Culture at York University. Current research projects include digital cities, focusing on the relationship between digital technology and multimedia cities; Canadian sexual assault law and contested boundaries of consent: legal and extralegal dimensions (with Dr. Lise Gotell), investigating women's organizations and legal discourses; the Mobile Digital Commons Network (MDCN), exploring relations of mobile technologies and cultural production; and most recently, the Community Wireless Infrastructure Research Project (CWIRP), exploring Wi-Fi as public infrastructure. She was president of the Canadian Women's Studies Association, 2002–2004.

Sheryl Cunningham is a PhD candidate at the University of Washington in Seattle. Her main research interest is in political communication, with a focus on how gender functions as a subtext within American politics. She often studies the rhetorical strategies of political candidates and how such strategies both (re)produce and maintain gender ideals. She also does work in the area of media studies. In this research she often focuses on the politics of representation as well as the political economy of both news and entertainment media outlets.

Margaret Gallagher is an independent researcher and writer specializing in gender and media. She started her career at the BBC (London), before moving to the Open University, where she was deputy head of the Audiovisual Media Research Group. For the past twenty-five years she has been a freelance consultant, and has carried out research, training, and evaluation projects for the United Nations and its agencies, the European Commission, international development agencies, and broadcasting organizations. Widely published on gender and media, her recent works include *Gender Setting: New Agendas for Media Monitoring and Advocacy* (Zed Books, 2001) and *Who Makes the News? Global Media Monitoring Project 2005* (WACC, 2006). She serves on the editorial boards of *International Communication Gazette, Feminist Media Studies, Media Development, Communication for Development and Social Change* and *Communication, Culture and Critique*. She is a member of the board of trustees of the Panos Institute.

C. Anthony Giffard, PhD, is a professor in Communication at the University of Washington in Seattle. He studies international media policy and systems, with a particular interest in media in Europe and developing countries. After a career in journalism in South Africa and London, Giffard received his Ph.D. from the University of Washington in 1968. He then founded and directed the Department of Journalism and Mass Communication at Rhodes University in South Africa, before joining the faculty of the School of Communications at UW in 1978. He also has been a visiting professor or scholar at the University of Wisconsin (Madison), Johannes Gutenberg University in Mainz, and the University of Rome (La Sapienza). Giffard has been a consultant for several UN agencies and international NGOs; in addition, he has served on the editorial boards of *Telematics and Informatics* and the South African journal for journalism research, *Ecquid Novi,* and on the board of directors of Inter Press Service.

Mary Griffiths, PhD, joined the University of Adelaide in July 2006, from senior positions in Screen and Media at the University of Waikato, NZ, and Monash University's international communications program. In Adelaide, she is leading development of new degree programs and research based on participatory media. Media democracy and digital citizenship, e-participation, digital storytelling, mobile interactive technologies, and social media are current research interests. She has worked for several years on the European E-Government Conference committees, and is a member of the editorial boards of *Southern Review: Communication, Politics and Culture; EJEG: The Electronic Journal of E-Government;* and *The Journal of E-Government,* recently guest-editing special issues for both *Southern Review* (Media and Belief) and *Media International Australia* (A Clever Little Country). Recent work includes the "pastoral" in the virtual classroom, visualizations of the mobile environment of Adelaide, and the impact on the reinvention of government through the use of social intranets.

Ursula Huws is the director of Analytical Social and Economic Research and an associate fellow of the UK-based Institute for Employment Studies. She has been researching and writing about various aspects of the development of the information society for over two decades for a variety of clients, including the European Commission, the UK Government, and various United Nations organizations. Details of her publications and past research commissions can be found at www.analytica.org.uk.

Yasmin Jiwani, PhD, is an associate professor in the Department of Communication Studies at Concordia University, Montreal. Prior to her move to Montreal, she was the executive coordinator of the BC/Yukon FREDA Centre for Research on Violence against Women and Children. Her recent publications include *Discourses of Denial: Mediations of Race, Gender and Violence* (UBC Press, 2006) and (coeditor) *Girlhood, Redefining the Limit* (Black Rose, 2006). Her work has appeared in *Social Justice, Violence Against Women, Canadian Journal of Communication, Journal of Popular Film & Television,* and the *International Journal of Media and Cultural Politics.* She serves on the editorial board of the *Canadian Journal of Women and the Law; Simile;* and the *Canadian Journal of Communication.* She is a board member for the Überculture Collective and Media Watch, and a steering committee member of RACE (Researchers and Academics of Colour for Equality).

Valentina Marinescu, PhD, is reader at the Faculty of Sociology and Social Work, Bucharest University (Romania). She teaches undergraduate and graduate courses in media and society and methods of researching mass communication. Her interests lie in media and communication studies in Eastern Europe, particularly in Romania, and in gender studies. She has also published articles and book chapters on those two subjects: "Le 8 mars roumain-Un concept publicitaire" (in *Revue Sciences de la Societe,* Universite Toulouse Le Mistral, France); "Les enjeux pratiques et interactionnels du chat présenté par la Délégation de la CE en Roumanie: les questions divisent" (in R. Patterson, *Enjeux et usages des TIC— reliance sociale et insertion professionnelle*); and "Rumanien" (in U. Hasebrink and W. Schutz, *Internationales Handbuch Medien*). At present she is working on a comparative project on the mediatization of domestic violence in Romania and Canada in a postdoctoral fellowship at Universite de Montreal-Canada.

Catherine McKercher, PhD, is associate professor in the School of Journalism and Communication at Carleton University in Ottawa, Canada. She is the author of *Newsworkers Unite: Labor, Convergence and North American Newspapers* (Rowman and Littlefield, 2002) and coauthor of the popular journalism textbook *The Canadian Reporter,* now going into its third edition. She is coinvestigator with Vincent Mosco on a research project funded by the Canadian Social

Sciences and Humanities Research Council to examine trade unions and convergence in the communications industry.

Lisa McLaughlin, PhD, is an associate professor at Miami University, Ohio, where she holds a joint appointment in Mass Communication and Women's Studies. Her scholarship focuses on feminism and the political economy of transnational public space and the gender implications of the corporatization of development. McLaughlin's current research concentrates on women and ICT work in the global south and specifically on gender and ICT training initiatives originating through public-private partnerships. She is coeditor of *Feminist Media Studies*, an international peer-reviewed journal published by Routledge.

Vincent Mosco, PhD, is Canada Research Chair in Communication and Society and professor of sociology at Queen's University. He is the author of numerous books, articles, and policy reports on the media, telecommunications, computers, and information technology. His most recent book, *The Digital Sublime: Myth, Power, and Cyberspace* (MIT Press, 2004), won the 2005 Olson Award for outstanding book in the field of rhetoric and cultural studies. He is also the author of *Continental Order? Integrating North America for Cybercapitalism* (edited with Dan Schiller and published by Rowman and Littlefield, 2001) and *The Political Economy of Communication: Rethinking and Renewal* (Sage, 1996), which has been translated into Chinese (in two editions), Spanish, and Korean. Mosco is currently working on two books on knowledge labor and a revised edition of his political economy book.

Simone Murray, PhD, is a lecturer in the School of English, Communications & Performance Studies at Monash University, Melbourne. She is author of the first critical monograph analyzing gender politics and the contemporary book publishing industry, *Mixed Media: Feminist Presses and Publishing Politics* (Pluto, 2004). *Mixed Media* was awarded the 2005 DeLong Book Prize by the international Society for the History of Authorship, Reading & Publishing (SHARP) for "the best book on any aspect of the creation, dissemination, or uses of script or print published in the previous year." Her research into the interface of the book with other media industries appears in *Publishing Research Quarterly*, the *International Journal of the Book, Women's Studies International Forum, European Journal of Women's Studies,* and *Women: A Cultural Review.* She has also published widely on the multiplatforming of media content and its effects on a variety of communications stakeholders in the journals *Media, Culture & Society, Convergence, Media International Australia Incorporating Culture & Policy, Continuum* and *M/C: Media/Culture.* She has recently begun a three-year Australian

Research Council Discovery project on the adaptation industry, titled "Books as Media: The Cultural Economy of Literary Adaptation."

Danielle Newton, from Green River Community College in Auburn, Washington, is a published writer and poet interested in educational issues of diversity, including investigating the most promising factors to close the academic achievement gap. Her consultancy, project, and policy-related work involve key opinion leaders and funders of national and international leadership, especially in higher education. She writes in the areas of organizational design, especially in how education is organized and adapts to student learning challenges and improvements. Although this is her first media study about international development, she is increasingly focused on how the role and nature of educational leadership results in policies and global mandates, such as universal education. Other research interests include how federal, state, and local policies involve international networks of funders, NGOs, and scholars, as well as how college leaders develop skills and resources to attain equity and excellence.

Nikki Porter is a doctoral candidate in the Department of Communication Studies at Concordia University. She is currently investigating the history of temporal logics within the television industry. Her other research and publications have focused on audience negotiation of women and power in *Buffy the Vampire Slayer* and domestic Internet use by young people. She holds the position of senior editorial assistant at the *Canadian Journal of Communication*.

Kiran Prasad, PhD, is associate professor in Communication and Journalism, Sri Padmavati Mahila University, Tirupati, India. She was awarded the Commonwealth Academic Staff Fellowship and was Visiting Research Fellow at the Centre for International Communication Research, Institute of Communication Studies, University of Leeds, UK. She was also Canadian Studies Research Fellow at Carleton University, Canada. She is author/editor of over fifteen books. Her recent books include *Communication and Empowerment of Women: Strategies and Policy Insights from India* (2004, in 2 vols.); *Information and Communication Technology: Recasting Development* (2004); *Women and Media: Challenging Feminist Discourse* (2005); *Women in Rural Development: Contemporary Social Policy and Practice* (2006); *Women, Globalization and Mass Media: International Facets of Emancipation* (2006); and *HIV and AIDS: Vulnerability of Women in Asia and Africa* (forthcoming). Her areas of research include communication theory and policy, communication policy for development, and international and intercultural communication.

Jayne Rodgers, PhD, is a lecturer in International Communications at the University of Leeds. She specializes in research into the impact of the Internet and other global media on political activity, focusing particularly on the production, design, and development trajectories of online news. She has published widely in this area, in book form (*Spatializing International Politics: Analysing Activist Use of the Internet,* Routledge, 2003), and in many book chapters and journal articles. For several years, she taught in the Canadian university system, designing online programs in Communications Studies and researching the role of the Internet in higher education. She is the cofounder of Zydemia Media (www. zydemia.com), an organization that promotes equitable access to online news and provides media training courses for nonprofit organizations.

Katharine Sarikakis, PhD, is senior lecturer in Communications Policy and Director of the Centre for International Communications Research at the Institute of Communications Studies, University of Leeds. Her research interests are in the field of international communications and the role of institutions in supra- and international communications policy processes. Currently she is working on a project on the role of communications and cultural policies in the materialization of citizenship rights and in particular in women's citizenship rights. She is the coauthor of *Media Policy and Globalization* (Edinburgh University Press 2006), author of *Powers in Media Policy* (Peter Lang 2004), *British Media in a Global Era* (Arnold 2004), the coeditor of *Ideologies of the Internet* (Hampton Press 2006), and the managing editor of the *International Journal of Media and Cultural Politics.* She is the chair for the Communications Law and Policy Section of ECREA, has served as an elected vice president of the International Association of Mass Communications Researchers (2000–2004), and became Honorary Research Fellow at Hainan University, China, in 2004.

Kim Sawchuk, PhD, is the current editor of the *Canadian Journal of Communication* and associate professor in the Department of Communication Studies at Concordia University, Montreal. Her research involves the close study of the relationship between embodiment, social practice, and discourses on technology. Sawchuk has an unusual passion for methodology, particularly qualitative methods. In the context of her participation of the research team, the Mobile Digital Commons Network, she has been experimenting with the potential of open-source software and multimedia tools for collaborative research and developing research protocols and processes for better understanding how to enhance user participation with locative media projects. *When Pain Strikes* (1999, with coeditors Cathy Busby and Bill Burns) and *Wild Science: Reading Feminism, Medicine and the Media* (2000, coedited with Janine Marchessault) are two of her many publications. In addition to her academic interests, Sawchuk has been a new media activist. In 1996 she cofounded StudioXX, a feminist research and media arts center in Montréal.

Leslie Regan Shade, PhD, is an associate professor at Concordia University's Department of Communication Studies in Montreal. Her research and teaching focuses on the social, political, and ethical aspects of ICTs, with a focus on gender and globalization. She is the author of *Gender and the Social Construction of the Internet* (Peter Lang 2002), coeditor of *Mediascapes: New Patterns in Canadian Communication* (Nelson Thomson 2006), and coeditor of the Communications in the Public Interest series published by the Canadian Centre on Policy Alternatives. She is the past president of the Canadian Communication Association and a coinvestigator in the Canadian Research Alliance for Community Innovation and Networking.

Zeenia Shaukat has studied economics and international communications at the University of Karachi and the University of Leeds. She has worked at different editorial and research positions with leading media organizations in Pakistan, including *She Magazine, The News International,* and Pakistan Television. Shaukat worked with Katharine Sarikakis at the Centre for International Communications Research, University of Leeds, on a research project investigating the financial and business aspects of the global pornography industry. She also presented a paper at the annual meeting of the American Anthropological Association of 2006, exploring the reactions in Pakistan over the publication of Prophet Mohammad's cartoons in European newspapers. She is currently working as a research assistant with a prominent member of the Parliament of Pakistan, Sherry Rehman. Shaukat is based in Karachi, where she works with Rehman on a range of issues concerning legislation and politics in Pakistan.

Andrew Stevens is a doctoral candidate in the department of sociology at Queen's University in Kingston, Ontario (3ajrs@qlink.queensu.ca). He is currently researching international trade unionism in the call center sector.

Nancy Van Leuven recently received her PhD in communication at the University of Washington in Seattle after a career in journalism and public relations and is now an assistant professor in Communication Studies at Bridgewater State College. Her main research areas are how mass media are involved in issues of globalization and inequality, feminist theory, and communication models of news flows, framing, and indexing. Other areas include development communication and issues of national identity, American Indian culture, and power relationships of gender and race within international relief and development efforts. She is especially interested in the cultural narrative of manifest destiny, especially in how developed countries now talk about the need to convert Africa and other "developing" areas to modernity. In addition to recent academic publications and conference presentations, including the 2006 World Congress on Communication for Development, Van Leuven has worked as a writer/author for newspapers, national and regional magazines, and books.

Gillian Youngs, PhD, has taught in the British and American university systems, including in Hong Kong, and is currently a senior lecturer in the Department of Media and Communication at the University of Leicester, UK. She has previous professional experience as a journalist and communications consultant in the civil aviation, high-technology, and media sectors. A founding coeditor of *International Feminist Journal of Politics*, she was lead coeditor, 2003–2005. She has been an associate editor of *Development* since 2002 and serves on the editorial boards of *Political Geography* and *Global Ethics*. Her main research areas are feminist international relations, globalization and inequality, global political economy, information society, women and feminist theory, and information and communication technologies. Her policy-related, consultancy, and project work has involved her with the cultural, communications, and education sectors of UNESCO and UK and international NGOs. Her major publications include *International Relations in a Global Age: A Conceptual Challenge* (Polity, 1999); the edited volume *Political Economy, Power and the Body: Global Perspectives* (Macmillan, 2000); the coedited volume *Globalization: Theory and Practice*, 2nd ed. (Continuum, 2003); and *Global Political Economy in the Information Age: Power and Inequality* (Routledge, 2007).